MARKETING LOGISTICS AND DISTRIBUTION PLANNING

Other books by Gordon Wills

Bradford Exercises in Management
(with Thomas Kempner)

Handbook of Management Technology
(with Ronald Yearsley)

Pricing Strategy
(with Bernard Taylor)

Technological Forecasting: the art and its managerial implications
Technological Forecasting and Corporate Strategy
(with David Ashton and Bernard Taylor)

Sources of U.K. Marketing Information
Marketing Through Research
Marketing Research
(with Joseph Siebert)

Management Thinkers
(with Anthony Tillett and Thomas Kempner)

Organizational Design for Marketing Futures
(with Roy Hayhurst)

New Ideas in Retail Management
Long Range Planning for Marketing and Diversification
(with Bernard Taylor)

Contemporary Marketing
Exploration in Marketing Thought
Fashion Marketing
(with David Midgley)

Creating and Marketing New Products
(with Roy Hayhurst and David Midgley)

Other books by Martin Christopher

Marketing Below-the-Line
Total Distribution
Research Methods in Marketing
(with C. K. Elliott)

MARKETING LOGISTICS AND DISTRIBUTION PLANNING

Edited by

Martin Christopher and Gordon Wills
University of Bradford Management Centre

A Halsted Press Book

JOHN WILEY & SONS
New York

First published in 1972

Published in the U.S.A. by
Halsted Press, a Division of
John Wiley & Sons, Inc.,
New York

Library of Congress Cataloging in Publication Data

Christopher, Martin.
    Marketing logistics and distribution planning.

    "A Halsted Press book."
    Bibliography: p.
    1.   Physical distribution of goods—Management.
I.   Wills, Gordon, joint author.   II.   Title.
HF5415.7.C56   1973   658.7'8   73–6674
ISBN 0-470-15631-7

Printed in Great Britain
in 10/11 point Times Roman type
by The Aldine Press, Letchworth

Dedication

This book is respectfully dedicated to all who find its message threatens their conventional view of distribution. This most certainly excludes some folk we would specifically wish to include, however. We, therefore, further wish to dedicate our efforts to friends at NEDO who have done so much to stimulate the new approach to distribution in Britain, and who encouraged us to prepare this title at its outset; to members of the EDC for the Distributive Trades who encouraged our efforts at Bradford University by making a £4000 grant for the preparation of teaching and research materials in marketing logistics and distribution; to friends at IPC Transport Press who backed the 1970 launch of our new *International Journal of Physical Distribution*; to all involved since 1971 with the work of the Centre for Physical Distribution Management in the U.K.; and to all members of the NEDO Working Party on PDM who have proved such stimulating commentators on our efforts. A future in literary criticism undoubtedly awaits them all, particularly Roy Close, Denis Vidler, Keith Read, Tommy Thomas, John Tunstall and Harold Nockolds.

Contents

CONTENTS

Introduction

This book offers a new perspective to the management of corporate affairs. Marketing logistics or physical distribution management (PDM) is a totally new concept to almost every sector of British business. It promises rich rewards to those who study it closely. It has been suggested that distribution is the economy's last dark continent, where dramatic cost savings can be made. PDM seems set fair to become a crucial management issue of the seventies, in the way that marketing and exporting dominated in the sixties.

Hence, we have produced the first thorough analysis attempted in Britain of this new focus of corporate concern. It is intended at once as a guide for action for all concerned in business where distribution costs are anything but absolutely very small; as a textbook for graduate and undergraduate students in management and business studies; and as a manual for the manager, furthering his understanding of the role of distribution in the business.

With these audiences in mind, we have not attempted to write the whole book ourselves. We have asked the experts in each sector to distil their views and to cite the cases which they know or have lived through.

In recent years increasing attention has been paid to the role of distribution in the corporate activities of the firm. New developments in transport technology, and the growth of the acceptance of a total approach to corporate activities, have led to a realization that distribution involves more than the problem of transporting the product of the firm from the factory to the customer. Now the accent is tending to be upon the integration of distribution, marketing, purchasing, and corporate strategy. Distribution planning is now seen to encompass decisions on plant location, depot location, inventory control, and customer service levels. New techniques, described in the chapters of this book, have enabled the firm to treat the flow of a good or service, from its basic input components to its final consumption, as one integrated system. The systems concept, for so long a subject of mainly academic interest, is now an operational reality for many firms. Marketing logistics, as the science of physical distribution management has been dubbed, has grown to be a managerial aid of crucial importance. The purpose of this book is to describe the setting of physical distribution management in the corporate context, and to suggest ways in which distribution cost savings of considerable magnitude may be made.

The Total Distribution Concept
Within the company many activities exist which have not traditionally been considered as being within the province of distribution management. Such activities as production scheduling, warehouse location, and inventory control

have generally been treated as unrelated components, not as part of a total system. However, if the assumption is made that final output is a function, however complex, not only of final demand but of all intervening inputs, it becomes clear that in order to achieve the objective of maintaining 'the best possible customer service at the least cost', it is necessary to view as interconnected all within-firm activities as well as extra-firm activities.

Similarly, when alternative distribution systems are being considered it is necessary to consider the *total costs* of these systems rather than just the costs of transportation. Road transport may be cheaper than rail transport for a particular product market situation but when the costs of handling, transhipment and packaging are also taken into account, a containerized system using Freightliners may be cheaper overall. It is simple to postulate other such possible savings by employing this total overview of distribution.

Such a view of distribution is entirely compatible with the new total corporate concept of a firm's activities. Corporate planning has received considerable attention of late and the total orientation that this concept involves necessitates that any plan must include the role of distribution. Many firms, particularly North American ones, are building their organizations around the distribution function, believing that distribution is the key to success in competitive markets. Whilst such an orientation may be extreme, there are sound grounds for viewing PDM as central to the success or failure of a company's marketing effort. It is useful to view PDM as the bridge between production and marketing:

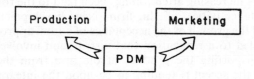

The role of production generally being to create goods, and the role of marketing to create customers, it is necessary that these two corporate functions be reconciled as efficiently as possible. This reconciliation is achieved by PDM—how it does it and how efficiently is determined by the company's approach to marketing logistics.

Cost-savings Through Marketing Logistics
A recent study of UK companies' distribution costs revealed that, on average, distribution accounted for 16 per cent of the cost of sales of those companies. It is obvious that even a reduction of a few per cent could lead to savings of many millions of pounds that could be used more profitably elsewhere by the companies concerned. The body who made the survey, the EDC for the Distributive Trades, was created with the specific purpose of bringing about such cost savings.

Because the whole orientation of the total approach to distribution management is centred around the objective of cost reduction, it is of obvious relevance to UK management. The profit leverage resulting from the release of funds in this way can be considerable. For too long distribution has been viewed as a cost centre within the company. Whilst not going so far as to suggest that it could well become a profit centre, it can sensibly be seen as a potential revenue-generating centre, in the sense that distribution can be used as a powerful marketing weapon. The obvious example of the company which can meet delivery dates one month ahead of its competitor with a near-identical product shows one way in which distribution can be revenue-generating. Traditional methods of distribution cost and revenue accounting fail to take into account the role of service in distribution and the effect that it can have on costs and revenue. A decision on whether to maintain a service level of 90 per cent as against 95 per cent could result in phenomenal cost savings and only a slight fall in revenue. We should never neglect exploring such possibilities.

Expenditures on distribution should be viewed in the light of their 'opportunity cost'—what return could they be making if they were employed elsewhere? This figure should be a constant inducement to make cost reductions in distribution quite apart from the revenue-generating possibilities arising from a more efficient distribution system.

Changes Outside the System
The dramatic changes in transport technology in the last decade have had far-reaching consequences for distribution. It is no exaggeration to say that the changes in these ten years are going to be as important as the total sum of change in transport technology over the last 100 years. The implementation of the 'through' concept of transportation, whereby goods are loaded into containers at the point of manufacture and not unloaded until they reach their final point of distribution, has made radical differences to many a firm's marketing effort, and this revolution is only just getting under way. 'Roll on-Roll off', massive cargo jets, containerization: these are some of the innovations in transport technology that demand an immediate reappraisal of the company's distribution function.

A further external influence on the shape of distribution systems is the growth of international marketing. Exports from the UK to markets overseas are currently growing dramatically, and the signs are that this growth will continue. Overseas markets are often unsuited to traditional distribution methods and, in addition, the further the market from the factory the greater the percentage of the cost of sales that is accounted for by distribution.

In any market, home or export, distribution can be a competitive tool in exactly the same way as price or promotion, and the purpose of marketing logistics is to secure more fully an integration between production and marketing. The role of marketing logistics is clearly outlined in the following quotation:

The physical distribution mission of the firm is to develop a system that meets the stated corporate customer service policy at the lowest possible cost. Development of a satisfactory programme requires two levels of adjustment: (1) integration of the logistical system with other corporate systems, and (2) development of total cost balance between logistical system activity centres.

> D. J. Bowersox, E. W. Smykay, and Bernard J. La Londe, *Physical Distribution Management*, New York, Macmillan, 1968, pp. 113–14.

The purpose of this present book is to suggest the means whereby this mission may be implemented successfully.

We gratefully acknowledge the assistance we have received in preparing this book, and in deciding its structure, from our colleagues at the University of Bradford Management Centre, participants at University PDM Seminars and Conferences and our regular one-week course for practitioners. In particular we are grateful to Drs Wendell Stewart, Donald Bowersox and Bernard La Londe—all North American academics who have taught with us at Bradford. Finally, and especially, we are grateful to Dr Philip Schary, who visited us as Senior Teaching Fellow in Marketing Logistics from January–June 1970, and has enormously aided the development both of our research and our studies at Bradford University. Our continuing research efforts at Bradford are now coordinated in the Marketing Logistics Systems Research Unit, whose work is currently supported by Tate and Lyle, NEDO and the university's own research resources.

Margaret Firth, Heather McCallum, Shirley Wraith and Helga Werwie provided excellent and timely secretarial support throughout, and the authors met deadlines as profit centres meet budgets.

Management Centre
University of Bradford

Martin Christopher
Gordon Wills
November 1971

The Authors and Contributors

Martin Christopher, B.A., M.SC., is lecturer in Marketing Logistics, University of Bradford Management Centre, where he has been responsible for developing the post-graduate course in marketing logistics and distribution. He has written and lectured widely on quantitative aspects of marketing.

I. M. Churcher is Director and General Manager of North Sea Ferries. Before establishing North Sea Ferries in 1964 he was with the General Steam Navigation Co. as General Manager in the Netherlands.

Andrew Dare, David Hedges, and Alan Slater at the time of writing were research associates in Marketing Logistics at the University of Bradford Management Centre. They are now involved, separately, in the organization and management of their respective companies' logistics and corporate planning functions. Andrew Dare is Head of Marketing Planning, Unigate Ltd. David Hedges is involved in logistics planning with United Glass and Alan Slater works in the Overseas Operations Division, Planning and Programming Department of Plessey Telecommunications.

Peter Detmold, B.SC. (ECON.), C.ENG., A.F.R.Ae.S., F.B.C.S., is Director of Economics and Systems Analysis with the Canadian Transport Commission. Prior to this he served in a planning function with British Railways.

Michael Graham, M.A., is Economic Adviser to the Board of Overseas Containers Ltd. He has worked with Shell International, The United Nations and NEDO.

John Houston, M.A., is Director of the Industrial and Construction Machinery Division of Massey-Ferguson (Export) Ltd. He has held several major marketing posts in the UK and Europe.

Keith Howard, B.SC., M.SC., is Lecturer in Management Science at the University of Bradford Management Centre. He has worked in Operations Research in this country and South Africa.

David Hussey, B.COM., A.C.I.S., is Planning Manager with A. Wander Ltd. He lectures and writes on management matters, particularly corporate planning, and has a book *Introducing Corporate Planning* published by Pergamon Press.

Paul Jackson, DIP.INST.M., is Head of European Development, BOAC. Prior to this he was Head of the International Cargo Advisory Board of BEA.

Brian McKibbin is Managing Director of Planned Warehousing Ltd. PW is a consulting group offering a range of services in warehousing and distribution management, materials handling and control engineering.

G. J. Murphy, B.SC. (ECON.), is a Lecturer in the Department of Business and Legal Studies at the Lanchester College of Technology. Prior to this he was Associate Editor of *Freight Management*.

Philip Schary, B.A., M.B.A., PH.D., is Associate Professor of Marketing and Logistics at Oregon State University. He has served as a Transportation Officer in the US Air Force and later as a Market Analyst for Douglas Aircraft Co., Lockheed Electronic and Avionics Division, The Flying Tiger Line and as a Business Economist for the Richfield Corporation.

T. E. Stephenson, B.A., is Lecturer in the Department of Management Studies in the University of Leeds. He has had wide experience of retailing and has published numerous articles on this and related topics.

C. D. T. Watson-Gandy, B.SC., M.SC. (ENG.), M.PHIL, D.I.C., is Lecturer in Management Engineering at Imperial College of Science and Technology. He has worked as a mining engineer in Zambia and as a consultant on distribution problems.

Gordon Wills, B.A. (POL.ECON.), D.M.S., F.INST.M., is Professor of Marketing Studies at the University of Bradford Management Centre. Professor Wills has held marketing research positions with ICI, Sales Research Services and Foote, Cone & Belding. He has written on a wide variety of topics and lectured in the Jnited States and Europe.

SECTION A

The Corporate Context of Marketing Logistics

Chapter A.1

PHYSICAL DISTRIBUTION: THE ENVIRONMENTAL CONTEXT

by David Hussey

The Importance of the Total Physical Distribution Concept

Physical distribution, or marketing logistics, is a subject which has been increasingly receiving management attention in recent years. Modern companies have realized the enormous importance of that section of their activity which physically moves the product from the factory through to the consumer; an importance as an area for top management strategic decisions, and with great potential for cost reduction and improvement in efficiency. This development is in line with two principles of modern management which are now permeating through to all areas of corporate activity: careful planning and objective decision making. To this philosophical development can be added the growth in computer usage, and the numerous quantitative techniques which managers can use to aid their decision processes. The means are now available whereby every company can put its physical distribution function under a microscope with the object of truly managing and controlling it.

The traditional approach to physical distribution has been to consider only a part of it: the transport element. It has always been recognized that the cost of transport is a determinant factor in the location of industry, and in the ability of a producer to sell profitably in the various markets available to him. The modern view accepts that the transport element is a vital, important part of the total physical distribution process, but stresses that it is only a part. A study in the USA by the consultants A. T. Kearney and Co.[1] showed that transport was in fact less than one-third of the total physical distribution cost in the 270 corporations in the sample.

What constitutes the remaining two-thirds or so of the total cost? The answer is: all the other activities that have to be carried out to move the product to the consumer, to give it utility of time and place. The total process includes many functions: items such as warehousing, the internal movement of goods within depots, the loading and unloading of lorries, methods of packaging, and—most important—the control of inventories. Consideration of all these as a total physical distribution concept has led to a new, positive way of controlling the function. Physical distribution is not a relatively passive last link in the chain of production, but a highly

17

important sector of the total business, with its interactions with every other aspect of corporate activity. This concept can make a unique contribution to total profits, and can lead the company to the discovery of new opportunities.

It is fair to say that at the present time there are many companies who do not know the true cost of physical distribution to their organizations. Accounting systems are rarely designed to provide this information, and seldom show more than basic transport costs. Even at this level, management information is frequently inadequate for control purposes, dealing in global averages and cost allocations of doubtful validity. Perhaps worse is the fact that different parts of the physical distribution function are managed by executives who have no direct link with each other, and who are under no obligation (and may not even see the need) to coordinate their activities.

Acceptance of the total physical distribution concept can bring a completely new approach to problems. For example, on a rate for rate basis, the cost of air transport may be considerably higher than that of other modes, and it is possible to discount air freight as being only suitable for high value/low bulk or emergency goods. Consideration of the distribution function as a total system may alter this thinking. Firstly, the cost of packing for air may be considerably cheaper than the stronger cases needed for sea transport. Secondly, the use of a regular speedy air service may mean that inventory levels can be reduced and warehouses closed: if a British manufacturer can put his product in any country in Europe within a few hours, he may not need warehouses in the receiving countries. The *total* cost of distribution by air could, conceivably, be lower than distributing by other means.

The system may be changed in other ways. A new approach to lorry routing, a change in the level of customer service, or some other factor may also mean that overheads can be reduced by the rationalization of warehouses. Every one warehouse less brings a lower level of direct storage costs, reduces working capital necessary to maintain inventory levels, and removes some of the risk of deterioration, pilferage and damage that occur whenever goods are stored.

Not all actions to improve efficiency result in reduced customer service. A study by a firm of food wholesalers[2] showed that they were giving some retailers a better van selling service than they, in fact, wanted—both parties benefited by a reduction in calling rate. Overall delivery times may be improved, because of speedier transit times and more effective inventory control. The least the total physical distribution concept can do is to identify the cost and profits of any change in the system, so that different levels of customer service can be evaluated by the marketing management as an aggressive element of total marketing strategy. This becomes one of the variables to be considered with the other variables—product changes, price movements, promotion advertising and the like.

The total physical distribution concept will assist companies to identify areas where change has to take place for progress to be made. Channels of distribution used by a company, or indeed an industry, are frequently the result of history. Every link in the chain has an effect on physical distribution costs. The adoption of a different channel might lead to reduced inventories or less handling.

Change might also be necessary in other areas of marketing strategy. The interaction of dynamic physical distribution management with other marketing decisions can lead, for example, to different price structures, or the introduction of other measures, to increase drop size.

Perhaps the most exciting thing about the concept is its ability to increase the scope of the company. Reduction in unit costs of delivery can give the organization a competitive edge. It may be possible to reach into markets previously barred by high distribution costs. Return on investment may rise because capital locked up in over-large inventories, or under-utilized lorries and other assets, may be released. The efficient organization can always find more opportunities for profit than its inefficient counterpart.

Physical distribution is a very heavy area of cost in most operations, and the transport element at least has had to withstand a rapid escalation of costs owing to the implementation of various government policies. The Transport Act, training legislation, fuel tax increases and the selective employment tax are all measures which have had a profound effect on the cost structure of many companies. Not all industries or companies feel the total effect of physical distribution costs in the same way, and the total intensity varies with the type of product handled. But as it is largely a hidden cost for most companies, it is a dangerous cost: management can only control the factors it is aware of.

The cost of transport to British manufacturing industry amounted to £600 million in 1963.[3] To this must be added the enormous, but undefined, expenditure by other sectors of the economy, such as agriculture, mining and distribution. When the 'hidden' elements of cost are taken into account—and the A. J. Kearney study suggests that they are the major part—it becomes apparent that the total costs of physical distribution to the nation are of enormous size.

An American study[4] gave the following estimates for total physical distribution costs in the USA:

Industry	% of Sales
Food and food products	29·6
Machinery	9·8
Chemicals, petroleum, rubber	23·1
Paper and allied products	16·7
Primary and fabricated metal	26·5
Wood products	16·1

Although a UK study might well reveal a different pattern, the American research can be taken as an indicator of the enormous burden of physical distribution costs which face today's managers. No one can seriously argue that an area of costs which may range from 10 to 30 per cent of turnover should not be a subject of great interest to top management.

The consideration of global figures leads to another view of the total distribution concept, one which has been touched on in the discussion of the

19

possible need to change channels of distribution. Besides being applicable on a company basis, the concept extends to the total economic process in an entire industry. Thus the distribution of food can be looked at as a total system from growing, through processing, wholesaling and retailing, until it reaches the ultimate consumer. This concept crosses the boundaries of individual firms, and is essentially a national problem, although the individual enterprise can take an active part in making changes. Cooperation with other units in the process is possible, ranging from such areas as bulking shipments, through to agreements on the use of non-returnable packaging.

This field is a neglected one. The sort of 'unnecessary' costs which an industry may incur can be seen by following the possible progress of a case of apples from grower through to consumer. The orchard in Kent may send the case to a market wholesaler in Covent Garden. There it may be purchased by a second wholesaler who may remove it back to Kent. He may sell it to a retailer who might be located next to the orchard. An even worse tangle is possible. The second wholesaler could sell the apples to a central depot of a chain of supermarkets on the outskirts of London—who might then send them back once again to Kent to their branch there. This is a probable but hypothetical example. Later in this chapter a real example is given of the action the world banana industry has taken to achieve economies in physical distribution, and to take the total concept into areas outside the scope of any one firm in the chain.

There is no doubt that attention to the problems of physical distribution can have far-reaching effects on the results of the individual firm. It is very much in a company's interests; but it is also in the interests of the economy at large, since a national improvement in distribution efficiency could represent a major increase in the overall productivity of British industry.

No company operates in a vacuum, and all its decisions are affected by events in the environment in which it operates. Physical distribution decisions are no exception. If outside happenings influence future profits, it seems logical for them to be taken into consideration during the decision process. This involves looking into the future a little more carefully than many firms have been in the habit of doing. All management decision is based on forecasts and assumptions, and it is as well to try to apply a logical process of evaluation to identify the factors which influence future results and, in the process, to try to define the results which are expected from the major actions being undertaken in the present.

It is one thing to claim that looking a little wider and a little further ahead is essential for effective management. It is another thing to actually do it. The rest of this chapter will identify some of the factors in the environment which a company should study, and will try to provide a logical method of actually bringing these factors into the decision process.

Environmental Factors Affecting Physical Distribution Decision
Figure 1·1 gives an outline—in broad category headings—of the environmental factors facing every company when it considers physical distribution policy. Each of these categories is discussed in greater detail to give an

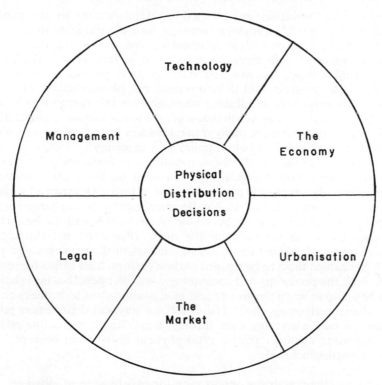

Figure 1·1   Factors in the Physical Distribution Environment.

appreciation of the type of effect it might have. This, of course, is only indicative, as the true result will vary with every company.

It is very easy to move into the realms of science fiction in this sort of discussion. One is aware of environmental forecasts of the shape of cities in the year 2000 that read something like this:

—All cities will be concentrated in single buildings up to one mile high.
—All cities will be underground.
—All cities will be built under (or on) the sea.

In the year 2000 it may be necessary to know whether to change the lorry fleet to helicopters, submarines or pit-ponies, but for most companies this sort of forecast is moving beyond the realms of usefulness, at least as far as physical distribution is concerned. For those who must take serious account of such possibilities, there is the technique of technological forecasting, which provides a reasoned method of evaluating the possible and the probable; but for the purposes of this discussion only things which affect the relatively near future have been considered. The emphasis is on areas likely to concern the majority of companies.

Technology All businesses are affected by developments in the world's technology. The word 'technology' tends to lead the thoughts to the more glamorous developments, such as hovercraft cargo vessels, electric vehicles, jumbo-jets, super-jets and outer space travel. It is very easy to slip into a world of semi-fantasy. The new and startling developments *are* important and essential to progress, and therefore must not be overlooked, but most companies are powerless to influence them, and for this reason they should also think of the technological environment on a much simpler plane. Outside the 'glamour' areas there are many other advances in technology which can alter the total physical distribution policy of a company.

An example from the world banana industry may make the point clearer. Not so long ago, most bananas were imported on the stem—misshapen bundles frequently wrapped in plastic. Because of their awkward and variable dimensions they were difficult to handle mechanically, and a large part of each bundle consisted of waste vegetable matter which had to be thrown away once the hands were cut off the stem. Then came a technological advance—a way of packing the hands of bananas in the tropics, and a process which enabled them to be ripened in their cartons. This called for investment in both the producing and consuming countries: new 'boxing' stations had to be set up to serve the grower and modifications had to be made to the existing banana ripening plant. The effects on physical distribution policy were far reaching, stretching right through from the grower to the retailer in the importing country—truly a total physical distribution concept.

The economies included:

—easier handling, with the opportunity for palletization at all stages
—more payload per cubic foot of shipping space
—more bananas could be fitted into a given area of warehouse space, thus boosting capacity of existing facilities
—saving in internal movement because bananas are handled in the carton throughout ripening
—containerization becomes a possibility
—there is an end to dealings in returnable boxes, with consequent savings in working capital, warehouse space, lorry space and clerical operations.

The members of the world banana industry could have ignored this technological advance, particularly as for many of them it meant some form of negotiation and cooperation with others along the channel of distribution. Or they could do what virtually all the leading firms and most of the minor ones have done, and move wholeheartedly to harness the forces of change to their benefit.

Such relatively minor technological developments—minor that is in the history of man, but major to the individual company—are within the scope of most firms and can be actively sought. New methods of packaging, new packaging materials, improvements in internal handling machinery, modifications to road transport vehicles can all have far-reaching effects on physical distribution policies.

Sometimes the new policies can change the market. The growth in the use of oxygen in steelworks arises partly from new methods of steelmaking, and partly from a new approach to distribution: in some cases the atmospheric gas plant is taken to the steelworks, in others networks of steelworks and other large consumers are connected by pipeline to a number of oxygen plants (for example the British Oxygen Company's pipeline systems around the Tees, and in the Sheffield district). Like the banana industry, the atmospheric gas industry could have insisted on sticking to its original methods of distribution—in this case in cylinders: if they had done so, their volume of business today would be much, much smaller.

It is important not to lose sight of the total distribution concept, and to make sure that improvements in one area are not lost by cost increases in another. For example, a speeding up of the discharging operation of a ship through an investment in port unloading facilities, might mean that ships can be turned round quicker. Such a benefit could well be lost if the faster flow of goods raised unloading problems at inland warehouses through night arrivals and bunching of consignments. Only when this factor has also been taken into consideration can the correct decision be made.

Urbanization We need the forces of technology to help overcome another problem that besets us: how to live in an island that is becoming more overcrowded each year.

The motor vehicle has added to the speed and range of the distribution function, and is certainly more effective than the pack-horses of our ancestors. At the same time it has caused a large part of the population to live with a high degree of traffic congestion which in some towns approaches conditions of chaos. The number of vehicles on the road has been doubling every ten years or so, and is nowhere near saturation point. At the same time the average annual distance travelled per vehicle has not decreased. Many roads used by motor vehicles were designed for a more leisurely age, and the programmes of road building and modernization are not keeping pace with traffic increases, so the position must inevitably become worse.

Physical distribution policies must not only take into account the many problems caused by present traffic conditions, but must also consider the additional difficulties in the future that the trends in ownership and the use of the motor vehicle suggest.

In the London area alone the number of goods vehicles is expected to reach 320,000 by 1981, compared with 190,000 in 1962. Trips by these vehicles will be up by one and three quarter times over the same period. In addition to these forecasts (taken from the London Traffic Survey), there is a prediction of a further million cars, making trips both inside and outside the central area.

Changes in the economic climate may accelerate or delay the achievement of these forecasts, but that they will be achieved within the next ten to fifteen years is almost inevitable.

It is possible to predict with confidence that the centres of other major conurbations will also become more difficult for the commercial vehicle operator. The increase in the sheer volume of traffic will almost certainly lead to longer delays, an increase in one-way streets and in more streets or traffic lanes which give preference to buses. An even more basic effect on the business of most vehicle operators will be additional restrictions on vehicle loading and unloading during peak hours, and possibly the complete prohibition of day-time delivery operations. Those receiving deliveries, particularly at night, will increasingly insist on suppliers' attending at scheduled times. If matters can be worse, there is always the possibility of a congestion tax for those using city centres!

It would be disastrous for any company to ignore the effect of traffic congestion when considering the location of depots. Currently profitable warehouses may become less economic in the future, or traffic regulations may make an existing depot impossible to operate. For example, I know of one company which has to re-locate one of its depots on the south coast because, within two years, it will no longer have vehicular access. In this case there was adequate warning, although the timing of the move to new premises was a complex exercise in management judgement.

Government strategies show that there will be certain changes in population locations, with the growth of new towns. Plans, in varying degrees of detail, have been published to show certain towns that will be developed to a considerable size, in order to relieve pressure on the larger cities. These shifts, depending of course on the nature of the individual company's business, can have an important influence on lorry operations and depot siting.

For many businesses, all these trends in urban development and traffic congestion will have a far-reaching effect on policy decisions. They may change not only operating costs, but the way in which the business sells (will van-salesmen be able to sell at night?), and its approach to depot size and location. A new pattern of decisions will emerge about the mode of transport to be used. Results need not always be adverse: an increase in night working could lead to a double-utilization of some lorries, while the out of town super-store movement will bring a new area of problems and opportunities to many firms.

Undoubtedly there are many imperfections in our knowledge of future events: but failure to consider this sector of the environment is very likely to lead to wrong decisions. Wrong decisions can add to the costs of the firm, and—perhaps even more important—can mean lost opportunities.

Economy Traffic congestion, though a national problem, is regional in its occurrence. The next area for discussion is of much wider incidence—the national economy. Every business is affected to a greater or lesser extent by the changing fortunes of the countries in which it operates, and there are many good reasons why each company should establish what this effect is. It is not the same for all businesses (the down turn of the trade cycle costs the motor industry more than the basic food industries), and indeed may vary between firms in the same industry.

Leaving aside, for the time being, those factors concerned with the market, I think there are four areas worth particular attention. Firstly there are the changes in the pattern of general costs. These always seem to move in one direction only, which is upwards, and every business has to run very fast to stay in the same place (to borrow from Lewis Carroll). But the rise in costs brings a challenge to management to find ways of meeting profit targets through increased productivity. How can cost projections alter corporate policies?

1. They may cause a change in capital appraisal decisions, changing the expected returns from a new project: labour saving equipment not at present economic may be worth installing.
2. There will be a greater impetus for the application of modern techniques to physical distribution, in particular the use of mathematics. This in turn should lead to the development of new aids to decision making.
3. There will be a more careful consideration of the costs of delivering to certain customers, in relation to the profits derived from them. This may well mean, for example, the elimination of small retailers from a delivery service. On a national basis this could mean that the 'cash and carry' wholesalers become virtually the only source of purchases to the very small retailers.

The second area is the way in which the population structure is going to change over the next few years. Total numbers will increase, but mainly in the 'under fifteen' and 'over sixty-five' groups. There will be very little difference in the size of the working age group, at least over the next five years. If the economy is to expand, it follows that more married women must work, or productivity must rise, or both. It is my opinion that in some sectors there is a shortage now in certain types of employee, despite the fact that nationally there is more unemployment than we care to see. This frictional unemployment is likely to continue since there are certain changes taking place in British industry. Each company must examine what effect variations in manpower patterns will have on their distribution policies. My own feeling is that certain jobs will become very difficult to fill, and that changing supply/demand patterns will mean that some unskilled jobs could become socially unacceptable. At the same time, the country will face an economic and social challenge in the necessity to find employment for those people displaced by the process of change in traditional industries.

Table 1·I

ESTIMATED POPULATION OF THE U.K.: '000[5]

				% Change Over 1967	
Age Group	1967	1972	1977	1972	1977
0–14	13,015	14,098	14,980	+8%	+15%
15–64	35,357	35,311	35,904	—	+ 2%
65 and over	6,773	7,368	7,898	+9%	+17%
Total	55,145	56,777	58,782	+3%	+ 7%

25

The third point is that British industry is undergoing a structural change. The trend of continued growth in the size of business units is likely to continue. In addition, various sectors of industry have to adapt to technological advance. The docks have begun to move towards new patterns of capital and labour usage; the steel industry faces a modernization programme which will reduce its labour requirements; the textile industry has changed considerably since the 1950s, and is still in a process of re-organization and re-grouping. Even agriculture is not exempt—for example the glasshouse sector, originally established in relation to distribution by horse and cart, is now subject to pressures from urban development and technological advance. The Lee Valley is declining in importance and many producers are re-locating in areas of better climatic and light conditions.

The fourth area takes into account the problems of EEC entry. Every company should be aware of the effect which entry to the EEC would have on its business. Some companies stand to gain, others stand to lose, and the way in which they consider this problem can have a profound effect on their physical distribution strategies.

The Market   In this focus on the physical distribution concept, it is easy to lose sight of the fact that the movement of goods is only part of overall marketing activity, and not an end in itself. Consumer needs have a determinant effect on all businesses, and it therefore becomes necessary to look at the physical distribution function through the eye of the marketing man. The activities of any one section of a business must be subjugated to the achievement of total corporate objectives, and it is very important that sectional interests should not prevail. It is very easy and very wrong for physical distribution decisions to be taken without knowledge of, or concern for, marketing strategy: similarly marketing strategy must consider physical distribution factors, if it is to make sound business sense.

This philosophy means that physical distribution policy will have to take into account the changing pattern of the market, the activity of competitors, the growth which the company plans to achieve, and variations in the traditional channels of distribution.

If a company really thinks about physical distribution policy, it must base its actions on the forecasts of the volume of sales it expects to achieve in the future. If sales are to grow, the means of getting the goods to the consumer must keep pace. Indeed, as we have seen, distribution policies can be used dynamically to help the company to attain its sales targets. The development of new products cannot be ignored; neither, of course, can the decline of sales caused by the obsolescence of products, competitive activity, or general falling off in demand. The longer the time-lag between the decision to alter physical distribution facilities to meet the new requirements (for example delivery time for a new lorry, construction time for a warehouse), the more important it becomes to base decisions on carefully formulated forecasts.

Channels of distribution in many sectors are in a state of change. Reference has already been made to structural changes in British industry, and similar forces are at work in the wholesaling and retailing sectors. The supermarket movement has brought about a considerable difference in the normal pattern of household shopping, and it has been accompanied by the physical removal of many small shop premises through the process of urban renewal and re-development. Concentration of purchasing power of retail outlets, and the tendency to larger manufacturing companies, has put pressure on the traditional wholesalers. Some have altered the objectives of their businesses (for example, some have turned into cash and carry wholesalers), others have left the industry, still others have themselves set out to become larger units, in order to be able to take advantage of modern business methods, and to enable them to afford the type of technical service demanded by the retailers or industrial users who are their customers. It is possible to argue that transfer of business from a traditional type of outlet to a supermarket is a matter for marketing people: but is it really of concern only to them? The sort of changes that are inevitable mean alteration in the location of customers, a decrease in customer numbers, an increase in customer size, and a new pattern of risks. All these are very much matters of concern to the physical distribution function.

The consumer influences the way in which goods are packed. The channels have an effect on the size and shape of trade packing. What suits the physical movement of goods best is not necessarily what will prove most acceptable. Changes here mean that there are more problems to be considered because the product must yield maximum utility to the consumer—or sell at a lower price.

I have already suggested that more firms will pay attention to the costs of delivering goods with their own transport to individual customers, and perhaps this should be elaborated on, since it is an area where distribution and marketing policies interact.

The starting point of the analysis is the realization that costs do not fall in a normal curve, and that it costs more to serve some customers than others. There are two elements for consideration. Firstly, it costs something to call on every customer, both in terms of the variable cost caused by travelling to him, and the standing cost incurred while travelling and while with him. Actual studies[2] showed that it took five-and-a-half minutes to deliver one unit to a customer, but only twelve minutes to deliver five units and fifteen minutes to deliver ten. Unless the sale to the customer contributes more in margin than the expense of getting to him, a loss situation occurs, which for most companies can only be revealed if they set out to study the economics of serving each customer.

Secondly, there is an opportunity cost in serving any customer. While the lorry is with him, it cannot also be with another. In some types of business it might be more profitable to give up a customer who yielded a low margin over delivery costs in favour of one who yielded a higher margin (although such a decision would have to be balanced against the probable effect on the corporate image).

How companies change their policies to meet this sort of situation is a matter for individual decision. Perhaps drop size can be increased by selling more to the small customers; perhaps a higher charge might be made for

27

small orders; perhaps customer service might be reduced, or withdrawn altogether. The important thing is acceptance of the problem: many companies have yet to do this.

Legal The legal environment is another area of change which must be taken into account. It is not always possible to predict what new laws are to be passed, but there is often an early warning of major pieces of legislation. In some cases it may be possible to anticipate changes in the laws.

Of course, the example which is familiar to all is the recent Transport Act, and there can be few companies which have not changed their policies to comply with this. But the law affects physical distribution decisions. There is likely to be further legislation in the area of vehicle safety. The traffic congestion discussed earlier will produce a crop of regulations, and predictions have already been made of the nature of some of these. There may also be attempts to control vehicle noise.

Another area of interest is the industrial training boards. Many companies will already come under a training board, and it is a fair guess that the rest will be brought into the system in the fairly near future. Training itself is a good thing, and there is no need to wait for government compulsion before introducing the type of programme which will be acceptable once the board is set up. Of course, if a company opts to do no training, it must consider training board levies as an irrecoverable element of cost.

All businesses are affected by prices and incomes policies, and these influence a company's freedom of action in its relations with employees, and its ability to recover costs through increased prices. One very important effect on distribution policy is to drive companies to greater efficiency, since this may be the only option open if profits are to be maintained or improved.

Management Perhaps it may seem to be stretching a point to include management in the study of environmental factors, but it is worth stressing that there is a continual development of new techniques and ideas which should be considered as a means of improving physical distribution decisions. For most companies this is not a question of predicting techniques as yet uninvented, but instead it is the diligent seeking out of existing methods—and using them. So often it is not the new and flamboyant 'breakthrough' which is required, but the application of techniques which are well established and well proved. A technique seldom solves a problem, since there is still a place for management judgement, but it frequently enables a better solution to be found.

Management should actively consider the application to physical distribution of operations research, new organizational procedures, organization and methods, work study, better management information, value analysis—in fact any improvement available in the general management field.

Later chapters in this book describe the use of various techniques to specific physical distribution problems. From these examples alone it is possible to obtain an appreciation of the scope of the kit-bag of tools already

28

available to every manager. It is quite safe to forecast that the future will provide management with many new developments, since the minds of many men in private companies, government and the universities are being applied to the solution of many of today's difficult problems. Keeping abreast with new ideas is a difficult task for many managers, and in practice there is often a wide gulf between knowing of the existence of a technique and its application. Enlightened management will always have to steer a difficult course between the latest 'fad', and new methods of real and lasting value; at the same time no management can afford to turn down an idea simply because it is new.

Taking Account of the Environment in Physical Distribution Decisions
The trouble with a long list of factors, such as has been set out above, is that it tends to depress. There seem to be so many things which are completely outside the control of management, that there is a very real danger that managers will throw up their hands in horror, decide that the whole thing is impossible, and rely on luck and intuition to help them make the right decisions. When it is remembered that there are numerous factors which are not included in the discussion in this chapter, it is possible to view this attitude with understanding, although this is not to imply acceptance of it.

What is needed is a logical way of assessing the environment, and identifying which of the many factors apply to the individual company. Of course, not all companies are affected by the same things, and the intensity of the effect will also vary from one business to another. A factor which hurts one company may provide a profit opportunity for another.

So the first step in the process of planning for change is to analyse the probable changes in relation to the physical distribution function. If a factor can be seen to have little or no effect on operations it can be omitted from the calculation. Now this raises a problem for the company which has no central system of corporate planning. A factor may be of great concern to a company's overall well-being, without having a direct effect on physical distribution. The indirect effect might be serious, and where the physical distribution manager is making the assessments, he must be very careful not to dismiss a factor too readily, and must put himself in the shoes of managers in other key areas.

In considering the intensity of the effect, it is important to assess the degree of risk connected with taking action, delaying action, or taking no action at all. It is worth remembering that the longer it is possible to defer a decision *without impairing subsequent results*, the more likely it will be that the company will make the right decision. There is no merit in being more hasty than the situation requires: but nor is there any merit in deferring action beyond the point when decisions should be made.

The policy of the company in relation to innovation is also important. Some companies take to new things quickly, to cream off the profits of being first. Others argue that it is more profitable to be second in the field, to introduce a new product after others have proved the market, to adopt a new technique only after their competitors have ironed out the snags. There are potential dangers and potential rewards in both policies: the skill comes in defining the policy. This definition must affect the individual company's appreciation of the environment; there must, for example, be a vast difference in approach between the company operating the new container service to Australia, and those who still see themselves as operators of 'traditional' ships. There is obviously more short term risk in backing something new— but probably more long term risk in sticking to the old methods.

Environmental factors may be put into two preliminary groups—those the company can affect by its own changes in policy, and those over which it has no control.

Where the company can influence future events, it should decide what it wishes to achieve, and then change its policies in order to accomplish the aim. The application of new technology (and in some cases the deliberate seeking of a technological advance through its own research and development), or the alteration of a marketing strategy to make a change in a predicted course of events are examples. This is when there is a clear difference between a forecast and a plan: a forecast may show results unsuitable to the firm, and a plan may set out to change the forecast to something more acceptable. I regard forecasting as a passive function, and planning as something very active indeed.

Over a large area of functions that will affect its operations the company may have no control. Of course, it may use its influence to persuade government or some other body to change its mind, just as many people lobbied against the Transport Bill. It may join with others (in, for example, a trade association) to do the same thing. The larger the company, the more influence it will have, and the more likelihood it will have of being successful in bringing about such changes. Even the small people, through combinations, can sometimes win, and the reconsideration of the siting of London's third airport at Stansted was a good example. But for most of us, changes in the economy, in traffic engineering, in social attitudes, and a thousand and one other areas, are completely beyond our sphere of control.

All business is a matter of management judgement, and it is judgement which has to be used to form workable assumptions about future events, and to base policy on these assumptions. To make assumptions a company requires all the information it can obtain, and the skills necessary to interpret this information and to make the necessary predictions and forecasts. There is, of course, a distinct difference between planning on an assumption, and making no judgement about environmental factors at all. The company that gives no thought to the problem is really assuming that present events will continue uninterrupted into the future: this has less likelihood of being correct.

Information for making assessments of the environment may come from a variety of sources, and it is possible to distinguish a number of different problems:

—Some environmental changes are virtual certainties, and an early warning mechanism operates. An example is decimalization, the date for which was announced well in advance, and the expected effects of which were analysed in numerous publications. This type of event is, of course, the easiest to foresee, although assessment of its influence on corporate policies may not be so simple.

—Certain types of forecasts are produced by government statistical services. Future population changes are predicted regularly by the government. These, at least in the medium term, have a high probability of being right. In the population table shown earlier it is really only the children who present a problem, since some of these are not yet born and past trends offer no guidance to the size of families under the influence of modern birth control methods. All those in the 15–64 year group, and the over 65s, are already born, and barring a major catastrophe we *know* that there will be a greater increase in the over 65s than in the working age group. Various other predictions are made from time to time by other government departments, and all that is needed to consider these factors in relation to a company's own operations is a little time and the collection of the necessary information—and of course a critical evaluation of the likely accuracy of the prediction.

—In some cases a study of past trends from available statistics may provide the best clue to the future. An example is the effect of weather on sales forecasts, where the patterns of previous years may be expected to be repeated in the future.

—Frequently, the statistical and background data available are insufficient for a reasoned assessment. Marketing research may be required to provide the company with a base on which to build. Besides the use of marketing research to establish the present pattern of events, its value is well known for the development of market and sales forecasts, and in studying competitive behaviour. Of direct benefit to physical distribution is the use of marketing research to study changes in the channels of distribution. If physical distribution is regarded as a marketing activity, it follows that there is also room for study of the impact of that activity on customers. What, for example, do a company's wholesale and retail customers require in the line of customer service? Such items as speed of delivery, employee attitudes, the corporate image, and time and frequency of delivery are vital parts of the physical distribution environment and can be studied through marketing research.

—Other assumptions have to be built on a study of the background of events. An assessment of the likelihood of UK entry into the EEC should be made after a study of the available political, social and economic facts, and a consideration of the opinions of experts in the field.

It is obvious that there is no universal, simple way of studying the environment. A number of different methods are needed to approach different environmental problems. The study itself can be conducted at various levels of complexity. For instance, there are many commonly used methods of making a sales forecast. These include:

—guessing (not recommended)
—grossing up salesmen's estimates
—extrapolating a time series of statistics by one of the numerous available mathematical methods
—extrapolation, amended by judgement factors
—building forecasts of individual market segments, and grossing these to arrive at a total forecast
—using a mathematical model which takes into account many of the key factors influencing the trend of events.

One important point is to ensure that forecasts provided by other areas in the company are based on common assumptions. It is difficult for a physical distribution manager to make the best decisions if he is basing his ideas on a predicted growth in per capita national income while the marketing manager's sales forecasts are based on an expected fall in economic performance.

When assumptions are defined they should be accompanied by an estimate of probability. The certainty of decimalization as discussed above would present a different sort of problem to management than an event which the assessment shows has only a 50 per cent chance of occurrence. This is highly relevant to defining the acceptable level of risks in any decision.

The last step in the process of environmental appraisal is to evaluate in money terms the effect of acting or not acting on the assumption. If the assumption is that there will be a shift in certain population centres, causing a change in depot siting, what would the penalty be for failure to act? Conversely, what costs would be incurred by acting now, what gains would accrue if the assumption were right—and what would the cost be if the assumption were subsequently proved to be wrong?

This sort of assessment will vary with the alternative actions open to the company. It is very rare that only one course is available, and all sensible possibilities should be examined before a decision is made. In this way the company is performing part of the process of preparing a long range plan for the physical distribution element of its activity. The corporate self analysis, and the appreciation of the future consequences of today's decisions which are occasioned by even this partial approach to corporate planning, can lead to better management.

Planning for environmental change should be taken a stage further. It is frequently possible to develop contingency plans which can be speedily brought into effect if assumptions prove to be wrong. This means that a predetermined alternative course of action is available for immediate implementation. In other cases, 'hedging' actions may be taken—a way of doing things which is not costly now, but which will stand the company in good stead if certain events do take place. This is rather in the way that a buyer will often refuse to place all his orders with one supplier, however acceptable the terms, so that he has some safeguard against failure. More appropriate to physical distribution is the hedging action that might be taken in relation to the siting of a new depot. Evaluation on the basis of the present might show two or three sites of approximately equal effect on corporate profits. If a study of the

32

environment revealed the probability of a new population centre being built in an area that could be reached conveniently from only one of these sites, it might be sound business judgement to locate the depot there. This decision would require little value judgement on the likelihood of the new development: in either event the company would be fully covered.

Modern managers simply cannot afford to ignore the changing world in which they operate. While the best of environmental appraisals may still leave large areas of uncertainty, many decisions will emerge that will be different from those arising from a less far-sighted management. The 'hedging' example above is a relatively painless decision, and perhaps gives the most apt perspective on the whole problem. The majority of decisions that physical distribution managers have to take are not matters of life and death. Multi-million pound investment projects that will yield good returns only if a certain event happens in the environment, and will cause loss of profits and capital if the event does not take place, are few and far between. Most decisions are not as drastic as this: it is simply that the best decisions will lead to higher profits than would otherwise have occurred. In the depot-siting example it is probable that any of the sites would have yielded a profit, even if the new town was built. There is, however, one course of action that would yield more profit than the others. By taking into account environmental factors, managers can often reach this 'best' decision, when otherwise they might have committed their company to something less than the best that is achievable.

A quotation from Peter Drucker[6] concisely sums up the situation faced by every manager and every business:

—But tomorrow always arrives. It is always different. And then the mightiest company is in trouble if it has not worked on the future. It will have lost distinction and leadership—all that will remain is big company overhead. It will neither control nor understand what is happening. Not having dared to take the risk of making the new happen, it perforce took the much greater risk of being surprised by what did happen. And this is a risk that even the largest and richest company cannot afford and that even the smallest business need not run.

References
(1) Wendell M. Stewart, 'Physical Distribution: Key to Improved Volume and Profits', *Journal of Marketing*, Chicago, USA, Vol. 29, No. 1.
(2) D. E. Hussey, 'Physical Distribution—the Effect on Marketing Decisions', paper presented at the British Institute of Management Physical Distribution Forum, February 20, 1968.
(3) 1963 Census of Production, Board of Trade (quoted in B. T. Bayliss and S. L. Edwards, 'Transport for Industry', Ministry of Transport, 1968).
(4) Richard E. Snyder, 'Physical Distribution Costs', *Distribution Age*, Vol. 62, December 1963.
(5) Government Actuary's Office (quoted in 'Food, Women and Shops', Lintas Special Projects, 1968).
(6) Peter Drucker, *Managing for Results*, London, Heinemann, 1964; Pan Books, 1967.

Chapter A.2

THE MARKETING CHANNEL
by Martin Christopher

... a channel of distribution embraces both intracompany organisation units and extracompany agents and dealers. Another way to look at it is that a firm's marketing organisation consists of (a) one or more organisation units within the firm and (b) a system of business units outside the firm, both of which it uses in its marketing work. If a company's marketing programme is to be effective, the activities of the inside units and those of the outside units must be closely coordinated so as to make a single, forceful impact on the market. A manager who thinks of the inside organisation units in one frame of reference and of the extra-firm units in another is likely to be handicapped in achieving such coordination.

> Ralph S. Alexander and Thomas L. Berg, *Dynamic Management in Marketing*. Homewood, Ill., Richard D. Irwin, Inc., 1965, p. 271.

The total approach to physical distribution management is a global managerial philosophy which views the movement of the product from its original basic sources to its ultimate consumption as a continuous system. What happens in the factory, in the warehouse and in the retail outlet (if there is one) and what happens in between are only sub-sets of the total system. It is possible to have a highly efficient materials handling system in the production shop and an equally efficient vehicle routing programme, and yet not achieve an optimum distribution system overall.

To optimize a distribution system essentially requires that a series of objectives must first be set by the firm. This may not simply be an objective of maximizing profits, or more likely of minimizing the costs of distribution, but may also include such constraints as maintaining service levels and delivery times consonant with the requirements of the product-market situation. In addition market conditions will almost certainly be dynamic: what is an efficient distributive channel today may, because of the intervention of a competitor for example, become outmoded tomorrow. It will not usually be the case that one channel unit has complete control of the channel. Thus, for example, the small manufacturer may be reliant on agents in the distributive network who, working to optimize their own sub-systems, throw the total system out of gear.

The situation for many marketing and manufacturing units is therefore likely to be unstable in the sense that unless they have complete control over the whole channel, they will be trying to achieve objectives which are in conflict with the objectives of other units. The aim of the body of concepts and techniques that is now springing up under the umbrella of the total approach to physical distribution is to achieve some sort of system stability and optimality. The ideas of strategy, borrowed from military science and games theory, are therefore obviously of some major importance to channel selection and operation.

The purpose of this chapter is to describe in operational terms how channel strategy may be used as an integral part of the marketing mix. Just as price and promotional policy are generally given a great deal of attention in the company's marketing effort, so too should channel strategy.

What is the Marketing Channel?

Every producer of goods, every provider of services and every agent who handles such goods or services, whether finished or not, is part of a distributive channel. It may be that these units view themselves as the centre of the system with flows coming in and out, or they may see their role as being integrative. In either case the distributive network, or marketing channel, exists to move goods or services spatially over time from their basic raw components to their final consumption. For example, the distributive network for a motor car is not just that method whereby the finished car leaves the end of the production line and arrives in the dealer's showroom. It includes the whole complex of networks whereby components are brought into the factory, stored and utilized. It includes the movement of materials into and out of the factory making the components and so on. When it is realized that the average car contains something like 5000 separate components, it is apparent that the complete distributive network for such a product is tremendously complex. The importance and the implications of this complexity are brought home when, for one reason or another, production at a firm of component manufacturers is halted, thereby bringing each unit in the channel to a halt. It is probable that a close examination of this particular channel would reveal it to be less than optimal by any of the usual criteria.

There are no hard and fast rules as to which particular units should constitute a particular channel. For example, it has been suggested by many writers that certain products, particularly in consumer markets, are sold via an influence process. In other words it is the effect of 'influentials' in a market that determine the final sales level of many products. These influentials may themselves form only a minute segment of the total market but their influence over the rest will be great; perhaps therefore these influentials should be treated as a separate unit in the channel. This idea is reinforced if we consider a distributive channel as acting as a communication channel as well, i.e. news about the product will flow through the channel preceding the actual flow of goods.

Such considerations bring us to a more sophisticated concept of the end unit of the marketing channel: it is not a homogeneous unit but may contain

35

many diverse and discrete segments. The manufacturer or retailer may there-fore be wise to treat each segment as a different channel unit, and possibly even set up separate channels if it is found that the needs of the market can best be catered for by so doing.

Product/Market Influences on Channel Choice

The peculiar features of the market and the product line that the manufac-turer offers to it are key determinants of the choice of marketing channel. To a certain extent, generalizations may be made concerning the effect of product/market features on the type of channel employed. Short channels with a minimum of intermediate units are more likely to be found where the product is high in value, or of a size or nature that makes storage impractic-able and for custom-built, one-off jobs. A highly technical product such as an electrical transformer will generally move directly from the production floor to the user, though the parts involved in the manufacture of that transformer could well have flowed through channels of some complexity. On the other hand, certain low value items of a perishable nature will also have more or less direct routes from manufacturer or processor to the ultimate consumer, for example milk or fashion items.

Associated with the product offering will be the degree to which the com-pany is established in the market. Smaller, newer companies will have a greater need for the specialist services of the wholesaler or agent in order to ensure an adequate distribution for the product. The better established the company is, both in terms of resources and consumer acceptance, then the better is it able to use more direct links with the ultimate consumer. The organizational effectiveness of the company will be of importance in deter-mining the extent to which it can rely on its own ability to set up and operate an independent marketing channel.

The nature of the market, too, is crucial in the choice of channel. There are three major aspects here: firstly the type of customer comprising the market; secondly the location of these customers and thirdly their buying and con-sumption habits.

The customers who make up a particular market are only rarely likely to be homogeneous. There will be no one 'typical' consumer but rather a collection of individuals whose requirements and characteristics may be highly diverse. The idea of market segmentation is not new, and has been the foundation for marketing success in a large number of businesses. The con-cept involves the identification of discrete and differing segments or groupings within the total market. These groupings may differ from each other in terms of age, income, social class or whatever; they may differ in their expectations towards the product; some may be price conscious, others may not. The identification of these segments will require careful research. Similarly, the exploitation of these differences will require careful planning. It may be that different segments can be reached simply by changing the label and selling at a different price in different outlets, as witness the growth in private branding. Another way of acting upon these market differences is to use different channels of distribution; an example here could be the selling of shoes at the same price but to highly different market segments by selling through high class shoe shops as well as through mail order chains.

Conversely, the wrong choice of channel could lead to marketing disaster. The type of customer purchasing a highly priced limousine would not respond favourably if the same product were widely available and at different prices. Nor would one expect a low price, low quality good to sell particularly well in an exclusive store. These may seem obvious considerations but they are deliberately chosen in order to emphasize the fact that the type of customer and the type of channel must be compatible.

The geographical location of the customer is of obvious importance. A highly concentrated urban market poses distributive problems of a different nature to those presented by a market where distances between prospects are greater, such as one might find in rural areas. In concentrated situations it would probably be possible to operate a highly effective, possibly individual, delivery service to customers. In rural areas it would be highly costly to maintain the same service and in this case the customer may have to collect from a central point. A wholesaler in the grocery market might find it optimal to deliver to retail stores within a town or city, but may require his rural customers to use a cash-and-carry service operated by him—possibly buying the goods at a discount. In some instances, where customers order low quantities regularly but are many miles distant from the depot there could be savings made by requiring the customer to hold greater stocks. If the goods are perishable or of a sort difficult to keep as stock, then further special problems will be raised.

The third market feature that we isolated as being important in the choice of channel was the buying and consumption patterns of the customers. A product which is bought once a week will require a different method of distribution from one which is bought once a year. In turn the stockholding habits of the customer will influence the purchasing pattern: for example, the pantry of any housewife will invariably have large stocks of canned fruit although these will probably be consumed irregularly and infrequently. The distribution problem is frequently analysed as being one of inventory, and this is true to a certain extent. The requirement of intermediaries to carry stocks will vary from product to product and from market to market, but in all cases the intermediary will be attempting to pass the stockholding function to the next unit down the marketing channel. The ultimate unit is, of course, the end consumer and the problem of inventory can be ameliorated to a certain extent by persuading the consumer to fulfil a stockholding function.

Clearly the foregoing comments have generalized on what are often highly complex situations but it is valid to suggest that most distribution problems can be analysed from this simple product/market viewpoint. How, then, may such distribution problems be resolved?

Choosing the Marketing Channel
Given that a firm or organization has a particular product/market framework upon which it wishes to base its distributive activities, how best may this be done? Mention was made earlier of how the total distribution system

37

comprises a number of sub-systems and how in order to optimize total channel efficiency, it is not always the case that the efficiency of each sub-system need be optimized. Thus in the situation where the firm does not have complete control over the other units in the network there may arise a situation in which each unit is trying to *sub-optimize* at the expense of the total optimum. Yet again, those units in the channel that are within the control of the firm may, through lack of central control and coordination, be attempting to sub-optimize without regard for total system optimization. Maybe the purchasing officer is acting independently of the transport manager, who is likewise acting independently of the production scheduler. All are attempting to perform their own task efficiently, with a minimum of inventory and a maximum of service. However, if the purchasing officer is trying to keep inventory at a minimum, this may lead to problems in production scheduling where the material inputs will vary from day to day. In the same way the transport officer, by trying to minimize vehicle routes and the storage of finished inventory, is throwing an extra spanner in the works. It is easy to envisage a completely inefficient, non-optimal logistics system arising between units within the control of the firm, as a result of each unit acting on its own with its own set of objectives.

It is apparent therefore that the logistics function within the firm must be viewed as being the control of a flow of inventory through the firm from basic input to finished output. The volume of entry of the basic input is a function of the demand for the finished output, but this is not a direct relationship. The nature of the equation between input and output is determined by what happens in the middle, by factors such as storage space, by the number of shifts available, by the size of the transport fleet and so on.

The optimal solution to this equation lies in the family of techniques which for want of a better term may be called *logistics systems engineering*. By adopting the systems approach to channel management we are stressing the importance of interactions within the system's technology. To make this clearer: we must first of all view the distribution system as an interaction of many sub-systems; we must also realize the utility of the channel as a means of providing information feedback as well as enabling the flow of materials; and, most importantly, we must be able to adapt existing distributive systems to our own product/market requirements. The techniques themselves will be described in detail in later chapters. Here we shall confine ourselves to the qualitative basis for choosing the channel of distribution.

Berg[1] has produced a five-step procedure for establishing a marketing channel. This firmly places distribution planning in the wider framework of the corporate plan. Berg suggests that the first requirement is for the development of an overall channel strategy. This will be a review of the company's product/market situation, an examination of the internal and external constraints upon its actions, and a review of the company's standing *vis-à-vis* other members of possible distribution networks. In the language of corporate planning: step one is the position audit.

Step two involves a movement from the general to the specific. The channel requirements of the firm should be stated as a set of objectives, detailing cost

38

constraints, profit requirements, service levels and so on. This statement of objectives is essential if the later step of channel control is to be meaningfully implemented.

Next Berg suggests that the alternative methods for meeting the requirements in step two should be considered. This appraisal should take the form of a distribution cost and revenue analysis whereby activity centres are identified within the systems, and an analysis of the costs and revenues accruing is made in the light of the product/market situation pertinent to the firm. It cannot be overemphasized how important this particular step is, since analysis of this kind will often lead to distribution modes being considered which would not otherwise have been considered, and vice versa. Against this cost analysis must be held the constraints of service commitments already agreed upon in the previous step. Figure 2·1 shows the interaction in this

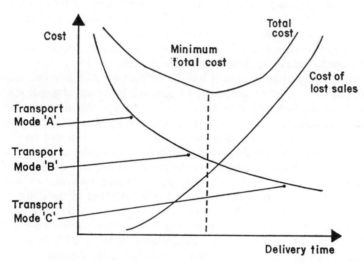

Figure 2·1   Cost Function for Product/Market 'X'

type of analysis between the cost of distribution and the cost of sales lost through longer delivery times. These costs of lost sales, whilst not costs in the usual sense, are nonetheless real costs—the economist would term them 'opportunity costs'. They represent revenue lost through not being able to meet customer requirements.

Thus transport mode 'A' has the shortest delivery time but at the highest cost; mode 'B' has a slightly longer delivery time but costs are lower; whilst mode 'C' is the lowest cost form of transport but takes the longest time. For a particular product these modes could well relate to Air, Rail and Road transport. To this cost function is added a further cost—the cost of sales lost through longer delivery times. This addition produces an aggregate total cost curve which will generally have a parabolic characteristic with a point of minimum cost. Other things being equal, this minimum point will indicate the suitable transport mode for this particular product/market situation.

39

This analysis is restricted in that it only examines two variables, but it does indicate the basis for the more sophisticated cost and revenue analysis that is essential to the proper selection of a marketing channel.

The fourth step in the channel selection procedure is to allocate roles to the various units within the total system. If control can be exercised over these units, then they should be made to adhere to the total overall objectives of the firm.

The final step is to set up the continuous feedback and control mechanism that will enable management to make adjustments, major or minor, to the channel structure and operation. Control of the marketing channel and the sources of channel malfunction will be examined in more detail later.

Improving Existing Channel Efficiency

In the majority of cases the firm will not be operating under conditions of complete flexibility regarding channel structure, and will often have to take its existing channel or channels as given. In circumstances such as these the firm will be more interested in how to get the most out of what may be a bad job than how to introduce change into the system.

The effectiveness of any channel will be a function of many factors, some of them peculiar to a given situation. In general, however, channel efficiency can only be judged in terms of how well it meets the requirements or objectives of the firm. Effectiveness will therefore be assessed in terms of a ratio between costs and benefits. The costs may be real and/or opportunity; the benefits may not always be measurable in money terms, as in the case of customer goodwill or the number of customers generated as a result of good delivery performance. In a sense we are looking for some measure of *marginal* efficiency, that is the payoff accruing to the investment of an extra unit of resource in the distribution effort. When the marginal benefit from that extra unit equals the marginal cost of employing it, then that should be the cut-off point for further investment. Such a marginal analysis is difficult to apply in reality, but work that has been done in this field has yielded encouraging results. Artle and Berglund,[2] working from different precepts, produced a model for channel choice which was based upon the construction of in-difference states between the choices open to the manufacturer. Here they used profit and cost of competing channels as the criteria for comparison. The result was the derivation of a set of decision rules for the particular hypo-thetical example that they took, which allowed the relative sales effectiveness of each channel examined to be assessed. Their model was incomplete in that it considered only the cost of a field sales force rather than taking a more total approach. Nevertheless, it provides a useful starting point for a marginal comparative analysis of marketing channels.

A further important concept for logistics systems engineering is that of the *trade-off*:

Trade-off is the term that describes how objects and attributes are methodic-ally manipulated to determine the full range of system characteristics.
Trade-off may be defined as the exchange of one set of values derived from

40

the relationship of a set of objects and attributes for another set that is to be similarly valued.

> S. L. Optner, *Systems Analysis for Business and Industrial Problem Solving*, Englewood Cliffs, N.J., Prentice-Hall, 1965, p. 105.

Putting this in operational terms it may be that the optimum number of delivery vans operating out of a warehouse in terms of stock carried is three, although this means, say, that the retail shops are serviced only once every five days whereas the volume of sales from the shops is such that stock-outs are likely to occur if they are not serviced every four days. A delivery every four days, however, would necessitate the purchase of a further van. The purchase and operation of this van would be a 'trade-off'. We are exchanging maximum efficiency in one sphere, vehicle scheduling, for a greater total pay-off, i.e. sales revenue. This analysis assumes that the extra revenue generated by eliminating or reducing stock-outs is greater than the cost and operation of the additional van. Another example would be the situation where the firm has limited financial resources and it can either build another regional warehouse or increase the field sales force. The determination of the best trade-off could only satisfactorily be resolved by marginal analysis. The marginal costs and the marginal benefits of the two strategies would need to be compared. The analysis would have to include the possibility that the extra sales generated by the enlarged sales force would not be met through the existing warehouse arrangement. Could an extra warehouse be paid for out of the new revenue generated? Would stock-outs be more frequent and thus lead to a fall-off in sales? It can be seen that in reality trade-offs are often difficult to calculate yet are vitally important in achieving maximum system effectiveness.

Questions should be asked which query the very basis of the existing channel. Why are we only selling via a warehouse; why do we not sell part of our production direct? Is the use of the middleman making our system more efficient or could he be dispensed with and savings made? It is all too often readily accepted that distribution system A, below, is better than system B (Figure 2·2). The thinking behind this is dominated by ideas of costs saved through minimizing transportation by the firm. Thinking globally,

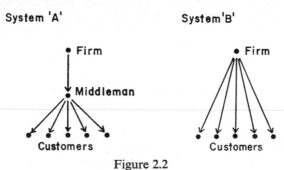

Figure 2.2

however, we may postulate that in some instances the manufacturer could sell more by selling direct to the ultimate customer, increasing revenue more than proportionately to the increased cost of delivery; as witness the success of mail order. Size of order, durability of product and delivery time requirements are also going to affect the differential cost and revenue structures of the two systems. It might be that a dual distribution system (System C, Figure 2·3) is optimal in terms of profit for a particular product:

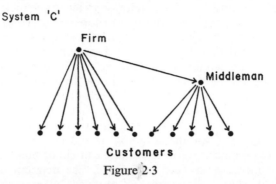

System 'C'

Firm

Middleman

Customers

Figure 2·3

We are now in effect segmenting our market by type of delivery.

An essential feature of all attempts to improve channel efficiency should be that all alternatives or trade-offs are considered and evaluated in cost/benefit terms. In many cases the options open to the firm are limited, but often even these have not been fully explored. In addition, given that a system can be improved, it is crucial that the improved version is flexible enough to meet the requirements of dynamic market circumstances.

Those elements of the channel which are not easily amenable to change are usually the bar to maximizing channel efficiency. In the majority of cases these elements are the other members of the channel over whom little or no control is presently exercised. It is therefore important that the logistics systems engineer understands how channel relationships and power structures can impinge on channel effectiveness.

Channel Relationships
The importance of interface relations in the marketing channel is not always realized. All too often relationships between channel members are taken as given and it is assumed that wherever two entities meet to exchange goods or services for payment there will be natural disharmony in that the goals of one member must necessarily conflict with those of the other. The entity selling the product wants to maximize his margin, whilst the purchaser is attempting to minimize his outlay. What happens according to traditional economics is an uneasy compromise. To a certain extent, where these entities are independent of each other, conflict is more likely to occur than cooperation. What the logistics systems engineer must be concerned with if he is to proceed with his plans for channel optimization, outlined in earlier sections, is to strike a balance between channel conflict and cooperation.

42

Conflict within the channel can come either from the manufacturer or from intervening units. The manufacturer may decide to sell directly to the middlemen's customers or may reduce the margin available to the middlemen. In defence the middlemen may strengthen their links with the next unit in the channel, say the retailers, and attempt to deny that particular manufacturer an outlet or at least to reduce the number of outlets available to him. The source of conflict may come from the end of the channel by retailers banding together to form voluntary chains with greatly increased purchasing power and thus extracting sizeable discounts from the next unit up-channel. Alternatively, particularly in the field of grocery trading, a large retailer may be able to demand that the manufacturer's product is sold under the retailer's own label, i.e. as a private label. Nielsen in a 1969 UK survey[3] of eighteen product classes accounting for over 10 per cent of total grocery business found that private label brands accounted for just under 30 per cent of those products stocked by multiple grocers in terms of sterling value, and for 35 per cent in terms of units. This represents a rapid growth over the last half-dozen years.

A plausible explanation for this pattern of activity has been advanced by J. K. Galbraith[4] who has asserted that where one channel unit becomes of such a size that it is the effective source of power in the channel, then it will eventually be countered by the actions of those who are subjected to its power. In other words 'private economic power is held in check by the countervailing power of those who are subject to it'. The effect of countervailing power must obviously be to produce an equilibrium within the channel, although this equilibrium need not be a stable one. The entry of a new competitor, or a slight change in the balance of power, will lead once more to channel conflict.

Such explanations of channel behaviour bear a certain resemblance to political processes generally, and often an understanding of such processes can lead to a greater understanding of channel conflict. The analogy with political systems has been made by McAmmon and Little[5] amongst others who have shown that channel relationships are determined by much more than the conventional cost, revenue and profit considerations. They state that a channel is a 'political, social and economic complex, and the alignments that prevail reflect all these influences'. This assertion is based on three precepts. Firstly the banding together, whether in a formal organization or informally, of channel members with similar interests, will inevitably lead to bargaining situations. Secondly, in order that a channel unit may achieve its objectives, tacit or overt, it will attempt to control the behaviour of the other members. Thirdly, channel units are economically motivated and will compete for the most favourable terms of trade.

Palamountain[6] has shown that channel conflict will usually take one of three forms:

—Horizontal competition—that is competition between middlemen of the same type; for example, discount store versus discount store.
—Intertype competition—that is competition between middlemen of

43

different types in the same channel sector; for example, discount store versus department store.

—Vertical conflict—that is conflict between channel members of different levels; for example discount store versus manufacturer.

Conflict and competition within the marketing channel are thus likely to be the outcome of the dynamic process that occurs in any exchange and bargaining system where complete control is not exercised by any one unit. Control of the marketing channel thus presents itself as the only certain way of ensuring system effectiveness. However, control need not only come through physical ownership of the marketing units (i.e. through vertical integration), but may be achieved by a system of rewards and sanctions which will bring about a state of viable cooperation. It is to these possibilities for gaining channel control that we now turn.

Controlling the Marketing Channel

Control through cooperation is a concept not often encountered in essays on channel management. Yet cooperation may provide a means of achieving corporate goals without recourse to the more elaborate exercise of achieving power through integration. The dominant unit in the channel is in a position to encourage cooperation in many ways.

Marks and Spencer is an example often taken to show how channel power is achieved through economic strength manifested in a system of sanctions (removal of business) and rewards; however, this organization is also committed to a policy of cooperation within the channel. For example, in order to ensure that they are able to stock new products in the numbers and form that they require, they are prepared to underwrite the financial risks that the producer incurs in setting up a production line for the product.

More common examples are to be found in manufacturer–retailer relationships, where the manufacturer is attempting to achieve or maintain wide distribution for his product in retail outlets. For example, it is not uncommon for the manufacturer to give help to the retailer in advertising the product locally. Often company advertising will prominently mention stockists. Help may be given to the retailer in the display and merchandising of the product; below-the-line promotions in the form of dealer incentives are a common phenomenon, and such incentives may take the form of quantity discounts, free gifts to dealers and so on.

These forms of cooperation are straightforward and uninvolved, but there is no reason why the manufacturer cannot extend his influence over other channel units by cooperating in more radical ventures. Examples that come to mind are the provision of management services to these other units, such as vehicle scheduling for wholesalers and stock control systems for retailers. Indeed cooperation of this sort is one way of achieving the total system optimum discussed earlier in the chapter. Help can be given to retailers in the training of staff, especially where the product is technical or innovatory in nature.

44

Risk, too, may be shared through cooperation. Sale-or-return is a good example of risk-sharing where the manufacturer reduces or removes the risk of loss from the retailer. The retailer will still have to meet stockholding costs and the opportunity loss of not being able to display or stock other items which may sell better. Understandings of this sort can often be mutually beneficial and, indeed, any form of cooperation within the channel may be viewed as being risk-reducing in one form or another.

One spin-off from intra-channel cooperation is that the distribution channel can double as a communications channel. If, underlying the formal system of relationships within the channel, there is an informal system, then information can flow freely both ways. Consumer complaints, middlemen complaints and reactions to the product generally at different stages in the channel can be communicated speedily to the unit concerned and remedial action promptly taken. Figure 2·4 illustrates the concept of a flow of information between units. This flow of information should be two-way and

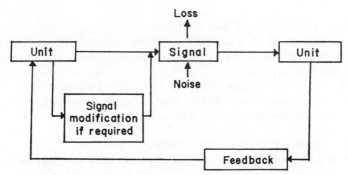

Figure 2·4   The Channel as a Communications Network

should be the raw input of the channel unit's control system. 'Signal loss' is that part of the information flow which is lost—information which could be potentially of use to the unit at which it is aimed but for one reason or another is never actually received. Similarly 'signal noise' is the irrelevant and/or inaccurate information which may seep into the flow of information and cause confusion at the receiving unit. Obviously the most efficient communications network is that which minimizes both signal loss and noise.

Social scientists have for long adhered to the view that 'democratic' systems will function more effectively than 'autocratic' systems. The same may be said for distributive systems. A democratic channel system would be one where the dominant channel unit encourages cooperation and partipation, whereas in an autocratic system the dominant unit acts unilaterally in attempting to achieve goals which may be at variance with the goals of the other channel units. The former system is more likely to achieve better pay-offs all round, in that it tends to the total systems view of channel management where overall functional efficiency takes sovereignty over unit efficiency. Cooperation, or democratic control, involves the recognition of mutual goals

45

by individual units. Under autocratic channel control, antagonism is likely to be aroused and no mutual goals recognized. Activities such as attempting to cut retailers' margins, cutting out middlemen, etc. ar more likely to be dysfunctional and result in a less favourable final position for the dominant unit.

The more usually accepted method whereby a channel unit extends its influence over other channel members is through vertical integration. The unit may integrate backwards and/or forwards. The manufacturer may wish to ensure his supplies by taking control of his suppliers, or he may wish to ensure his outlets by taking over his retailers. The retailer, too, may grow strong and may take control of his manufacturers. Vertical integration implies financial and managerial control: other channel units so integrated become part of the total entity of the dominant unit. In an important study of vertical integration in the marketing channel, Sturdivant[7] has found the following factors to be of major importance in influencing moves towards vertical integration:

A. *Factors External to the Channel System:*
  —The threat posed by a competing system—if retail integration is undertaken successfully by one channel, competing channels are also under pressure to integrate.
  —A change in market conditions—as new market segments, new products, and new product uses appear, marketing problems are created which may best be solved through integration.

B. *Factors Internal to the Channel System:*
  —The presence of firms with a broad market base which permits them to integrate profitably.
  —The existence of channel conflicts, particularly with sources of supply.
  —The presence of aggressive innovators in the system, who are willing to try new channel arrangements.

This classification neatly identifies the major motivations to integration. The only criterion for integration, however, should be financial. 'Can we more nearly achieve our system optimum by pursuing such a strategy?' should be the question uppermost in the logistics systems analyst's mind. By engaging in vertical integration of any sort, the firm is automatically closing its options for change. A vertically integrated firm is not nearly so well placed for taking action to meet changed circumstances that are likely to arise in a dynamic market environment. On the other hand, the non-integrated company faced with a competitive integrated system may find itself squeezed on prices, its supply source cut off, and its outlets reduced.

The key to market success in the distribution context is not solely a function of control. A considered strategy for channel management is essential if corporate goals are to be achieved and maintained. The concluding section of this chapter is concerned with the broader aspects of strategy beyond considerations of channel behaviour—be it control or cooperation.

Channel Strategy

The concept of the 'marketing mix' is not new, although some controversy exists[8] as to whether the practice is applied operationally by many UK firms. Most firms, however, would probably agree that by the manipulation of the various marketing inputs available to them they can have some effect on sales. What elements are actually perceived to be available to the firm will vary from company to company. Most firms, for example, would accept that price, promotion, packaging and customer service are variables over which they have a certain degree of control. Few firms, however, would list 'channels of distribution' as an element in their marketing mix—yet it should be. The choice of channel and the control of its activities can most definitely have an effect on sales. We have discussed earlier how the wrong initial choice of channel can have an effect on sales; we have also seen how a lack of awareness of the dynamic business environment can lead to an atrophy of the channel. It is essential that distribution is included in the total planning and control activities of a firm.

Channel strategy requires a systematic procedure for preparing, implementing and controlling programmes which will more efficiently fulfil the corporate objectives that were discussed in the opening paragraphs of this chapter. What this means is that channel management should be based upon a 'planning-programming-budgeting sequence' (PPBS). This highly successful strategic tool, developed originally by the US Department of Defence, is now the basis for many business and government agencies' operations. The key elements of this process are:

—Systematic decision making
—Goal-oriented programming
—Measurement of programme performance against actual performance.

How may this be applied in the planning of distribution strategy? The first step is to identify the mission or missions that the firm is pursuing (i.e. the determination of goals for the company's products or services) in terms of the needs that they are intended to meet.

Next should come the distribution position audit: an exercise the intention of which is to examine in detail the marketing channel(s) presently used, the degree of utilization of the channel, its advantages and its disadvantages, relation to competitors and so on.

Following this is the environmental forecast which looks at present and future needs of consumers, likely technological changes that may affect the suitability of a particular channel to the product, and the possible direction of government regulation of channels.

The synthesis of these three operations should result in the identification of challenges to the existing distribution system. Sometimes these challenges will come from the actions and activities of other channel members, or perhaps from competitors, at other times changes in the technical nature of the product will require changes in the structure of the channel. The perceived existence of challenges and the examination of possible futures affecting the

47

firm's missions will result in a definition of goals to be met by the distribution system. These goals will be expressed in operational terms, e.g. minimum service levels required, maximum ratios of distribution costs per unit sold, stock levels allowable and so on.

The firm's next step in the strategic process is to list alternative distribution strategies available to it—no matter how unconventional or unconnected with existing channels these may be. To each of these alternatives is applied a

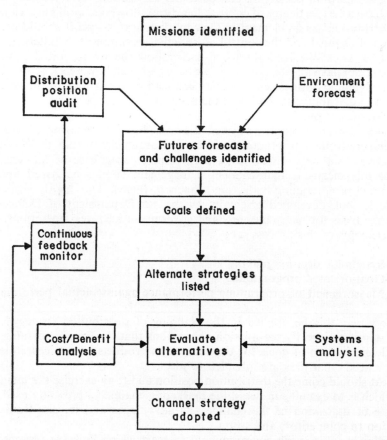

Figure 2·5   The Strategic Approach to Dynamic Distribution Programming

rigorous cost/benefit analysis which will perform a distribution cost and revenue analysis on each alternative proposed. A simple example of a cost/ benefit analysis in this area would be the case of a firm which has three distribution strategies available to it; one of these strategies is of lower total cost to implement than the other two but would result in a lower service level being maintained. Both the other available strategies are high cost ones but would adequately meet the service level required. The choice should be based on the following decision rule: 'Would the cost of lost sales through adopting the first strategy be greater than the additional cost of the cheaper of the two alternative strategies?' Systems analysis can be used to provide estimates of comparative system effectiveness.

Whilst these sophisticated quantitative techniques should be employed as groundwork, the final decision will always be qualitative. The question asked must be, 'Is this choice of channel strategy realistic for this firm given its present and future product/market situation?' The answer to this question is not available through quantitative analysis, but must be based on the experience of the firm and its competitors, upon their present strategic posture and upon the ideas of channel control and cooperation discussed earlier.

The analytical study of marketing channels is a new science and in comparison with some of the other, longer-established management sciences it is puny and unsophisticated indeed. Nevertheless, there is a growing recognition that a fuller understanding of its relationship to its marketing channel can help the firm achieve greater effectiveness in meeting its objectives. Eventually the techniques available to the logistics systems engineer will be comparable in their efficacy to, say, the tools available to the capital investment analyst. Nevertheless, the cost to the firm of developing a systematic approach to channel management need not be high but the payoffs will surely be great.

References
(1) T. L. Berg, 'Designing the Distribution System' in W. D. Stevens (ed.), *The Social Responsibility of Marketing*, Chicago, American Marketing Association, 1962.
(2) R. Artle and S. Berglund, 'A Note on Manufacturers' Choice of Distribution Channel', *Management Science*, July 1959, pp. 460–71.
(3) *Nielsen Researcher*, July–August 1969.
(4) J. K. Galbraith, *American Capitalism*, London, Hamish Hamilton, 1957.
(5) B. C. McAmmon and R. W. Little, 'Marketing Channels: Analytical Systems and Approaches' in G. Schwartz (ed.), *Science in Marketing*, London, Wiley, 1965.
(6) J. C. Palamountain, *The Politics of Distribution*, Harvard University Press, 1955 (quoted in B. Mallen, 'Conflict and Cooperation in Marketing Channels' in L. G. Smith, *Reflections on Progress in Marketing*, Chicago, American Marketing Association, 1964).
(7) F. D. Sturdivant, 'Determinants of Vertical Integration in Channel Systems' in *Science, Technology and Marketing*, Chicago, American Marketing Association, 1967.
(8) R. Hayhurst and G. S. C. Wills, *Organisational Design for Marketing Futures*, London, George Allen & Unwin, 1972, especially Part C.

SECTION B

Transport Modes

Chapter B.3

RAIL TRANSPORT
by P. J. Detmold

Why Rail?
The first step to considering the place of the railway in physical distribution management is the identification of those reasons which justify the existence of this means of moving freight.

There are two fundamental reasons why—all other factors ignored—it is more efficient to draw steel wheeled vehicles along steel rails than to haul pneumatic tyred vehicles along a concrete or asphalt surfaced road. The first concerns resistance to motion; the latter concerns the greater productivity obtainable from rail guidance. The resistance to motion of a rail vehicle at 60 m.p.h. on level track may be as low as six pounds per ton (eight pounds is a typical figure). The resistance of a road vehicle is roughly five times greater.

The productivity argument is much less clear cut. There is no mechanical reason why a one-man train crew should not guide a load of several thousand tons, thus achieving a productivity many times greater than that of the largest road vehicle. (There are of course plenty of political reasons why this is not so and even in North America large freight trains are not usually single manned.) Even with a two- or a three-man crew, it is possible to obtain productivities in terms of tons of payload per crew man hour well in excess of trucking standards.

Crude assessments of this kind conveniently ignore the man hours expended in signalling, in track maintenance and in transferring loads between road and rail, which dissipate the advantage of rail over road and may even vitiate it altogether if rail is not used to its full advantage.

It must be obvious at the outset that if a modern road system is essential to a modern industrialized society then the retention of a rail system on a nationwide scale must be justified by demonstrating that the additional advantages to society are an adequate return on the additional expenditures. The criteria for this justification may not, of course, be merely commercial but may also take social factors into account.

At this point the professional may suspect that there is to be some new exposition of the time-worn road and rail arguments. Be reassured! The essential point is merely that no country would seriously consider disbanding its road system, but however desirable a rail system may be it is physically possible—no more than that—to do without it. Rail must justify itself.

53

The justification may be on social grounds, but in a book on physical distribution management, lengthy discussions of community benefit would probably be out of place and it will be assumed that the railway must be financially self sustaining. That is to say, it must generate a cash flow from its receipts which exceeds the huge outgoing flow in direct operating expenses, new investment, maintenance of infrastructure and management.

Objectives
In the exploitation of the advantages of rail transport for physical distribution, the objectives of the trader and the railway differ radically; one must consider each separately before considering how they interact to evolve the distribution pattern. One of the railways' primary objectives in hauling freight is to make a surplus. This they are most likely to achieve at close to the maximum utilization of those assets which can be used profitably, provided that traffic which cannot pay more than the bare cost of its movement is excluded.

A balance must be found between the utilization of passenger trains, freight trains and track. If profitable inter-city services demand higher speeds, then less paths may be available for other trains. Against the maintenance of high utilization of passenger trains must be offset the poorer utilization of track. If freight train paths are obstructed and demand lengthy waiting periods then this must be taken into the reckoning.

The manner in which a railway may compute the policies which lead close to this profitability objective will evolve as this chapter proceeds; suffice it here to express the view that in the majority of cases the objective will be best achieved by the concentration of traffic on a small number of intensively used routes. Contributing routes may be regarded on their merits but, where alternative routes between two urban centres must be maintained (whether for commercial or political reasons) to serve intermediate points, some specialization of the through traffic on them may be advisable. The railway will also be concerned with maximizing the throughput on other infrastructures, such as marshalling yards and terminals.

There will thus be pressure from the railway toward the development of an intensive operation of high volume long-haul traffic on main lines between principal areas onto which traffic is induced by local feeder networks, each judged on its merits by its overall contribution to revenue and to cost.

From the 'demand' viewpoint the ultimate objective must be to maximize the profitability of production by producing to the point at which no greater profitable output is possible, and to move this production in a manner which minimizes the total cost of distribution. That is to say which minimizes the combined cost of all modes of transportation employed, the use of all load transfer and storage facilities, insurance cost and that of the financing of production (insofar as it is influenced by distribution). The last of these will include the interest payment on goods in transit, the conservation of working capital and the cost of maintaining stock at points of sale which will be less the faster it can be replaced after sale.

Where regular and substantial flows of heavy freight between rail-connected points is concerned (coal, iron ore, semi-finished iron and steel, heavy chemicals, oil, and cement to quote a few) it seems probable that an efficient modern railway will hold the balance of advantage over road transport (though in the case of oil and possibly, coal slurry, very high and even flows may justify pipelines as still more economical).

This is because the mechanical advantage of 'steel wheel on steel rail' is at its greatest with the high axle loads and ratios of load to tare weight consistent with heavy freight, and the productivity advantages of rail are at their highest where the 'unit train' can be used from one large scale plant to another.

In the case of lighter merchandise the mechanical advantage tends to be lower. Where the distribution of finished products is concerned, reduction in trunk haul cost by the concentration of loads into a small number of rail hauls between principal centres is offset by higher load transfer, local delivery and possibly warehousing cost. The advantage may often be small by comparison with direct road transport and it is likely to be very sensitive to journey distance, and size, frequency and regularity of flow.

Markets and Interrelationships
In a country the size of and with the cost characteristics of the UK, the truly 'captive' market for merchandise by rail may be confined to a narrow band of traffic on the longer inter-city hauls, and even here the profitability will be held down by the narrowness of the cost advantage over road transport.

Over the remainder of the market a complex and volatile commercial pattern emerges in which the railway will try to expand its traffic by quoting rates which are often much less than 'full' cost. The pattern will be 'volatile' because both rail and road costs will depend on the volume and the regularity of the flow, and whether it necessitates increases in their respective fleets or can be accommodated by 'back loading' existing vehicles which would otherwise return empty. The situation will constantly be changing as new products come onto the market and existing ones break into new market areas, altering the disparity between outward and return haul and creating the need for an organization capable of adjusting to a changing distribution pattern.

The railways' success in competing with smaller more 'mobile' road haulage organizations will depend in no small measure on its ability to assess its own and its competitors' cost and capacity situation rapidly and accurately. More of this will be said later.

The development of a highly efficient railway system will, however, have a profound effect on the distribution pattern. A fast low cost service will increase the number of nationally distributed products and encourage the rationalization of manufactures into a small number of large plants taking full advantage of scale economies; component and 'semi-finished' products will also concentrate, serving final assemblers further afield. Steel rolling mills and blast furnaces will become fewer in number and will be served by possibly two or three huge ore ports capable of handling the largest ore carriers.

There are certain to be some long time lags in the rationalization of the physical distribution process, however. When factories, their labour forces and ancillary industries are entrenched in certain areas (albeit uneconomical

55

areas) the cost of re-location and the political pressures against it may hamper movement for many years. A high cost railway with an illogical, inflexible tariff may influence the distribution pattern many years after its worst characteristics have been eradicated. Similarly, a highly efficient, low cost railway may fail to generate its potential traffic because it is unable to charge the rates that would ultimately be possible. The sum of the prospective later years of profit discounted at current interest rates may be insufficient to compensate for the certain early years of loss. The sins of the railway fore-fathers may be visited upon the railway sons.

The maximization of profit is concerned with maximization of the gap between the price charged for the service and the cost of supplying it on the one hand, and the extension of the business to include all applications which contribute more to revenue than to cost on the other. The successful operation of a modern railroad is strongly dependent upon its ability to minimize the cost of its operation and to understand its market—the distribution cost of industry in particular—with sufficient perception to pin-point profitable new applications, to understand how much its customer can afford to pay for its services, and to influence industrial location in a manner which favours the profitable exploitation of rail services.

Much work has been done during the last ten years on the means of analys-ing total distribution costs in individual cases which makes it possible to predict the most economical—not necessarily the cheapest—means of transport with reasonable accuracy and reliability. The electronic computer makes it a practicable operation for a transport operator to mass produce these calculations, grossing up the collective reaction of traders to its pricing and other policies.

Alan Stratford referred in his book, *Air Transport in the Supersonic Era*, to developments of these techniques by M. E. L. Spanyoll and the writer, in which freight on the North Atlantic was analysed with the object of determining, for any projected aircraft, the tonnage it could expect to capture on various assumptions regarding the rate structure, the revenue obtainable and the cost. This followed earlier work on this subject by K. R. Sealy and P. Herdson.* There is no reason why these techniques should not be applied to inland transport also.

Of equal importance is the impact of computer technology on the cost side of the equation. Combined with adequate demand analysis it becomes possible to determine an ideal railway system, the specification and performance of the trains and certain significant points regarding the operating pattern and assembly techniques. Much more will be said later in this chapter about the computational methods and the reader is also referred to 'Optimizing Railway Strategies' (in *Long Range Planning*, March 1969) in which the writer describes this work.

Some Fundamental Relationships

As computer programmes conceal their *modus operandi* in their listing, it is intended here to consider some of the fundamental physical relationships

* *Air Freight and Anglo-European Trade.*

which constrain the options open to the railway planner in his search to extract the maximum saleable product from his operation at minimum overall cost. The building up of the relationship step by step should not mask the essential truth that the operation can only be optimized if the whole package of decisions regarding the choice of routes, the routing of the trains, the track layout, train size, speed, operating patterns, etc. is determined as part of one computing process.

What are the criteria to be optimized? This could be the profitability of the railway or, ideally, benefit to the community. To concentrate first on merely minimizing cost is a less pernicious shortcoming than it might at first appear, because it will be seen that the performance standards shown to be desirable are at least as high as the very best on any European railway today.

The maximum throughput on a two-track railway would be achieved if all trains, whether passenger or freight, ran at some uniform speed. The longer the train, the higher the throughput; but this is a point of minor importance because a one-speed railway would have a capacity many times in excess of any needed on any main line in the UK today.

The principal difficulty is that there is no standard of performance that is both satisfactory for the inter-city business traveller and economical for freight. Passenger services today often average around 80 m.p.h. and there are indications that this may have to increase to 100 m.p.h. if the market share is to be retained. For a freight train to average 80 m.p.h.—even though this is now technically possible with recently designed suspension systems— is nevertheless highly uneconomical. This is partly due to the cost of providing the higher power to weight ratio needed and partly because of the higher cost of the wagons per unit of payload. The cost increase would depend amongst other things on the nature of the gradients on the route, but would often exceed twice that of a train averaging 40 m.p.h.

There is a strategic choice therefore when two-track routes are concerned between:

1. complete specialization for passenger or freight purposes
2. providing some pattern of non-stop paths. The longer the two track route, the greater the speed difference between passenger and freight trains, and the greater the frequency of the former, the fewer the freight paths that are available
3. abandoning non-stop paths for freight trains, which would be drawn into 'loops' or sidings for passenger trains to pass.

The principal difficulty of 3. is that, because at least half the cost of moving a freight train is in time-dependent items (such as the standing charges on the train itself and some large part of the wages of the crew), the delay involved in the passing operation is very costly apart from its effect on the service provided to the customer.

Strategy 1 is rarely a practical possibility. Often there is only one route and the passenger service cannot be abandoned. (It might even be profitable!) The cost of maintaining an alternative route solely for route capacity purposes would seldom be justifiable out of the additional revenue obtained (on British Rail, for example, one would deduce from the published accounts that to maintain an additional 100 miles of track and to provide signalling costs, rather more than a million pounds a year would be needed). If this were apportioned, for example, over fifty trains a day, operating 250 days a year and each hauling 500 tons of freight, then the additional cost per ton over and above that on the main line would be some forty pence.

This might be regarded as a 'marginal cost' of operating a fast and frequent passenger service on the main line but it is doubtful if on many routes the contribution of passenger revenue (the direct cost of movement and of maintaining the main line having already been deducted) could support a million pounds per 100 miles of alternative freight route. It is equally doubtful if there are many routes where there is a sufficient volume of profitable freight to support this cost.

The provision of alternative routes and the operation of freight trains which stop frequently for passing purposes are both high cost solutions compared with an integrated service of non-stop passenger and freight trains between main centres. There may be occasions, however, in which it may be necessary to retain alternative routes to serve intermediate points and here some degree of specialization may be possible of through-passenger services on the one and through-freight services on the other.

Some Operating Considerations
The problem of 'marshalling' (sorting) freight traffic must also be considered and its cost must be taken into the reckoning, as appropriate, whenever optimal strategies are to be considered.

The railway has the basic option of adjusting the number of rail-connected terminals and the size of consignment accepted at each. It will compare the additional cost of serving additional points and the greater cost of sorting single wagons against the additional revenue thereby obtained. It will compare the cost of running 'sundries' and parcels depots in order to obtain even more single wagons against the revenue.

The starting point on the chain of marginal cost/marginal revenue considerations is the direct train between the points where the freight enters and leaves the railway. If the maximum accepted load were, say, 250 gross tons this 'no marshalling at all' solution is not as ridiculous as it sounds, although movement cost would be very high and if operated in combination with faster passenger trains this arrangement would be grossly wasteful of route capacity.

There are, of course, a number of circuit-type operations in Britain; for example between coal pitheads and power stations of less than fifty miles in length where the size and regularity of flow justifies rail operation, but the journey distance and the cross-country route makes it not worthwhile to consider any combining of the traffic.

Excluding this type of operation from consideration there are in Britain some twenty-five major industrial areas (the precise number depending on how one groups them) which any national railway system would wish to serve. The second option is therefore to combine all traffic in each such area to each other area in one train a day. If a minimum gross load limit of, say 200 tons were set with scheme 'C', shunting would be of a rudimentary kind, involving much less delay than a full hump yard operation.

An obvious improvement to this system would be to combine traffic between one area (e.g. London) and areas lying on the same route (e.g. Newcastle, Edinburgh, Dundee, Aberdeen). Each area removing a section from the train could replace it with another, but could adjust the power-to-weight ratio by reducing the overall load where the route between major areas is severely graded.

In each stage of development of the system, the additional cost of the sidings needed for the sectioning operation and the additional *time cost* of delaying the train and its crew would be set against the saving through the more productive movement of the larger train.

The reader may wonder at this stage where the benefit to the trader of fast service enters the calculation. The writer believes that with a very smart sectioning operation the overall journey time would, in a country the size of Britain, be highly acceptable to the customer so long as there were no delays for passing and provided that average speed over clear sections averaged not less than 40 m.p.h. Almost all delivery between these areas, even on the longest Anglo-Scottish services, would be within twenty-four hours, private siding to private siding.

What happens to the small consignment? It would be containered, either on its own, or if very small through consolidation at a sundries depot.

The next alternative to this type of arrangement is the wagon load marshalling system with possibly some thirty-five hump yards in a country the size of Britain. It has the advantage that any load down to a single wagon load with a gross weight of some twenty tons can be accommodated. But against the additional revenue this facility attracts must be set:

1. the very high cost of maintaining local networks to collect and deliver very small loads
2. the cost of maintaining and operating the yards (stated to be more than £11 million in the B.R. accounts for 1968)
3. the huge time cost of the standing wagons. (The net book value of the B.R. fleet was approximately £157 million at December 31, 1968, which suggests a standing charge per day of roughly £50,000.)

As in any other industrial process, the value of the input to the system must be considered against its cost.

The main alternatives are therefore (a) no marshalling, (b) local marshalling in industrial area with a set minimum consignment and only sectioning at intermediate points and (c) a full hump yard system.

It remains to point out that any diversion of more highly rated traffic to some premium service will influence the number of points which can be served by the remaining system at any given minimum consignment size specification. The smaller volume of traffic remaining for 'non premium' service between

59

any two points will make the service less marketable either because smaller, higher cost trains will be used or because it will be less frequent.

Before such a service is introduced, its effect on the overall economy of the system should be compared with upgrading the standard of service on the system as a whole. In the past it was usually assumed that a slow service was cheaper to operate than a fast one. The paramount need in present day conditions to maximize productivity of men and machines casts doubt on the continued validity of this concept.

Mr R. A. Long, when chief planning manager to the British Railways Board,* said that 'considering the engineering factors in isolation' a speed on level track of 60 m.p.h. with a gross load of 2500 was the most economical for trunk movement in Britain. If one also took account of commercial factors it would hardly be likely to *decrease* the speed, which suggests that the best compromise between the dictates of cost and of demand lie within the narrow range of Mr Long's 60 m.p.h. and the Freightliners 75 m.p.h. maximum. Not very far from a single uniform speed for rail freight!

In cases where the total freight moving between each pair of principal industrial areas exceeds 2500 gross tons a day, then what would be the point of offering other than direct service or of dividing the traffic into higher and lower categories for movement purposes? (Traffic might continue to pay premium rates for movement at the most popular times of the day or night.)

It will be apparent that the optimization of the railway policies toward passenger and freight train performance standards, route network and track layout, train length, service frequency and marshalling arrangements, and technical specification of equipment, are all part of one massive problem in which each decision taken reacts and interacts with others sometimes in very complex relationships. The repercussions throughout the system of the large number of decisions required can only be estimated with the speed and frequency needed for efficient management if the system can be simulated by electronic computer. These decisions vary from the planning of the next day's operation to long term strategies; the computer system needs to be able to operate both rapidly with the constraints of the short term situation and also to provide the more comprehensive analysis appropriate to the larger numbers of 'degrees of freedom' of the longer term.

Some Criteria for Transportation Demand

To this point the railway's place in physical distribution management has been viewed mainly from a cost standpoint. Rigorous analysis from a demand point of view requires the thorough study of total distribution cost of all potential rail user industries to establish the precise user criteria and constraints within which the use of rail is advantageous. In the absence of this, analysis can at best be rudimentary.

The two most fundamental criteria for comparison between road, rail, and combined use of road/rail are transport charge and transit time, though service frequency, reliability of transit, freedom from danger and pilferage,

* In his paper 'Corporate Planning in Railways' to the Institute of Transport, November 1968.

and maintenance of suitable temperature provide constraints, often of a *sine quâ non* kind.

Where the movement of such basic 'heavies' as coal and iron ore between rail-connected ports and pits at one end and integrated steel works and power stations at the other is involved, an efficient, intensive rail operation can still undercut road haulage in price when the throughput is several thousand tons a day, even where journey distance may be as little as thirty miles. In these circumstances differences in road and rail transit time may be of little significance. Although in theory stockyard area could be reduced with the greater delivery frequency of road haulage, it is doubtful if the risk of holding less than, say, eight hours supply would be acceptable, because the cost of an occasional unscheduled shutdown would heavily outweigh any saving.

At the other extreme end of the scale, transit time will be at its most important where high-value goods are to be moved over 'long hauls' such as Glasgow–London and Edinburgh–London. Here the journey by freight-liner averages in the region of 45 to 50 m.p.h., but there is also time at terminals and collection and delivery to consider.

It must be pointed out at once that road can only achieve this kind of performance where well-organized haulage firms have sufficient and regular traffic on the route to change crews within the length of one working shift. The smaller firms involved in roadside rest periods would, of course, take very much longer for a 400 mile haul. Road is also subject to delay through fog and ice, though it must be admitted, if in a whisper, that rail has also been known to have delays under such conditions.

Rail may also have a time advantage in long haul block traffic between private sidings. Motor cars, car parts, oil and heavy chemicals are examples. On the other hand this is offset by the additional time to load an 800 ton train by comparison with a road vehicle.

Outside these classes of traffic a large proportion of rail freight has the time disadvantage of having to be 'marshalled' into trains in the vicinity of the pick-up point, possibly again close to the destination and in really bad circumstances at one or more intermediate points. This process can only be short-circuited (1) by containerizing the traffic, in which case against the saving in marshalling yard time must be offset the time spent in container terminals, or (2) by running a train which is marshalled at one end of its journey straight into a road/rail terminal at the other. Some finished steel traffic is handled in this way but there is, of course, the time in the steel terminal to consider.

When it is borne in mind that the overall time in a marshalling yard will usually be upwards of four hours, one reaches the unhappy conclusion that a haul of 150 miles at an average of 25 m.p.h. net of marshalling and with three 'sorts' at four hours apiece will have a gross average speed of just a little less than $8\frac{1}{2}$ m.p.h.

What is the value of time? Where reduced transit time enables bills to be paid more quickly then the capital moves back into the materials entering the production cycle at an earlier time. If the firm's production is limited by the length of its order book, then only the interest on the capital value of the goods in transit is concerned. Where the firm is short of working capital the value of time saving is very much greater, but case studies are needed to evaluate it.

By this means it can be shown that for a daily consignment of 120 type-writers, weighing 2 tons, valued at £30 each to a warehouse 150 miles away serving fifty retail outlets, if transit time from plant to warehouse is three days and from warehouse to outlet is one day, the cost of carrying inventory is £24 per day. If transit time from factory to warehouse were reduced to one day, the cost of inventory would become £16·4 per day.

The differential saving per ton/mile between a three-day haul and a one-day haul is around 2½p. Clearly the value of time saving will heavily outweigh any small cost difference between transport modes. Fast transport will get this kind of business.

After working out a few examples of this kind one rapidly reaches the conclusion that as more and more manufacturers apply total cost analysis to their physical distribution problems, the market for third day delivery, wagonload traffic carried in elderly wagons and hauled at 25 m.p.h. average speeds will virtually disappear where high value : weight ratio products are concerned.

The Development of the Marketing Approach

British Rail have made a very substantial and effective marketing effort in recent years and many lucrative contracts have been gained. But if the company train concept is to be extended to part loads too small to be hauled as 'block loads' but sufficiently large to be assembled with other part loads by a fast and simple 'sectioning' operation, then their interest must extend to the production process itself.

Production may be considered in three broad categories:

1. homogeneous products
2. batch processes
3. multiple production-line products.

Where homogeneous products (e.g. soda ash) are concerned there is no *physical* reason why production for the London area, for example, should not be produced two days a week, for the Midlands once on a third day, the north-east on a fourth day, and so on.

It will become necessary to carry larger stocks at the receiving plant, but against this the total quantity in transit at any one time will be much smaller with one through load a day than with two- and three-day transits. British Rail have made some notable developments with products of this kind in cooperation with some of Britain's largest and most efficient manufacturers.

Where batch processes are concerned, clearly this kind of rationalization cannot be achieved to any substantial extent. If, for example, a steel works produces beams of one particular size on one particular working shift, then they will execute all orders for that product. To carry out all London orders on one day would involve re-setting machinery several times each shift, or

62

carrying some substantial buffer stock at works. The former would be very time wasting; the latter not very attractive to the steelmen unless accompanied by some substantial incentive.

Where multiple production lines are concerned it again becomes possible to dispatch orders in sequence to all areas, although inventory and warehouse cost would have to be analysed with various possible rail and non-rail solutions.

The most that may be said with conviction is that it might reward the railways very handsomely to get into the business of distribution cost analysis on a large scale, to identify fields in which rail movement can be sold in a total production package.

The Contribution of Systems Planning

Systems Planning assists a large organization with a very complex operation to compete with smaller organizations with more simple problems. The railway needs to understand the consequence both of its own decisions and also of changing circumstances outside its control, firstly upon its own cost and secondly upon those of its traders who will be influenced by the service the railway offers and by its charges.

The railways' 'own decisions' must be evaluated in the same degree of detail as that in which they are taken and those in financial, commercial, operating and technical fields must be considered as inseparable parts of the one overall problem of running the railway.

It will already have become apparent to the reader that each decision in any of the above-mentioned fields will influence cost and constrain the range of choice decisions in each other field. They are all interdependent. Almost every decision regarding the specification of technical equipment links into this nexus of complex relationships, expanding it until it covers the full spectrum of railway operation.

Consider a few examples. The type of signalling system will influence the spacing needed between the trains, and therefore the paths available, whilst the cost of providing and operating it feeds back into the fare and rate structure.

The specification of locomotive also has some significant side effects. Diesel-electric locomotives designed for speeds of up to 75 m.p.h. (and not suitable, therefore, for express passenger trains) generally haul larger freight loads than those designed for 100 m.p.h. or for higher speeds. The key factor here is the minimum speed at which full power can be delivered for sufficient time to climb the most severe inclines. The specialized freight locomotive, because it can deliver its power to a lower speed, generates a greater tractive effort and hauls a greater load. But against this advantage must be offset (1) the effect upon traffic demand of an (admittedly small) increase in journey time, (2) the possible loss of train paths and (3) the possible loss of utilization resulting from largely separate passenger and freight power, all of which—you will have guessed—redound on the level of cost, charges and, therefore, traffic.

I have involved the reader in what may seem an inappropriate degree of technical detail to show him how complicated the railway decision-taking

63

nexus must inevitably be. Inevitably, that is, if the exploitation of the fundamental advantages of rail is to be optimized.

Some Further Implications
British Rail has, in recent years, tried to use the computer in a number of ways to tackle this problem. The F.R.A.T.E. system of programme, for example, tries to cost a railway as far as possible from 'first principles'. It costs each of a huge permutation of choices available to the railway and tests them in a variety of circumstances beyond the railway's control. It then establishes the strategic combinations of decisions which are either optimal economically in a predicted set of circumstances or, as is often preferable, establishes the strategies which stand up best in the broadest variety of foreseeable circumstances.

The programme starts work on the dimensions and density and other physical characteristics of the load to be hauled, and simulates its accommodation in wagons of all suitable kinds and any projected new designs. It simulates the haulage of these wagons in trains of every length within constraints of technical possibility.

The programme proceeds to consider physical characteristics of the route in terms of curvature and gradient, and experiments with each design of locomotive, finding the maximum load for one, or for two, or even three coupled together, assuming various standards of performance. It can be used to specify the leading characteristics for a new design of locomotive.

In each of a huge permutation of wagon types, train length, locomotive types, performance standards, it works out the cost of providing, manning and maintaining the locomotives and of the fuel which would be consumed. Other programmes performing similar tasks for computer services are used in conjunction with the one described, and others which work out how many trains can be run over each route. It is thus possible to proceed from the individual freight loads to be hauled, to the overall cost of running the railway and then, by costing each of the feasible combinations of decisions, to discover the best.

It follows very importantly that plans made to optimize the operations of any one department of the railway (e.g. to minimize the cost of providing wagons) will not necessarily maximize the overall economy of the railway. In fact it would be a quite extraordinary coincidence if they did. There are no grounds for supposing that the best overall combination of decisions will minimize the individual cost of each individual technical department. It is, in fact, far from certain that the plans of each business department to optimize their financial position will necessarily optimize the railway economy as a whole, because each makes a competing demand on jointly used resources which will be used more profitably in one way than another.

What is required, therefore, is a corporate pattern of decision-taking in which each department states the full range of alternative decisions available in its specialized field, with the investment and operating cost needed for each of a range of future years. Forecasts are needed of the probable revenue to be expected at each standard of service from each class of traffic.

The function of the planner is, then, to compute each alternative set of compatible decisions and their financial implications. Various degrees of 'technological forecasting' can be built into each alternative on the advice of the technical departments, taking note of the risk and the consequences of failure to achieve the technical targets set thereby.

It is incorrect to assume that this procedure is solely concerned with long-term planning. Each time the marketing department spots some opportunity, the implications on the overall plan, the adjustment needed on the decision sequence, and the consequence on revenue and cost, must be evaluated in order that the favourability of the business may be assessed and the lowest rate limits established, below which it would not be profitable.

The difference between the system I have outlined for central planning computation and an arrangement whereby central planners assess plans produced by each individual department, is a subtle one. My experience is that in the former case, cooperation between individual departments and the computing team can be very effective, because working closely together, they evaluate the overall effect of each of their decisions. They are no less involved than if producing the plans themselves. The essential difference is that the whole of the business of railroading is looked at as a single problem.

The implications on organization are profound. In any large business responsibility for advice on policy matters is divided between departments either on a 'functional' basis (e.g. production, sales, distribution, etc.), or on a 'professional' basis (e.g. mechanical engineering, economies, etc.), or on the degree of '*futurity*' (e.g. long range planning, line management, etc.). What will be the effect of fitting into the organization a central 'think sink' involving itself equally with short- and long-term problems concerning the professional and functional departments in a manner which frequently cuts across boundaries between one manager's responsibility and another's?

By removing much guesswork from the routine task of predicting the outcome of decisions, this arrangement frees managers to exercise more studied judgment on the quality of their initial assumptions and the nature of their objectives. But at the same time, it broadens the business and technical character of these assumptions, involving managers much more closely with one another in the achievement of their objectives and much more closely with the achievement of the objectives of the business as a whole.

Where the railway is concerned the most significant influence of all may be on philosophy. Although specialists will remain, the pervasive idea that a man and even a manager is fundamentally an engineer, or an 'operator', or 'commercial' may be undermined. The railways' educational system has long recognized the approach of the inter-disciplinary age in the curriculum of staff and management training courses. Central computerized planning provides the tools whereby broader ranges of interest can develop and on which ideas can be tested. We look backward to the age of the railways but forward to the maturity of the science of rail-roading.

This development may be expected to increase the mobility of the large business when competing with the small, and to decrease significantly the reaction time in which all railway departments deploy in response to changes in a fast moving market environment, linking their actions to the needs of a changing pattern of physical distribution.

If full advantage is taken of development in modern management techniques, then the railways still have a vital part to play in the management of physical distribution, in the rationalization of industry and in the development of the intra- and extra-European trade pattern.

Some Criteria for Choosing the Transport Mode
To conclude, it seems desirable to develop some general principles for deciding when rail transport may be advantageous, though these will summarize and therefore repeat some of the earlier content of this chapter.

At the onset it must be emphasized that the very best basis for decision must be to analyse the advantage and the cost of the distribution system using each combination of road, rail and, where appropriate, air transport. This analysis would consider rail transport in each form suitable for the goods in question (e.g. freightliner, company train, etc.)

Any general criteria must be a poor substitute for total distribution cost analysis. Rail transport over hauls of under 100 miles will in Britain only normally be advantageous for a heavy and regular flow, such as the merry-go-round coal operation.

Where bulk commodities are concerned, the longer the journey distance, the greater the size of each consignment to each destination, and the higher the frequency and regularity of shipment, the more probable it becomes that rail will be part of the best transportation arrangements.

Where manufactured goods are concerned, the above principles will hold good, but here there is the additional possibility that containerized rail transport might be preferable to the use of rail 'vans', whether operated in unit 'company' trains or in smaller formations. Where it is possible to operate a unit train directly between private sidings it seems doubtful if any other solution involving rail transport would be preferable.

Where this is not possible and goods would have to be transferred to road vehicles at one or other end of the journey, then freightliner might well be advantageous, more particularly where fast high quality transportation benefits the economy of the distribution system.

Chapter B.4

ROAD TRANSPORT
by Andrew Dare, David Hedges and Alan Slater

Road transport is the major transport mode within the United Kingdom. The Ministry of Transport Industries has calculated that road transport accounted for no less than 82 per cent of the total inland freight tonnage in 1966. It is estimated that transport costs typically account for one-third of the total physical distribution cost and, therefore, road transport is the major cost element in most companies' physical distribution system.

The road haulage industry in Britain is being increasingly affected by new government restrictions and heavier taxation. The restrictions are designed to minimize the socially undesirable effects of large lorries on our roads and to make rail transport more attractive. These restrictions include legislation for the prevention of noise and pollution, for the easing of road congestion, and for prevention of accidents.

The total number of goods vehicles on the road in 1968 was estimated to have been 1,565,000 vehicles, which was 11 per cent of the total vehicle population; but of these over 50 per cent were of less than 30 cwt. unladen weight.

We intend to examine road transport in four major sections. The first will deal with the structure of the road haulage industry and the major changes caused by the 1968 Transport Act. The second section considers the determinants of the transport mode to be used. In particular it examines the costs and the advantages of road haulage. The third section covers the supply aspects of roads and equipment. It further investigates the organizational techniques that can be used to make more efficient use of the available resources. The final section deals with the future development of roads and road transport. Throughout this chapter road transport will be considered in the context of the total physical distribution system.

THE STRUCTURE OF THE BRITISH ROAD HAULAGE INDUSTRY

Pre-1968 Transport Act
The Road and Rail Traffic Act of 1933 introduced a licensing system to road haulage for the first time. This and various other provisions were consolidated into the Road Traffic Act 1960. Under this Act there was a three-tier system of licences. There was an 'A' licence which was for public carriers who carried

other shippers' goods for reward. There was a 'C' licence for carriers who only carried their own goods and there was usually little difficulty in obtaining this licence. Finally, there was a hybrid 'B' licence which allowed carriers to carry both their own and other shippers' goods, and these licences were usually restricted to certain categories of goods and to specific geographical areas.

The 1968 Transport Act

The 1968 Transport Act affected the entire transportation system within Britain. It reorganized the nationalized transport companies, created passenger transport authorities, established a new goods vehicles licensing system, and gave new powers to local authorities to regulate road traffic.

Part I of this Act set up the National Freight Corporation to provide integrated road and rail freight services. This body took over the Transport Holding Company's road freight and shipping subsidiaries. It also, in effect, became the retailer for the majority of the railways' freight interests in that rail only retained the responsibility for obtaining 'private siding' traffic. The National Freight Corporation, therefore, is a direct competitor of road hauliers through their ownership of British Road Services and Pickfords, etc. and an indirect competitor through their ownership of National Carriers Ltd and Freightliner Ltd.

Set out below are the main requirements for operator's licences, special authorizations and driver's hours, although for a full understanding the reader should consult Parts V and VI of the Act.

Operators' Licence

The operator's licence must specify all vehicles and trailers owned, hired, or loaned by the operator. The operator can later add vehicles to his fleet provided the licensing authority is notified within one month of the acquisition, and the total fleet size specified on the licence is not exceeded. It appears, therefore, that a margin for future expansion of the total fleet should be allowed at the time of application to avoid frequent variations of the licence. A person may apply for an operator's licence to the licensing authority in whose area his operating centre is situated. If he has operating centres in various licensing authority areas, then application has to be made to each relevant licensing authority. Applicants must be prepared to give details of:

—the purposes for which the vehicles are to be used
—the arrangements for ensuring that drivers' hours regulations are complied with and for ensuring that vehicles are not overloaded
—the facilities for ensuring that vehicles will be maintained
—activities previously carried on by applicants
—convictions during the previous five years for failing to maintain vehicles, breaking speed limits, illegal parking, etc.
—financial resources of applicant
—names of directors and officers where the applicant is a company.

Part V of the 1968 Transport Act superseded most of the previous regulations applying to road haulage. This section removed the requirement for separate commercial licences for all vehicles below 30 cwt. unladen weight. It is estimated that this exempted 900,000 vehicles as, from the passing of the Act, they were treated in the same way as private motor cars. The Act completely changed the system of licensing for vehicles above 30 cwt. Its primary purpose was to ensure road safety and, therefore, a system of quality licensing was established whereby all hauliers had to apply for an operator's licence. A secondary purpose was to encourage bulk long-distance freight to be sent by rail, and so special authorizations were to be required for vehicles over 16 tons plated gross weight.

Part VI of the Transport Act introduced new regulations for drivers' hours. The primary purpose was to improve road safety by eliminating excessive driver fatigue.

The licensing authority will normally publish all applications and only the following bodies can object:

—certain prescribed trade unions
—the Road Haulage Association
—the Freight Transport Association
—the Chief Officer of Police
—a local authority.

The burden of proof lies with the objector. Grounds for objection are that the applicant cannot meet one or more of the safety criteria outlined in the previous paragraph. Before granting a licence the licensing authority have to satisfy themselves on these safety criteria, as well as satisfying themselves as to the competence and suitability of the transport manager and the proposed holder of the licence. An operator's licence, if granted, will normally be valid for a period of five years.

In all operator's licences one person must be nominated as responsible for the operation and maintenance of the vehicles. This person must hold both a transport manager's licence and a responsible position within his company. Operators who contract out their maintenance will still be required to have a transport manager and will still be held responsible by the licensing authority for the condition of their vehicles.

The licensing authority can revoke an operator's licence for various reasons, including failing to maintain vehicles adequately, convictions for speeding, failing to keep proper records, giving false information, and bankruptcy. When the operator's licence is revoked, the licensing authority can disqualify the holder for any period. It also appears that the transport manager could have his licence revoked if his vehicles fail to comply with the safety regulations.

Special Authorizations
The Transport Act included provisions for the use of 'special authorizations'. However, there is some controversy at the time of writing as to whether this section of the Act will be implemented.

Special authorizations are required to use a vehicle of 16 tons or more plated weight for journeys of 100 miles or over and for loads exceeding 11 tons for any journey length.

69

Applications are made to the licensing authority where the operating centre is based. Details of the vehicles to be used and the service proposed must be given, e.g. goods to be carried and the places between which they are to be moved. The licensing authority then sends a copy of the application to the Railways Board and the National Freight Corporation. The Transport Act states that these bodies must object within fourteen days, if at all, 'on the ground that the service or part can be provided by that body, or a subsidiary of that body, wholly or partly by rail'. The objection must be accompanied by a statement of the charges that would be levied by the railways and the authorization is to be refused unless it is less advantageous for the shippers to use rail. The relevant factors to be considered by the licensing authority in deciding on whether the service is less advantageous are speed, reliability, and cost.

To aid in the enforcement of the 'special authorizations' no goods are to be carried in a vehicle of 16 tons or more plated weight unless the driver has a properly completed consignment note.

Drivers' Hours

The objective to improve road safety is met by Part VI of the Transport Act 1968 which brought in more exacting requirements as to drivers' hours.

The Act placed a limit of sixty hours of duty a week on drivers. It specified that there must be at least eleven-hour rests between each working day and that a working day was to be no more than eleven hours. Further, in a working day no driver may actually drive for more than ten hours.

To assist in implementing these regulations a mechanical recorder was to be fitted to each vehicle and no driver was to drive a vehicle unless this recorder was in working order. However, this provision created much unrest amongst the drivers and so was not implemented. To ensure that drivers' hours were enforced the Drivers' Hours (Goods Vehicles) (Keeping of Records) Regulations 1970 replaced the 1935 Regulations. These regulations did away with the old system of loose-leaf sheets and introduced a record book with each page serially numbered. This is intended to overcome the problem of where the driver had one set of records for his employer and another set for the police! The employer must keep a record of the books he issues; the driver must enter his name and address on the front of his book and fill in the details of the day's work as he proceeds. This book is the driver's record and hence he must enter all his driving in this one book, even if he drives for two or more employers.

Current Situation

No vehicle below 30 cwt., whatever its purpose, need have an operator's licence. From February 2, 1970 heavy goods vehicle drivers were required to have special licences and from March 1, 1970 the new driver's hours and records regulations took effect. As previously mentioned, the use of mechanical recorders for driver's hours has not been made mandatory.

From March 1, 1970 the 'O' licence replaced the old 'A' and 'B' licences and from June 1, 1970 the old 'C' licences were gradually replaced.

The transport manager's licence has not been introduced. It is anticipated that those persons already holding such positions on the date of the introduction of this scheme will automatically get a licence. Others will have to pass examinations to obtain the licence. It is not yet known what the syllabus will be for those examinations, but it is expected that it will concentrate largely on the safety and legal aspects of road haulage.

The maximum weight at present allowed on the road is 32 tons but it is thought that during the 1970s this will increase, first to 38 tons and then, perhaps, to 44 tons to bring the United Kingdom in line with Continental standards.

To ensure the safety of commercial vehicles the Construction and Use Regulations for Road Vehicles 1966 made it mandatory from 1968 for all new vehicles to be 'plated', and laid down minimum braking requirements for all vehicles on the road. Now all commercial vehicles above 30 cwt. must be 'plated'. 'Plating' is merely the fixing of a plate about six inches by four inches to a vehicle which specifies the maximum gross weight that can be carried and the axle weight limits. This is to prevent overloading and unequal load distribution. The Road Safety Act 1967 introduced an annual testing system to ensure the observance of these regulations and other maintenance and safety requirements such as noise and smoke emission, lighting, etc. The Ministry of Transport operate testing stations for these annual tests, which became compulsory for all commercial vehicles from April 1, 1970. The Ministry of Transport inspectors are also empowered to carry out spot roadside checks, both of the condition of the vehicle and its load.

The Main Ramifications of the Transport Act 1968

The distinction between public hauliers and own account fleet operators has now disappeared in law for vehicles under 16 tons, and hence own account operators can now carry goods for reward. Further, there is now usually no restriction on the use to which the vehicle can be put. This gives scope for the own account operators to reduce the costs of distribution by carrying other shippers' goods on the back haul. The number of own account operators wishing to find back hauls could well be significant, as many vehicles make regular runs and return empty. This in turn could lead to the expansion of clearing-house type agencies to ease the task of finding back hauls.

The Transport Act increases the cost of maintenance and record keeping. Further, the penalty of poor maintenance and incomplete records is to lose the 'O' licence altogether. A cheaper and safer alternative for many companies may be to sell off their fleet and to buy their transport from specialists. Alternatively, certain routes may be more economically served by specialists, whilst other routes are better served by owned vehicles. The Act gives greater flexibility to the distribution managers but to realize the benefits the distribution manager must have an accurate and detailed knowledge of all the relevant costs.

The ten-hour driving day regulations have a greater effect on the long-distance hauliers as drivers for short-distance hauliers rarely drive ten hours in a day. However, the limit of sixty hours per week on duty will be the main obstacle for short-distance hauliers. To overcome these increased labour

71

restrictions, hauliers will have to pay more critical attention to routing, scheduling and minimizing idle time both at the customer's premises and at their own depots.

The requirement for a transport manager to be named on the operator's licence and the proposed licensing of transport managers will raise the status of this position. Further, as transport managers will face the risk of losing their licence, they will expect to be able to take what action they consider necessary without hindrance or pressure from other functions within the company. It is, therefore, probable that many companies will have to pay higher salaries to the transport managers in order to compensate them for their risk and expertise, and to re-arrange their internal organization to give the manager the necessary authority for him to be able to discharge his new responsibilities efficiently. The establishment of the National Freight Corporation and the introduction of the special authorization procedure is intended to divert bulk long-distance freight onto rail. However, it will still be necessary, in most cases, for goods to be taken by road to the nearest freightliner terminal and to be collected by road at the other end. Hence, although the long-distance haulier may well suffer, the main impact on road transportation would appear to be the greater use of inter-modal transport on the longer journeys. The National Freight Corporation are in a unique position in that they alone are retailers of road, rail and sea transport and should, therefore, be able to lead the way in developing inter-modal transportation.

Every mode of transport has to have a motive power unit, a terminal, and a track. Unlike rail, road transport does not require massive investment in a track, as this is provided by the state. As a result the fixed costs of the operation are relatively small. This allows easy entry to the industry, which makes it very competitive. However, the new licensing system lays down severe maintenance regulations to ensure vehicle safety. The need for proper service facilities increases the fixed costs of operation which will tend to restrict entry to the industry and favour the larger operator as he can spread these fixed overheads over more vehicles.

DEMAND FOR ROAD TRANSPORT

Demand for road transport in the United Kingdom has risen considerably over the last ten years. This is illustrated by the fact that in the period 1957–67 the total tonnage carried by road transport has risen from 1300 million tons to 1787 million tons. There are a number of reasons why this has occurred and these will be discussed in the following sections.

Advantages of Road Transport
Road transport has a number of advantages over other modes of transport. These can be listed as:

—speed
—flexibility
—control
—adaptability.

72

Road transport has the advantage of speed and the use of containers is helping to cut down handling times—which in turn enables maximum use to be obtained from the vehicles.

Flexibility is an important advantage of road transport. Vehicle bodies can be built for specialized purposes, such as refrigerated vehicles and tankers for transporting powders in bulk. This flexibility is less easily obtained in some of the alternative modes of transport.

An essential element of any transport system is control, and road transport, particularly in the case of own fleet operations, has the advantage that control can be fairly easily maintained. There is less risk of delays or interruptions through strikes with this mode of transport.

Road transport also has the advantage of adaptability. Vehicles can be moved around the country to adjust to changes in demand and also road transport enables the service level to be adjusted to the individual customer needs.

DISADVANTAGES OF ROAD TRANSPORT

Road transport has, however, a number of disadvantages. Firstly, the size of the load is at present limited to a maximum of 32 tons (including the weight of the vehicle). Secondly, there are distance constraints, as the restrictions on drivers' hours limit the distance that can be travelled in one day. Additional costs are incurred when vehicles have to be away from base for periods greater than a day—such as parking costs and drivers' allowances for overnight stops. Thirdly, limitations of road conditions and parking facilities can reduce the speed advantage of transport. The development of the inter-urban road system is tending to reduce this disadvantage.

Choice of Mode of Transportation
There are five basic modes of transportation for goods—rail, motor carrier, water, pipeline and air. Table 4·I illustrates the percentage of goods moved by different modes of transportation in the United Kingdom in 1967.

Table 4·I

COMPARISON OF TONS AND TON MILES MOVED BY VARIOUS MODES OF TRANSPORT—1967

Transport Mode	Tons millions	%	Ton miles millions	%
Road	1,500	84	43,000	58·7
Rail	201	11	13,600	18·6
Coastal shipping	52	3	15,500	21·2
Pipelines	27	1·6	1,000	1·4
Inland waterways	7	0·4	100	0·1
Air	—	—	10	—
Total	1,787	100	73,210	100

Source: Road Transport Federation, *Basic Road Statistics*, 1969.

Factors Affecting Choice of Transport Mode
The following are the main factors affecting choice of transport mode:

—product characteristics
—length of haul
—cost of alternative modes of transport
—service and reliability
—stage in manufacture.

Product characteristics   Product characteristics play an important part in the selection of a given mode of transport. This is particularly true in the case of perishable goods such as foodstuffs: 97 per cent of all foodstuffs in the United Kingdom are transported by road. Fragile goods, bulk liquids and powders are also dependent upon road transport, although some liquids are increasingly being transported in bulk by rail. The relationship of the cost of transport to the product sales price again affects the mode of transport used. Products with a low selling price and low density tend to utilize relatively low cost forms of transport, such as rail and water, whilst products with a high selling price and high density, such as transistors, are more able to utilize more expensive forms of transport because the additional cost of transport is relatively small per unit and is often more than offset by savings in inventory costs.

Length of haul   The length of haul is often the most important factor in the selection of the transport mode. The use of road transport reduces the cost of materials handling through its ability to make door-to-door deliveries. As materials handling is the critical cost on short hauls, road transport predominates in this sector. The average length of haul for road transport is about 25 miles and 84 per cent of the goods transported by road travel less than 50 miles. This can be compared to rail where length of haul is about 70 miles for general goods and 135 miles for specific products.

The nature of the end market often determines the mode of transport selected. Where the end market is highly dispersed, as in the case of foodstuffs and building materials which have to be delivered to many outlets, road transport is often the only feasible mode. In both cases deliveries tend to be over short distances not only because the destinations are dispersed, but also because there are numerous origins, which again favour road transport. On the other hand, where the end market is concentrated, larger volumes are usually moved over greater distances, enabling the shipper to consider alternative modes for the line haul.

It has been estimated that in 1966 approximately 80 per cent of all long distance haulage, measured in tons, was carried by road, whilst rail accounted for 20 per cent. Thus, it can be seen that road transport is playing a major part in both short and long haul transport, but this situation may be altered by the implementation of the special authorization procedure which aims to encourage long distance freight to go by rail.

Cost   Costs of alternative modes of transport should be considered before a specific mode is chosen. It must be realized that the mode with the lowest freight rates may not necessarily result in the lowest total distribution cost. Transport cost has to be related to costs in other parts of the distribution system. The effects of a given mode of transport on other parts of the system such as warehousing, inventory levels, packaging and administrative costs have to be considered so that the overall system is optimized to produce maximum profit. Higher speeds and smaller loads lead to increased transport costs, but they can also lead to significant savings in inventory costs. This trade-off should very often work in favour of road haulage.

Other factors   Such factors as service and reliability are playing an increasingly important part in the selection of the transport mode. The mode of transport used has to be selected so that either service is maximized given a cost constraint, or a given service level is obtained at minimum cost. The flexibility of road transport enables companies to adjust their transport requirements so that customer service levels may be matched with customer needs. Goods to be transported can be classed as raw materials, semi-finished products, or finished products. Each class may require a different mode of transport and a different service level. With the introduction of operator's licences, own account operators will no longer be restricted to the type of goods they can carry. With increasing costs of transport, companies may find it profitable to use their own vehicles to collect raw materials from suppliers. The profitability will depend essentially on the material cost savings, the nature of the product, and the presence of spare capacity.

Choice of Road Carrier
Once a decision has been made to use road transport, a second decision has to be made among:

—own fleet operation
—hired contract transport
—leased vehicles
—combination of above.

As was pointed out previously, the 1968 Transport Act allows own fleet operators to carry other shippers' goods for reward. In 1962 it was estimated that empty running accounted for one-quarter of total road transport mileage. There are, however, considerable organizational difficulties and rate setting problems associated with trying to fill return loads. These problems must be overcome if such arrangements are to be both convenient and profitable to both parties. Other problems would be the time spent in finding back hauls and the handling time associated with these loads.

   The decision between running one's own fleet and hiring one's transportation requirements depends on the financial position of the company, the nature of demand for transportation within the company, and the total operational costs associated with each alternative. One common combination

75

is to use own fleet operation for the average level of demand supplemented by hired transport to cater for seasonal fluctuations.

The length of haul also affects whether one's own vehicles or hired transport is utilized. The greater the length of haul, the higher is the probability that hired transportation will be used. This is related to the requirement for either relief drivers or night parking facilities for long hauls and public carriers are often more able to provide these services. When hauls are less than fifty miles, road transport on own account predominates. Further, many companies employ driver/salesmen to distribute their goods and this again favours own transport.

Advantages of Leased and Hired Transportation

Leasing and contract hire are alternatives to owning one's own vehicles. Leasing is normally associated with rental of a vehicle, the capital cost of the vehicle being borne by the lessor, who then hires out the vehicle, over a longer period of time than is generally the case with hire purchase.

Contract hire can be custom-arranged, the contractor may provide the vehicles, which are taxed, insured, maintained, garaged and complete with driver. Contract hire companies can provide a complete operating service and some offer warehousing facilities as well.

The main advantage of leasing is that if capital is limited within a company, vehicles can be acquired without capital expenditure. Operating the leased vehicles would be the same as for own fleet operations. Contract hire, on the other hand, can include all operating costs and in this case the company's transport requirements are being provided by an outside organization. Contract hire is advantageous for both small firms where capital is limited and for larger firms where capital can be employed with a greater return elsewhere. Further, contract hire provides the complete transport system for the company at a previously agreed cost.

The decision to own, lease or hire is very complex, and cost is not the only factor to be considered: service and reliability of the contractor have also to be taken into account.

Costs Associated with Road Transport Operations

A basic understanding of road transport costs is required when choice of either mode of carrier is being considered. These costs can be divided into static and running costs, as Figure 4·1 illustrates.

Operating costs are those directly related to the vehicles, whilst the fixed costs include such items as buildings, power, office expenses and salaries. The various fixed and operating costs have to be combined to produce an overall cost per vehicle mile, or cost per vehicle hour. Vehicle depreciation has been shown as both a running cost and a static cost. Usually the vehicle engines and transmission are depreciated on a mileage basis and are, therefore, a running cost. Vehicle bodies, however, are normally depreciated on a time basis and are regarded as static costs.

It has been estimated that transport costs are typically about 30 per cent of total distribution costs. For this reason, it is essential that transport costs

76

should be continually monitored and any adverse variances should be analysed and corrective action taken if necessary.

Costs can also be broken down on a percentage time basis and as an example the figures for a four thousand gallon oil tanker are shown below:

	%
Loading	6·5
Moving	57
Unloading	12
Maintenance	14
Idle	10·5

(Assuming a 24-hour day)

Source: Freight Management, April 1968.

From these figures it can be seen that for maximum utilization of the vehicle, the time spent on loading, unloading and maintenance should be kept to a minimum. Driver productivity schemes can also help to maximize the utilization of vehicles by increasing the average speed travelled on the road.

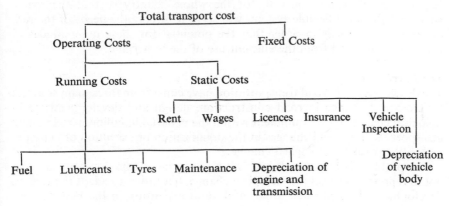

Figure 4·1

SUPPLY OF ROADS AND ROAD TRANSPORT

For the last decade Britain has had a large and ever-expanding road building policy, based on new motorways connecting urban centres, and on urban improvement schemes. The motorways form part of a programme designed to provide a national network of modern inter-urban routes. In the urban areas, the improvement programme is designed to eliminate some of the heavy congestion and to give free access from the cities to the major inter-urban routes. In a number of cases this has been done by building urban motorways, some of which are already open as in London, Leeds, Manchester and Newcastle.

The main objectives of the government's road development schemes are: to improve communications; the rehabilitation and improvement of town and countryside; the improvement of access between the home and work;

the reduction of traffic congestion; and improvements to assist industrial development generally, and development areas in particular, including better access to ports and large market areas.

The present position, therefore, is one of heavy congestion in towns. However successful the railways are in recapturing the long-distance goods traffic, the volume of commercial traffic in towns will hardly be affected. The increases in population and the rising gross national product will also cause an increase in the private car population. To ease congestion, the loading and unloading of goods at business and commercial premises in towns is increasingly being controlled, and companies are being encouraged to move into rural areas. However, this movement of commercial enterprises to rural areas increases the number of rural origins and destinations, which in turn increases the total amount of traffic on the rural roads.

The main problem is that the road systems have in the past been developed from projections of urban growth and associated traffic predictions for individual towns rather than from planned urban growth for the country as a whole. Now each regional infra-structure is being developed to meet the requirement of planned growth for the whole country so that the roads, which are the most flexible system, will serve to supply the needs of the rail, air and sea terminals in order that the potential for these other modes of transport is realized from the efficient use of the hinterland.

The Developments

The developments in road transportation have come from three main sources: technological change in road construction, design and development; technological change of the equipment within the material handling, terminal and transport facilities; and changes in the organization or execution of activities with little or no technological change.

The problem is how to integrate all three forms of development in order not to repress or restrict technological change, but rather to adapt the various developments into planned urban and rural expansion in the best possible way.

Since distribution covers the transfer of goods from the point of manufacture to the final consumer, each development must be considered in the light of its total costs and benefits which should include the indirect social costs and the creation of demand in associated industries. All developments in the field of transportation should be designed ultimately either to reduce the total costs of the physical distribution system or to increase the service level and thereby expand the market.

Technological development in all three forms outlined above will affect the choice of the transport mode, the route, the warehouse and factory locations, primarily by widening the choice of possible alternatives, and by altering the relative attractiveness of the various possible alternatives for each of the above elements. For example, changes in handling costs relative to movement costs may affect the choice of route and the location of warehouses. The pressure of adapting to this technological change will be intense, and the price of using obsolete methods high.

Road Patterns

The government policy for roads is to develop a national network consisting of urban and inter-urban roads. The object is to stimulate economic growth and reduce prices by reducing transport costs. This can be achieved through easier accessibility, improved service level and reliability of service, reduction of the necessity for warehouse facilities and associated inventory, and the reduction of the capital employed in distribution. The effects of the proposed road improvement schemes on the physical distribution system will, however, be even greater in scope. Larger and faster vehicles may be used, and working capital in the distribution process could be reduced. There will be greater savings in time and operating costs, there may be fewer accidents and reduced insurance costs. Regular delivery schedules will be possible, and as a result may lead to reduced inventory.

It can be questioned whether the transfer of vehicles from a congested road to a new route will facilitate the circulation of other vehicles. E. J. Mishan argues that road improvements would be nullified by increases in traffic according to Parkinson's Law—that vehicles expand to fill the road space made available—and indeed there are indications that the generation of traffic is a function of the resources available.

The optimum allocation of resources for roads, however, would be related to the speed of vehicles and the cost of congestion. The road design should, in the first instance, be related to the maximum permissible speed of vehicles. Secondly, it should aim to reduce congestion costs so that the density of traffic at any point on the road is so low in relation to the capacity of the highway that one vehicle in no way impedes the speed or progress of another. Obviously, the optimum situation would require so many resources, and in particular a large acreage of land, that it is impossible to achieve; but the urban and inter-urban road proposals for the seventies are striving towards this goal.

The inter-urban roads will be a network of high-quality roads, mainly motorways, to provide vital access between major cities, ports, and industrial regions. The future development will be concentrated on a number of carefully selected trunk routes and will provide a high-quality road system to all existing and planned centres of population. These routes are outlined on the map at the end of this chapter (Figure 4·3); the motorways and dual carriageways being those completed or proposed and the 'strategy routes' being those roads to be improved in order to establish a comprehensive national network.

The urban roads are the main problem for the future, since urban areas are already congested. The Buchanan Report outlined the problems and proposed a number of road design solutions, but the main way to relieve the long-term traffic congestion must be by technological change in material handling, terminal facilities, transport facilities and improved organizational methods.

The basic urban problem of congestion could be solved by a system comprising urban motorways, primary distributor roads, district distributors, and local distributors (see Figure 4·2). The motorways and clearways will provide an immediate and effective solution to the congestion problem on main traffic routes, but the district and local distributors will have to be of a high enough standard to clear the traffic leaving the clearway, otherwise blockages will occur.

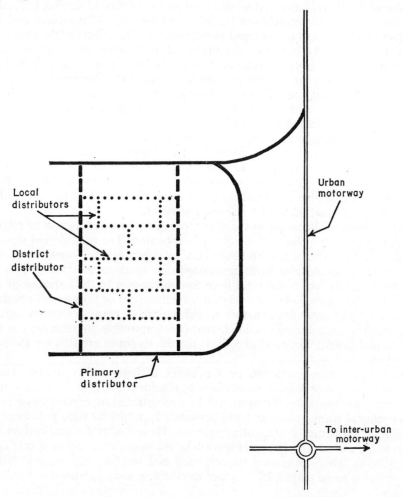

Figure 4·2   Road Network Design in Urban Areas

New kinds of town centre and suburb designs allocate special areas at the rear of shops and commercial premises to allow deliveries to be undertaken away from other traffic and pedestrians, thus facilitating a secure and rapid delivery service. Wider roads and new one-way systems improve traffic flows and increase access routes to manufacturing, commercial and warehouse sites. This enables larger commercial vehicles to be used, and thereby encourages greater economies of scale.

The relief of urban congestion will also be assisted by the introduction of computer controlled traffic lights, police controlling traffic from helicopters, improved communications between traffic police and the road user by radio, new traffic signs and improved road markings.

It is anticipated that the construction of the urban road system will accommodate the planned traffice expansion. Any unplanned traffic expansion can, therefore, be met only by improved materials handling technology, and new organizational techniques in order to improve the utilization of the planned road system.

Equipment

At present there is a rapid movement towards technological developments and improvements in the equipment used for materials handling, terminal and transportation facilities. By reducing the turnround time and increasing the speed of vehicles the total vehicles required for a given demand can be reduced which, in turn, helps to reduce congestion on the roads.

There may be a need in certain industries for developments in automatic warehousing, and more efficient systems of moving goods from the warehouse to the transit vehicle. There will also be a need to develop more powerful and efficient vehicles with power steering and braking, automatic gear change, and either electric or gas turbine engines if they can be proved to be more efficient than existing petrol and diesel engines. Such developments may be encouraged by the government: either by easing the regulations, for example, by allowing larger containers up to 45 feet long and vehicles of 44 tons gross laden weight, or by more severe regulations such as the enforcement of new noise limits which may encourage the introduction of gas turbine powered vehicles.

Organization

The most important area of development is that of changes in the organization or execution of an activity by making use of the current technology within the physical distribution system. An important example of such a change is the use of containers and detachable bodies for internal and international freight transport.

Possible future changes in techniques may include: improved training of vehicle operators; increased vehicle utilization and the use of detachable trailers on the back haul; the use of computer techniques for vehicle routing, depot siting and vehicle fleet planning.

One organizational technique which has been considered in the last few years is the delivery of goods to destinations in urban areas at night in order to avoid traffic congestion. The operators will be able to run two or three shifts and maximize their vehicle utilization, but the retailers and wholesalers may have to be persuaded to accept the system because they have to pay for night staff.

81

The Tendency towards Inter-Modal Operations

Road transport is often the only way of moving goods from the origin to the destination, but roads may not be used through the entire transit process. Rail, air and sea terminals use road systems as a vital link in the transport chain and, as previously mentioned, the 1968 Transport Act aimed at increasing this type of transport. This leaves the road systems with the short hauls of origin to destination; longer hauls of origin to destination which could only go by road due to the physical characteristics of the products; and the shorter hauls of origin to terminal, terminal to destination, and in some cases terminal to terminal. Shorter line hauls are going to promote faster and more efficient material handling methods in order to maximize the time utilization of the motive power unit and greater productivity of labour. Transit containers will be required to match both the international standard dimensions and the characteristics of other modes of transport.

THE FUTURE OF ROAD TRANSPORT IN THE PHYSICAL DISTRIBUTION SYSTEM

In the future, rail may be able to increase its share of long haul traffic. There will, however, be an increase in urban and short haul traffic of which the vast majority will go by road. In order to accommodate the increasing goods traffic, pressure will be applied to encourage a number of changes in the country's physical distribution system, such as new urban motorways, clearways and through-ways in order to avoid the hazards of congestion and its associated costs; improved methods of material handling in order to facilitate increasing inter-modal transport; and improved organizational techniques to maximize the use of the resources available.

Two current major changes in the pattern of distribution will affect the road transport system of the future. The first is the rapid expansion of freightliner, air freight and international container freight traffic giving rise to inter-modal traffic flows on an ever-increasing scale. The second is the trend in urban development towards large groups of retail stores within a concentrated area with special unloading facilities. This may lead to the use of multi-product delivery systems on a large and more frequent scale from a large town depot.

Another major factor is that as Britain grows closer to Europe in trading links, there is a need for vehicle weights and dimensions in Britain to match those of the continent. If the road systems were to develop as far as the building of a channel tunnel, then a new pattern of European export distribution may develop using long hauls by road as the basic physical distribution transport system.

Eventually, however, the same technology which develops new road system designs and new or improved methods of materials handling, terminal or transportation facilities, may direct a large part of freight transport away from the road to an old or a new system of transport. Pipelines may be used to transport bulk liquids like oil or beer to the local distribution centre, or a freighting hovercraft may be used from coastal, inland river- or canal-side sites for a one day European delivery service.

In the shorter term, there is likely to be a tendency towards larger fleets within the road transport industry because of continued pressure on costs, the competitive structure of the industry and the ramifications of the Transport Act 1968. This Act, in particular, specifies the need for adequate maintenance facilities. This inevitably increases the overhead costs which tend not to vary directly with the number of vehicles and hence economies can be achieved by expanding fleet sizes as the fixed element of overheads can be spread over more vehicles. The larger operator should, therefore, be able to offer lower rates and so attract a greater proportion of freight. Further, these higher fixed costs will tend to make entry to the industry more difficult, and so reduce the number of new entrants, who are usually small in size.

To forecast the relative movement as between public hauliers and own fleet operators is more difficult. For the reasons mentioned in the previous paragraph, the own fleet operators with few vehicles are likely to find it more economic to contract hire their transport from large specialist hauliers. Larger own fleet operators have to trade-off the likely cost advantages of using specialists against the benefit of increased control of using their own vehicles. The cost advantage of using specialists is likely to be greatest where the own fleet operator is unable to secure regular back hauls.

There is no reason, of course, why transport specialists should not themselves expand to cater for more elements in the physical distribution system. There are already many companies which offer both warehousing and transport facilities, and there are several organizations who provide other services as well such as packaging, inventory control and even the selling of the product. As such companies grow, so more own fleet operators will have to review their distribution policies and decide whether it would be more advantageous to contract out the whole physical distribution process to specialists.

Conclusion

Transportation is often considered a necessary cost and, as has been seen earlier, it is a major element in the cost of physical distribution. Transport however, can also generate revenue through service. Transport provides a service by adding time and place utility to products through the movement of goods. Consequently, economic rationality dictates that road haulage can pay only when goods are on the move to their destinations. The 1968 Transport Act, by increasing the potential competition for carriage of goods and by increasing the costs of carriage through more exacting safety requirements, puts more pressure on hauliers to improve efficiency. Improved efficiency can be obtained by reducing costs whilst maintaining the service level, alternatively increasing the service level whilst maintaining the cost, or a combination of both. Frequently hauliers talk only in terms of cost and forget that they can also compete through the service that they offer. Further, if it is remembered that transportation is part of the total distribution system, then the opportunities for 'service' are enormous. For example, more careful transportation can reduce breakage and packing costs, quicker transport can reduce

83

Motorways and dual carriageways
(completed or proposed)

Strategy routes (completed or proposed)

Figure 4·3   Inter-Urban Road Proposals for the Seventies

inventory, and containers reduce handling costs. In other words, hauliers may often be able to reduce the total distribution costs of their clients by offering higher cost/higher service facilities, but they must understand the costs and the trade-offs involved to be able to sell the idea to potential users.

By 1985 the government will have spent £3400 million to provide 4000 miles of new or improved inter-urban roads. Even this may not be enough to face the mounting problem of road congestion, and pressure will be applied to the technologies of vehicle design, material handling, road design and to the improvement of organizational methods in order to maximize the use of the additional resources which will be made available. The problem is to plan the future road development to meet planned expansion in total vehicles, and any excess unplanned demand will itself necessitate changes in technology and organizational methods within the industry. Planning for the future will necessarily direct technology towards the goal of minimum cost and maximum vehicle utilization; and towards the reduction of social hazards such as noise, pollution and accidents. These goals are critical because, even by the year 2000, road transport is still likely to be the major transportation mode on our island due to the dispersed pattern of retail distribution and the fact that road haulage can offer speed, flexibility, control, and adaptability.

References

R. V. Arnfield, *Technological Forecasting*, Edinburgh University Press, 1969.
R. W. Faulks, *Elements of Transport*, Shepperton, Ian Allan, 1969.
G. A. Hughes, *Company Freight Management*, London, Gower Press, 1969.
E. J. Mishan, *Growth: the Price we Pay*, London, Staples Press, 1969.
F. Wentworth, *Physical Distribution Management*, London, Gower Press, 1970.
British Road Federation, *Basic Road Statistics*, 1969.
'Vehicle Fleet Management', *Financial Times*, 24 February 1970.
National Computing Centre Ltd, *The Impact of Computer Technique on Road Transport Planning*, 1969.

Government publications:
Survey of Road Goods Transport, Final Results, Part I, 1962.
Transport for Industry (Summary Report): B. T. Bayliss and S. L. Edwards, *The Transport of Freight*, Cmd 3470, 1968.
Traffic in Towns (Buchanan Report), 1963.
Road Safety Act, 1967.
Transport Act, 1968.
Goods Vehicle (Plating and Testing) Regulations, 1968.
Transport for Industry (Summary Report): B. T. Bayliss and S. L. Edwards, *A study of the determinants of demand for transport in manufacturing industry conducted for the Ministry of Transport*, 1968.

Chapter B.5

SEA AND CANAL TRANSPORT

by Ian Churcher

1. SHORT SEA TRADE (SHORT DURATION SEA PASSAGE)

A different approach is necessary in dealing with traffic moving by short sea routes (up to 36 hours on passage) to that for deep sea routes. A different description, such as 'short duration' and 'long duration' services, better expresses the differences, and these terms will be adopted for greater clarity. On short duration sea passages, where goods are not packed conventionally, it is better that the equipment used to carry the goods should be owned by the through-carrier, in order to meet the varying packaging needs of the product. On long duration services it is probably better that the shipowner provides the equipment, where durability is a major factor. There is an overlap on certain services where either can economically supply the equipment. There are also certain cases where the shipowner can and does offer the whole through service from door to door.

The main types of equipment used to carry goods are as follows:

1. Semi-trailers (including tank, bulk, powder, tilt, refrigerated)
2. Articulated vehicles with their own driver
3. Lorry and trailer with their own driver
4. Containers (normally complying with the ISO requirements)
5. Flats (some do and some do not comply with the ISO requirements)
6. Pallets.

Containers can, of course, be in many forms: tank, bulk, powder, refrigerated, etc., and with doors or lids in every position.

For short duration voyages, in view of the wide market to be covered, it has been found that a more efficient and economic service is available to the client if the through-carrier provides the equipment, the land transport, and the customs clearance and is therefore the only contact the shipper (or receiver) deals with to move his goods. This simplifies documentation and pinpoints responsibility.

Certain shipowners do provide these services but it depends very much on the volume of flow there is on the short duration sea passage—the larger it is, the more difficult it becomes for the shipowner to provide an efficient, economic through service. The exceptions are where the shipowner also owns the rail service and, to a much more limited extent, the road service connecting with the sea service. Even here there are exceptions.

2. DEEP SEA TRADE (LONG DURATION SEA PASSAGE)

Where the goods are not moving in a conventional vessel, the shipowner invariably provides the equipment in which to move the goods, as the standardization of the size of containers (for container services) is most important for the efficient utilization of space in the vessel. Tied to this factor is the need to pass certain of the containers to and from depots in the hinterland for packing and unpacking.

The shipowner can arrange to deliver door to door, depot to depot, or quay to quay. The choice is left to the client which firm he uses for the land haul (i.e. the shipowner's service or a through-carrier's service). [Through-carriers are also called 'forwarding agents' or 'freight forwarders'.]

3. ROLL ON–ROLL OFF

Services are available on both short and deep sea routes for drive-on drive-off freight—though it appears that this facility can be at its most efficient in the short sea trade. However, if the shape of existing trailers changes (e.g. if wheels get smaller and axle loadings increase, without increasing the point loading on the road) there will certainly be a re-examination of their use in the deep sea trades.

Flexibility
The advantages of this mode are that anything that has its own wheels or tracks can be driven, towed or pushed on or off the vessel. This avoids packing, lifting/lowering and labour costs. For these reasons the goods can be transported more cheaply, as no expensive cranes and strong berth foundations are required to accept the loads imposed, and the labour force is kept to a minimum.

The most common means of moving general cargo is in the semi-trailer, which is parked on the quay prior to departure by the land haulier. The shipowner then uses a tractor unit, usually provided with a fifth wheel-coupling which can be raised or lowered about 3 feet, which couples on to the semi-trailer, hydraulically raises it so that the landing wheels are well clear of the ground, and tows it on board the vessel. There it lowers the semi-trailer on to a special trestle to bear the weight of the forward end of the trailer and disconnects. The unit is then lashed into position.

Discharge is effected by the same method and the land haulier at the port of destination picks it up in the usual way. Earthmoving equipment, export cars, caravans, etc., can all be driven or towed on and off quite simply. Ro-Ro ships are frequently used to carry pallets, which are moved on and off the vessel by fork trucks. At a certain point it is more economical to put the pallet loads in trailers or containers/flats at the point of origin and move them as a larger unit. In addition the shipowner can also carry containers, flats and pallets by placing these on ship's trailers (or slave trailers).

The client's vehicle, with the container on it, arrives at the quay, and the container is lifted from the road trailer on to a ship's trailer, which is then handled in the same way as the semi-trailer described above. At the port of destination the container is lifted on to the road trailer for onward carriage. The same system prevails if the container is moving by railway wagon. However, at a certain level of traffic flow it is more efficient for the container to move in a specially constructed ship and for special fast-working gantry cranes to be used (see below).

It will be appreciated that by carrying containers and flats on Ro-Ro ships, cranage (secondary handling equipment), labour and ship's trailers have to be provided by the shipowner, thus raising the cost as compared with the handling of semi-trailers. However, to handle pure Ro-Ro traffic it is necessary to provide a vessel with strong decks to accept high point loads and high axle weights, and fitted with ramps and shorebridges. The cost of this may be partly offset by using the same vessels for the carriage of passengers with their own cars. However, this restricts the carriage of cargo which might prove hazardous. Obviously, the Ro-Ro vessel is extremely flexible as compared with a specialist type of ship constructed to take only a special type of cargo-carrying unit. Again, the choice is made by the shipowner in favour of that ship which gives a reasonable economic return and can cope with the traffic flow in the most economic way for the client.

Control
The control of a unit moving by Ro-Ro is simple, as the vessel is no more than a bridge. If the semi-trailer has its own tractor unit and driver, it requires just the same control as if it were on a normal road journey. Otherwise, it is handled by the through-carrier's tractors, and no unnecessary freight need be paid for the carriage, by sea, of the tractor unit.

The shipper also has the same control over his goods that he has for a normal road haulage movement. He knows where to go to secure retribution if there is any delay in the delivery of his goods, he can ensure that delivery dates to his client are kept, and if there is any pilferage or damage he deals with one man—the through-carrier. He who pays controls.

Fleet Utilization
Certain firms who carry their own products by road find it efficient and economical to use Ro-Ro vessels as a bridge, and the receiver has no fear that the sea passage will cause any more delay than a land haul. Water is no longer a barrier to trade. It is, in fact, probably safer to move units by water than by land. The average overall speed of a vessel is no less than for a road vehicle. Furthermore, on short sea routes the driver can often have his rest period, when he cannot legally drive, on board the vessel.

Through-carriers who are hauliers themselves can utilize their tractor units efficiently and secure the maximum load-carrying work out of their semi-trailers by using Ro-Ro. On a typical overnight Ro-Ro service 4–6 semi-trailers can be served by two tractors. The advantage of trailers over containers is the better utilization that can be obtained by quicker positioning for return loads. Conversely, the advantage of the container is the lower initial cost and the supposedly lower cost of maintenance [though insufficient experience has yet been amassed of container use to state this latter point with confidence].

TIR Convention (Customs Convention on the international transport of goods under cover of TIR carnets).
The specification for the construction and sealing of semi-trailers (and containers) to enable them to be approved for the carriage of goods over frontiers sealed and unexamined is laid down by the International Road Union operating from Geneva.

The TIR carnet is issued by the authority of the Ministry of Transport through the Road Haulage Association and the Freight Transport Association Ltd. This covers passage through Continental and, in certain, circumstances, UK ports. Not all countries are signatories to the agreement.

Conditions of Carriage
Whilst goods are carried by sea, the conditions laid down in the bills of lading issued by the shipowner apply. However, the through-unit operator is usually carrying goods under CMR conditions (convention on the contract for the international carriage of goods by road) which impose greater responsibility upon him.

Low Cost
By using the Ro-Ro system, stock holdings and capital invested in this operation may be substantially reduced, and so released for alternative investment opportunities.

Speed
Transit times of 7 to 10 days from despatch in the UK to arrival at the customer in Germany, for example, were common with conventional vessels. By Ro-Ro this is now reduced to a matter of hours—36 hours being quite normal. This has enabled markets to be found by UK exporters which are closer in time to the customer than their competitors on the land mass of Europe. If control is good, the unit is moving all the time at a steady average speed, and up to 21 tons of goods are delivered at one time.

Unit Hire
It is normal for the through-haulier to quote a fixed price or contract price from door to door, and the unit is supplied by him. Naturally, if the client wishes to utilize the unit to store his goods for a certain time, demurrage or hire is charged.

Operators in the Ro-Ro trade invariably own their own trailers and do not hire them as container operators sometimes do.

Special Traffic
a. *Bulk Liquids*   Beer, edible oil, chemicals, etc. are carried in considerable quantities. Steam-heated tankers are being replaced by electrically-heated

90

ones. Many vessels provide steam (typically at 80 p.s.i.) but it is necessary to check the pressure required and available, and to confirm the diameter of the coupling used, as this may vary.

Tanker operators should ensure that the manhole covers are tight and do not leak. Thermometers must be provided on the unit. Operators are also required to provide clear, written instructions and any special equipment that may be required in case of accident.

Electrical power is usually available (at 380/440 V, 3 phase, 50 cycles), but this has to be checked at the time of booking. It is equally important to check that the tanker's plug connections suit those provided on the vessel, and that power is also available at the vessel's berth in case of delay.

b. *Heavy Lifts* Indivisible loads are ideal for carriage on low loaders on Ro-Ro vessels. The dimensions of doors may vary and deck capacities also vary but in the main both the linkspan and the vessel's decks are constructed to the HB loading standard (British Standard 153/1954) as laid down for bridges on the public highway.

c. *Animals* Anything from dogs in kennels to a complete circus is carried. In the former case the crew usually attends to the wants of the animal for a small fee, whilst in the latter case the attendants will, of course, accompany the units. The equipment used to move animals on the road is invariably acceptable by Ro-Ro vessels.

d. *Mobile equipment* Under this heading are included cranes, bulldozers and the like. Depending on the dimensions of the doors of the vessel and the wheel/trackloadings, these are normally carried without major difficulty.

e. *Controlled-temperature units*, usually refrigerated units—these are provided with electrical connections and dealt with as described above in the case of bulk liquids.

4. CONTAINERIZATION

Cellular Container Vessels

These have been found to be economic to maintain where a high traffic flow occurs or can be created by using the service to link land terminals which are road- and above all rail-served. Containers complying with the International Standards Organization (ISO) requirements as laid down in British Standard 3951/1967 (Specification for Freight Containers) with top corner lifting are normally the only type acceptable by these vessels. There are five types:

Designation	Height	Width	Length	Rating Kgs	Tons
A	8′	8′	40′	30·480	30
B	8′	8′	29′ 11¼″	25·400	25
C	8′	8′	19′ 10½″	20·320	20
D	8′	8′	9′ 9¾″	10·160	10
E	6′ 10½″	6′ 10½″	7′ 10½″	7·110	7

Normally only types A, B and C are accepted and used.

The vessel's holds are provided with guide rails to hold containers in position when stowed under deck. The lengths of the cells holding them can be varied. Containers are also carried on deck and secured by special lugs to the hatchcovers or by special couplings and lashing chains when double stacked. (More than one can be stowed upon another if required, and if the vessel's design permits.)

The handling is usually effected as follows: from client's unit to quay trailer (or on to quay) by straddle loader, gantry crane, mobile crane, etc. The quay trailer is then towed under the gantry crane loading the vessel. The gantry crane picks the unit up by the top corners, transports it over the cell required and lowers it into position. Discharge is exactly the reverse. The working of the vessel varies but either the gantry crane moves on rails as each set of cells is completed to the next set of cells, or the vessel itself is moved to bring the required set of cells under the crane.

The gantry crane is usually able to accept lifts up to 32 tons under the twist locks. A spreader is used with guides to locate the corner twist locks on the container's corner castings. Some spreaders are hydraulically or mechanically extendible to enable them to take lengths of 20 feet, 30 feet, 40 feet under the control of the crane driver. The crane itself often extends sufficiently far over the vessel to permit it to handle containers to and from a barge moored outside the vessel. It also extends sufficiently far landwards to land or pick up from a number of traffic (road or rail) lanes as well as from/to stacks of containers on the quay, within the travel of the crane.

The quays have to be specially strengthened to take the imposed loads. Containers are stacked on the quay up to six high for types A, B, C and D and up to three high for type E.

In practice it has been found unsatisfactory to work directly from/to rail wagons as this slows down the working. A normal cycle takes two to three minutes from pick up to uncoupling, if loading and discharging are being carried on at the same time. There are certain vessels with their own handling equipment on board which are capable of handling units of up to 25 tons each.

Flow

As mentioned above, it is the large flow that makes this types of vessel economic. This and the handling equipment required on the quay entail considerable capital expenditure. However, the saving is in labour power: the pattern of handling has to be very carefully planned and controlled to avoid delays both to the vessel and units. The container technique is still in its earliest stage of development. The need for customs control, examination, and lock-up storage imposes more problems in the UK than on the Continent, where containers very often pass the ports on transit documents and are examined by customs at the destination or depot serving the area of the destination, often deep into the heart of the Continent.

Many factories are now using this system as part of their production line with specially designed interiors to the containers which facilitate their easy loading/discharge as part of the flow pattern. The fact that the container happens to have crossed the sea is not significant.

Low Cost
There is a continuity of flow, and the contents of the container remain undisturbed by intermediate handling; costs are cut and the risk of damage minimized. Some of these savings have to be invested in capital equipment, control, etc., but practice has proved the rightness of the system so far.

Control
The unit owner has to ensure that he has an active agent at the point of origin depots and destination, mainly to ensure correct stowage, but also to ensure that there is no delay in the unit's movement, re-employment and re-positioning. These operations must all be effected in the most economical way if competition is not to attract the traffic away.

Modern methods for producing consignment notes, way bills or other documents to title, by using lightprinting or other methods have to be employed, otherwise the unit moves more quickly than the documents. In the short sea trade this is one of the more prominent problems and has been the subject of special study. The customs authorities have cooperated by the acceptance of telex declarations or deposits. If the regulations were applied to the letter, the system would undoubtedly grind to a halt. Documentation on deep sea voyages has been the subject of active investigation to try to provide one document issued by the shipowner to cover the movement door-to-door or depot-to-depot including insurance. Up to now this has not been solved satisfactorily.

The control of the condition of the container and recording at the various stages of its movement is effected by the shipowner (or his agent) at the point of receipt for shipment and handover to receivers. This interchange form records the difference in condition and narrows down the cause or place of damage. Any damage to the container's corner casting can result in serious accidents occurring, and any shell damage could cause damage to the contents. Certain owners X-ray their corner castings regularly to guard against fatigue.

Unit Hire
There are a number of container owners who lease containers to large and small users on a daily hire basis. Naturally, the longer the contract, the better the conditions. The emergence of this service has meant that units do not always have to be returned to the point where they were hired, but can be returned to the owners at various places around the world.

Special Traffics
Containers (and other units constructed within ISO limits) are being used for a vast number of special traffics. Most kinds of traffic that can move by trailer can now move in containers.

a. *Lids* The provision of lids—to facilitate the easy loading of individual pieces of considerable weight—means that machines, for example, can be carried with virtually no packing. The machine must be firmly secured to the container, of course, to avoid it being thrown around during transport.

b. *Doors* Doors are often provided at the sides as well as the ends of containers. This can be very important if two 20-foot units are being transported on the same rail wagon or road vehicle, by facilitating access.

c. *Shelves* For products which cannot be overstowed, shelves can be slotted into position to facilitate their safe carriage.

d. *Lashing and securing* Webbing straps and lugs can hold products firmly in stow. The movement of vessels at sea can be very considerable and rolling, yawing, pounding, pitching and heaving all at the same time impose forces not met with on land transport.

e. *Pallets* (*British Standard 2629*) There are five sizes of pallets recommended for use in general purpose freight containers. They are as follows:

    1100 mm × 800 mm
    1100 mm × 900 mm
    1100 mm × 1100 mm
    1100 mm × 1400 mm
    1000 mm × 1200 mm

The loading of pallets has to be carefully calculated, and the recommended loadings can be ascertained by consulting BS 3951. If the nature of the goods permits two-high stacking in the container, naturally a separate calculation has to be made.

One first ascertains what can be loaded in the container, i.e. by deducting the tare weight of the container from its rating. The design and the construction should be such that the pallets can be handled by suitable equipment designed to load and discharge containers, such as fork trucks. All pallets should be constructed to permit fork entry on the 1100 mm side (i.e. two-way entry only is required). However, for the 1000 mm × 1200 mm type, four-way entry is essential.

The disposition of pallets within freight containers in order to fully utilize the floor space (and if possible the headroom) is also covered in BS 3951. By following this advice, depending upon the type of pallet used and the type of container, 82–91 per cent of floor space can be utilized.

f. *Flats* Flats are usually the same as an open lorry floor with a fixed headboard. The remaining three sides are of steel mesh locking onto corner posts. The whole is demountable minus the headboard. A further type, constructed for top corner lifting and complying with the measurements laid down for ISO containers, is also available. These are conveniently used where the contents do not have to be protected from the weather. Loading and discharge are facilitated by the ability to work from three sides at the same time. If the goods have to be given protection from the weather, special sheets are provided like an inverted box to fit over the whole. Flats are useful for the carriage of products such as tomatoes, lettuce, copper ingots, wet hides,

94

etc. Their advantage is that, when empty, the three sides can be folded inwards and the flats stacked one upon the other, thus saving shipping space.

g. *Humidity* Humidity still causes trouble—particularly on deep sea voyages. Silica-gel in bags has been found to be an effective antidote in the case of machines, but each product requires a special study. Certain timber products or, more particularly, sawn timber can suffer distortion if dampness sets in. Labels on canned goods can become unglued and the tins themselves may become rusty—thus reducing their marketable attractiveness.

h. *Controlled temperature* Products requiring temperature control can be carried by containers provided with electrical systems which are connected with the vessel's power supply. (Power points are also provided on the terminals.) Clear written instructions have to be given to the shipowner specifying the shipper's requirements.

In deep sea trades these units are invariably supplied by the shipowner, on the short sea trade by the through-carrier.

i. *Bulk Liquids* These are carried in tanks built within the ISO standard design for containers, except that the sides and roof are not usually closed in. Temperature control, if required, is invariably effected by an electrical system.

5. CONVENTIONAL VESSELS AND MIXED CONVENTIONAL/CONTAINER VESSELS

Naturally, conventional vessels can also accept containers. However, the advantage of the pure container-vessel is that the labour element is drastically reduced and replaced by capital equipment enabling larger units to be handled. If the vessel is full of containers the fastest turnround of the vessel can be obtained.

By mixing conventional packaged cargo with containers, the actual turnround of the vessel in port is dictated by that hold which takes longest to discharge/load, the conventional. So even if the containers are discharged/loaded quickly it does not result in proportional advantages. It does help to reduce labour costs, but the vessel is still not moving at sea, and is not generating revenue.

However, in many ports of the world there is neither the flow nor quantity of the right type of product to permit full containerization of the trade. For many years to come there will be a need for vessels which carry conventional and containerized cargo.

It is quite clear that the most fertile area for container services is between countries in the industrial or post-industrial stage of their development, where the flow is great and can justify the very considerable capital outlays in containers, berth, cranes, and vessels and the shore handling gear. In the developing countries, or those in their early industrial period, the flow has not reached the required level.

Transition

How long the transition to containers will take is difficult to assess. Each route requires separate study. Raw materials move one way and finished products the other. Wool is being packed in containers, palm kernels will no doubt be carried in roof loading-floor flap discharge containers (trailers). If the savings on ship's time warrant it, then a way will be found to carry fish, meat and fertilizers in containers over long ranges. But there is still a definite place for the conventional dry cargo vessel for many years to come.

These vessels are often used as floating warehouses and serve as a floating part of the pipeline of physical distribution. If they moved more quickly between two highly developed container ports, they might well cost more to the through-carrier than by serving a greater number of ports in a more leisurely fashion. Economics will probably force a change in the long run, at the expense of some aspects of flexibility in operation.

Higher Costs

The economics of size and flow have a great effect upon the freight rates, and thus on the through cost. Competition keeps prices down, whilst labour in the West costs more than in the East and capital equipment is more easily maintained and replaced in the West than in the East. Thus trade between the Western nations (possibly with the exclusion of Japan and Australia) tends towards containerization and lower costs per ton than could be achieved by using conventional vessels with expensive labour and lower carryings per vessel per year. The time spent in port by a conventional vessel can be many times that of a container/Ro-Ro vessel. This is not to say that the container/Ro-Ro vessel always provides the answer.

Control

Conventional handling of cargo reduces the control and increases the risk of damage or pilferage. The number of handlings of the package means that it has to be strong. This is expensive in labour and materials. It has to be examined each time the responsibility for the package changes; the condition and number have to be recorded. A large flow of bagged cargo is easy to control, whereas a flow of cased goods of mixed dimensions poses problems for watchmen and tallyclerks. In the deep sea trade, packages have to be measured individually in order to charge freight. This is a very tedious and time-consuming task. It can also lead to underhand practices.

Special Traffics

a. *Heavy Lifts* These have to be handled at special heavy craneberths or with floating cranes. The expense of hire and insurance is very great, and so far as the short sea trade is concerned, the Ro-Ro system is superior. For deep sea traffic the problem remains unchanged, except on certain routes where Ro-Ro vessels provide an alternative service.

b. *Bulk goods* So far as liquids are concerned they have to be carried in special tanks. The cleaning of heated double-bottom tanks is not an easy task and can be expensive in labour.

Bulk powders can be more easily handled now by loading the produce into a large plastic bag lining the tanks.

c. *Controlled temperature cargo* This type of cargo is normally carried in refrigerated or cooled lockers which entail a very labour-intensive operation to load and discharge, each package or carcase having to be man-handled. Special vessels for the carriage of bananas have improved their turnround time. They are carried in cartons instead of in bunches, which eases the handling problems.

d. *Dangerous cargo* The so called 'Blue Book'—'the Carriage of Dangerous Cargo in Ships', 1966—has been produced to guide all who carry dangerous goods. The Merchant Shipping (Dangerous Goods) Rules 1965 (si 1965 No. 1067) lays down the British government's requirements and states what cargo is unlawful.

In addition, as a result of the International Conference on the Safety of Life at Sea, held in 1960, the Inter-Government Maritime Consultative Organization in London has produced the 'International Maritime Dangerous Goods Code' (imco) which is recommended to be adopted by those governments party to the 1960 Safety Convention. It is an excellent guide, but so far as British vessels are concerned the 'Blue Book' is still the law. In case of difficulty the Ministry of Transport should be consulted as they will interpret the regulations or agree to the packing and safe carriage of new products. The regulations apply however the goods are carried, and whatever the type of vessel.

e. *Full dry cargoes* Where a cargo of one product is involved, which moves in sufficient quantities to warrant the chartering of one or more vessels (i.e. from 100 tons on the short sea trade upwards), then shippers should contact a shipbroker of repute who is a member of the Chartered Institute of Shipbrokers in London. The market will be sounded through, for example, the Baltic Exchange and the most suitable vessel found at the market price. The charter party will then be drawn up to define the responsibilities of the two parties in, it is hoped, unambiguous terms. Most disputes are settled by arbitration and few reach the courts for settlement. It is a flexible and efficient system tested by time.

f. *Full bulk cargo* In response to need there has emerged a vessel called an obo (ore, bulk, oil) with a capacity of 10,000 tons and upwards. These vessels are flexible enough to load bulk grain or ore one way and return with oil, whereas in the past the ore- and grain-carrying vessel was separate from a tanker. The use of these vessels is open to anyone and the same system applies as mentioned in (e) above.

These vessels are cleaned in special berths, and certificates are issued by special surveyors who inspect them and attest their suitability for the carriage of the cargo specified.

97

6. SPECIAL VESSELS

Heavy Lifts

There are now a number of deep sea vessels available on the market which can lift pieces up to 500 tons with their own derricks and safely stow and carry them. On the short sea trade vessels are available to carry indivisible loads up to 300 tons.

Lash

This is the system whereby barges are floated into the after-end of the vessel and then lifted by the vessel's own transporter crane(s) and stowed for carriage to the destination port. They are then discharged into the water and towed or pushed to the final destination. The first service of this kind started with the movement of wood pulp in bales as a basis, but it can be adapted to any trade. It avoids the need to proceed to a berth to work cargo, or to fully enter a port. The barges can be distributed to smaller ports, thus cutting out expensive calls at many ports by a large vessel. The barges are then loaded/discharged at a variety of berths or alongside factories, thus keeping transport costs and handling to a minimum.

7. PACKING QUESTIONS

As the reader will know, packing of products has to be adjusted to suit the handling, route and buyers' requirements, so that the product arrives in first-class condition. Each consignment is worth considerable attention, not just to protect the contents but to economize in packing where possible.

In the UK/Continent trade, domestic cartons are used more and more, thus simplifying the production scheme. However, a package carried in a trailer or container still needs substantial packing. The good stowage of the carrying unit is always vitally important, for time spent on mastering this technique will bring its own reward in satisfied clients and reduced insurance premiums.

Taint is a problem that should not be forgotten if there are a number of dissimilar products moving in the same unit. On a short journey of 24 to 36 hours this may not be so important, but on a longer voyage of 24 to 36 days it can be disastrous. All shipowners or through carriers are pleased to use their experience to help shippers to achieve the best result, which is in everyone's interest. The British Shippers Council and other similar bodies can also provide useful service.

8. RELATIONSHIP WITH SERVICE SUPPLIER

The working relationship has to be close, and the character of those providing the service well known. The savings and efficiency can be greater if the relationship is right. Nevertheless, the shipper must shop around and play off one service provider against another if he is to have the full advantage of the free market. All quotations must be kept under close and regular review.

It is essential to understand what is involved in a particular quotation, what is included and excluded, and where responsibilities fall. It is important, however, not to squeeze the service provider too far, otherwise the service received may be below that required because the rewards are not there.

9. CLIENT RELATIONSHIP

A close personal relationship with the client is equally important for the supplier to get the most efficient results. The personal contact must be regular and must ensure that the client outside the UK feels that a UK supplier is just as accessible as a local supplier. So far as the Continent is concerned this can be easily achieved, and with the speeding up of transport there is hardly any place in the world which is not accessible within hours. The organization and methods applied in the shipper's firm soon become apparent to the buyer, so the need to make the right impression and follow it up with facts is quite obvious.

10. THE FUTURE

As the gross national products of the industrial and post-industrial countries grow, and the developing countries enter into the pre-industrial and industrial period of their histories, the demand for manufactured products will multiply tremendously.

The problems of moving vast quantities of similar products look as if they can be solved by the use of the unit-load system. The ideal is that as soon as a product is manufactured, it is packed for transportation in the safest, largest legal unit, and moved from door to door without breaking bulk. It is a nice problem for the physical distribution manager of the future to solve in the most economic way.

It seems as if the sea will continue to be the element in which the largest units can be moved safely, reliably and swiftly. However, whether the unit moves on an air bubble on the water, in the water or under the water will be determined by the economies involved. There are great advantages in underwater movement for deep sea voyages and it may very well be that this mode of movement will win the day. Possibly a lash submarine will be the normal mode of transport before the end of the twentieth century.

Allied to the increased use of container-vessels (or container/lash/submarines) there may be a change in the present practice where shipowners' containers (of standard size) gradually collect together in the port of shipment, awaiting shipment in the interests of the vessel's quick turnround. We may see the standard size container per shipowner changed to take advantage of cost savings to be achieved on the land haul section of the through carriage. This factor is receiving attention now, and if construction and use or rail regulations permit larger units to move, those shipowners whose module does not allow for the largest units to move, by land or barge (at the most economic price) may find themselves with large numbers of the wrong-sized unit on their hands. As 40 feet would appear to be the greatest length which will be acceptable for some time, those with 20-foot or 40-foot containers may be in the best position.

99

We may also see a considerable growth in the pre-stowage of containers in lash barges during the build-up period, prior to the deep sea vessel's arrival in port. The turnround time in port will be much shortened by loading such pre-stowed barges in 400 ton units, instead of waiting as now, for 1000/2000 containers of 12–28 tons to be loaded individually, unit by unit. How swiftly one can continue to raise the size and weight of the unit to save in-port time for the deep sea vessel will presumably be determined by technology. The object of the whole exercise is, of course, to keep the vessel moving at sea as much as possible in each 24-hour period. If the logistics are right, the best market conditions can be offered to the distribution manager.

The same rule applies to carrying bulk raw materials: vessels will surely become faster, carry more payload and be loaded and discharged more quickly.

The short sea trade between the UK and the Continent, as well as the overlap area between voyages of long and short duration, may be affected by a surface link across the English Channel. The assembly areas for using this link, which will presumably be built one day, may be better sited well away from the commencement of the link passing the water barrier. This would have a considerable effect upon the shipping services. However, there should be ten to fifteen years' notice of its completion date, so that the necessary action may be taken by the shipowners.

It would appear that over the next 10 to 15 years the roll on-roll off/lift on-lift off specialized vessels can and will deal with the carriage of assembled vehicle and general cargo trades, and that they will not vary very much in design from those we now see in service. Roll on-Roll off vessels will probably have wider door openings and more deck space for the carriage of 'dangerous goods' on deck. Lift on-Lift off vessels for the carriage of ISO containers will be provided with a cell system for safety, which can be easily changed to accept a variable mix of container lengths both on and under the deck.

The imponderable here is which length of container is going to be predominant or whether there will continue to be a varied mix on different routes. As the through carrier on the short sea trade will almost certainly continue to provide the containers (unlike deep sea) the mix will be determined by the land haul factors: accessibility for factories, vehicle availability, rail wagon size and barge size.

A change in the 'construction' and 'use' regulations for road vehicles or a change of view by the railways on the standard preferred size of containers will have profound effects on the final outcome of the size, shape and cell system of the short sea cellular container vessel.

Will we have smaller vessels with quicker turnrounds in port? This may very well be the answer for the very short voyage (1 to 6 hours), whilst larger vessels may be employed on the short voyage (7 to 36 hours). There are arguments both ways. But expensive shore-handling equipment and vessels must be used 24 hours per day, and they must form a continuous link with the physical distribution system.

The feasibility of this ideal will depend on whether the port operation can continue round the clock and not, as now, cause peaks to be created as the through movement of traffic bunches up towards the end of the normal day shift. If the flow can be smoothed out the very short sea trade should have small (70–100 20-foot containers) sized vessels and the short sea trade probably medium (140 20-foot containers) sized vessels.

By any analysis, the future for shipping and shipping technology is challenging and dynamic.

11. INLAND WATERWAYS

UK

The British Waterways Board have been doing their utmost to encourage the use of canals. However, compared with the Continent, their range and possibilities are not so great and thus, as usual, nature and geography play their part and for bulk movements, for which canals are particularly suited, pipelines and the siting of factories near the ports tend to syphon off traffic which could move by canal. Nevertheless the tonnage moving by canal is still measured in hundreds of thousands of tons per annum.

The advantage of using craft to move primary products from deep sea vessels to riverside/canalside warehouses is that in the major UK ports wharfage is not chargeable—a significant saving. However, the distribution from the warehouse sometimes causes extra expenses which cancel out the advantages. It would appear that there will be a steady decline in the use of barges—but this may be halted by the adoption of some techniques from the Continent. The distances hinterland/port and vice-versa are relatively so short in the UK that waterways are not capable of very considerable exploitation. As mentioned earlier, the siting of factories which consume bulk products at the port, on the waterside, has had a great effect in limiting canal use.

Storage

The use of craft for storage of products where the supply of material needs to move only slowly does, apparently, achieve considerable savings in labour and warehousing. The dumb barges once loaded can remain untouched until wanted. However, each situation needs to be studied to see if savings can in fact be made. There are a large number of craft about with unused capacity, but this is bound to decline if injections of capital are not regularly made.

Continent

The use of rivers and canals on the Continent for the movement of bulk goods is very great indeed. Liner barge services are operated, particularly in the Netherlands, guaranteeing regular sailings and calls at various places *en route*. These can be used to link up with ocean services and, though some are duplicated by road services for the carriage of general cargo, there are many in regular use. Through bills of lading are obtainable by certain of them.

The Rhine and the other major rivers have been linked by canals and are used mainly for the movement of goods in craft on charter. Charters both for full and part-loads are made on the barge exchanges, or 'bourses', in all the main centres daily. The barges are sometimes owned by the bargemaster himself who attends the bourse, but in the main a central agency looks after the interests of the bargeowner, be he the bargemaster or a company.

Very many factories are water-served and this method of moving irregular quantities is very extensively used. For example, drilling pipes will move from a factory in France to the natural gas fields in North Holland, whence a load of strawboards will be taken to one of the upper Rhine ports such as Strasbourg, whence sawn timber will be moved to Antwerp for shipment and so on. Most people in the UK do not appreciate the many uses made of chartered barges over the whole Continent, and how convenient this method can be. Vehicles are moved in large numbers on the decks of these barges.

Craft owned by users of the product they carry are very numerous, the food grains, oil and steel companies being the largest. The latter move coal and ore in vast quantities. Naturally, this is particularly attractive for very large bulk movements. The latest 'pusher' types are capable of moving 8000 tons at a time. The technical advances have been very great, and barges are available for the carriage of compressed gas, chemicals in liquid form and bulk and have a range of facilities very nearly as great as those of sea-going vessels. The tonnage moving by water on the Continent is measured in terms of millions of tons.

The future appears to be assured for the use of barges in Western Europe as a means of the bulk carriage of raw materials, and there are strong possibilities for the successful development of canal craft to carry containers.

Chapter B.6

AIR TRANSPORT

by Paul Jackson

Any business that increases at 20 to 30 per cent annually deserves some recognition, but when it is a sector of a primary industry as important as transportation, it requires attention from every business executive. Air cargo transportation is a product of modern technology, serving, and growing with, the modern growth industries. It is a newcomer to the transport scene and consequently tends not to be hampered by tradition, yet it is, at the beginning of the 1970 decade, still trying to find a firm base for its development. This chapter will set out to show briefly the conflicts within the economics of the industry itself but, more importantly, it will show the marketing executive how he should use this industry of speed. No discussion of the air cargo scene can take place without a look at the future, when some predict air cargo will dominate the world trade flows of finished goods.

History
Some historians trace the birth of air cargo to the Berlin airlift of 1949, although freight had been carried on aircraft since the first aircraft flew with passengers. The most significant thing about this massive air operation was that it was carried out at all; it proved that the aircraft had a role to play in the movement of goods even if the circumstances were unusual. It is interesting to note that the entire operation, which originally took some one hundred aircraft operating round the clock to complete, could now be carried out by only one of the modern jet freighter aircraft.

From this time airlines, or should we say shippers, began to take a larger interest in the movement of goods for non-military purposes, and as aircraft became bigger by advances in airframe and engine technology, so did the space available for freight under the passenger cabin, a function of the necessity for aircraft to be of an aerodynamic shape. So the airlines in the 1950s had a by-product of their operation of moving people from A to B, and they set about obtaining business by offering rates that took no account of the operating costs of the aircraft or what the market could afford. The case was simple—the aircraft was flying with a load of passengers which met the costs of the aircraft, so anything obtained from the freight was pure profit providing the handling costs had been met.

This short-sighted thinking tended to start the air freight business off on the wrong foot. The cargo business lacked management attention, which in turn caused a lack of capital investment. The business developed through the 1950s to the early 1960s, when the introduction of faster jet-powered aircraft meant many piston-propelled aircraft became redundant for passenger service. The airlines decided that they could use these aircraft, which still had some years of life ahead of them, to carry air freight, as by then the demand was beginning to outstrip the supply of space in the passenger aircraft. So began the start of what can be called the primary product era in air cargo: the operation of aircraft for the carriage of goods had to make a reasonable return in its own right. It is not surprising that the airlines even now find that they are still not able to make a profit with freight-only aircraft, although the break-through does not seem to be far away. They offer more or less the same rates that were available when they were reducing rates in the by-product era.

How is all this significant to the present-day marketing and distribution executive? The answer is simple—air cargo is here to stay, it is now an industry and is investing large sums of capital in terminals and new freighter aircraft. This means that the marketing man can consider with confidence what it has to offer.

Even now air cargo moves about 12 per cent of all United Kingdom exports, London (Heathrow) Airport is the third largest port in the country and, for example, some 30 per cent of all trade with France moves by air. Table 6.I shows the increasing penetration of air freight transport, both in the export and import sides of United Kingdom trade.

More than any other form of transport, the selection of air cargo warrants a full investigation into the implications of its use throughout the whole business system—the total integrated approach.

Table 6·I

TOTAL U.K. TRADE BY AIR

Year	Exports		Imports	
	Value (F.O.B.) £m	*% of Total* U.K. Exports	*Value* (C.I.F.) £m	*% of Total* U.K. Imports
1962	257·7	6·6	270·7	5·8
1963	289·2	6·9	305·8	6·1
1964	292·2	6·6	376·3	6·6
1965	370·5	7·8	438·3	7·6
1966	483·1	9·6	545·9	9·2
1967	539·7	10·7	640·9	9·9
1968	750·4	12·2	930·0	11·8
1969	978·9	13·3	1082·6	13·0
1970	1095·2	13·6	1220·2	13·5
1971	1304·3	14·2	1342·2	13·6

Source: Board of Trade.

Transport Quality Criteria

In any evaluation of air freight one has always to keep in mind that it usually costs more on a direct comparison with surface costs; but it is a superior quality of transport. The problem is to assess this greater quality and relate its value to the business organization, playing off the greater costs against the benefits obtainable by using air freight.

An examination of transport quality criteria subdivides into the following:

—Speed
—Frequency
—Reliability
—Environment.

Most will agree that air cargo is the fastest, most frequent and reliable service available today. Environment is, however, open to discussion. The advent of containerization on sea and rail routes has brought a resultant improvement in environment, most akin to what has existed for some time in air freight. In other words, factors influencing the environment of the mode of transport are now at a common base—the container or lorry that is at the beginning or end of the journey, whatever the intermediate form of transport.

Factors which are quantifiable under environment are packaging, insurance and pilferage represented by the appropriate costs. Not so easily quantifiable, but nevertheless a most significant factor, is the condition of goods on arrival in terms of customer satisfaction.

Without any doubt the aircraft's greatest value is its speed and ability to cross physical and political barriers, which often present considerable obstacles to other forms of transport. This speed only has a real value in a planned environment, when it is assessed within the total system of physical distribution. Although air freight is increasing rapidly, it is mostly on account of companies using it on an emergency basis. The future for air freight lies in companies accepting air freight's greater quality and incorporating this in a total approach. The danger is that most management like to have something in reserve, and air freight as a speedy efficient form of transport is very convenient to recover from the unexpected. Management will need to sail closer to the wind to obtain the benefits of lower costs and improved customer service, but then if management did not accept increased sophistication and tighter control, society would not have developed.

After speed come reliability and frequency, and these two are treated together because of their inevitable interaction. The greater frequency of the transportation, the greater is the reliability factor, setting aside the fact that aircraft are normally more reliable as, although hindered by weather during certain periods, the high frequency of services gives a quicker opportunity to recover.

These factors give the marketing executives greater flexibility to meet fluctuations in demand usually reflected in lower stocks. This important aspect will be dealt with later in the chapter. Before examining elements of a distribution system requiring greater management attention, it would perhaps be worthwhile to set out the role of transportation in distribution strategy.

105

Distribution Strategy

Typical of what was referred to earlier as the by-product era was the view that distribution was purely a problem of moving one's products from the factory floor to the customer at the cheapest possible price; the other main factor, speed, was only taken into consideration when, for one reason or another, an element of emergency was introduced into the system.

It is a sad reflection on modern management that this short-sighted attitude is all too prevalent as we move into the primary product era; this is manifested in the fact that 'emergency' shipments still constitute a high proportion of air freight traffic.

Fortunately industry is at last gaining speed in its efforts to introduce sophisticated strategy into the distribution decision-making process. The leaders have, quite naturally, been those companies for whom distribution is the greatest commercial headache—the spare-parts industry, for example— but others are now moving in the same direction, probably due to the squeeze on liquidity brought about by a high interest rate trade environment.

The essence of the distribution problem is liquidity. Distribution can be described in terms of a 'gap' between a financial commitment and the revenue return on that commitment. Examination of the nature of this 'gap' gives us insight into the fundamental problem of distribution strategy. This problem is as follows: the need for sophisticated management accountancy, though it is obviously accentuated by high interest rates, is of paramount importance regardless of credit facilities. Over the past ten years industry has fully realized the importance of managment accountancy, a fact which is evident from the growth in importance of budgetary control specialists and the fact that financial control is no longer confined to the desk of the accountant. The trend towards educating all types of management to a greater or lesser degree in the principles of financial control is growing rapidly.

As pointed out earlier, this is all evidence of the greater need for financial planning to forecast cash flows with greater accuracy, in order that the best possible use be made of financial resources. It is not to detract from the complexity of the budgetary controller's task to say that he is fundamentally concerned with ensuring that the level of 'idle' capital in the business is at the minimum without bringing undue strain on resources. If the amount of 'working capital' is more than is required to ensure the smooth day-to-day running of the company, then there is a quantity of 'idle capital', capital which if it were re-allocated could earn the company a useful return. Alternatively, if the amount of 'working capital' is too low, if developments arise which require financing and for which the company has made no plans, then money has to be obtained probably at a premium price—a price much higher than if the contingency had been anticipated and provided for. It is in the light of these facts that one must view distribution strategy, because this requires that a certain level of financial resources is continuously unproductive. The executive who has more than the absolutely essential amount of unproductive capital in his system is like the man who keeps his life-savings under the mattress. The two are also alike in that neither has a

106

necessity to retain his capital in this form: both, were they to give the matter consideration, would realize that a proportion of this capital could be allocated to an area where it would be financially productive, only keeping the minimum amount to satisfy day-to-day needs.

Both men are also similar in that, while the capital is unproductive, it is also likely to be reducing in value. This is more serious for the executive, for his 'locked-up' capital is quite likely to lose its value completely, i.e. become obsolescent.

Concentrating now on the executive we see that by virtue of the separation of the supply and demand sectors, there is inevitably a certain level of unproductive capital. The formulation of the distribution strategy requires that utilization of the components of the distribution system which will optimize the strategy, and two of the most important decision making areas are:

(i) the stock-control system
(ii) the transport mode.

In this section we are concerned with the part played by the transport mode, and later we will examine stockholding problems. It is important to emphasize that in the past, and largely at the present time, most attention is paid to stock-control techniques. Evidence of this is to be found in the fact that while sophisticated electronic data processing techniques have been evolved to 'optimize' the stock control system, none of these incorporates the crucial influence of varying lead-times.

This immediately raises the question, 'How, then, can the stock-control system be optimized by the use of electronic data processing if no account is taken of varying lead-times?' The answer is, of course, that it cannot.

However, what we can do is gain a fuller understanding of how the lead-time—a direct function of the transport mode—affects distribution strategy. With such an understanding, the distribution decision will become much more rational. It is now time to examine more precisely the influence of transport mode selection on distribution strategy, but before doing so we must have clear in our minds that, though the influences are the same in all types of distribution, their effects vary in degree according to product-market characteristics. These characteristics will be dealt with shortly when we discuss a suggested approach to the formulation of distribution strategy, but it is as well to bear in mind that the appropriate transport mode will differ according to such factors as product value, price and perishability, the importance of customer service, the degree of sophistication already present in the system, and so on.

Why, then, should this be so? Why should not one transport mode, because of certain critical influences that transport has on distribution, be the optimum for every firm? If it can be shown that it is more profitable for the car-parts distributor to use air freight, should it not also be so for the coal distributor? The answer is that one must take into account the relationship between:

(i) the effects of the transport mode in the light of the product-market characteristics such as those outlined above

(ii) the difference between prices charged by alternative transport modes.

The transport mode is critical to distribution strategy because it has a direct influence on the distribution 'gap'. Let us examine this influence. We began by noting that the 'gap' was a lag between financial outlay and the corresponding revenue return. If a company ships a box of cigarette lighters between London and Germany, and the time elapsed between the two ports concerned was ten days, the company's capital, represented by the cigarette lighters, would be unproductive for ten days. This unproductive period would be no more than ten days were the revenue from the sale of the lighters to appear in the hands of the manufacturer on arrival of the goods in Germany, but clearly this is unlikely to be so. Another time lag appears between arrival at the German port and the receipt of the goods by the distributor, wholesaler, retailer, or individual customer. If the lighters go direct to the buyer, then the gap will be significantly less than if they were to go to the buyer via distributor, retailer, etc. In normal business practice the goods are unlikely to go direct to the customer and so we see a second time lag emerging. But even when they reach the retailer, the goods will not be sold immediately and so there is another lag. Let us assume that the goods have been sold, then there is a further lag between the time of purchase and the manufacturer's receipt of revenue, and we have as yet ignored the fact that the goods do not get shipped to Germany as soon as they come off the production line: they are only shipped when the customer requests them and so we see that once more the distribution 'gap' has widened.

All the time that those goods have been produced but are not sold the company has a quantity of capital invested which is not earning money, and it is the job of the executive to minimize this quantity, to reduce his unproductive capital allocated to distribution to the minimum safe level.

Throughout this discussion of the distribution system it has become clear that the significant factor is the relationship between time and levels of unproductive capital. If the distribution 'gap' is narrowed with a corresponding adjustment in levels of unproductive capital—e.g. stock in transit, static stock in warehouse—then capital will be released for allocation to more productive areas. The significance of the transport mode to distribution strategy is its effect on the distribution 'gap'. Now it can be safely reckoned that the justifiable cost of a transport mode varies in proportion to the contribution it makes in reducing the distribution gap, and the distribution decision involves the very important trade-off between:

(i) the increased cost of greater speed, reliability and frequency

(ii) the resultant cost reductions brought about by narrowing the 'gap'.

This takes us back to the all important consideration of product-market characteristics because these will dictate whether or not the reduction in the distribution 'gap' is beneficial in terms of a reduction in total distribution costs and an increase in profitability.

We have enough knowledge about these characteristics to analyse a distribution system, and to establish which transport mode is likely to be the most effective for a particular firm. It is now proposed to show in more measurable terms when air cargo should or should not be used.

Suggested Approach
It has been said that air freighting offers a fast, reliable and frequent transport service, and whilst they are not individually important factors, their combination in the distribution cycle is significant.

To bring to the attention of the reader when a company should use air freight it is now proposed to suggest a logical sequence of analysis. This could be divided as follows:

   (i) comparison of actual rates
  (ii) comparison of the environmental costs
 (iii) capital commitment reduction
  (iv) marketing.

Given that the mode of transport is the artery of any distribution system, it follows that the choice of transport is crucial and affects every part of the system. Any system as wide ranging in its effect as distribution is inevitably complex and it is proposed, in this analytical appraisal, to highlight the more common aspects in general terms. Obviously what is of little significance to one company could be the major reason for using air transport to another. The first stage, comparison of actual rates, is what people have been doing for a long time. As we have already pointed out, many people will still only compare the actual transport rates involved in using air or surface transport. The charges collected by air on the odd minimum emergency shipment are often compared with the bulk surface rates obtained. The optimum surface container rates are usually highlighted, ignoring the fact that a container rarely moves fully loaded to obtain the cheapest rate. The volume-density rates, particularly on some of the longer routes by sea, are very severe and rates are often compared taking no account of the density of consignments. Air is generous towards the lighter weight-to-volume goods.

The second stage is a comparison of the direct costs involved by varying criteria of quality (see Table 6.II). This will involve mainly packing and insurance, and one should be aware that often the respective weights are different for the competitive modes. In fact the airlines have a scheme where they will recommend certain size packing, which will allow the tare weight to be free of charge, along with some discounts off the rates for good measure. One factor which people tend to overlook in transport costing is that there are considerable reductions available for air freighting as the consignment size increases. This is not only reflected in the respective airline tariffs but also in the operation within the company itself, such as the avoidance of special handling charges caused by the emergency characteristic of the operation. If, by this stage, there is no case for air freight the cost accountant will probably move away from the shippers department to the corporate planners

109

in the marketing departments. This is because, as mentioned earlier, the biggest advantage air freight can and always will offer is speed, reliability and frequency. This is particularly highlighted where goods are replenishing a stock-holding point rather than serving a customer direct, although distribution direct to the customer, at least in terms of improved service, is also significant.

Distribution is the employment of capital just like any other part of the business system. The fact that it is a service function makes it more difficult to define and more importantly, difficult to make accountable. How does one really know if the distribution system is at its optimum if it is, after all, only

Table 6·II

TRANSPORT COSTS ANALYSIS

Confidential

Part 'A'

Description of goods..........

Declared value for carriage ....

Originating at ....   Destined for..........

Weight in rail/sea packing ....   Nett weight..........

Charges payable by exporter ....   Annual tonnage ....

Charges payable by importer..........

Part 'B'	£	p	Part 'C'	£	p
By surface			By air		
Packing costs—inclusive of labour and materials			Packing costs—modified to show any labour and material savings		
Transport costs to docks—inclusive of waiting time costs			Transport costs to airport		
Charges at port of shipment—inclusive of loading and incidental charges			Charges at airport of shipment		
Agency fees for export clearance			Agency fees for export clearance		
Insurance at %			Insurance at %		
Surface freight charges By weight volume *ad valorem* or minimum quantity rate			Air cargo charges By weight volume or *ad valorem* at per kilo		
TOTAL			TOTAL		
Average elapsed time door to door..........days			Average elapsed time door to door ....days		
			Estimated time saving ....days		

a buffer between production and consumption? If the demand for a product was predictable and matched by production, and the customer collected it himself off the end of the production line, then the distribution system would be unnecessary. Of course in practice this is not so, hence the reason for warehousing in particular, which is dealt with in some length later.

The fourth and most important assessment, certainly to the marketing logistics executive, is the effect air freight can have on market development, customer service and pricing margins.

As a marketing tool in the development of a market it is invaluable. No longer is the world measured in distance—the time that a product can be in a customer's hands around the world is now probably the most significant fact in export marketing. With air freight every overseas market is the home market, but at a price. The price, of course, is increased transportation costs and, even allowing for capital saved in transit and in warehouses, it could still be too much. But organizations spend millions of pounds creating and containing a demand for their product, and yet so often they do not have it available when the customer requires it. So with air freight, companies can confidently test-market an area or boost the demand in their more stable markets. Retailers are renowned for ordering replacement products when they have run out and if the product is substitutable, then somebody is missing a lot of sales while the goods are on their way. Similarly, retailers will tend to order on the shortest re-order cycle in the particular product group, so if your product is the one with the shortest re-order cycle with air freight, there is good chance of maximizing your sales to the detriment of your slower moving competitors. Added to this is the greater responsiveness one has to change— change in fashion and technical innovation. Obviously the shorter the lead time, i.e. the distribution 'gap', the less committed you are to write-off or price reductions. Pricing is, of course, set by the consumer in broad terms and mark-up levels are usually a measure of the amount of time in ware- housing and the risk of not selling the particular product. Significant in determining mark-up levels is the level of stocks, and it is fair to say here, and not in the section on stock control, that air freight could well develop a market so that, for example, mark-up (price) could be reduced by a quarter: if sales doubled as a result and the other quarter covered the increased costs involved, one would maintain or increase the profit level.

It could be said that such a proposition could not be accomplished, but discount houses and similar organizations have done this very thing. They cut prices with larger volume, and took business away from the other retailers. If by doubling the turnover rates (sales) one can see that beans have increasing demand and peas have a lowering demand—then both buyer and supplier should switch the working capital to beans instead of peas. Organizations will appreciate that quicker turnovers give valuable information nearer to the time of sale. If one firm had the courage and conviction to go ahead with this sort of programme, it would clean up the market before its competitors could act in the same way. A prime reason for wholesale and retail organiza- tions is to offer a bigger variety of goods to choose from in particular localities. By doubling turnover and using air delivery (or any faster delivery

111

for that matter) a firm could carry twice the variety that it had been able to carry before. This alone could give it twice the amount of sales compared with past performance. A higher rate of turnover means that goods are going to be nearer to the customer choice at a given time. This means that through continuous testing of the retail market with more turnovers, each successive turnover will contain more and more of the goods that are in demand. It follows that less and less goods with each successive turnover will need to be marked down and therefore with less mark-downs as a result, one does not have to double unit sales to get double the sales revenue. This is not stating that turnover is the panacea for the successful business, it is after all only a guide, but it is hoped that this has shown that the executive should be alive to the opportunities in the world of every wider range of consumer choice.

Some basic parameters which favour the use of air freight include:

    (i) Above average value-to-weight ratio
   (ii) Competitive market
  (iii) Service sensitive product
  (iv) Fluctuating demand
   (v) Above average mark-up levels
  (vi) Constant production
 (vii) High growth or developing market
(viii) Time limited product
  (ix) Above average obsolescence.

Stockholding
The failure to maintain the investment of stock at such a level as to provide a balance between profitability and service to the customer, is one of the prime causes of business failure, and a frequent cause of frustration in an expanding company as rising profits are absorbed by corresponding rising stocks.

The following sets out to show that, by the application of various techniques, air freight can contribute towards the solving of this and other problems which continually plague the sales manager, who wants a higher level of customer service, and the managing director, who wants a better return on investment. Stock is essentially a buffer between supply and demand, the size of which is a measure of the continuous gamble of balancing supply with demand. Air freight, if used selectively, can shorten the odds considerably by reducing the lead times involved to a minimum.

Capital is becoming more difficult to obtain and is costing more. The world is also becoming more competitive, products are now more varied and are generally of a shorter life span, causing the size and costs of stockholding to increase.

Meanwhile there is always the objective to meet of improving rates of turnover, level of customer service and return on capital investment. Yet reducing stock at the same time as increasing sales is a goal that until now was hard to realize. But now, by examining what actually makes up the stock level and how this would be affected by the planned use of air freight, the goal of a higher capital return on investment along with increased sales could well be achieved.

An attempt will be made to show what the planned use of the fastest, most reliable and frequent transport service available today means in stock reduction, and how the savings in many cases are more than enough to pay for the additional costs of using this premium service.

Determining the Size of Stock
Firstly it is as well to consider what actually determines the size of stock and the constituent parts of a satisfactory level. In a simplified example Figure 6.1 shows that the two main constituent parts determining size of stock in any

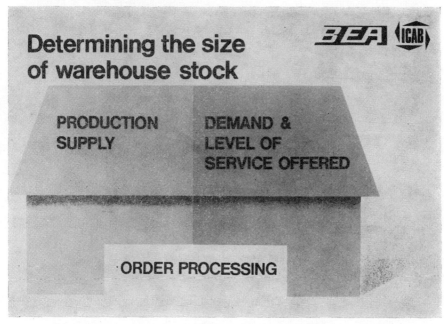

Figure 6·1

warehouse are the production supply considerations, the nature of the demand and how well it is to be met. The other point is the efficiency of order processing within the warehouse. The amount of stock held against order processing is not normally affected by the lead time.

A closer examination of the stock held against production supply would show continuity of production to be significant (Figure 6·2). This will be a function of the level of service provided. Where a company arranges for all the warehouses or group of products to be replenished by air freight then the level of service provided by the central source will actually decrease.

This is simple to understand, as the demand for a product is being centralized at one point and therefore a broader demand can be met more often. This

113

improves the few stockholding points that exist in the total distribution chain. The order processing time at the original source is often the major portion of the total lead time. It is quite common for the stock which is in the system being processed, to be more than the actual stock level it is replenishing. Therefore, when reviewed on an annual basis this transit stock becomes as significant as the actual static warehouse stock at the point closest to consumption. This is another point in favour of pre-selecting stock for air delivery, as time is saved on the ground as well as in the air.

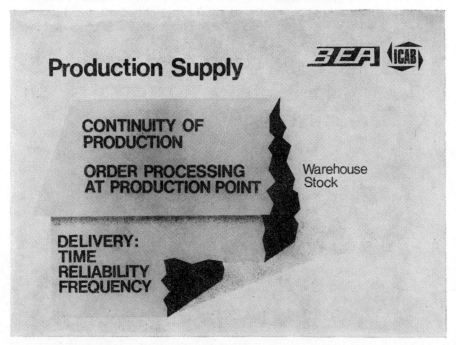

Figure 6·2

The key to faster order processing is not to overload the system. This is where the maxim of a little but often by air fits in perfectly. The significant factor is the principal of the familiar 80–20 rule whereby 80 per cent of a company's sales come from 20 per cent of its customers.

Equally, this invariably applies to warehouse stock with 80 per cent of sales being attributed to 20 per cent of the items which could be served by 40 per cent of stock. Conversely 20 per cent of the sales representing 20 per cent of the annual shipments, if moved by air, would have a more significant effect on the 60 per cent of stock, this being the slower moving, than if the 80 per cent moved by air replenishing the faster moving 40 per cent of stock.

In this way only a comparatively small amount is sent by air, which would not overload the order processing system. The 60 per cent of stock which is the slower moving is the real capital that is tied up, which could be earning

114

profit elsewhere. It could be argued that this philosophy could equally apply to a total surface movement. This is not so. The essence of the operation is the total delivery time between production and the warehouse and as shown in the pictorial presentation it is the time, reliability and frequency that are the factors that go to make up what can be called a standard transit time, i.e. the average plus the standard deviation. A simple table will serve to make this point. It must be remembered that what are being compared are the varying times for smaller shipments, any under half a ton. Surface transport is not suited to this market, its rates are not as competitive as for larger loads; packing will also be necessary because of the rougher handling expected for non-unit loads, and most of all there is an extreme likelihood of the goods being delayed in the system; a system geared to the movement of 20-ton container loads. On the other hand, air freight is very much suited to this size consignment. The rates are competitive and it is able to offer containers (some would say large boxes) to suit the size of the consignment—containers in fact that could be loaded direct from the store shelf saving a separate packing process.

COMPARISON OF STANDARD TRANSIT TIMES—SMALL ORDERS

(The basis of planning, with order processing time, the applicable stock levels)

| | London–Paris | | Manchester–Vienna | |
	Air	Surface	Air	Surface
Time: preparation for despatch transit	1	2 2	1	2 7
Frequency	$\frac{1}{2}$	1	$\frac{1}{2}$	6
Reliability	$\frac{1}{2}$	1	$\frac{1}{2}$	3
Standard Transit time	2 days	6 days	2 days	18 days

Technical Notes

Time It is a simple fact of life that preparation time is a function of transit speed. Air transit by its simpler documentation, booking service and lack of packing is easily accomplished in one day anywhere in Europe. On the other hand, surface transport is slower and normally requires more notice to obtain space.

Frequency and reliability. There are over thirty services a day between London and Paris. Thus, not only is a service available at the moment it is required but should it not be available, or should it be delayed as has been stated, the ability to recover (reliability) is easier than with surface where frequency is lower and is more subject to delays. The Manchester–Vienna example makes this point clearer, the service here is available weekly and it takes seven days with possible delays of three days. Thus goods will take between nine and eighteen days—the eighteen days is the basis on which stock levels are determined—not the seven-day transit.

As with the supply stock, air freight can also make reductions in the stock held against demand (Figure 6·3). The amount of capital which is to be made

115

available for stock, and the average level of service that the company intends giving to its customers (i.e. the percentage of customer requests that can be met from stock) are the basic decisions upon which the distribution system is set up. The second decision is very delicate: it is simply impossible as well as uneconomic to satisfy every demand from the customer. A great deal is known about the amount of stock that is necessary to satisfy the various degrees of demand. It is accepted, however, that there is a problem that the lower the level of service, the more lost sales result.

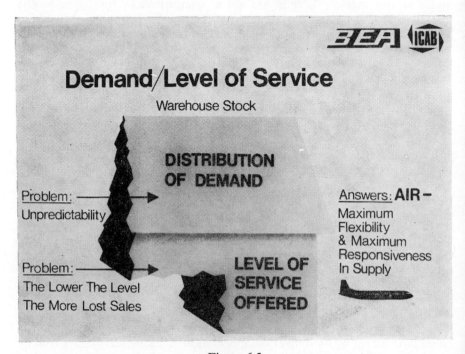

Figure 6·3

The other major problem with the distribution of demand is its unpre dictability. Air freight offers to both these problems maximum flexibility and maximum responsiveness in supply.

The level of service is improved by using air freight in the first instance, as the orders are received more frequently and there is thus less chance of a stock-out position, even if stocks have been reduced accordingly (see Figure 6·4 and Figure 6·5) referring to lead time stock showing lost sales avoided by a shorter order cycle.

There are two forms of level of service which go to make up the generally accepted term. The first can be called 'product range' level of service, and the second is the item level of service. Product range level of service is the percentage of a company's product range that it is prepared to offer 'off the shelf'. Air freight can, because it is reducing the scale of the operation, allow

116

companies to offer a wider product range as less is being held of each product, which means that products with a lower demand can be held economically. It is often these products that require market development, and air freight can assist with this, keeping the capital committed to the distribution system to a minimum.

The ratio of cost to item level of service is also significantly affected by lead time, and an improved level of service can be met by using air. The point where the stock increases rapidly to meet a 1 per cent increase in level of service is reached earlier with a longer re-order cycle. This is shown in Figure 6·6. Thus a 93 per cent level of service is achievable by air and surface,

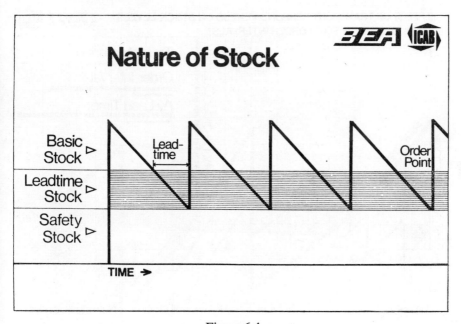

Figure 6·4

but a 98 per cent level of service with realistic stock levels, is only possible with a shortened lead time by air. Equally a 97 per cent level of service by air would be unsatisfactory. Whilst the vertical axis is showing total cost, it could equally show stock level although the scale would need to be adjusted.

Thus the more flexibility available to meet errors in forecasting, the less stock that is required to meet the unexpected. This now enables us to move onto the nature of stock.

Nature of Stock
Without actually specifying what the constituent parts for the control of stock are, we have so far shown the effects of air freight on the supply and demand factors influencing the size of stock. Looking at stock in a more

practical way, it can be divided into three main categories which are, how-ever, still affected by supply and demand. They are basic stock, lead time stock, and safety stock (see Figure 6·4). It is now proposed to relate time to stock level, and to show that this is the third factor after supply and demand influencing stock size.

Thus, it will be shown that air freight does more than just lower the stock held against lead time. It can, because of its responsiveness to supply and demand, reduce or even avoid the need to hold the safety stock. The portion of the stock that repeatedly increases or decreases daily is the basic stock, while the portion of the stock that serves to cover the demand from the time

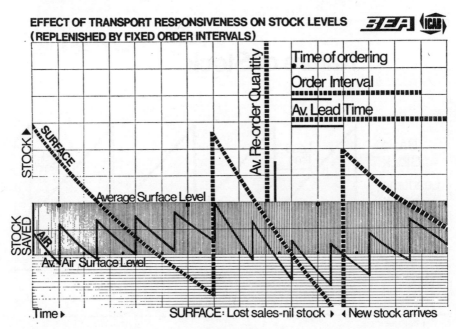

Figure 6·5

that products are ordered until arrival (the lead time) is, not surprisingly, called the lead time stock. In practice, however, the stock movement is in accordance with the fluctuations in demand, and traces an irregular pattern as shown in Figure 6·5, so that in order to assure a certain degree of safety, extra (safety stock) must always be maintained for this purpose. Viewing this diagramatically (Figure 6·4) the ideal condition will be when the stock drops down to safety stock. The new stock arrives, but stock shortage will come from the situation shown in Figure 6·3 where demand increased rapidly after the regular order was made, the order level being basically the lead time plus the safety stock as shown in Figure 6·4.

All this serves to show that the stock saved on the graph (Figure 6·5, the horizontally and vertically shaded) possibly only by use of air freight, is taken from the basic stock (note the difference between the respective stock level peaks); lead time (smaller shipments, quicker and more often); and safety stock (risk is minimized).

Basic stock reduces in direct relation to lead time; it is difficult to quantify in advance. Lead time stock, on the other hand, is not. If two months average consumption is being held against a lead time of six to eight weeks, lead time by air would reduce the stock by seven-eighths. The amount of safety stock sometimes tends to be an arbitrary management decision based on many factors, one of which is the time available to replenish the stock. Nevertheless many companies have found that on using air, this is the first area in which they can make reductions. It is, after all, a simple management decision to ask, 'Do we continue to hold two months safety stock or reduce to two weeks with air freight?'

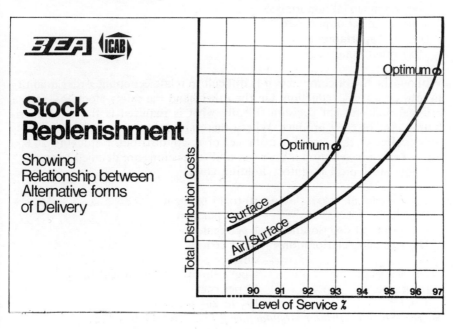

Figure 6·6

How Much Reduction is Possible

Having established that air freight reduces basic lead time and safety stock, the problem now is to determine how much stock, i.e. capital, can be released without jeopardizing the level of customer service. The savings have, of course, to be at least enough to pay for the increased freight charges normally incurred by using air freight.

If available, the use of electronic data processing makes this a simple task. Alternatively, data is fed into the necessary ordering formula and both the IBM's IMPACT and ICL's SCAN inventory programmes are able to show the

119

appropriate stock level reductions. At this moment they are not able to evaluate the varying total distribution costs of each item.

Manual selection is more time consuming. The use of the Cardex type systems precludes an instant answer and the appropriate reductions may best be established by selection of various groups and stock reduced by proportions based on management's view of the lead time and safety stock savings.

Some Methods for Selecting Groups Susceptible to Air Freight Replenishment
   (i) rate of turnover
  (ii) varying levels of service
 (iii) age of product
 (iv) value/weight ratio
  (v) physical shape, size and fragility
 (vi) commercial importance
(vii) technical importance
(viii) transportation costs
 (ix) order quantity.

Without the use of computers it is difficult to relate economic order quantity to lead time stock reduction. On the other hand the safety stock saving is a rational management decision. Ideally what is required is the total distribution cost of each product. Where there are only a few products, this is feasible but in the case, for instance, of a car distributor stocking 20,000 items, some pre-selection is essential and suggestions are detailed later.

Below are typical inventory holding costs:

Cost of capital	10 to 15 per cent
Warehouse space	1 to 3 per cent
Prevention of deterioration	1 per cent
Damage and deterioration	1 per cent
Pilferage	small
Obsolescence	5 per cent except for special cases
Insurance	$1\frac{1}{2}$ per cent
Total	$19\frac{1}{2}$ to $26\frac{1}{2}$ per cent

Source: *Stock Control in Manufacturing Industries*, Gower Press.

The cost of capital is clearly the major inventory cost. A profit minded company will tend to place a value on capital in stock, of what it would earn if it was redistributed throughout the company—the 'opportunity cost' of capital. Others take the view that the value of capital is the cost of borrowing, and that if the stock was reduced less capital would be borrowed. The warehouse space cost of 1 per cent to 3 per cent is really only reduced over a long period with the use of air freight. Stock can be halved relatively quickly but warehouse space cannot be halved overnight. The other major cost, obsolescence, is of course related to the importance of the changing demands of the consumer as well as to the passage of time. Either way there are several products of time-limited and fashion markets that use air freight

120

regularly because of the high risk and, therefore, eventual cost of obsolescence. Obviously, reducing the capital commitment in stock reduces the amount as well as the degree at risk.

Transportation costs, the other major part of distribution costs, vary with the distance and the environment of the mode. The shorter the distance the more significant packing, insurance, handling and delivery charges become. Often over the shorter distances this means that air freight is cheaper even without stock savings. Between the UK and Europe, for goods requiring packing of FOB value of £1 per kilogram (100 cubic feet per ton), transportation costs would range between 5 per cent and 10 per cent of the FOB

Maximising Profits
with Planned Air Replenishment

(Actual Case Study: UK to Denmark)

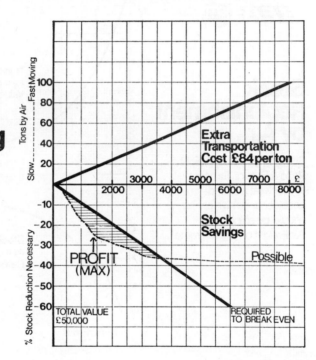

Figure 6·7

price for distances around 300 miles for air as well as surface; for distances of 500, air would be about 15 per cent, surface 10 per cent and around 1000 miles 25 per cent for air with surface 15 per cent.

Figure 6·7 attempts to show for a particular distributor in Denmark where he can achieve the most profit by using air freight. It should be noted that this is not at the point of the highest stock reduction, but is where the least sent by air produces the largest stock reduction. In this case, air transport costs were 30 per cent more than the equivalent surface costs. The stock to move by air was simply phased through by rate of turnover in groups already established for stock control purposes, and varying obsolescence

121

costs were apportionable. Due to the lack of the value/weight ratio of each part, this grouping was the only way to select at that time. Selection depends largely on the information available and with this very much in mind we move on to the ideal methods of selecting items for air freight.

This is graphically expressed in Figure 6·8 and is a method of relating distance to time. The data refers to a particular flow of parts to a stockholding point, and attempts to show the break points in value/weight ratio or rates of turnover that should move by air.

Stock Replenishment by Air

Showing the Value/Weight Ratio & Rate of Turnover of Stock (at a stated obsolescence) which should be shipped by Air Freight on a given route

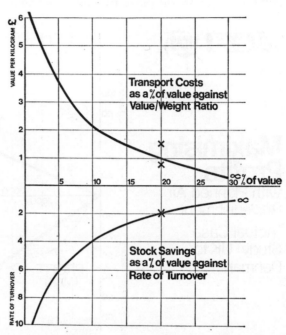

Figure 6·8

The positive part of the graph is simple, i.e. transport costs directly relate to the value of the part. The negative part (the lower half) is based on the case that air could move all parts at a lower cost with the subsequent reductions in stock related to the rate of turnover. If air was used for all parts, even the stock levels for the fast movers would be reduced. Then, by putting the two halves together and using the same base line, the break point when air should be used would be obtained. Thus any part above a certain value at a fixed rate of turnover could move by air, or if it is simpler, parts below a certain rate of turnover at a fixed value/weight could move by air.

There is a problem of obtaining the information for the negative part of the graph, but with the use of modern electronic data processing techniques, and random sampling, it can be achieved.

122

No apology is made for discussing the stock level content at some length. It is without doubt the most significant tangible factor influenced by air freight.

The Role of Air Distribution in Service Sensitive Marketing
During the last decade, customer service has emerged as the prime element of competition in marketing. It now assumes even greater importance than the classical considerations of advertising quality and price. Customer service is customer satisfaction, which means having the right goods, be they consumer, capital industrial or spare parts, at the right place at the right time. A planned air cargo distribution system will always enable the ultimate in customer service to be achieved.

The role of any fully integrated physical distribution system must be profit maximization, surely a more realistic approach than cost minimization. The key to successful planning is the estimation of elasticity of demand with respect to service in each market. This section sets out to indicate how service sensitive situations may be identified, and to show with actual case studies how companies have exploited them with air cargo to maximize profits.

We all agree that speedy delivery boosts short- and long-term sales. We all assume speedy delivery costs a high premium. None of us knows precisely the interrelation between demand, and speed, and reliability of delivery.

The most logical approach is to identify the markets and products most likely to respond to service first. This can be achieved simply by answering the questions below:

1. Degree of substitutability of your product in this market
2. Customer dependence on your product
3. Do customers specify mode of delivery and take active interest in it?
4. Is there a high incidence of last minute rush orders?
5. Is traffic often re-routed at customer request?

Affirmative answers indicate a service sensitive product.

Once alternative air and surface based supply systems have been costed and estimates of their relative effectiveness considered, a decision as to the optimum level of service to offer then has to be made. This is best achieved by examining customer requirements and reaching a conclusion which is wholly consumer oriented. It is then a marketing decision to predict whether the higher distribution cost can be offset by increased sales. Actual case studies are examined later.

Once the plant is put into operation, valuable data can be accumulated as a basis for further decision making. A word of warning here: the full effect of improving service will not be felt for some time as the reputation develops. A graphical presentation of this data might be expected to look something like Fig. 6·8 but will vary with product and market.

The customer will appreciate improved service, not only because it will enable him to reduce stocks but because it will help him solve his major problems. These solutions result in:

123

1. Fewer lost sales and double deliveries
2. Better production planning
3. Less effort and more peace of mind
4. Gives competitive advantage.

The following examples serve to illustrate how the well-known problem of eliminating the lost sale can be combated to some extent with air cargo.

A company with business in France found that they were able to sell only a limited range of their products, but in relatively high volume. The items concerned were permanently in stock in the UK and it was a simple matter for French customers, having placed their first order, to place a repeat order by post, telex or phone. Because this was an 'in-stock' business it was of paramount importance that the customer did not miss a sale. Now, as is frequently the case, all customers are not as efficient nor financed for good stock control as they might be, and it happens that they do not place a repeat order until they have actually run out of stock. It follows that these customers will be missing sales during the period when replacement orders are being processed and delivered. For this reason the company concerned does all its business with France using air freight and finds that the increase in business which they achieve by enabling the customer to achieve maximum sales outweighs the premium which they pay for air freight.

As has been said, air transportation can also enable an existing market to be stimulated and expanded. A company selling in Switzerland reached the classical situation where their products were reaching the peak of their life cycle, and were facing the possibility of a decline in sales. The response to this was to step up their advertising and try to give the products a second lease of life. Normal advertising in the national press was inadequate and it was decided to use television which is more powerful; this enabled them to boost sales through established outlets on the strength of their decision to advertise this new and powerful media.

This was the marketing plan and then came the question of how much sales would increase. The answer was, of course, imprecise but what was known was that to service this sudden increase in demand a certain level of stock would be necessary. This stock would have to be maintained plus the additional stock that would be required because the goods would take ten to fourteen days in transit. Their answer was arrived at by calculating the cost of stock levels and stock in transit at a discounted cash flow rate of 10 per cent against the air freight premium. To stay in their established market needed a marketing boost, and to capitalize on this increased tempo air cargo was an essential element of customer service.

Fast reliable customer service has, in addition to the short term effect of eliminating lost sales, considerable effect on long-term demand.

A shorter order cycle time and greater reliability enable a customer to receive good service. Distributors who received good service are less susceptible to approaches from alternative manufacturers.

One export manager of a large company recently summed up his company's attitude to air freight by stating that the company owed it to its customers, its products and itself to use the best form of delivery available. Undoubtedly this attitude will gain strength as customer service becomes more and more significant, particularly to those companies competing in service sensitive markets.

Future

So what of the future? It seems that the air cargo industry will continue to grow at least 20 per cent per annum for some time to come. It will, by the middle 1970s, have purpose-built aircraft with lower operating costs than present day with the capability to carry the ISO container, making inter-modal transport a reality. The existing terminals at airports will be run down and off airport preparation of load and customs clearance will be carried out at specially sited depots. The expected decline in business travel, when audio-visual telephone links are established, and the greater growth rate in the cargo sector of the airline business will see the world scheduled airlines earning more from the carriage of freight than passengers by 1980. Just as the 1970s may well be called the customer service decade, the airlines them-selves will continue to attract some business by their superior service even though it could still be cheaper overall to use a slower form of transport.

The development of air freight on a planned basis will stimulate the demand for charter aircraft capacity possibly operating out of lower cost airports. Management techniques will have to incorporate the value of time into their distribution systems. Distribution will attract far more management attention. It will be commonplace for the computer not only to handle inventory levels, but also to minimize total distribution costs as a sub-routine before showing the system that will optimize the business system as a whole.

Chapter B.7

THE THROUGH TRANSPORT CONCEPT
by M. G. Graham

Through transport is a very important aspect of total physical distribution, important to the actual physical process of distribution and important to the way of thinking which is summed up in the initials 'PDM'.* The value of through transport to industry will not be appreciated fully if the principles of PDM are not understood. Conversely, to the extent that shippers and transporters who are involved in through transport grapple with its problems and develop its techniques, they will be helping to create the climate in which PDM can flourish.

This chapter aims firstly to examine the essential features of the concept which has become known as through transport; secondly to identify the advantages offered by through transport to traders, to attempt to show how they came about and to demonstrate the importance of an awareness of PDM on the part of the trader, if these potential benefits are to become real; thirdly to consider the influence of through transport on the location of inland distribution facilities; and fourthly to draw up a short summary list of relevant actions which a dutch uncle might proffer to a trader. The through transport idea can only become a physical reality through the agency of the unit-load systems which have been developing in recent years. Through transport has its root in the efforts made to improve the efficiency of handling goods, identified by transport men as their major cost problem; but it has come to mean much more than the unit-load systems themselves and that 'more' is the part which is particularly relevant to students of PDM. It would be wrong to ignore the unit-load systems altogether, and some comparison of them is made in an Appendix to the chapter, where the reader will not be distracted from the main question: what is the significance of through transport to the concept of total distribution?

Through Transport Described
Through transport means a system by which goods can flow smoothly from origin to destination, with the minimum of transhipment, under unified responsibility. The first is a physical characteristic, the second a characteristic of management organization, also having commercial implications. They are

---

* In this chapter the initials 'PDM' will be used as a convenient short description of the concept of total distribution.

126

related. From a PDM point of view the second is the more important. If the goods are transhipped many times from one mode of transport to another there is a presumption of divided responsibility. In conventional transport this has been the case. Responsibility has been shared between shippers,* forwarding agents, hauliers, rail operators, port authorities, stevedores or wharfingers and shipowners, who hand the cargo over in the country of destination to another set of agents, hauliers, etc. In the through transport system, responsibility is unified in the hands of one operator who takes charge of the cargo right from origin to destination. Attention focuses upon the consignment, which must be steered safely and with despatch through its journey, and not upon a form of transport such as a lorry, train or ship; these are important only as physical agents with which to get the job done.

Logically the unit to be considered should be the total journey of a given consignment rather than merely a part of it. The 'product' of a transport service is obviously a journey, and to a road haulier or a shipowner in the conventional system the unit is naturally enough seen as his own service. To the trader on the other hand these individual services are emphatically not the total service; each is useless without the others, like components of a manufactured product in relation to the finished product itself. The concept of the road service or the ship service as the unit is therefore producer orientated and not consumer orientated. In reality 'production' is useless except in relation to its market opportunity, and the transport industries, just as much as manufacturing industries, must study the total needs of the consumer. The only thing the customer is really interested in when considering his transport problem is the best way of getting his goods from his factory or warehouse to his market. The through transport concept embraces this logic and does regard the total journey as the unit of product. It follows that a through service which equates more or less exactly with the customer's requirement for transport from factory to market has a better chance of meeting his needs than one which is piecemeal in nature.

Once this is accepted, it follows that responsibility for the unit task should reside in one clearly identified quarter, and not be divided between several operators none of whom will accept responsibility for providing an efficient service over the whole journey. To pursue the analogy of a production process, under modern principles of production control the manufacturer who is selling the good accepts responsibility for the efficient production of the good concerned as an entity. He must see that sub-contractors provide sub-units that are satisfactory in terms of quality, cost, quantity and delivery time. He must monitor progress through the production process. In the short-run he must have contingency actions that he can take when anything fails to come up to standard. In the longer run he must set adequate standards

---

* Shipper is a word easily misunderstood and may even be confused with a shipowner. Literally, the shipper is the man who organizes shipment (movement) of cargo and may be the middleman rather than the exporter. In this chapter we are interested in the person who makes the product and sells or causes it to be sold abroad (the exporter) and the person who wants to use it or incorporate it in another product at destination (the importer). In this chapter the exporters and importers together will be referred to as *traders*.

127

and only pick sub-contractors who meet them. In other words he must accept responsibility. If things go wrong he cannot turn to a customer and blame someone else. The customer has a right to be uninterested in such excuses, and to be concerned only with the total result. In short, without unified responsibility there cannot possibly be total efficiency; and unified responsibility by definition imposes the burden of ensuring the efficiency of the total unit concerned. Thus in the transport field, the through transport operator has a total responsibility for the efficiency of the unit, the consignment-journey, not carried by the conventional operator of a modal service.

The label 'unified responsibility' carries a message for the trader as well. A task of senior management is to seek to achieve an optimum balance of functions within the firm. The study of PDM underlines the importance of the distribution function, hitherto often neglected. Those responsible for physical distribution within the firm must seek a balance between the transport function, defined in the strict sense of the carriage of goods, and the other elements of distribution in the wider sense, including stock control, patterns of ordering and the like, but the overall balance between main functions such as production, marketing and distribution can only be achieved at a level senior to the levels of management of the individual functions; in effect this means at board level. For some time the criticism has been made by transport specialists that transport has been neglected in the board room, that it has been left to the shipping clerk to look up the rate of freight with less than satisfactory results. PDM will help to change all that. The principles of PDM widen the concept of transport, erect the result as a main function and cost centre of the firm, and bring the overall policy issues between that function and others into the board room where they properly belong. Thus the principles of PDM do a service to those of through transport, for the reason that the full benefits of through transport require consideration of many things which bear upon total distribution, and of some things which bear upon the total balance of functions within the firm.

The *physical* aspect of through transport centres on the dual problem of minimizing the number of separate cargo handlings and increasing their efficiency. It is only in the past few years that transhipment between modes has been recognized as the great destroyer of efficiency in transport. Removing cargo out of one sort of vehicle in order to put it in another, which usually means putting it down on the ground somewhere, perhaps for minutes, often for days, and re-sorting it before the second vehicle comes along (or worse, long after it has come along) is what runs away with money in excessive handling cost: this is where time is lost, and where cargo is damaged, pilfered or misdirected. At least three kinds of inefficiency can be discerned in the above. Firstly, the customer receives a relatively high cost and unreliable service. The word relative is an important qualification because within the limits of the system a wide range in the standard of service has been provided by operators, good, bad or indifferent. Secondly, the operator incurs direct charges which have tended to increase much faster than the average of industrial costs and prices; these particularly relate to the costs of direct handling, a labour intensive operation subject to cost increases which reflect

128

rising living standards and therefore tend to be above the average increase of industrial costs. Thirdly, he also incurs indirect costs because of the relatively inefficient use of this equipment. Lorries stand in queues waiting to load or unload and at the end of the day may be told to come back and try again in the morning. Ships take too long in port to load and unload cargo (and turn-round times seem to have lengthened with the years rather than improved) with the result that they have spent in some cases as much as half their life in port and not at sea. Ships and lorries are expensive pieces of equipment. While they are in the queue and on the berth, these lorries and ships are not earning. The opportunity cost of their wasted time is a real cost, albeit an indirect one, to the operator.

In these two examples the port appears to be used as the whipping boy. It is not the intention to imply that port operators are less efficient persons than other men, although it could be argued that some ports have perhaps been run a little too much by the city fathers, and not quite enough by their more commercially minded managers. The point here is inherent in the conventional transport system. The port is a magnet attracting cargo from many inland points and many overseas destinations. Everything meets there. It becomes a warehouse, a sorting shed, a customs house and much else besides a place to load and unload ships. The tasks multiply and with time the volume of trade expands, but often the port area itself remains physically restricted, hemmed in by works of nature and of man. The result is a built-in tendency towards congestion. Further there has been a history of divided ownership of facilities and responsibility for labour in ports in Britain and elsewhere which in some important cases have soured labour relations with well-known results in the incidence of strikes and restrictive practices. From time to time these have accentuated congestion to the point of national crisis.

All these are important reasons why no one today believes there is a future for loose cargo. The handling of too many pieces of cargo too many times during a journey is the root of the trouble. The solution that has been sought is to unitize cargo and to rationalize its flow. Pre-slinging of cargo, pallet loading in conventional ships—or better into specialist wide hatch or side-loading ships, rolling lorries, on and off specialist 'Ro-Ro' ships built on the car ferry principle, the use of containers and cellular containerships, lash ships, these have been the developments in unitized cargo. No doubt ingenuity will provide yet more means of handling. A great deal has been written on the subject and the chapters immediately prior to this one in this present book have described them. Naturally there has been a certain amount of taking sides by operators as to the relative merits of different systems. It would not be appropriate to use this book as a medium to put forward a particular case. The main aspects are in the Appendix to this chapter. The reader may then apply judgment according to PDM principles to suit particular circumstances or to decide between a series of situations which might arise. The important point to emphasize here is that the creation of unit loads as a convenience to handling paves the way for the through-transport operation by removing important elements of handling away from the port area, eliminating others altogether, and avoiding some of the incidental port uses like its use as a warehouse. More than this it places positive emphasis on points at or near the origin and destination of the cargo.

In short, unit loads and unified responsibility pave the way for rationalization of services. This has both provider and user connotations, and concerns both operations and procedures. To take a deep-sea ship operation: where the focal point in a conventional service has been regarded by shippers and operators as the port, ships have tended to call at any and every port, now disrespectfully referred to as 'the milk-round', thereby multiplying the number of port handling operations almost to the nth degree and contributing heavily to the very high proportion of unproductive port time. Once the port becomes a less important focal point than the inland loading and discharge points, the way is clear to rationalizing ports of call, moving cargo to a smaller number of ports to and from 'inland groupage points',* factories or warehouses and increasing the amount of time the expensive ship is earning revenue. For the trader, rationalizing the flow calls in question traditional routes and distribution patterns. The need to re-assess these is an important aspect of the PDM approach to through transport, and will be reverted to below. For operators and governments the rationalization process also raises fundamental questions concerning the exact number and location of ports that are required for through transport systems, but this lies outside the PDM framework of decision-taking by the firm.

The *commercial* implications stem from the fact that an exporter using a through transport system has an opportunity to sell on a through transport basis. Traditional FOB selling, virtually ex-works selling, reflects in many cases the production orientated philosophy; not in all cases it must be conceded, because the importer may insist on buying FOB country of origin. If the producer of an export good regards his responsibility as ending when the product leaves his factory, then he will be content to sell FOB and leave the problems of forwarding, freight and export procedures to others. Where cargo is shipped by traditional methods, multiplicity and division have of necessity made for a complex system of commercial procedures. Specialist firms have developed who advise on the best way to ship abroad and handle procedures and documents on behalf of traders. Given the complicated system, they perform a legitimate function and fulfil an economic need; many shipping and forwarding agents will rightly claim that they give excellent and necessary service to their customers. Here we are concerned with inherent weaknesses in the system, not to judge where quality of execution is good and where it is faulty. There have been several such weaknesses. A complex system invites over-complication. A divided system means separate, perhaps conflicting, procedures. Over a period of time these procedures proliferate and there exists no ready-made focal point for rationalization. Where the exporter is prepared to abdicate responsibility outside the factory

---

* In the UK the term inland clearance depot was used initially, as the idea first took shape, in trying to frame rules for customs clearance of mainly inward cargo. Some of the container operators have preferred the less restrictive name of containerbase. In the US they are more loosely called terminals, in Australia depots, and in the Far East container freight stations.

gate or where he is too daunted by the prospect to act or simply has not the resources to do so, then the effectiveness of competition between agents as a spur to efficiency is reduced. Some agents may even see inefficiency as a form of bread and butter.

A smoother and faster flow of goods under a through transport system builds in an incentive for operators to improve procedures. The unified responsibility provides the means for rationalizing them. For the trader, greater simplicity will bring greater clarity of options open to him. Many firms will find an advantage in quoting delivered prices and monitoring the flow through the system. This last is not an onerous task for him, since an essential part of through transport is the passing of information back and forth through the system by the operators to users. The specialist agent will still have a role to play, particularly in serving the smaller firms. In a market where the trader is aware of the need for a quality service, competition between agents will exist; in these circumstances the agent has every incentive to maximize the efficiency with which he handles his clients' goods.

The commercial procedures 'live' by means of documents or other means of passing information. The smooth, speedy flow of goods by through transport requires an equally smooth, speedy flow of documents. They are parallel flows and the second will show up the first if it is wrong. The documents should follow rather than lead the procedures. The factor which is emerging as crucial in the streamlining of commercial procedures is the use of documentary credit (a document in the system against which producers, merchants and buyers can raise money). The bill of lading, issued by the shipowner to the shipper, as a document of title to goods against which credit can be raised, has played an important role in international trade in a slower age than the present. On the short-sea trades and on the North Atlantic it is now being found that with through transport systems there is neither the time nor the need to sell against bills of lading which must follow right through the commercial system and be presented to the operator at destination, before he releases the goods. Only about 12 per cent of goods in these short-sea trades, we are told, are now moved in conjunction with documentary credit. Necessity has found the answer and the old procedures are being dispensed with, the taking charge and delivery of goods being made against a simple receipt. In the longer sea trades shippers and importers are still requiring documentary credit. The real problem lies in the grey area of trades that are neither particularly long nor short in terms of distance. It is in such cases that it is particularly important that management think in terms of what the new situation produced by through transport really requires, and whether or not traditional commercial practices are still desirable. This is another example of the need for a conscious approach by management to a physical distribution problem.

The above paragraphs have attempted to show that through transport is not only a new system of transport in a physical sense; it is also a new commercial system *and*, perhaps most importantly, a new philosophy for management in dealing with the problem of moving its products to foreign markets and of receiving overseas goods into its system.

131

Through Transport, the Trader and PDM

At this stage in the argument there is some value in listing more specifically the possible advantages to traders of the through transport system and noting where an awareness of PDM has relevance in promoting an understanding of these advantages. The phrase 'possible advantages' introduces a tone of caution. There is always a danger, particularly in time of rapid change, of overselling a case. Clearly the incidence of claimed benefits is not going to be uniform. It will vary with the geography of the service, the quality of the operator, the type of product and so forth; while time and experience will no doubt mark up some of the claims and mark down others. This is inevitable. What does matter at this stage is that everyone is *aware* of the possibilities. Here we are concerned with the educative role. Once awareness has been established, traders will be in a position to judge cases and to see that through transport serves their several needs. Having said this, the points to be made can be listed in a series of desirable attributes: speed, reliability, safety, simplicity, cheapness. These are considered in turn. In each case, the nature of the improvement is taken first, and its significance to the trader second.

Speed   The speed of a through transport service is not really a function of increasing in-movement speed, although this may be done marginally, but of decreasing non-movement time. Handling, sorting, storing,* waiting time, are all unproductive in terms of movement. Efficiency is increased if 'non-movements' can be reduced in number, cutting out certain transhipments and shortened in time by mechanized handling. The total effect of such time savings will be a function of the length of journey. The shorter the journey the smaller the ratio of in-movement time to total time and therefore the greater the incidence of non-movement time savings. For instance, the UK–Australia container service is reducing the door-to-door transit time by about one-third, from nine weeks to six weeks, with only a marginal increase in ship steaming time. On the short-sea trade to Europe the reduction in door-to-door time due to unit load services† is from ten days by conventional modes to four days, on average (i.e. a reduction of 60 per cent).

The value of speed to the trader is difficult to generalize about. Quite obviously speed is a selling point. Conventional cargo liner sailing speeds, for instance, have been rising in recent years, often at considerable cost; this has been a competitive response by shipowners to what they believe to be the demands of the trading public for increased speed of service. How much this increase has cost the trader and whether any advantage has been 'swamped' by delays elsewhere in the system have not, one suspects, been very closely pursued in a good many cases. As part of the PDM concept, the subject would repay study by traders. The psychological effect on the

---

* There is an important difference between stockholding by a company as a matter of policy and storing in transit warehouses and quayside sheds as a matter of operating convenience or necessity; although it is true that a change in the latter may affect the former and traders quite often (successfully) attempt to use the latter facilities to perform their own stockholding functions.

† Source: see References, item 3.

customer (the importer) may turn out to be considerable. The inquiry instituted by the EDC for the Movement of Exports into moving exports to Europe showed that many importers thought that transit times from British shippers were generally bad, whereas journeys sampled suggested they were not so. The fact of Britain being an island and of goods requiring to be transhipped through ports, coupled with the periodic, but not continuous, difficulties at British ports, led to 'a perceived view' on the part of importers at variance with the facts. The moral is the need to sustain a good level of operating and to ensure, as part of a firm's marketing effort, that the facts about real transit times are put over to the customer.

Similarly there may be a psychological advantage to UK shippers on the Australia trade. The UK and Australia are at opposite ends of the earth. The old political ties of Commonwealth are loosening, and Australia is turning to trading partners closer at hand, namely Japan and the United States. The speeding up of the UK service by the through container service may bring delivery times into a band where, for many products, a few days' disadvantage against the competition from America and Japan is no longer an important factor in an importer's decision as to where to buy from.

Having said all this, it is probably still the case that the advantages of speed have been overplayed. The EDC inquiry referred to above found that whereas the average conventional transit time was ten days, the average time between the placing of an order and despatch from the factory was fifty days. Although the EDC rightly pointed out that 'it may be easier to reduce transport time from say sixteen days to six days than an order-to-despatch time from sixty to fifty days', the average findings do suggest that for many products speed for speed's sake in transport may not confer great benefits. Moreover half the goods to Europe were found to go into stock. This may suggest that where speed is needed the cost of stockholding on the Continent rather than in the UK has been weighed by exporters and found to be worth it. Alternatively it may suggest that for too many products the conventional service has been inadequate, and that through services may well reduce by a significant margin the need to hold stocks abroad. The lesson is one of need for a *conscious* cost and convenience trade-off between overseas stockholding and speed of the transport service.

Reliability The claim for greater reliability of through transport services compared to conventional services rests on several factors. First, as already noted, handling, sorting and storing are all opportunities for goods to be damaged, stolen, misdirected or otherwise lost. Obviously, in reducing the number of handling operations a through service is reducing the chances of this happening. Secondly, the nature of the operation is itself changed. The through operation is a mechanized operation and the human element is reduced. Machines are, of course, not infallible and only as good as those who operate them. On the other hand the task of control is made more wieldy for management and on average an improvement in handling efficiency has been seen to result. Thirdly, as far as container transport is concerned, each container carries a unique number. This seemingly simple fact is of the utmost

133

importance. It means that consignments or small groups of consignments can be monitored by EDP control methods right through the system. Throughout control makes for greater reliability. Wrong marking by the shipper is rendered largely irrelevant. Misrouting is minimized and correction made easier. Fourthly, the removal of important functions away from the port area relieves congestion at the most vulnerable point and helps prevent (indeed should avoid altogether) the periodic build-ups of cargo in port to saturation levels. The worst of the congestion build-ups have not only caused direct harm to the economy but also an indirect psychological harm—going back to the 'perceived image'—out of all proportion to actual delay.

As more through transport services are introduced, experience in devising and operating them grows. True, each trade has its own particular problems, while in some cases operators—and traders—are involved who have not had previous experience. On the other hand, the rapid growth* of through transport services of one kind or another suggests that operators and traders are succeeding in producing reliable services.

It is only fair to examine the degree to which through services may be vulnerable to interruption. Where economies of scale are leading to a marked rationalization of port and shipping services, the eggs are being put in fewer baskets, in some cases only one basket. What happens when there is mechanical failure or if labour disputes immobilize facilities? Indeed, does not the single berth approach invite labour trouble by creating a monopoly opportunity? Again the problem is mainly transitional. It is a truism that with larger units, the short-run effect of immobilization of a unit, for any reason whatever, is increased. Reliability is damaged if facilities cannot be switched quickly or if the proneness to difficulty is in some way increased. As services grow in size and number, more specialist ships, berths, even port complexes will become available and the ability to switch a ship into a gap filled by one put out of service or to switch ports is increased. Some of the specialist berths are exclusive user berths designed for the needs of particular operators, but competition is increasing the number of ports on a common user basis. Operators are finding that they can adapt to these berths.

The labour problem is related to fear of redundancy. Bulk handling of raw material cargoes, mechanization of across-the-quay movement, unit loading of general cargoes, are contributing to a redundancy problem in the ports, already an industry with an historical tendency to be dispute-prone. The UK mining industry shared similar attributes, yet a reduction in the labour force has been achieved with marked success. There is no reason why, with good management, a reduction cannot also be achieved in the ports. In the longer term, the prospects for good labour relations ought to be

---

* Statistics of growth are very quickly going to have a dated look at a time of rapid change. Emphasis upon them is therefore deliberately avoided in this chapter. The reader is referred particularly to the 1969 Port Progress Report of the National Ports Council, where he will find that the tonnage moved by unit loads in UK foreign trade grew from 3·5 million tons in 1965 to 6 million tons in 1967. He will also discover the paucity of information as yet on unit load statistics. The NPC and others are continuing their efforts and the available data will doubtless improve.

improved by the capital intensive nature of the operation. A labour force of economic size should be able to earn high wages, without a general need for overtime, for work which carries relatively high responsibility (operating expensive equipment) and relatively low physical effort compared with that required from the traditional docker. This is the climate for good labour relations, and it has been observed that relations are usually better in industries where the ratio of capital to labour is high. There is reason to anticipate that through services will engender more reliable labour relations, not less.

For the exporter and importer, recent researches suggest that reliability of service is more important than speed. The customer wants to know when goods will arrive, and to be reasonably confident that delivery will take place as stated. To be able to plan on that near-certain knowledge is usually more important to him than shaving a day or two off the average delivery time. If delay should take place, then he is probably still satisfied provided the number of instances is not large and he is told in good time of the change in the arrival date. An exporter should himself be aware of his customer's interests and needs concerning information about and reliability of delivery. If he is in the habit simply of waving good-bye to his goods when they leave his factory, his own responsibility discharged to his satisfaction, then he is unlikely to be interested in reliability of delivery. When he is rung up with the news that something has gone wrong, he will just blame someone else and probably show irritation at the implication that he is in any way responsible. But whether he knows it or not, his goodwill will suffer. Worse, other people's will suffer. The work of the Movement of Exports EDC, referred to earlier, suggested that the harm done by the talk of slow, late deliveries to Europe was out of proportion to their occurrence in the system. At least for those importers used to fairly short average delivery time,* in many cases the 'perceived image' of British reliability tended to align with the tail rather than with the average journey. On deep-sea trades it is probable that the tail again has a disproportionate influence. It is important that the tail is kept as short as possible, that the true picture of overall reliability is put over as part of marketing effort, and that where delay does occur the customer is given as much warning of it as possible.

Our exporter who waves good-bye to his cargo may concede the case thus far, but still claim that he has no direct influence on the transport operator. This is only true in the very short run. The normal commercial pressures can be brought to bear in a system where competition on service is present, and in the longer run the standard of service is responsive to that pressure. There is one field in which the action of the shipper is of immediate and direct significance—documentation. Incomplete or inaccurate documents or non-compliance with standard procedures is a great cause of delay. Many of the

---

* Since journey lengths to Europe are unlikely to be widely different, 'short' and 'long' delivery must refer mainly to different product types. It is only natural that customers buying product types wanted on short delivery should be the ones who are most aware of delivery time. The point may well remain valid on other and longer trades, even though statistical support for saying this is lacking.

135

occasions when goods are 'held up in the Customs' or 'not cleared by the shipowner' are directly due to faulty documentation by the shipper. There is more to say on this subject under the heading of simplicity below.

Safety Safety is here used in the sense of minimizing loss or damage to cargo through physical means of handling and transit and through pilferage. Loss or delay through misrouting or wrong marking has been included under the heading of reliability. Nor are we here concerned with the subject of safety at sea as such. One of the claims for through transport services is that they do give greater protection for cargo. Handling is the point of maximum risk of damage. Reduce the number and increase the quality of handlings and the risk is reduced. A container, or articulated trailer in the case of Ro-Ro services, does itself provide a great deal of protection to cargo. The box is of reasonable strength, weatherproof and, travelling under customs seal, pilfer proof. Crushing of cargo by loose stacking is eliminated. The safe packing of containers is important. Loose cargo of manufactured products in the container could easily damage itself to destruction under the rolling motion of a ship. Many containers are packed by expert packers in inland clearance depots or groupage facilities of forwarding agents. Shippers who themselves pack their exports are quickly becoming expert, and container operators offer specialist advice to them. Experience on the North Atlantic, and on the Irish and short-sea trades has been building up. In the new deep-sea container trade to Australia, shippers carried out extensive experiments in sending packed containers by cargo liner in advance of the service, and at the time of writing the cargo out-turn of the new service has been good. In all these cases exporters and importers are finding greatly improved quality of cargo, and much reduced insurance claims. As would be expected, the improvement with the breakage record is greatest with fragile goods like furniture, gramophone records, ceramics and glassware. Quite how dramatic in some cases may not be realized. For glassware, breakages of 30–40 per cent had been accepted as normal by conventional service, even where expensive crates were used; one container out-turn in Australia of tumblers packed in light cartons showed only four broken out of 10,000. An improved damage rate is not confined to the fragile cargoes. For instance, bagged cargoes often suffer loss where bags split open. In containers the bags get much greater protection. Pilferage has also been a cause of heavy loss on some cargoes, for instance whisky. Container shipment can virtually eliminate this.

All this experience is at variance with a body of opinion in the insurance market which has said that the advent of containers has brought higher claims. This opinion may stem from experience of the carriage of containers in considerable numbers on non-specialist ships, particularly on the North Atlantic. In such cases the containers may be handled by a wide variety of equipment not specially tailored to the system. The view of the vast majority of through transport operators is that the system must be a specialist one; in this way containers, trailers (if they are used) and cargo can be adequately protected.

136

For the exporter and importer the safety aspect is important in reducing the number of insurance claims. In time this must have an effect on insurance premiums. On the glassware example above this surely must have been at a high rate. Nevertheless insurance of freight cannot be said to be a very large item in the total delivered value of most products and it may be that indirect benefits are of even more importance to the trader. A low damage rate will improve an exporter's goodwill with his customers, and his competitive ability against equivalent locally produced goods. Where prompt delivery of a particular consignment is important, both the cost of replacement and the cost of delay may be high; improvement leads to an overall improvement in economic efficiency.

Simplicity There are two or three rather disparate things which can be said under the heading of simplicity; these concern the service itself, procedures and rates structure.

It is worth underlining the basic simplicity of the through transport concept. The idea of pre-packing goods in boxes which can be put on a standard rail flat-car or road 'frame' trailer and slotted into a cell in a ship, with the process being repeated at the other end of the trade, is so simple and has a look of being so convenient as to prompt the question: why was it not all thought of before? The answer, as the literature on container transport seldom fails to point out, is that the container *was* thought of some time ago. What was not thought of, which is sometimes, but less often, pointed out, was the system of through flow from origin to destination. Containers were heavy objects which stuck about in quays and warehouses and yards, did not improve transit conditions and did not pay for themselves. The crucial part of the 'simple idea' did not come until economic pressures on the conventional system caused operators to look round for something different and better, and to follow the lead of a perspicacious American trucker who proved that he could beat inland transport rates across the United States by a coast-to-coast containership service. To make the change in international trade has not been so simple, and is still not proving so simple. Demands are being made on numerous people. Much traditional practice has had to be changed and changed in important respects by cooperative action between operators of different modes and between them and traders, port authorities, governments and government agencies—engendering much discussion and much committee work. The simplicity is to be found in the basic idea, not in the implementation. The idea is compelling because of the strength which simplicity brings.

Once a through transport system has been decided upon the complexity of ensuring a smooth physical flow of traffic is the through operator's responsibility. For the trader the system *should* look simple, and successful services are operating today in which this is the case. Where the trader is directly concerned is in the procedures and rating structure.

The unified responsibility of the through operator eases some problems and removes some from the shoulders of the trader. Satisfactory internal procedures (based on a.d.p. and numeric control) between modes and at

137

interchange points are, of course, still required. Regularity of flow through a particular chain of facilities, exclusive user berths or depots, long-term contracts with sub-operators, all give sufficient continuity of contact between a through operator and other transporters for such procedures to be worked out and adhered to.

Simplification of external commercial procedures will be greatly helped by agreement on standard terms of liability for through carriage of cargo which are now being devised in the appropriate fora. These draft rules set out the responsibilities of through carriers and of traders and state the principles upon which through operators' liability rests. Agreement will pave the way for issuance of through bills of lading upon terms which are immediately recognizable as internationally acceptable, and will therefore facilitate the use of these bills for raising credit.

Further work is also proceeding in various quarters* to simplify those documents relating to through transport which pass between traders, operators, government agencies, etc. The aim is to produce the minimum number of documents consistent with satisfactory operation of through transport systems; to standardize and align documents where practicable and useful; and to make proper use of modern mechanical methods of data processing and transmission.

Finally, there is simplicity of rates structure. By this is not meant reduction of unit load rates to a freight of all kinds (FAK) rate—the FAK concept pays scant regard for degrees of price elasticity of demand† which is a normal feature of pricing theory—but rather some rationalization of rates and greater clarity in expressing total through charges. The second is the vital point and stems from the ability of the through-service operator to quote a through rate from door-to-door, inclusive not only of the land-sea-land legs, but also of various additional items like warehouse or wharfage costs in the port, insurance, etc. In other words he is able to quote a price for

---

* In the UK, under the auspices of the NEDC, a UK Committee for the Simplification of International Trade Procedures has been formed with a membership as widely based as possible. A similar body called the NITCD exists in the US, though it does not contain government membership. Further work is also done in committees of the ECE, the Customs Cooperation Council, etc.

† The elasticity of demand for transport services will depend on the elasticity of demand for the final product in question. This latter elasticity is not a function of the value of the product. Nevertheless, because a given level of freight is a smaller proportion of the final price of a high value product than of a low value product, there is a presumption that a high value product is more easily able to bear a higher freight charge than is a low value product. An equal percentage increase in the rate of freight will have a smaller effect on the final price of the high value product than on that of the low value product. Where conventional cargo liner tariffs pay regard to value of cargo as well as to its volume and/or weight, they are paying some regard to price elasticity of demand for transport, and discriminating according to ability to pay. 'Fair' competition is a practical limitation on the amount, and especially on the character of the discrimination applied between cargoes. A container service is more capital intensive than a cargo liner service; fixed costs are high and avoidable costs low. Provided they cover avoidable costs, there is considerable incentive to charge down to this level if this is what is required to secure the cargo. The low level of avoidable cost means that the least cost system may be arrived at by a charging basis more discriminatory than in the case of the cargo liner.

the consignment-journey as a whole which, as we have seen, is the real unit of product to the trader. For many exporters this is the first time that they have readily been able to compute the real price of their goods in overseas markets. The importance to efficient marketing of being able to do so is obvious. An exporter, even in a small way of business, is enabled to see the selling price of his own product in the market against the price of competing products produced locally, or imported from third countries. He is thus able to assess his true situation against the competition. He will not be able to do this if he is only interested in an ex-works price or if the number of on-cost items are so complicated that he cannot get the final figure right. There is a a second angle. Being able to express total delivery charges simply and accurately enables an exporter to know easily and quickly what are his own distribution costs as a proportion of the total cost of producing and delivering a particular good. The effects of changes in either element can then be related. In short the through price is an important management tool for his own internal cost control. What has been said of exporters, can, *mutatis mutandis*, be said of importers as well.

Cheapness For most people the crunch comes with the price. It is quite fair that this should be so, provided the trader is asking himself the question in the right way—how does it affect my *real* costs overall, not simply the direct cost of freight?—*and* provided he is also assessing some measure of worth to him, however difficult to quantify, of the factors we have been discussing above. A conscious effort is required within the firm to identify indirect cost savings and benefits.

First, direct cost to the trader, i.e. the level of freights. Here cost and competition are the factors to consider.

Concerning costs, the savings to be made are in better utilization of the more expensive items of hardware, namely ships and berths, and on direct handling. Most of these savings occur at the terminals rather than at sea. Therefore, as a general rule, the shorter the route and therefore the greater the weight of terminal costs in total costs, the greater will be the saving in cost on a through transport service. On the other hand through transport systems are capital intensive, and the operators are moving into fields new to many of them, such as provision of inland depots and inland transport facilities. More money is required and in larger lumps. In the early days of development some of these facilities will inevitably be under-utilized, while recent investments made elsewhere, notably in conventional cargo lines with an uncertain future, will suffer premature obsolescence. The necessary capital will only be attracted if rates of return look reasonable in relation to other opportunities, and this means a share in total rewards higher than many of the operators, mainly shipowners, have been receiving in recent years. Operators are also currently faced with a good many cost unknowns, e.g. speed of terminal throughput in various parts of the world, the rate of packing containers in depots, the precise length of time containers will be out of operator's charge on the inland legs of the journey, the physical life of containers, the economic life of container and other unit-load ships at this

139

early stage in the development of the technology and so on. In short it is early to say with any assurance how costs will move. Indeed comparison in detail between an old port-to-port type service and a through service is not possible. They are too different in kind.

Concerning competition and the sharing of rewards, in the past traders (at least European traders) have clearly preferred stability of rates in wooden liner trades to rock-bottom prices, and have in general given their support to the conference system which has evolved over the years in international sea-borne trade. Competition has remained on service, in shares of trade between operators and in some respects on price. Some people see the growth of through transport services as heralding monopoly, because economies of scale are demanding rationalization of services, equipment and companies. This could possibly be true, but even then not necessarily so, if separate trades existed in water-tight compartments. Under the traditional conference system trade routes have indeed kept separate identities and liner companies have retained corresponding identities because they carried rights on the trade, even after they have been absorbed into larger financial groupings. Even under that system the compartments were not water-tight. The situation *is* changing, but not towards monopoly, and is changing in different ways on deep- and short-sea trades respectively. On deep-sea trades the likely evolution is the emergence of a relatively few powerful companies with world-wide interests. Because these companies are operating through transport services, they will be concerned with the marketing and operation of their services in the principal countries to and from which they operate. The pressure on them is to become more conscious of marketing than in the past, to establish certain territories which will become strong bases from which to operate world-wide services. The port industry, too, is feeling the competitive pressure of unit-load services and few ports of significance in international trade will feel it prudent to be without specialist facilities to serve unit-load ships of one kind or another. The new specialist service operators will thus still retain flexibility to operate all round the world. This means an increase of at least the potential competitive position between the major companies. As of now it is too early to discern any trend in the level of unit-load rates. On the North Atlantic, which is a medium-length route and the first international route of significance to enjoy a significant number of unit-load services, a 5 per cent discount is given on all unit-load cargoes. On the new UK–Australia service, full container load consignments are also discounted.

On the short-sea trades, through transport is enhancing the importance of many land-based operators; the sea leg being essentially a bridge operation, the weight of investment and of expertise lies in the land legs rather than the sea leg. Certainly, on the trade between the UK and the Continent, freight forwarders, hauliers and others are entering the trade as through-service operators and seizing an opportunity hitherto not open to them: the indications are that the competitive position between operators is having an influence on price.

Therefore, if one is to hazard a guess as to the movement of direct costs for the trader, as reflected in through service rates, on both short- and deep-sea trades there will soon be a period in which the movement of operators' costs and of competitive forces is such as to bring about a reduction in freights in real terms. How successful operators will be in continuing to achieve reductions once the new technology has been widely adopted remains to be seen. Most new technologies sustain improvement in sophistication and in scale for a considerable time. Technological forecasting is today considered to be more than a game, but it does not appear yet to have been applied to this field.

Consideration must now be given to the very important area of *indirect savings*, of great relevance to the concept of physical distribution management. All these are cost savings that will be missed by the firm which is oblivious of the principles of PDM. First there is time, secondly, packaging, thirdly, goodwill and fourthly, location. Location is such an important aspect of PDM that this will form the last main heading of this chapter.

Time is money. An important saving to be made is through what is often now called the pipeline effect, that is the saving on the interest charges on goods in transit. In the Australia trade, for instance, the reduction in average transit times from about nine weeks to six weeks, means that at any moment only two-thirds as many goods as hitherto are tied up in transit. With interest charged at say, 8 per cent in the accounts of traders, the annual saving to a regular trader is obviously considerable. The value of a 20-foot container load may vary from two or three hundred pounds to ten or twelve thousand. To use the Australian example: if say twenty days' interest at 8 per cent is saved on a container load worth £500, the amount saved is £2·20. A low value good of this kind might pass in considerable numbers, and one shipper might, say, be regularly passing to one customer 100 containers a year, in which case the interest saving would be £220 p.a. The saving on a single container load of £10,000 value would be £44. The total saving will be shared between shippers and importers, according to their pattern of financing. The sooner the shipper gets his money the sooner will he be able to write the value of the goods off his books. He may be able to do this almost at once, in which case speed of settlement becomes the concern of the buyer who, even if he does not make payment until he takes delivery, may have to finance the credit established by a bank in favour of the seller. Who is liable for financing credit for how long a period depends upon the terms of sale, the type of credit raised, and whether middlemen are involved between buyer and seller through transferable credits. Documentary credits and bills are not the easiest subject for those without about half a life-time's experience in commerce. Its complexity does not invalidate the point being made; rather it affects the proportions of the total transit period shared between buyer, seller and any intermediaries involved.

In the case of container and Ro-Ro services it is now becoming established that most exporters are saving by being able to use lighter *packaging* than is necessary for break-bulk shipment. This is a multiple saving since he saves on materials, labour and freight involved in packaging no longer required. The amount of this saving must vary greatly from fragile goods at the high packing cost end, through anything that needs crating, to goods where perhaps a lighter fibre-board packing case becomes acceptable. For some raw commodites like wool it will be nil. For some bagged cargoes it may still be nil, but it must be remembered that out-turn may be improved. For many consumer goods and light engineering products, domestic packs have been used successfully instead of crates, with an overall packaging saving of the order of 60 per cent. For heavier machinery a very wide range of savings have been noted according to the characteristics of the machine, e.g. whether and how easily it breaks down into stowable parts, what sort of supports are needed in the container, how much dunnage, etc. Savings as low as £50 per machine and as high as £2000 (for a machine divided among several containers) have been recorded.

Goodwill has already been alluded to above. It is impossible to put a figure on it in the wide sense in which it is here used, yet any trader worth his salt will be acutely conscious of it. It embraces every aspect of efficiency in the through transport system which enhances relations between buyers and sellers of goods moved in the system: reliability and speed of service, information about delivery, good out-turn of cargo, simplicity of procedure, stability of rates. If these are present, goodwill is present.

Through Transport and Location
Through transport has a positive bearing on the subject of depot and warehouse location. Here the heading 'location' is used as shorthand to cover the question of the pattern of points at which goods are at rest along the transport chain and that of stocks, where and how much should be held. By definition through transport has the effect, as already noted, both of moving the points of making and breaking bulk away from port areas towards the main centres of gravity of supply and demand and of reducing the number of points along the chain at which goods are rehandled and/or re-sorted. Where volume is sufficient cargo can move in full unit loads, e.g. container loads between the port and exporters'/importers' factories and warehouses. Where volume is low cargo can be grouped and broken down in public inland clearance depots or forwarding agents' depots, a journey involving only one short haul, 'C & D'-type movement plus the through journey either direct to customer or with another short-haul movement at the receiving end of the journey. There thus is still an opportunity to reduce the number of intermediate points along the chain.

All major ports have attracted a number of warehouses to their vicinity. Road hauliers and others have found it convenient to establish these 'reservoirs' in the port area, especially for import cargoes. The logic of the current developments in through transport is for warehouses to be located near the inland clearance depots (ICDs), if possible just over the fence. The effect will be not only to move the warehouses closer to principal trading centres, perhaps cutting down on the need for an extra warehouse link in the chain, but also to break the warehousing function up into smaller units geared to the size of throughput of one ICD rather than that of a major port. The

142

optimum size of an ICD is probably of the order of half-a-million tons dead-weight throughput a year. This change has not yet taken place, but it is highly probable that signs of it will soon emerge.

Most wholesalers of general goods are probably still buying on a pattern which precludes direct ordering of a complete unit load (container or trailer load) at a time. It is, of course, possible that for some goods buying patterns may change. In the US, for some commodities, a container load is already becoming a unit of sale. In many cases a container load will be impracticable in terms of space and too costly in terms of turnover time to be economic. The size of wholesaling firms (units) will continue to be dictated by the size of the market within easy reach by road. In these cases wholesalers will con-veniently be able either to send their C & D vehicles direct to the ICD for a less-than-container consignment or collect from the adjacent inland ware-house. It could be argued that a smoother flow of goods associated with through transport systems will eliminate the need for a 'reservoir' warehouse, all wholesalers using ICDs or agents' depots. In practice, buying patterns are such that the inland warehouse has a genuine function, however smooth the flow. In the US warehouses of this type are certainly beginning to appear.

Foodstuffs present a particular case because of the significant proportion of perishables and other fast turnover goods involved. In this trade the supermarkets are now leading the trend in new patterns of distribution. For some commodities the supermarket groups are large enough to be taking container/trailer loads. The question is, where to? At this stage in through transport development there is clearly room for more than one view, but broadly the pattern which seems to be emerging is the establishment by supermarket companies of their own depots, each depot serving that number of retail outlets which can be reached by a daily road drop. The pressure in the high street is to keep down the number of vans parking and to reduce the amount of space for stockholding behind the shop. The more that can be brought in daily by one van to go straight onto the shelf and into the cus-tomer's basket the better. The depots will, therefore, act as the wholesale reservoir for storing, sorting and sometimes price-marking of goods. Full unit loads of imported canned food, cheese, even fresh fruit can be fed straight into these depots as customers' premises. Meat and butter present particular problems and may require an intermediate factory stage for making up of cuts, packing and blending as appropriate before going to depots. Neverthe-less, a flow direct from the ship to factory or depot, as the case may be, should be capable of being achieved with no intermediate handling of the contents and the minimum of transfer (it may be nil) of the container itself from one vehicle to another. For some commodities which require longer or specialist storage it may be convenient to make one depot within a chain a specialist depot for storing a particular good, from which it is sent to the other depots for sorting and sending out in mixed loads to retail outlets.

All this is illustrative of possibilities. The important point is that importers should be thinking about the location problem in their distribution pattern, and how through transport will assist in rationalizing it. The following quotation* sums up the line of thought: 'It should be possible to look at the through transport operation in question and to ask oneself whether it is any longer necessary to warehouse certain goods in location A for subsequent sorting and distribution to B, C, D and E. Could one not so organize the packing at origin that so many container loads could by-pass the delays and costs of A completely, and be sent direct to B, C, D and E? Or could a certain proportion be handled this way, sending the balance to A? But is A the best distribution centre any longer, or might it more profitably be located adjacent to a containerbase (ICD) in order to take advantage of its transport facilities and rates?'

The final part of the argument concerns policy towards holding stocks. It has been noted above that in the UK–Europe trade 50 per cent of goods are now sold out of stock and not on consignment. This method particularly related to consumer goods, which usually carry a bigger time premium than other goods. Quite obviously importers have found it worthwhile to hold stocks as the best way to ensure quick delivery and some exporters will have set up their own stockholding organizations on the Continent. The point is not confined to Europe. Indeed, it applies more strongly on the longer trade routes. For if, by through transport, reliable average transit times of four days or so can be achieved to the Continent, then buying on consignment except for very small amounts may stand up pretty well. The argument is one of degree. In many cases the cost of holding overseas stocks will be justified, but the speed and reliability of through transport services should reduce the *amount* of stocks which need to be held to give an adequate safety margin. There is a further point.† An importing company which buys for stock and not against a firm order takes a calculated risk. This risk is reduced if the service is speedy and less goods are tied up in transit (the pipeline effect), and also if it is reliable and his stocks can be held at a relatively low level. The interest he pays on goods both in transit and in stock is thereby reduced.

---

* K. St Johnston, a Managing Director, Overseas Containers Ltd, Lecture on 'Movement of Exports' at the University of Bradford Management Centre Conference on 'Developing Policies for Physical Distribution', January 1969.

† Perhaps two points, the second deserving only a footnote at present. Trade in certain foodstuffs like meat and fresh fruit tends to be seasonal and a large proportion of the commodities concerned are moved seasonally and stored in the country of destination. This has long created an awkward problem for shipping lines. The advent of capital intensive containerships (high fixed, low avoidable costs) increases the need for high load factors if they are to operate economically, and for a pricing mechanism to discourage peaking. To the economist it seems eminently reasonable that there should be an off-peak inducement to encourage producers to invest in greater storage capacity at their end of the trade (capacity which cubic foot for cubic foot is likely to be no more expensive and in some cases cheaper than like capacity at the consumer end). This would result in a lower cost total distribution pattern, the benefits of which may be presumed to be shared equitably. However traditional patterns of trading may be hard to shift in this respect; and there are some counter-arguments, like the need for fruit to hit the market in the season (this itself may change with more advanced storage techniques) and also some alternative solutions, like specialist non-container ships for peak cargoes and the flexibility of large-scale container operations (once they have become widespread) to switch ships between trades to meet peak requirements.

144

Conclusion

The argument is now completed; the reader may say 'the spell wound up'. The aim of this chapter, however, has not been to put him under the spell of an ideal world of through transport systems, removed from the realities of the imperfect world we all know. Rather, the aim, it is hoped legitimate for a contribution to a textbook, has been to describe the characteristics, aims and objectives of these systems and help to improve understanding of the possibilities they hold out for importers and exporters in improving the efficiency of distribution. Such an understanding falls best into place if it becomes a conscious part of the whole concept of physical distribution. It is then up to the trader to use his own sound judgment in deciding whether the benefits proffered are real, and if they *are* real, how he himself should adjust to gain maximum benefit.

It may be added that little attempt has been made to distinguish between problems of exporters and importers. A through transport service is a unit. If it has any excellence it will be of benefit to both exporters and importers. It is open to the exporter to sell it as part of his total product, and to the importer to demand a high level of efficiency, which may sometimes still mean buying FOB ex-works or ex-warehouse rather than accepting goods on a delivered basis. Much of what has been said on the commercial advantages of selling on a through basis may have more direct relevance to exporters than to importers; what has been said about location of distribution facilities, to the importer. But even that distinction is not entirely true. An exporter always has at least a latent possibility of setting up his own distribution facilities, directly or through an agent, in a country to which he is a significant exporter; in which case he becomes an importer. An importer is in a position to share to a greater or lesser extent in the financial benefits, direct or indirect, of through transport services.

This chapter concludes with nine precepts for traders about through transport. They have been used in more than one lecture, but perhaps will bear setting down in print by way of summarizing the argument. It must also be said that they owe something in spirit to the work of the EDC for Movement of Exports in pioneering the philosophy of through transport in this country:

1. Take transport to the Board Room. Don't leave transport to the shipping clerk
2. Look at total distribution. Don't just look at direct transport costs. In through transport indirect costs/savings are absolutely vital
3. Make total distribution a separate cost centre. This will enable you to strike a balance between physical distribution as a whole and your production and marketing functions. Holding the balance between functions is a Board responsibility
4. Look at delivered price. Don't stop short at the ex-works price. Quote a delivered price if this is advantageous to you. Benefits are: identifying your competitive price in the market and identifying your distribution costs as a percentage of total costs. Through transport helps you to quote delivered prices

145

5. Accept the responsibility for delivery. See that the operator monitors progress through the system and informs you of it. Advise your customer of the delivery date and of any delay

6. A look at transit time against the overall time from placing of order to delivery to customer. This enables you to see the total worth of saving X days transit and to quote realistic delivery dates which enable your customer to plan with safety

7. Think of stocks held in the country of distribution and the speed/ reliability of transport to it as complementary factors. The better the performance of the latter, the lower the former need be. Relative costs will decide where the balance should be

8. Look at your pattern of distribution. Will through transport systems enable you to eliminate some of the points along the chain of inland distribution, re-locate others to advantage and increase the efficiency of your own distribution system?

9. Promote distribution efficiency along with the excellence of your product. Make sure that the customer does not think that you are further away in time than you actually are. (He may still think of Britain as a far-off island.) In practice your delivery record may be excellent and compare favourably with that from other countries. Say so. Efficiency of distribution is an important part of the total effect which it is desirable to impress on the customer, and your promotional activities should lay some stress on it.

Appendix

COMPARISON BETWEEN TYPES OF UNIT LOAD

It has been shown that out-of-date handling methods have been responsible for the increasing costs of sea transport and the unreliability of services and congestion in the ports. The key to improvement is improvement in handling. The principle of the unit load is quite simply the putting together of cargo in larger and more convenient units which will decrease the number and increase the speed of handling operations, in short improving handling productivity.

An example of an effective and simple form of unit load is packaged timber, where timber is sawn in uniform lengths, bonded together in some way by straps leaving loops by which it can easily be slung on and off a ship. The productivity of packaged timber berths has increased remarkably. Figures of the order of 1000 standards* a day across the ship's rail are being achieved, compared with about 200 a day by traditional methods. Some large indivisible loads, whether in crated form or not, are also a form of unit load and usually require heavy lifting gear to move them. For general cargo, however, the term unit load is usually taken to mean pallets, containers and Roll on-Roll off trailers.

Pallets The essential feature of the pallet is that it should be strong enough to carry the cargo for which it is designed, or perhaps even several forms of cargo; it may have to carry loads of a ton or more, perhaps several tons when stacking is considered; a reasonable loading range is 0.5–2.0 tons per pallet. It must also be designed so that it can be lifted by fork-lift trucks and by slings. As such the pallet is not all that cheap. It may cost several pounds and although many pallets must make a good many journeys, recovery can be difficult and pools are complex to administer. Life may as easily end by being pushed aside out of the system as by damage and destruction. A good many shipping lines and some ports do give financial incentives to shippers to unitize their cargo on pallets, and some operate pallet exchange schemes. The best known example of the pallet pool is that operated by the European railways. A good deal of work has been done in recent years to find a cheap, disposable pallet for a price of $37\frac{1}{2}p$ or so, which represents an economic price

* A standard measures 165 cu. feet, about 4 measurement tons.

147

for one journey. For instance it is possible to give added strength to cartons by bonding them together with a glue so that the pallet with some fibreboard content would be strong enough to hold them. But no really satisfactory solution here has yet been forthcoming. Certainly nothing has been produced at that price.

There have been two important improvements in the handling of pallets on and off ships: pre-slung cargo and side- or end-loading by fork-lift truck. The so-called Scandia ship, as run by several Scandinavian lines, is an example of the former where palletized cargo with wire loops left in position can be slung straight on to the ship without further movement beyond the vertical plane. This means that the ship is designed with wide hatches, itself an advance in naval architecture. The fork-lift load system is able to run cargo quickly and economically under hatch coamings. Both forms have permitted impressive improvement in handling times, in gang productivity and in turn-round time of ships. It is possible to design low deck heads so that the stacking does not have to be high, thus minimizing crushing; and to put shrink-wrap covers on the pallets to improve protection. It is also possible in some cases to move the pallets to and from the port area as a unit load, and thus reduce congestion somewhat, but the pallets themselves must still be sorted to marks in the port area which takes space and time. The pallet is not truly an international unit and it has limits as a basis for a through transport system.

Roll on-Roll off transport has developed remarkably quickly in the short-sea trades, where a ship on the car ferry principle is economic because of the shortness of the sea leg of the total journey. The trailer is usually driven on and off the ship by a stevedore's tractor unit, to and from the trailer park where a haulier's tractor unit will collect it. Loading and unloading costs are low, but taking the wheels to sea is expensive in stowage space (any general cargo ship is selling space rather than weight) and locks up the capital invested in the trailers; this has prevented the extension of this system to deep-sea trades, except where motor-car exports are important (as on the North Atlantic, where specialist combination ships with both Roll on-Roll off and container space have been developed). It is possible, of course, to transport a container on a frame trailer by this method, but one of the essential and expensive features of the container itself is its strength for stacking, which is not required on a Ro-Ro trailer. Most Ro-Ro traffic is therefore by van-type articulated trailers of comparatively light construction such as are also used in domestic road haulage. (In the UK the flat trailer is still more popular than the van trailer, but the latter is on the increase). In the short-sea trades, lorry crews sometimes go with the trailers right through to their destination, and are thus able to look after the cargo; some shippers value this as a selling point, but the practice is believed to be declining in popularity. [See Chapter B.5 for more detail.]

Containers The rapid development of container transport in the very recent past in trades to and from the United States and in the UK–Irish trade (where

148

80 per cent of the trade is now unitized, much of it in containers) and the further developments going on in deep-sea trades suggest that containers are here in a big way, and are here to stay. Perhaps six characteristics of the container can be singled out to account for its success:

1. Strength, designed for stacking and protection of cargo, at the same time keeping a low tare weight/load ratio
2. Durability, giving it a reasonable economic life
3. Uniformity—ISO external dimension and corner casting (for top lift) standards now exist; this gives flexibility of use in the sense that containers can be used in trades of widely differing characteristics, and carried by many different modes of transport
4. Handleability, giving a potential increase in productivity of operations at terminals and other interchange points which is markedly better than any other system
5. Density of space utilization—by clothing cargo in units of 1000 cu ft. a much better use is achieved (a) of ship space than by packing cargo in 'tween deck spaces many times the size; (b) of terminal space
6. Identity—a unique number, important to the control and monitoring of container movements. An international standard system of numbering is in course of being agreed through the ISO.

A good many containers have been carried as deck cargo on conventional ships and handled on and off trucks by a variety of means. This, however, has led to a fairly high degree of damage and the acceptable container operation really requires the specialist cellular ship and the specialist handling top-lift equipment to see it smoothly through its journey. The cellular ship is a more expensive ship than, say, the Scandia pallet ship, and the cost of the ship, the containers themselves and the gear must be traded off against savings elsewhere for the system to be economic. A standard general purpose container 20-foot long may cost about £600 and an insulated 20-foot container £1000 or more. The life of a marine container is as yet uncertain; a prudent assumption is of the order of seven years. The containers are an essential part of a cellular ship which is of open construction, having no decks in the conventional sense. How many 'suits' are needed per ship depends upon the characteristics of the inland operation of the trade concerned in relation to the length of the sea journey; it is essentially a question of the ratio of the time a ship is at sea to the time it takes for containers to circulate inland and re-appear at the marine terminal. On a long-sea trade like UK–Australia about one-and-three-quarter suits are needed per ship. On shorter haul deep-sea trades the ratio may be as high as three. On the short-sea trades where the ship is acting as a bridge it is probably wrong to think of the containers as belonging to the ship at all (certainly many will be owned by through-service operators who do not own vessels).

The container ship itself is not only expensive; increased size to take account of scale economies also means that investment is 'lumpy' compared with conventional cargo liners. The trend to faster speed is accentuated in container ships, while the stress problems posed by the U-formation of the hull also cause expense.

Then there is the land-side investment of a through service, greater for a container service than for a Ro-Ro or pallet service. The cost of a single berth terminal as a turn-key job may be several million pounds. A five-high stacking system for containers such as devised by OCL is relatively expensive on works (stack, windbreaks, ground piling, etc.) and cheap on land; and a trailer park system as used by Sea-Land is expensive on land and cheap on works. There are variants in between these two systems. Inland clearance depots, again, are a necessary expense.

The trade-off against these costs is the greater productivity achieved. To take ship-side operations first. A conventional cargo liner may typically be worked at say five hatches by five gangs, each of seventeen–nineteen men, nearly a hundred men in all. It might take five days with work going well to unload the ship, carrying, say, 4000 freight tons. This might give up to 20 tons per gang hour, according to how many hours are worked per day. Obviously performance may vary from this for a variety of reasons. Pallet loading shows a marked improvement on these figures. Olsen's, who are acknowledged pallet experts, have given 60 weight tons per side front or top-lift on a Scandia type ship compared with 15 weight tons per gang hour by conventional means. Gang sizes can be reduced to seven, averaging about thirty-five men per ship. It is possible to work a large container ship with as few as eighteen men (ship- and land-side) per shift, multiplying this up for a two or three shift system. A shipside container crane works in a cycle, taking a container 'unit' off the ship and putting one 'unit' on in one cycle of two movements; for a comparatively few movement cycles only one container unit will be shifted while space is made in this ship for the double movement to take place. The real life requirement may also be to move more containers one way than the other. Theoretical cycle times on maximum crane performance may only be one-and-a-half minutes, but average time over a shift, allowing for crane movement along the quay, container imbalances, etc. may be more than double this figure. With twin-lift gear it is still possible to average thirty 20-foot container movements each way per hour. The maximum load per 20-foot container is 18 weight tons or about 26 measurement tons, although average figures will be considerably lower. Turn-round times for big container ships of 1300-C capacity of forty-eight hours are realistic, involving 10,000 weight tons or more of cargo each way. Better times are being achieved in ports where only part of the cargo is being transferred.

The effect of these handling improvements on reducing idle ship time and so increasing ship productivity is also great. On the long Australia run of 12000 sea miles, conventional cargo liners have been taking 120–130 days or even up to 150 days to complete a round voyage according to the number of ports of call. The Scandia pallet ships can reduce this to 80–90 days and the OCL/ACT container ships to 60–70 days, again varying with the number of port calls. Thus the container ship is doing roughly twice as much work in terms of

150

miles as a break-bulk cargo liner, some of the difference being due to increased speed but most to better turn-round and rationalization of ports of call. It is probably also achieving about twice the amount of cargo per voyage as a break-bulk ship, partly because the ships are bigger, partly because they are able to accommodate a large amount of deck cargo (a little under one-third of the total). A ship for ship ratio in terms of total work done is obviously a very loose term, but a 5 to 1 figure on a very long run would increase in favour of container ships as voyage length decreased and might be as high as 9 to 1 on short-haul trades. The productivity of short-sea container ships is thus very great. For instance the two British Rail ships built for the Harwich–Zeebrugge run (some 90 sea miles) and each with a capacity equivalent to 220×20-foot C, can complete a round trip in twenty-four hours and on a five-run week, given availability of cargo, could each make over 2000 container journeys a week, say 20,000 weight tons of cargo per ship. These sort of figures, of course, greatly improve the work done per voyage per crew member, although on deep-sea trades the short amount of time in port means that more home leave must be given, requiring one-and-a-half crews per ship. At a ship ratio of 5:1 the crew productivity factor is still about $\times 3$.

Obviously successful operation of such a capital intensive system as a container service requires a high rate of throughput. It is up to the operator to devise ship operating schedules which give good utilization, consistent with that frequency of service which is compatible with traders' requirements in a competitive market. Depot throughputs are more difficult to control, and the optimum number of depots required under given conditions is something which will only be learned with experience. It is important that the containers themselves are kept moving. The emerging pattern of charging for retention of containers for loading and unloading is of an initial fairly short, but adequate, free period and rapidly mounting demurrage charges thereafter, the same applying to equipment interchange such as trailers. To facilitate loading, operators are tending not to charge freight on pallets loaded into containers, the responsibility for the pallet remaining with the shipper.

The size of pallets in relation to containers has raised something of a furore with some shippers, who have been presented with the standard container 8-foot width as a *fait accompli*. The 8-foot width was the widest size which could reasonably be carried extensively on the world's highways and railways, and it was justifiably adopted after due consideration by ISO. This does not present a neat fit for certain standard pallet sizes currently in use like the 40 inches $\times$ 48 inches. Moreover insulated containers do not as yet have standard internal dimensions, the thickness of the insulation and the degree of the refrigeration applied being interdependent but variable factors. (It is, in fact, probable that shippers wanting to pack their own containers will receive only general purpose containers.) However, the number of pallet sizes in general use and the particular predilections of shippers for a given cube unit of cargo, of which the container internal cube should be a multiple, are too diverse (particularly the latter) for a solution to be found to please everyone. Pallets are much cheaper and less durable than containers.

151

The trend will be for pallets to be devised for use in conjunction with containers, the pallet sizes being those which fit the internal GP dimensions well. Traders are also already adjusting pack sizes to be a convenient module of the container cube.

Because the container is an identifiable, internationally interchangeable strong box, it has a potential not really shared by other types of unit load. A new unit of international transport has been born. The trader is in a position to equate a consignment with a container or number of containers. Operators are emerging whose prime interest is in the movement of the boxes, each and every one, rather than in a given mode of transport, and who are developing control systems designed to achieve an orderly flow of containers round the world. The importance of the combination of the uniquely numbered and identifiable box and the development of ADP systems of control cannot be emphasized too strongly.

The whole is a radically new concept and justifies the now well used phrase 'the Container Revolution'. For students of PDM the more usefully descriptive phrase for essentially the same concept is 'the Through Transport Revolution'.

References
Reports, articles, etc.

(1) Economic Development Committee for Movement of Exports, 'Through Transport to Europe', London, HMSO, 1966. This is one of the first authoritative statements of what through transport is all about and is still relevant.

(2) EDC for Movement of Exports, 'Exports by Air', London, HMSO, 1967: air freight in a through transport context.

(3) EDC for Movement of Exports, 'Delivering the Goods', London, HMSO, November 1968: the results and conclusions of an exercise to enquire on a quantitative basis into the movement of UK exports to the continent of Europe. Some of the findings have been quoted in this chapter.

(4) 'Containerisation: The key to Low Cost Transport', report by McKinsey and Co. for the British Transport Docks Board, BTDB, 1967. So far as the author knows, this is the only major consultant's report on containerization to be made available publicly. It is well presented but there has been no general agreement with its conclusions.

(5) John R. Immer, 'Container Services of the North Atlantic', Washington DC, Work Saving International, 1967: numerous facts, some of which are now out of date; others will remain useful background; understood to be in course of revision.

(6) *Jane's Freight Containers* (Jane's Yearbooks), London, BPC, each Autumn. As information builds up on container services, port facilities and equipment, this should be a useful reference work.

(7) 'An examination of some aspects of the unit-load system of cargo shipments: application to developing countries', New York, Department of Economic and Social Affairs, United Nations, 1966. Notable for giving some lengthy examples of liner conference tariff provisions for unit loads, but a little dated.

(8) (i) *Future Container Services; What Shippers Require:* two reports by the British Shipper's Council, London, BSC, 1967: exporters' views on the requirements of through container services. Inevitably this dates a little.
(ii) A Report by the National Shipper Councils of Europe on Containerisation, May 1967. This report is understood to be in course of revision.

(9) 'Moving Goods in the 1970s', supplement in *The Economist*, September 14, 1968. Available as a reprint. A good review with the accent mainly on developments based in the UK and on the continent of Europe.

(10) Report from the Senate Select Committee on 'The Container Method of Handling Cargoes', Commonwealth of Australia, Parliamentary Paper No. 46, 1968. The Australians look at their container problem.

(11) (India) and the Indians at theirs.

(12) Molyneux report on New Zealand Overseas Trade by the Container and Cargo Handling Committee, May 1967. Only a stage in the development of thinking about through transport services, but a useful case study.

(13) International Transport Workers' Federation, 'Statement on the Social and Trade Union Consequences of Containerisation', London, 1968. An assessment of the effects of the new system on transport workers.

(14) F. G. Ebel and M. S. Pennington, 'Unitised Cargo Transportation Systems', paper to the Society of Naval Architects and Marine Engineers, New York, June 1968: describes the various ship systems.

(15) Gctz. Erichsen and Heirung, paper to the Society of Naval Architects and Marine Engineers, No. 6, New York: a good statement of the case for pallet transport.

(16) (i) Trade Simplification Bill, introduced to us Congress by Department of Transportation, March 1968.
(ii) Hearings on the TS Bill by the sub-committee on Merchant Marine of the Senate Commerce Committee, June 1968.
(iii) Alan S. Boyd, us Secretary of Transportation, 'Facilitation of International Transportation in the United States', an address at the third International Transport and Export Services Exhibition, Rotterdam, October 23, 1968.
Although the Bill did not pass the last Congress of the Johnson Administration, and despite delay has still to be produced by President Nixon's Administration, the above sources do give a fair idea of the problem posed by through transport to the American concept of fair trading and the methods proposed to adjust their legal and administrative framework to the new requirements.

(17) 'Standardisation of Containers', hearings before the sub-committee on Merchant Marine and Fisheries of the Committee on Commerce, United States Senate, Washington DC, us Government Printing Office, July 13, 14 and 17, 1967; Serial No. 90–31. Interesting and ranging fairly widely in subject matter.

(18) 'An examination of the changing nature of cargo insurance following the introduction of containers', report by Advanced Study Group No. 188, the Insurance Institute of London, 1969. A good resumé of the insurance question.

(19) Report on the Tokyo Conference of the Comité Maritime International, March/April 1969, published by the Chamber of Shipping of the United Kingdom. The relevant part of the report discusses the question of cargo liability in through transport operations and reproduces the draft convention. This draft is subject to adjustment, but gives a fair indication of the way problems are being resolved.

(20) 'Goods in Containers: Customs Requirements, Procedures and Facilities', HM Customs and Excise, Notice No. 464, 1969. Customs rules in the UK devised in consultation with traders and operators.
This list is by no means exhaustive.

Statistics

(1) Port Traffic on unit transport services, Great Britain, 1965 and 1966, published by the National Ports Council, 1967.

(2) Port Unit Transport Statistics, Great Britain, 1968, published by the National Ports Council, 1969.

(3) Port Progress Report 1969, published by the National Ports Council: contains some forecasts.

(4) *Fairplay*, a monthly publication: they have been producing quarterly a useful compilation of container ships, combination ships, lash ships, etc. building and on order round the world. As a good many general cargo ships are being built with the ability to carry some containers and are listed, care should be taken not to aggregate in all this general tonnage as container capacity.

Conferences

There are a good many published papers from conferences and seminars which deal with aspects of the subject. Three organizations who have organized such conferences, sometimes jointly with other sponsors, are: the International Cargo Handling Co-ordination Association (ICHCA), the journal *Ports and Terminals* (published by McLean-Hunter Ltd, the journal *Freight Management* (published by the Temple Press London and a specialist journal in physical distribution from the trader's point of view).

Chapter B.8

TRANSPORT MANAGEMENT
by George Murphy

Over the past few years a profound change has taken place in management science's attitude towards the subject of transport. This trend has not yet fully worked itself out, and indeed many firms can still be found within which neither the subject, nor its implications for the good of the company, are yet understood, let alone subjected to intensive study. This is the result not so much of deliberate neglect, as of concentration on other areas of management opportunity, and the fact that many firms simply do not appreciate the importance which activities in this area can represent.

Until very recently transport, in common with many other related functions, suffered from the results of splintered authority. That is to say, the situation has been, and still often is, such that transport was looked upon as a compartmentalized area—as simply moving raw materials into the production point and finished goods out. In fact even these two functions very often worked in isolation.

The transport decision can have a very marked influence on the overall profitability of the firm. The effects will obviously vary between the various industries, even between firms in the same industry, but irrespective of how important it is for the individual, there is now no doubt whatsoever that this is a far more potent function than the majority of industrial firms realize. The basis of this belief in the importance of the transport function lies not so much in the absolute rates that have to be paid for the purchase of a transport service, but in the implications which this choice will have on many aspects of the firm's activities.

The basics of the Physical Distribution concept, or as it is often called the *Total* Distribution concept, have already been looked at in Section A. The PDE costs to the firm can be substantial, and the linch-pin of the entire TDC system is the choice of the transport mode. Table 8·I shows the TDC cost structure for the average United Kingdom manufacturing firm. As can be seen, this can amount to 16 per cent of the selling price of the product. The study from which these figures are taken illustrated that the TDC costs could be lower than this, but at the same time it also showed that they could be as high as 43 per cent of the selling price, and in very rare cases much higher.

From the table it can be seen that the absolute cost for transport amounts to only 5·5 per cent out of the total of 16 per cent, but this does not in any

155

way affect the previous statement that transport is the key to TDC operations. In Figure 8·1 this is illustrated. It is best to regard transport as the apex of an inverted triangle whose base is the Total Distribution Cost of the PDE system under consideration. The transport decision is taken within the framework of the policy structure of the firm as regards customer service, and the financial resources open to the department. This in effect means that the two most important factors to be reconciled are speed and cost.

It is a fairly safe generalization to say that fast transport modes are more expensive than slow ones. Given this fact it is not surprising that, very often, the mode with the cheapest transport rate is chosen. Follow the results of this up through the TDC triangle.

Table 8·I

COST OF DISTRIBUTION ACTIVITY AS A PERCENTAGE OF SALES
(*Excluding Retailing*)

		United Kingdom
Administration		2·0
Transport:		
Inbound	1·5	
Outbound	4·0	
	——	5·5
Receiving and despatch		0·5
Packaging and protective packaging		2·0
Warehousing:		
Factories	1·0	
Distribution depots	1·5	
	——	2·5
Stock holding:		
Interest on investment	2·0	
Taxes, insurance, etc.	1·0	
	——	3·0
Order Processing		0·5
Total physical distribution cost		16·0

As will be seen in Section C, one of the key factors deciding inventory levels is transport time, as this is an important component of total lead time. Increase the transport time and you also increase the lead time; as this becomes greater so does the amount of inventory that must be held to maintain a given service level. As carrying costs for inventory can be substantial, the transport decision has already affected an important area of cost. This increase in costs will not only be apparent at the stockholding points in the system, but because of the general slowing in pipeline movements there will be an increase in the level of inventory that is circulating within the distribution network, and an increase in 'tied money' will have taken place. Even from this very sparse outline of the effects of a transport decision on inventory levels it can be seen to be important, especially when it is remembered that carrying costs of 25 per cent are by no means exceptional in many industries. The next rank in the triangle is no less important. A transport choice will affect the warehousing component in two broad ways,
156

namely in location and in numbers. The whole concept behind the warehouse network is to allow the service policy of the firm to be carried out. If a very slow mode of transport has been decided on, then this means that there must be a sufficient number of warehouses available to cover all the market areas of the company; it is likely that there will be a higher number of warehousing points so that all the customers can be satisfied within a previously decided number of days/hours. A fast, reliable method of transport can frequently reduce the number of warehouses that are required. Moreover, from the layer below (inventory) the warehouse system has had certain requirements, capacity, etc., pre-determined.

TOTAL DISTRIBUTION COST

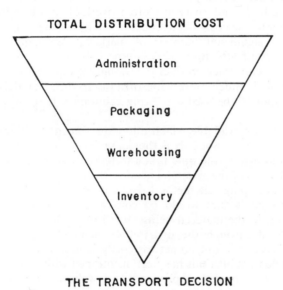

THE TRANSPORT DECISION

Figure 8·1   T.D.C. Triangle

In deciding the location of the warehouses within a system, a great deal of attention is given to the relative weights of the demand and supply points to be covered. This inevitably means that importance is given to the costs of moving materials from source to market, including the costs of 'in transit' inventory. Both these factors can be significantly affected by the initial transport decision. This in turn means that the locational pattern of the warehousing complex can be altered by the initial policy outlook of the planning body responsible for the implementation of the firm's distribution concepts. In the case where there is already a system in operation then, for the very same reasons, it is often possible to increase its effectiveness by an accurate appraisal of the transportation modes adopted previously. The most common advantage found here is that of being able to increase capacity without new building programmes. This is achieved through the use of a more efficient transport mode, reducing the inventory levels held in the past.

This allows a market expansion without the corresponding capital investment normally associated with it.

Deciding on the location and the number of warehousing points is only the beginning of the warehousing programme. The territory to be served by each location must also be decided. This again will be affected by the delivered cost of the products from each of the locations. In its turn, this will be greatly influenced by the choice of transport mode, the routing decison, the transport module, and the general effectiveness of the transport function within the firm. The relative inventory levels within the system will also have an influence here, and as has already been pointed out, these can be determined in part by the choice of transport.

Packaging methods and costs are often overlooked when investigations are being made into the cost-effectiveness of the firm, yet for a wide range of products, and a significant number of markets, they can be sufficiently important to warrant attention. This is especially true, of course, of those firms marketing a consumer product over longer distances, but the influence of packaging costs is much more widespread than this. The decision on the method of transport to be used can bring economies here or, alternatively, extra costs.

There are methods available which allow the transit of the product in its display pack. In this way, not only is there a saving in the absolute amount of material costs but also in the time taken to unload, unpack and arrange the material at both ends of the system. The most obvious of these methods is the container. By developing this method it might be possible for the company to construct a module that would be employed all through the network. This would result in the material being stored in module form at the firm's warehouse, moved through the distribution channel chosen, to the final point and displayed, without numerous costly handling stages. The savings here are self-evident. Whilst this has been mentioned with consumer products in mind, the same concept applies equally well to industrial products. Through modules would bring not only savings in the packaging sphere, but would help to increase the efficiency of the entire distribution function.

So far we have been looking at the influence of transport on various operating components that go to make up the distribution system of the firm. It will no doubt be noted that, very often, at the base of the activities being examined, is the question of time saving. This applies no less to the administrative function. Indeed, delays here can often wipe out any saving which mode choice has brought about; conversely, the choice of the method of transport can often influence administrative time. We have now arrived at the total distribution cost for the particular system under examination. It will be easily seen that transport, coming as it does at the point where all other factors are subsequently influenced by the decision, deserves a great deal of attention, for it has a most profound effect on the general efficiency of the entire system, which in its turn can substantially alter the overall performance of the firm. It is important to realize that the entire distribution function has suffered from a lack of attention over the past decade or so, except in those areas of activity where the proportion of costs that it swallows has forced

158

management to pay attention to it. There has been many an executive who, when shown the true costs of physical distribution, wondered why he had been so blind in the past. Many factors combined to ensure that transport and distribution were given second place to production.

The most obvious of these is, of course, that only in the past few years has the consumption society really matured. The Second World War and its aftermath tended to result in a production-orientated school of management thinking, in which all effort was directed to increasing the efficiency of production. Recently, however, there has been a tendency to diminishing returns in this field, and management has naturally turned to examine other areas where economies can be made for less capital investment. This is largely an environmental factor. However, there are other more 'in plant' reasons.

Increasing competition and decreasing profit margins have combined to ensure that all possible opportunities for economies are investigated. In the conventional accounting layout, there is very seldom a consolidated account showing the true costs of the distribution function as shown in Table 8·I. When, however, the subject is investigated its importance is at once recognized and some improvement attempted, although this can often be less than fully effective because of the lack of understanding of the need for overall coordination of the function. Attempts are often made to introduce total distribution thinking without changing the management structure to allow total distribution techniques to be put into practice.

The movement towards UK participation in European markets can effectively be regarded (from the distribution viewpoint) as simply additions to the home market with a more complex transport problem. This approach is gradually forcing firms into a reappraisal of the importance of the transport function.

This will be reinforced by the political moves towards larger markets, free from tariffs. This means greater competition for UK firms at home, and more opportunity to expand markets through the implementation of a more efficient transportation system. There is little doubt that one of the great problems facing any company executive trying to introduce a more realistic approach to the transport problem is the image which the transport function has inherited. This has built up over the years, as a result of the neglect that the area has suffered. It is often regarded as not of sufficient importance to warrant attention from higher levels of management. It is hoped that this brief survey of the wider implications of the importance of decisions taken in transport will help to illustrate the fallacy of this viewpoint.

Some of the blame for this attitude can be laid at the door of the people who are themselves interested in the subject. Even here it very often happens that full attention is directed solely on the transport function itself, without sufficient attention being given to the *influence* that the subject can have on the entire distribution function.

It is evident, however, that this whole outlook is changing throughout wide sectors of industry, and recent legislation in the field will, without doubt, lead to increased emphasis on the transport function.

The real purpose of this chapter is not to survey the importance of the transport function, but to discuss the implications, for management, of the implementation of the type of thinking that we have been discussing so far, and to look at some of the techniques available to aid them in its introduction and efficient operation.

Initially it must be emphasized that it is not sufficient to say that the transport function is going to receive much more attention in the future than it has received in the past. Management must not expect to achieve important new savings for the firm without there being significant changes in attitude throughout the company. Such changes are not easy to achieve, but this is an area for the individual manager to solve. The best plan, if it is at all possible, is to start afresh—not to attempt to graft new departments and personnel onto the old structure, but to build from the bottom up. The new system may then be introduced gradually and at least, in this way, all concerned will have some idea of what they are working towards, and their own eventual place in the completed structure. This is the first task that must be looked to: namely, the transformation of the general attitude of management in other areas to the transportation department. Without first achieving this, the entire project becomes more difficult, if not impossible, to carry out. Once the correct orientation has been developed, the objectives must be decided upon. Since the whole reason for the existence of the transport function is to satisfy the demands made on the firm for its products, we can reasonably assume that the most likely objective will be the maintenance or improvement of the firm's service levels, at the lowest possible cost.

These are the two basic constraints within which the transport function must operate. It is on these that the entire structure of the function will be developed, and it is with these two—costs and service—in mind that the position of the transport function within the wider company structure will be decided upon. The service level will be decided upon using methods similar to those discussed in Section C following, but once the decisions have been taken, they have a profound influence on the transport function, because they become targets towards which transport must work. It is not permissible to lower costs by lowering transport/service requirements. These must be adhered to—assuming that the points decided on were correct in the first instance.

In the same manner, the cost allocation made to the transport department will decide, to a great extent, the choices that can be made between the various modes of transport, methods of handling and so on. This appreciation of the constraints placed on choices and decisions must not be one-sided, however, and it is of crucial importance that other departments (or, more accurately, the higher management of other departments) fully appreciate the influence that their decisions might have on the transport department, for through this the total distribution costs of the firm will be affected. So before the marketing director decides to achieve sales through increased service levels or promotional campaigns, he must ensure that there is an opportunity to discuss and evaluate the influence of these moves on distribution costs. It is a commonly held misconception that distribution and transport costs decrease per unit with increases in volume. Some do, but others increase—and some of these latter can be of crucial importance.

The effect of increased service levels on inventory costs and through these on transport costs should also be considered. This introduces the second of the environmental structures that must be instituted before there is any work on the actual function itself. Provision must be made for the flow of information between transport and the other sectors of the firm. This does not mean simply passing on decisions taken. It means consultation, and multi-directional liaison. The penalty for ignoring this requirement is less profit. With an efficient system of consultation, however, there should be a general increase in effectiveness over the entire organization, as these meetings should give some flesh to the overall product marketing concept.

The question of organizing for the total concept of transport can be broadly divided into two interrelated sections. Firstly, the function itself, the scope and responsibilities to be delegated to it and the place of the function within the overall structure of the firm.

All decisions in these areas must be made against the general policies laid down for the company as a whole. Is the general structure one of centralized control or is it decentralized? Does the firm have a wide or narrow product range, and are the markets concentrated or dispersed? Within this list there will obviously be a wide variety of combinations, and because of this it is impossible to give any generally applicable solutions. Each pattern must be tailored to suit the individual firm's requirements. One important factor that must be examined is the stage of development in distribution thinking within the firm. If this has proceeded to a high level, then it is likely that the transport function will be one of many under the control of the distribution manager. At the intermediate stages a great variety of relationships can exist. There will be definite limitations on the extent to which the transport manager can coordinate activities, and this will help to decide the optimum structure of the function.

Ideally, the situation would be as illustrated in Figure 8·2. It can be seen that the transport manager has under his control all those functions which will be influenced by his decisions. This is, in other words, the completely integrated transport function, where all decisions can be seen to operate, and where there is the greatest opportunity for cost reduction through

Figure 8·2   Ideal authority for transport/distribution

161

coordination, within the general structure of policy decisions laid down by the firm. If the firm is centralized in its authority structure, having a reasonably homogeneous product range (as far as distribution characteristics go) and a concentrated market structure, then it might be possible to have just such an ideal structure implemented in practice. This would be the situation as shown in Figure 8·3. It can be seen that the transport function is again used as the key to the total distribution system, allowing the maximum use of trade-off methods and by the same means providing ample consultation

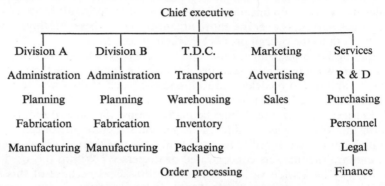

Figure 8·3   Centralized structure 1

time at the higher levels of management. Although this type of structure is probably the one most likely to achieve the greatest benefits from a total approach to the transportation problem, there are important obstacles in the way of its introduction. The first and most important of these is the fact that it requires a very specific set of conditions in the firm: namely, a narrow product range, concentrated markets and centralization of authority. If these are missing then the effectiveness of this structure decreases, because of difficulties in coordination.

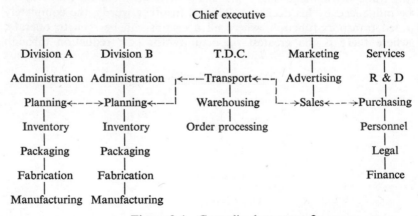

Figure 8·4   Centralized structure 2

Figure 8·4 shows a possible structure where the situation is similar to that above, the chief difference being that a more realistic view has been taken of the likely pattern of product range and market dispersion—there is still centralization. It can be seen here that the product and market forces have caused management to allow each area some degree of autonomy over some of the distribution functions, but that these are operated within a firm's overall policy. This is achieved in this case by retaining transport as a centralized service. In this way it can be used as the central coordinating function.

Much the same overall structure will be used when there is little centralization of policy. In Figure 8·5 a typical de-centralized structure is shown. Here we are assuming a narrow product range, and market concentration. In this situation it is likely that there will be little realization of the total

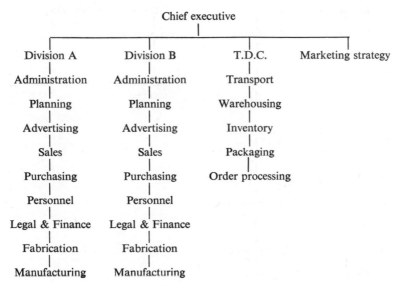

Figure 8·5   De-centralized 1

effects of physical distribution on the real competitive position of the firm. This is caused by the decentralized structure of authority. It is likely that the development of this firm has meant little coordination in the distribution field. With the type of transport organization illustrated, it would still be possible to decentralize those functions that benefit from this policy, whilst at the same time ensuring all the advantages of the local distribution cost concept.

As an alternative to this arrangement, again where there is product spread and market dispersion, the structure in Figure 8·6 might be adopted or adapted. This is also designed to allow autonomy in some functions, yet allows the transport function to act as coordinator both between the various distribution functions under local control, and the other departments of interest to the distribution function.

163

It will be obvious that the key to all these organizational types is the development of a distribution network under the transport umbrella. The implementation of any of these types (or variations of them) will depend to a great degree on how successful the original step (changing attitude) was, because they all imply a profound change in the organizational status of the transport man and, of course, in his remuneration and recruitment.

They also assume a willingness at top management level to accept the changes recommended. This, in turn, will depend on how much importance is accorded to an area which swallows up on average 16 per cent of selling

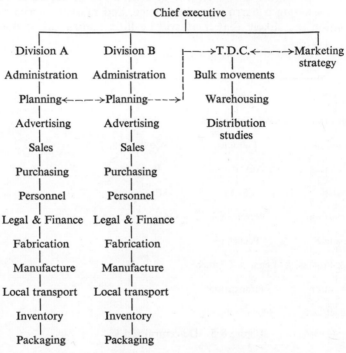

Figure 8·6   De-centralized 2

price for manufactured products, and which in the vast majority of cases is open to major increases in efficiency for modest outlays of capital. Nonetheless, there seems little doubt that industry is realizing the magnitude of the contribution which the transport man can make to the overall performance of the firm. As this movement progresses it will of itself cause recruitment of a more management-orientated type of transport man, and result in those already in the field becoming interested in the wider implications of the job. Assuming, however, that transport receives all the importance that it is due, there still remains the problem of technique.

As more and more attention is directed to the transport and distribution area, management increasingly expects the methods that it employs there to be as sophisticated as the techniques used elsewhere, and this means the adaptation of methods that have been used to solve management problems in other fields. Before this is put into operation, however, the transport man must ensure that he has systems available for the collection of all the relevant information. No method, however scientific and accurate, can give the right answer if the basic information which is being processed is either inaccurate or incomplete. In many manufacturing firms it is quite amazing the extent to which misconceptions exist as to what actually goes on once a vehicle has left the depot.

It is important that information should be available for this area, because it is the first step towards increasing the effectiveness of the transport fleet. Even before any major changes are introduced to the department, a simple and easy study of the existing system will throw up areas where efficiency can be increased immediately. Since any method of collecting information must rely a great deal on the people already doing the job, the way they have developed, and even the way they like to do it, it is of the utmost importance that their cooperation is secured in developing a new system. This is a point that is all too often forgotten, and it can be the source of a great deal of strife. Nobody likes to have their methods investigated. Nobody likes people gathering information about their job. Nobody likes the thought of new methods being introduced; but everybody would like to be informed of what is going on, and if changes are inevitable then at least they can be explained to the people who are to be involved. A manager can think up the most perfect scheme to increase efficiency, but if the operatives who are to give the idea flesh will not cooperate, the scheme itself cannot be effective and the hoped-for targets will not be reached. This is especially true of information-gathering practices in the transport field, because by the very nature of the task, the operatives are unsupervised for the greater proportion of their working day. For this reason the manager must rely to a very large extent on the information which his workers give him. If the idea behind the scheme is fully explained, then at least he is reducing the area of likely misinformation arising through lack of cooperation, and appreciation of the benefits that the idea might bring.

There are a great many methods and techniques used to collect detailed information about vehicles after they have left the depot. They are all based on some form of feed-back from the drivers themselves. This means that the drivers carry with them an additional 'log-book' in which the appropriate entries are made. It will now become even more obvious why their participation must be ensured—most drivers feel that they already have enough trouble with the compulsory log book without anything else—and one is bound to have some sympathy with their point of view in this respect; nonetheless, the job must be done. Each vehicle will be given an analysis sheet showing the vehicle number, and some also like to see the driver's name.This requirement is optional and can, under some conditions, give rise to 'bad blood'; moreover, if for some reason or other the name of the driver is required at a later stage, then little trouble should be experienced in finding it. Some managers prefer to have the name included for speed of reference,

165

however. Space will be allowed for delivery listing (start to finish), the time at which the delivery was made, and also the distance between drops. Space must also be provided so that the driver can note any occurrences which are of importance. At the briefing meetings he would have naturally been instructed as to the type of delay that should be noted. These sheets will be issued to the drivers on the various routes over a period of time so that any unusual quirks can be observed, and allowance made for them. The actual time allowed will vary as to the number of vehicle routes covered, and the amount of time that can be devoted to the subject—although accuracy should never be sacrificed in the cause of false economy.

Once the study has built up a sufficiently large number of sheets, an analysis of the information must be undertaken. The aim of this will be to uncover any obvious points which could be sources of economy within the department. An analysis of common statistics from the sheets will often point to a glaring need for improvement in one or more aspects of the operation. This could easily be in the form of more efficient loading methods at the depot, for example. It is not uncommon for this type of study to show that a high degree of inefficiency is involved at the depot. This might be solved by the use of articulated vehicles or by operating an earlier shift to complete the loading before the vehicles leave in the morning. This dis-economy will be shown up on the sheets by large gaps between the drivers reporting to the depot and actually leaving on the delivery routes.

Another factor that is often obvious after the first examination of the daily sheets is the varying amounts of time that the drivers may have to wait at their destination for unloading. The first step here is to check with the customers to see if some rearrangement of arrival times would alleviate the problem. The vehicle might be waiting at one point when a different customer a short distance away might be willing to accept delivery.

If these sheets are used on the longer distance routes, they quite frequently allow considerable speeding up of the operation by mid-route changeovers. If a firm is moving goods from and to many different points, it is highly likely that their vehicles pass each other on the way, perhaps involving two drivers in overnight stays. Many firms have found that swapping drivers mid-way results in greater utilization of their vehicles. The sheets also allow a great deal of consolidation to take place. It is not unusual for the routes that the vehicles follow to develop over time rather than from any planning in the past. This can often mean that some degree of duplication takes place, and if this is present it should become obvious in any examination of the daily delivery sheets. There are a great many further uses which these sheets can be put to, but it is extremely dangerous to make generalizations. Careful use of them should allow the transport manager to make a great deal of improvement with a modest outlay in terms of time and cost. It is worth remembering, however, that the whole idea will come to grief if the honest cooperation of drivers is not achieved in the first instance.

An efficient recording and analysis system can also show the transport manager the effectiveness of each of his vehicles. All that is required is a summary of the operating costs of the vehicle—including drivers' wages etc.—and the number of deliveries that the combination make. From these it is easy to calculate the cost per drop and one should then be able to see any improvements working themselves out in hard cash effectiveness.

It has been previously mentioned that the depot itself can very often be a great cost-creating centre for the transport man. This is becoming more and more apparent as the general move is towards a unified control for warehouse and transport functions. In many cases this control has always been evident, especially in the faster-moving consumer goods field, where coordination is vital. One of the greater difficulties facing the transport manager when dealing with this problem is the lack of definitive cost information on the entire operation. The first step in any programme aimed at reducing costs is, therefore, to identify the most important cost centres. Once this has been achieved, economies can be introduced at the relevant points.

The great difficulty with depot and warehousing operations is that they do not easily lend themselves to conventional costing operations. Variety of work task is the most common reason for this. There are, however, many techniques which can overcome this combination of diversity of task and volume moved to produce reliable cost figures which are of use to the depot operator.

The most commonly used of these methods is work sampling. This is a method based on the laws of probability. Its fundamental assumption is that a small number of occurrences will tend to follow the same general distribution as a greater number. Since the greater the number of the original occurrences, the greater the accuracy of the generalization, it follows that a greater degree of accuracy is required and that the study will be more prolonged and expensive. For carrying out the study it is necessary to subdivide activities going on in the particular depot into their work elements. There are two broad rules to be followed in this procedure: the first is that all elements should be clearly defined in writing at the outset of the study. In this way there can be no later confusion over the aims of the study. The second rule is that all the elements must be easily recognized visually; it is again important to gain the cooperation of those workers who are going to be under observation. Nothing is more likely to cause trouble than the unexpected arrival of an observation team. The reasons for securing this cooperation have already been mentioned.

A typical work element sheet might be as follows:

Handling in: Receive truck; open doors; check load
                 Sign receipt; direct lift truck to lorry
                 Travel to storage point
                 (and so on)
                 Storage area
                 Stack onto racking; remove pallet truck
                 (and so on).
Handling out: Order picking
                 Consolidation of orders
                 Load truck
                 (and so on).

This is a brief indication of the type of division into work elements which is referred to. The individual manager will, of course, draw up a form which will take into consideration the particular work conditions of his depot operation. The detailed breakdown is produced in a form allowing space for the observer to note which work element is proceeding as the observation takes place. At this point it is worth mentioning that the observer carrying out the study must record exactly what is going on at a work station and *not* what he *thinks* is going on.

The operatives chosen to implement the study are entirely at the choice of the transport manager—no special skill is required other than accuracy. Once the form has been designed, the basic observations can take place. The chief point to bear in mind is that randomness is of the utmost importance. In the normal warehouse situation, the distance to be travelled and the normal variation in the speed of movement will ensure that this condition is observed. If the depot is small, however, other steps may have to be taken. Randomness may be ensured by making observation trips at random times. This may be done by the good old-fashioned method of drawing the times out of a hat or, if more swift methods are required, by using a list of random times such as can be found in most books on forecasting. The next problem facing the originator of the study is to decide when the total number of observations has reached the point where the accuracy is acceptable for conclusions to be drawn from the results.

Again, there are many ways of determining this point, but one of the most simple is to use the occurrence graph. This requires little time to compile and is sufficiently accurate for the purpose. In other fields, where accuracy approaching 100 per cent is necessary, it is possible to read the number of occurrences for a specified accuracy from projections of the probability curve. The occurrence graph consists of the percentage occurrences of the

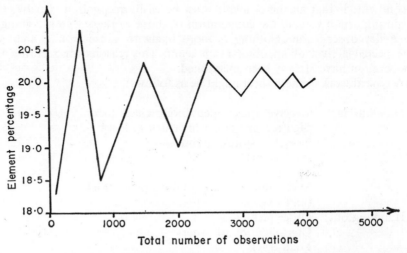

Figure 8·7   Occurrence Graph

various elements plotted against the number of observations. After each day's record of observations, the number of observations for each element is divided into the total number of observations (on an accumulated basis) and the percentage results plotted on a graph.

In the early stages of the project there will be great fluctuations (as can be seen in Figure 8·7) as the number of observations increases. However, these fluctuations will decrease until they eventually disappear entirely. When this point has been reached, observations for this element can cease as there will be no further increases in the accuracy of the data. It is quite permissible to stop observations at the point when the fluctuations become very small.

This procedure is carried out for all the elements involved in the study. At the conclusion of the study the data must be summarized so that the proportion contributed from each activity group to the total costs of the depot can be seen. This data is completed by dividing the number of observations of each element by the number of observations carried out and converting this result to a percentage: for example, if over the study it was observed that from a total of 5000 random checks, 1000 lorry unloading operations had been noted, thus $\frac{1000}{5000} \times 100$ equals 20 per cent. Under the particular conditions pertaining in that depot we could then say that, on average, 20 per cent of the time was spent unloading incoming vehicles. This calculation is completed for all the work elements that were included in the study.

The manager now has before him an accurate breakdown of the activities that go to make up the total time spent in his depot. Even at this early stage economies can be introduced. Very often depot managers receive a surprise when they see the operation presented in this fashion. It can certainly show up those areas where the greatest benefit will arise from the expenditure of some of the budget for investment in new equipment or, on the other hand, will provide him with useful information with which he can prove his need for more funds to top management.

The information collected can be used, as has been pointed out, to give the transport/depot manager a clearer picture of the costs involved. The first step is to develop an overhead weighting and this is done by dividing the total handling and storage costs (of labour+direct and indirect expenses) by the costs of labour. Next the percentages from the work-sampling study are listed together with their direct labour cost, and these are multiplied by the weighting factor to give the total handling costs, broken down by work elements. For example, let us suppose that for our lorry unloading element above, the weighting factor was three and the direct labour cost £12; then the total handling cost of this would be £36.

These figures will again enable the depot manager to tackle the problem of increasing the efficiency of the operation with as much information as possible. As a final example of the usefulness of this study, it can frequently be used to check that the rates charged by the depot to its customers are reflecting the changing costs of handling the materials. A breakdown by commodity will show up these variations and allow the adjustment in rates to take place on an economic basis, rather than by hit-or-miss methods.

169

Before leaving the internal operations of the depot, a word on work simplification might be useful. Work simplification is nothing more nor less than the logical application of common sense. A check-list is built up to channel the thought of the people involved along definite, logical lines. Its use in our context would be to help reorganize particular bottlenecks thrown up by the work sampling study. Given below is a typical check-list:

Select the problem
How complex is it?
Manpower and other costs compared to the likely benefits from improvement
Collect the facts
What happens and can anything be eliminated?
Is every action necessary?
Is the timing right?
Could the job be done by another method (costs-benefits)?
(and so on).

Although it is the logical application of common sense, it is amazing how helpful such a schedule can be when tackling problems. The contents of the various schemes vary a great deal but the individual can draw up one best suited to his needs.

So far we have been looking at the situation as if there were only one depot and a very limited number of customers. This is, of course, remote from the real work environment of the transport manager. He is usually faced with a difficult allocation problem. That is, he has a number of supply points of varying capacity and an even greater number of demand points with large variations in their demands. This type of problem is best solved by the application of one of the many linear programming techniques available. There are many such methods which the ordinary transport manager can apply to his situation. All have the same basic steps and all will provide the same solution. Their differences lie in the mechanics of solving the problem. For the purposes of illustration, we will assume a simple problem—irrespective of the complexities of the problem the steps employed in its solution will be the same as those used here.

At this point it might be useful to comment on a common attitude found among transport men, who seem to think that linear programming is only for the big outfit and that the smaller operator cannot use the method. This is just not true. Certainly, for a real-life problem the arithmetic required is longer than in our simple illustration; certainly, when handling nine or ten or more destinations and as many origins, a table calculating machine comes in useful; nevertheless, for the medium-sized firm the method is quite accessible by hand. The bigger firms' computers use much the same method—they merely provide the answer infinitely faster, and for a more diverse range. This is the only real difference. The first step in the application of any of the methods is to identify the problem as exactly as possible. Is the real object the reduction of transport costs to the minimum, or is it a reduction towards
170

a certain objective? An important customer might be more cheaply served by delivering to him last in line—but does this come within the policies laid down by the firm regarding service for this type of customer?

The next step is to gather the relevant data and to put it into such a form as makes it suitable for solving by linear programming. The greatest care should be taken at this point to ensure that the information gathered is as accurate as possible for, irrespective of how it is used after this stage, any inaccuracies here will inevitably result in the wrong solution being produced. From the transport standpoint the chief type of information to be gathered will be the cost involved in the movement of goods from the supply to the demand—whatever pattern this may take for the individual firm. Costs are taken per unit of merchandise moved. Once this basic data has been collected, it is drawn up in the form of a matrix, as illustrated in Figure 8·8(a). The costs are shown as minus values because they are in fact costs to the transport department. This matrix has a conventional terminology, as is shown in the illustration Figure 8·8(b). Here, 11 refers to the first grid square from the first supply point, 12 to the second and so on.

DESTINATIONS ORIGINS	D.I.	D.2.	D.3.	D.4	D.5	SUPPLY
S_1	-3	-7	-12	-10	-9	9
S_2	-14	-20	-13	-6	-12	4
S_3	-12	-15	-13	-9	-6	8
DEMAND	3	5	4	6	3	21

Figure 8·8 (a)

DESTINATIONS ORIGINS	D.I	D.2	D.3	D.4	D.5	SUPPLY
S_1	X_{11}	X_{12}	X_{13}	X_{14}	X_{15}	9
S_2	X_{21}	X_{22}	X_{23}	X_{24}	X_{25}	4
S_3	X_{31}	X_{32}	X_{33}	X_{34}	X_{35}	8
DEMAND	3	5	4	6	3	21

Figure 8·8 (b)

The next move is to develop a solution which is possible under the conditions of supply and demand pertaining, remembering that it is not necessarily the best solution.

We move onto the calculation of the best solution. The final step is the implementation of what has been calculated. This does not have to be slavishly carried through—there may be a good reason why the optimum solution is not possible in practice—but at least it will give a target at which the department can aim, and a measure of the efficiency of the real situation. For the purpose of illustration, assume that the situation is the one laid out in the costs matrix in Figure 8·8(a). Five demand points and three sources are required to be satisfied at the lowest possible cost.

The costs per unit are shown in the cost matrix, as are the respective demands and capacities. In the firm shown it is assumed that the aim is to satisfy all demands at the lowest cost; no further restraints are placed on the

171

transport man because of policy decisions. As has already been noted, the first step is to determine a first, or feasible solution. This is done by the application of the north-west corner method.

Starting at the north-west corner (X11), examine the supply and demand position: if the demand at X11 is less than the available supply, set X11 equal to demand, and proceed horizontally to the next grid square. If the demand at X11 is more than the supply, then set X11 equal to the supply, and proceed vertically to the next grid square. If the demand is equal to the supply, then set X11 equal to the supply and proceed diagonally to the next grid square. These rules are, of course, applied in order, so that the solution proceeds from grid square to grid square. Examine Figure 8·9(a). Commencing at X11 supply is 9 and the demand is 3. Therefore, we set X11 equal to demand and move to X12. Supply is now 6 (9–3), and demand is 5. Demand is still less than supply so we set X12 equal to demand (5) and proceed

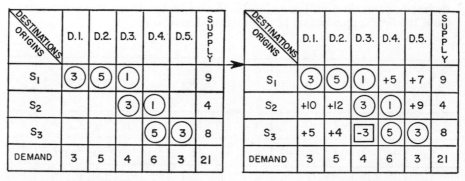

Figure 8·9 (a)   Figure 8·9 (b)

to X13. At this point demand exceeds supply (1); therefore we set X13 equal to supply (1) and proceed vertically to X23. At this point demand is 3, that is 4–1, and supply is 4. We can now set X23 equal to demand and proceed to X24. Here the demand is 5 but supply is 1 (4–3). We thus set demand equal to supply (1) and move vertically to X34. In this grid square the demand is 5 (6–1) and the supply 8. Therefore, we set X34 to demand and proceed horizontally. At X35 demand is 3 and the supply is 3 (8–5), therefore set demand equal to supply.

This gives us a first feasible solution—all demands have been met and all supplies have been used.

It will be noticed that the feasible solution digits have been circled in the grid. The reason for this is ease of identification—as will become more apparent as we proceed. At this stage we need only emphasize that it is of great importance to ensure that the data is so identified. This circle gives rise to those grid squares containing them being known as 'stone squares'— those which do not are called 'water squares'.

Select any water square, say X21; we evaluate this square in the following manner. Find the nearest stone square in the same row, which also has a stone square in the same column, move to this location and trace a path back to the original water square, stepping on stone squares all the time and only making right-angled turns. List the path with alternating positive and negative signs for each stone square. Substitute the costs related to each stone square and the final water square and add. This will give a value for the water square:

Thus for X21 in Figure 8·8(a) we move to X23 to X13 to X11 to X21.

$$+(-13)-(-12)+(-3)-(-14)$$

or 10 as in Figure 8·9(b)

For X15 we move to X13 to X23 to X24 to X34 to X35 to X15

$$+(-12)-(-13)+(-6)-(-9)+(-6)-(-9)$$

or 7 as in Figure 8·9(b)

It will be noticed that in both these examples the path is always traced with right-angled turns. As a final example, the path for X33 in Figure 8·9(b) is X34 to X24 to X23 to X33, giving a value of -3. All the water squares are treated in this manner as is shown in the figure. Select the most negative water square (if there are two equal, either will do) and mark it with a square as in Figure 8·9(b). Retrace the path that was used to evaluate this water square, marking the stone values with alternating positive and negative signs. Select the smallest positive stone value and move it to the water square containing the most negative value, leaving all other stones in their place. Reallocate supply and demand ensuring that row and column assignments are equal to supplies and demands, and continue as before.

Thus from Figure 8·9(b) the only negative water value is X33 (this is deliberate for simplicity). Mark for identification purposes. Retrace the path used in its evaluation X34 to X24 to X23 to X33—the stone values being $+5 -1 +3$; therefore the smallest positive stone value is 3. This is moved to the water square with the other stones remaining (unallocated) in their original positions. This is shown in Figure 8·9(c). The stones are then

DESTINATIONS / ORIGINS	D.1	D.2	D.3	D.4	D.5	SUPPLY
S_1	◯	◯	◯			9
S_2				◯		4
S_3			(3)	◯	◯	8
DEMAND	3	5	4	6	3	21

Figure 8·9 (c)

allocated as in Figure 8·9(d) and the water squares evaluated in the same fashion as before.

An optimum solution is reached when there are no more negative water values, the procedure being repeated till this happens. For the sake of simplicity, the optimum solution in the example is reached after only one operation of the procedure—in practice, of course, many grids will be required but the method is exactly as has been described: Reach an initial solution; evaluate all water squares; select the most negative (if two, use either); retrace the path alternating positive and negative symbols; select the smallest positive stone value (if two, use either); move this to the location of the most negative water value leaving the other stones in their place unallocated. Re-allocate stones and revalue water squares. If negative values are still present, repeat as before until all water squares have positive values. This is the optimum allocation.

ORIGINS \ DESTINATIONS	D.1.	D.2.	D.3.	D.4.	D.5.	SUPPLY
S₁	(3)	(5)	(1)	+2	+4	9
S₂	+11	+15	+2	(4)	+9	4
S₃	+8	+7	(3)	(2)	(3)	8
DEMAND	3	5	4	6	3	21

ORIGINS \ DESTINATIONS	D.1.	D.2.	D.3.	D.4.	D.5.	SUPPLY
S₁	(3)	(5)	(1)			9
S₂				(4)		4
S₃			(3)	(2)	(3)	8
DEMAND	3	5	4	6	3	21

Figure 8·9 (d)   Figure 8·9 (e)

In our example, Figure 8·9(e), S1 will supply D1 with 3 units, D2 with 5 units, D3 with 1 unit; S2 will supply D4 with its total supply of 4 units. S3 will supply D3 with 3 units, D4 with 5, and D5 with 3 units. These results are, of course, open to interpretation within the policies laid down by the firm.

One or two points must now be made about the method illustrated. In all cases the demand and supply totals must be equal. Since this is seldom the case in practice, a simple procedure must be adopted. This is simply to add a 'dummy' row or column so that demand and supply become equated. The important thing to remember is that ALL COSTS for the 'dummy' must be set at zero. In this way it will work itself out of the final solution. If, for policy reasons, a particular market supply combination is known to be undesirable, then at the start a very undesirable cost should be assigned to this combination—at least greater than any other cost on the matrix. The method which has been outlined is not the shortest technique for arriving at a solution; it is, however, one of the best for operating management unfamiliar with lineaɪ programming methods. The writer's opinion in this matter is based on the fact that other, shorter methods require mental inspection and selection of the grids. This is fine in the simple examples which are used here to illustrate, but in the real work situation can lead to mistakes. This method is long but it is based on very simple steps and equally simple arithmetic. It allows easy checking of the solution, and can be used by anyone.

The future planning of the transport department must also be considered. In this sphere it becomes increasingly difficult for the manager to make any reliable forecasts at all in isolation, but planning must be undertaken as the scope of the firm's activities increases. One of the most difficult areas here is planning the future choice of modes that the firm is to use. (Air/road/rail/ water—in what combinations?) To achieve a degree of effective planning, it is absolutely essential for the transport manager to adopt the total approach, otherwise the effectiveness of the firm must decline in the long run.

When making plans of any kind, it is essential to achieve flexibility, and this poses its own special problems for the transport man attempting to forecast future policies. In this respect it is necessary to remember that straight comparisons between alternative transport modes can be very misleading. It is much more accurate to employ an extended approach where all the factors which are influenced by the transport decision are included in the appraisal. This will include inventory, warehouse costs, packaging, insurance, obsolescence costs and so on. These costs are discussed in detail in other sections of this volume, but the implications of changes in them are of the greatest importance. By applying the total cost, a variety of changes in choice will come to light. This is especially true where there can be some reduction in inventory, and warehousing and obsolescence costs, through the use of a faster, more expensive mode. Very often, extra costs can be offset by more than proportionate savings elsewhere. The real point here is simply to emphasize that when applying the methods discussed below it is essential to take as wide a view as possible of the effect of the transport decision—within the structure of the firm under examination.

Irrespective of the present modes employed, there is always the possibility that, in the future, alternatives will be used. We must, therefore, use a method that will allow some quantification of the potential benefits. The chief relationship determining the effectiveness of the modes under consideration over a range of traffic loads is the basic relationship between their fixed and variable costs. These will determine at what traffic loads the firm would benefit by changing methods. Thus, in the long term plan of the company, investment decisions can bear in mind the possible future pattern of the distribution function of the firm.

Figure 8·10 illustrates this point. Here we have two modes differing in their composition of costs. The total costs associated with either of the modes will be given by the area under the variable costs curve, plus the fixed costs. It can be seen that up to the change point, A is the overall more efficient method of transport and distribution. Above this point, B becomes the more efficient. It will be noted that the variable cost curve of A is steep— indicating an expensive mode such as air; whilst at the same time the fixed costs tend to be low—indicating savings in the provision of warehousing,

175

safety stock and so on. Basically the method can be used to see if and when two modes change places as the more profitable for the firm. The total approach must be used when determining the cost curves, and the wider the base, the more useful the method.

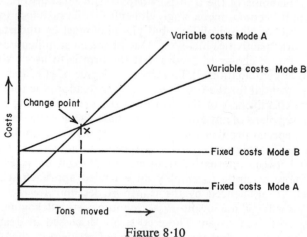

Figure 8·10

There are better methods available for determining the change points between various modes. A simple algebraic formula developed at the University of Michigan by Smykay, Bowersox and Mossman is often used, which again relies on the use of the cost characteristics between the modes under review. Let us assume that these are as below:

	Fixed costs	*Variable cost/ton*
Road	1000	1
Rail/warehouse	2000	0·5
Branch depot	3000	0·25

$$\text{Change point} \quad \frac{F2-F1}{V1-V2}$$

Where F1 is the fixed costs of the method with the lowest fixed costs
F2 is the fixed costs of the method with the highest fixed costs
V1 is the variable costs associated with F1
V2 is the variable costs associated with F2.

Change point Road-Rail/Warehouse

$\text{C.P.} = \dfrac{2000-1000}{1-0·5}$ giving a change point of 2000 tons.

Change point Rail/warehouse-Branch Depot

$\text{C.P.} = \dfrac{3000-2000}{0·5-0·25}$ giving a change point of 4000 tons.

Thus for the cost data under consideration we may conclude that, so long as the firm is moving under 2000 tons of material to this market, the most effective mode to employ is road. Over 2000 and under 4000 tons the best method would be rail-warehouse and for movements over this level, a branch depot is the answer. Any number of modes can be compared in this way to give the transport man an idea of theoretical choices in the future and these are, of course, open to adaptation to fit in with the policies of the firm. The greatest difficulty is flexibility. Obviously, the firm cannot change methods as quickly or as easily as is suggested by this analysis. But the purpose of this method is to give the transport manager some indication of the most profitable methods in the future—how he acts upon this information will be determined by many subsidiary factors.

One of the most important supplementary pieces of information to use in conjunction with the change point analysis is some estimate of the time scale over which the firm expects growth to move in the markets under consideration. If, for example, it was most unlikely that the firm would move over 4000 tons to this market in the foreseeable future, then the transport man might well work on the assumption that he can ignore the likelihood of having to invest in assets to meet this demand. If, at the same time, the firm expects very rapid growth from below the 2000 tons level to above it then he can either hire the required road transport or move straight away into the rail/warehouse medium. This will depend on the costs and time involved.

If it seems that the firm will quickly leave the warehouse method, then those premises may be leased, for instance. It is important that the transport man makes himself familiar with the more modern methods of investment appraisal, especially with respect to leasing—but these are outside the present scope of this chapter.

The method set out above is a starting point, no more; but with the required supplementary information and the correct approach it can be a positive aid in planning the distribution function. It would be difficult to say anything on transport and distribution today without a brief look at the problems of automation. There are, broadly speaking, three trends or stages to be seen in this area. The first of these is that the transport and distribution department is requested to provide greater and more detailed information for higher management than was ever the case in the past. This is a result of the greater interest being shown recently. These requests cause a great many problems for operating management because the information is not always available, and its collection often means that they are diverted from the actual administration of the department. Secondly, as this information reaches higher management, there is usually pressure for the reduction of the cost burden that the new data reveals from the department. This requires the use of modern management methods, which in their turn often cannot be used without some machine aid. The third stage is reached when it is realized that the total approach must be implemented. At this point the individual branches of the physical distribution function have had their efficiency pushed as far as is individually possible. It is recognized that further improvement can only come from effective coordination of all the functions involved.

Needless to say, the introduction of automation in the various sectors will not provide an easy answer to the problems mentioned above; indeed, because the use of such methods does allow an increase in the efficiency of operations and planning, machine aids can, in the first instance, temporarily increase the number of decisions that face the operating management. In the long run, however, the more sophisticated planning methods and the more accurate information will act as a boost to the effectiveness of the function within the firm. The 1968 Transport Act reinforced the move towards greater attention to the transport function within the firm. Briefly, the Act meant that firms operating vehicles of more than 35 cwts UW within a radius of 130 miles would come under Quality Licensing (i.e. they have to satisfy the local licensing authority that the maintenance facilities and general ability of the transport manager are up to the required standards). Ultimately, this will entail the transport man sitting examinations for his licence. Above these distances and above 16 tons UW, special authorization for the journey will have to be obtained.

These factors, coupled with those mentioned at the beginning of the chapter, are inevitably going to mean that greater attention will be paid to transport and its implications for the firm. Perhaps the transport function will at last receive the management status that it deserves.

SECTION C

The Logistics Function

Chapter C.9

INVENTORY CONTROL

by Keith Howard

The whole process of physical distribution can be seen as a dynamic mechanism with many constituent parts, each more or less vital to the efficient operation of the total system. In a sense the holdings of inventory can be likened to the role of a lubricant in the functioning of a machine. The lubricant is independent of the power source and similarly inventory, which is idle resources, would seem to make no contribution to the financial well-being of the enterprise. However, without a lubricant the machine would sooner or later grind to a halt, and without inventory an enterprise would be affected in similar manner.

Neglecting considerations of monopoly and limited promotion it would seem that a single unit responsible for the total production and distribution of goods could control its stock more effectively than a number of smaller units which, if integrated vertically and horizontally, would produce and distribute the same quantity of the goods. This is found to be true even though the configuration of the single unit is equivalent to the sum of the smaller units; this may be shown to be due in part to the influence of uncertainty on decision makers. In this chapter we shall be considering how inventory—or, more specifically, stock, this being the name generally given to goods which are 'in progress' or completed—may be controlled in such a manner that the greatest contribution is made towards unit operation.

An enterprise produces in response to innovate-push or demand-pull motives, or often a combination of both of these. It is assumed that demand-pull production is desired at the earliest possible stage, and it is in this environment that the control of stocks will be studied.

A further distinction needs to be stressed before the development of control procedures is commenced, namely, that between the objectives. Generally the aim is to minimize the total costs relating to the stock condition working within given dimensions of supply and demand. It may be, however, that the very holding of stock influences the framework and, in particular, demand. The presence of stocks in the hands of a wholesaler or retailer may have a promotional effect and hence in this situation the correct objective would be the maximization of profit. Discussion here, however, will be confined to enterprises working within fixed frameworks as defined above, always bearing in mind that if the dimensions of operation are altered then the stock control procedures should be reviewed.

It need hardly be stressed that for control to be a viable proposition, contra-directional costs must be involved in the holding of stocks. A *prima facie* case for this situation to exist may be made by considering what costs may be linked with stocks. These may be summarized as costs due to holding, procuring, and being out of stocks. All distribution managers are aware, if only subconsciously, of these three costs, but in different contexts. It is not unreasonable to state that, within the context of his own firm, the distribution manager generally considers the out of stock cost to outweigh by far costs of obtaining and holding stock. He is, however, likely to be made very conscious, by customers of his firm, of the costs involved in obtaining and holding their stocks by reason of the irritating manner in which they demand inconvenient quantities at specific times, perhaps on a scheduled delivery basis when the selling company is made to bear some of the holding costs.

At this point in the discussion it may be appropriate to consider in some detail the directional reactions which affect the distribution manager as a result of his operating environment. He will be aware (perhaps painfully!) of the consequences of being out of stock and, in a buyers' market at least, will have taken steps to protect himself against this possibility. He might think that he is providing for expected demand plus something to spare for above average demand. In fact, if pressed, he would possibly be prepared to talk in terms of a certain probability of providing a given level of service. This approach, the probabilistic, is, as we shall see, vital to considerations of controlling stock. Again, another variable will be highlighted, namely the time interval between the placing of an order and the delivery of the goods ordered into stock. The name given to this variable is 'lead time'. The distribution manager will naturally be involved more with lead times relating to the supply of his products to customers than to lead times involved in his company's purchases. Lack of attention to the lead times of his products may in fact be quite as harmful to his company's operating position as the inability to supply any goods at all.

Three costs are postulated:

C_1—the cost of 'obtaining' (ordering or setting-up for manufacture)
C_2—the cost of holding stock
C_3—the cost of being out of stock.

C_1, for example, may be related to the cost of placing an order; this cost may be, say, £20 and will include administrative and perhaps delivery costs. C_2 in this analysis will be expressed as a proportion of the annual cost of the item and may range from 0·10 to even 0·40 for a period of one year. These extremes arise as a result of the attitude held towards the provision of finance. If it is considered that loans cover the cost of stock, then some debt carrying charge as low as 8 per cent might seem appropriate. If, on the other hand, the opportunity cost of money tied up in stock is deemed relevant the charge may be 15 per cent or even 20 per cent. Additionally the costs of warehousing, insurance, etc. vary considerably with the type of good and the facilities available. C_3 is the most difficult to quantify (although this does not mean that no attempt at quantification should be made); it may even be negative if the customer is in no hurry and advantage is taken of the delay to smooth out production. More usually, C_3 will lie within the range defined by the cost required for emergency production to the cost of lost profit, perhaps permanently, as far as some customers are concerned.

In what respect are these costs contra-directional? It will be apparent that in many instances the cost involved in ordering and delivering 100 items should not differ markedly from the ordering cost involved in obtaining 10 or 1000 items. Thus on a per item basis (the usual way of describing C_1) this cost will decrease as the size of an order increases. However, for a given pattern of demand, as the order size increases the average level of stock held must increase as shown in Figure 9·1.

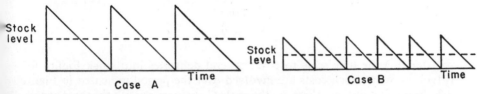

Figure 9·1

The broken line indicates the average level of stock held in the two cases A and B. In case B the number of orders is doubled and the average stock level is halved. Regarding C_3, this may be taken as a cost per item which, of course, produces an increasing total shortage as the shortfall increases.

As far as the distribution manager is concerned he is most aware of C_2 and C_3. If he is responsible for supplying a number of depots, however, he must take decisions as to the size and frequency of deliveries, and the latter involves C_1. He should also understand the implications of analysis involving C_1 in order to appreciate his company's overall attitude towards stocks from input to output, and additionally to be able to comprehend ordering decisions made by his customers.

The Patterns of Demand and Stock Levels
A prerequisite of stock control is that accurate records are kept of the movement of all items. This requires that records of stock level, demand, usage, placement of orders, etc. should be updated when any action involving a particular item of stock is taken. A useful lead-in to the study of stock control procedures is to extract the stock record cards of a number of items (these may be input materials or finished goods) and plot on a graph the changes in the level of stock over time. Three outcome are possible, and are shown in Figure 9·2 (a), (b), and (c).

Figure 9·2 (a) indicates that demand for the item is constant; say each day a fixed quantity is withdrawn from stock. Figure 9·2 (b) at first sight might appear highly irregular. In fact demand is varying about some constant value and can be described as 'statistically stable'. Figure 9·2 (c) demand is highly irregular; so irregular in fact that an out of stock situation arose on two occasions. The description 'statistically unstable' may be used in respect of this pattern of demand. The control of stocks of items in this category presents considerable problems.

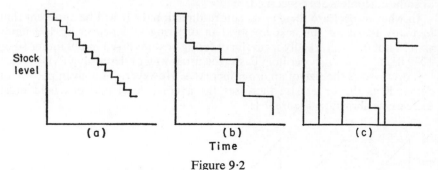

Figure 9·2

Extending the time scale to cover several deliveries into stock Figure 9·3 is typical. What stock costs are involved over the period indicated in Figure 9·3? In the first instance there are the costs C_1, associated with the three orders/deliveries. Secondly there is the cost C_2 arising from the total quantity held over the period (this is indicated by the area under the graph). There were no stock outs and thus C_3 is not involved. Is control optimal, and if not how could improvements be effected? We have already referred to numbers of orders *vis-à-vis* level of average stock and we must, therefore, come to some decision in respect of two points:

(a) the interval between orders
(b) the quantity to be ordered.

The discerning reader will also have drawn another conclusion. He will have noted that the stock level never fell below q_1 and will have guessed the relevance of this apparently 'dead' stock. If, over the whole period, the stock

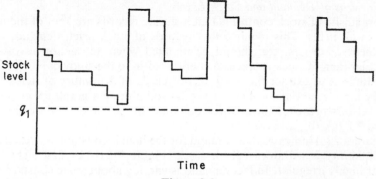

Figure 9·3

level had been reduced by q_1, unsatisfied demand would never have arisen and C_2 costs would have been reduced considerably. However, if demand during the third cycle had been higher, or during the first cycle a little higher, stock-out conditions would have arisen. As demand is very rarely constant the third major point to be resolved is

(c) the magnitude of the 'safety' or 'buffer' stock.

Much of the literature includes treatment of C_1, C_2, and C_3 together in the development of a single model. A strong case may be made, however, for using separate but complementary approaches to points (a) and (b) on the one hand, and point (c) on the other. This should appeal to distribution managers who are especially concerned with the latter.

The Size and Frequency of Orders

A company may be prevailed upon to supply certain quantities at fixed intervals of time. Its customers may turn a deaf ear to suggestions that bulk discounts are available if the size of the lots is increased. What might be the reasoning behind these decisions?

Assume that the company is purchasing R items per annum, and that the pattern of usage is statistically stable. Let p be the purchase price of an item, and q the quantity ordered. Deliveries into stock and usage may be represented in terms of average usage by the model depicted in Figure 9·4. Within each cycle, a cost of ordering and a cost of holding stock arise.

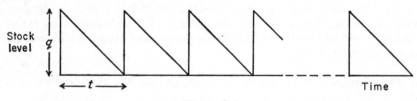

Figure 9·4

The ordering cost is C_1 and the holdings cost is $p \times$ (Proportion of year taken by cycle $\times C_2$) $\times$ (average level of stock). Thus the total cost per cycle is:

$$C_1 + p \cdot \frac{q}{R} \cdot C_2 \cdot \frac{q}{2}.$$

The total cost, K, over the year is determined by multiplying the cost per cycle by the number of cycle, R/q.

$$K = \left[C_1 + \frac{pC_2q^2}{2R} \right] \frac{R}{q} = \frac{C_1R}{q} + \frac{pC_2q}{2} \qquad (1)$$

K similarly reflects the two components due to ordering and holding stock, and these may be graphed in Figure 9·5 as follows:

185

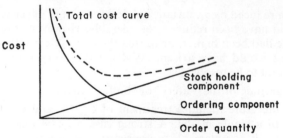

Figure 9·5

The minimum value of K occurs above the intersection of the component curves, that is when

$$\frac{C_1 R}{q} = \frac{C_2 pq}{2}$$

Denoting this special value of q by q_0

$$q_0 = \sqrt{\frac{2C_1 R}{C_2 p}}$$

By substituting this value of q_0 in (1) the minimum total cost is

$$K_0 = \sqrt{2C_1 C_2 Rp}$$

(This result may be established using the calculus and taking the first and second derivatives of K.) This 'square root formula' or 'economic batch quantity' has been much maligned but is nevertheless explicit or implicit in many current stock control schemes. Study of it with extensions can give a useful insight into problems which arise in practical situations. Three aspects are considered as follows:

(a) *The relationship between q_0 and R*   Assume that R is 4000 items per annum and q_0 is 500 then 8 orders will be placed per annum. If the demand for R now increases to 16000 items per annum q_0 will not increase to 2000 but to 1000 items, and the number of orders will be doubled. Having once determined q_0 this effect is sometimes overlooked.

(b) *The sensitivity of the total cost curve*   The annual demand for an item is 1000, the ordering cost is £10, the purchase price of the item is £25 and C_2 is 0·2.

Then $q_0 = \sqrt{\dfrac{2.10.1000}{0·2.25}} = \sqrt{4000} = 63·2$ or 63 to nearest unit

and $K_0 = $ £316 per annum.

The number of orders required is 1000/63·2 which implies an order interval of 3·28 weeks. In practice a more convenient interval would be required. One order per month (twelve per year) administratively would be more acceptable. What value of K would correspond to a decision of this nature? The order

186

quantity q will now be 1000/12 or 83 to nearest unit, and K will thus amount to (from (1)):

$$\frac{10.1000.12}{1000}+\frac{25.0\cdot2.1000}{2.12} = 120+208 = £328 \text{ per annum.}$$

A conclusion which at first sight might appear rather surprising is that total cost is insensitive to quite large changes in q. This is one advantage of the EBQ, in that the calculated value of q_0 may serve as an indication of the approximate size of the batch to be obtained. For example in the past batches of 2000 may have been despatched, q_0 is determined as 743 and hence a new batch size of 1000 should result in considerable savings.

This may be studied in the general case by considering a proportionate change in q_0, d, where d is not less than -1. This latter condition, the only one, implies of course that the batch size cannot be reduced by more than 100 per cent.

$$K = \frac{C_1R}{q_0+d.q_0}+\frac{C_2p(q_0+d.q_0)}{2} \quad \text{by substitution in (1)}$$

$$= \frac{2C_1R+pC_2q_0^2(1+d)^2}{2q_0(1+d)}$$

Putting

$$q_0 = \sqrt{\frac{2C_1R}{C_2p}}$$

$$K = \frac{2C_1R+2C_1R(1+d)^2}{2\sqrt{\dfrac{2C_1R}{C_2p}}(1+d)}+\frac{C_1R(1+(1+d)^2)}{\sqrt{\dfrac{2C_1R}{C_2p}}(1+d)}$$

$$= \sqrt{2C_1C_2Rp}\left(1+\frac{d^2}{2(1+d)}\right)$$

Thus the total cost has increased by

$$\frac{d^2}{2(1+d)}.K_0$$

The sensitivity of total cost K to proportionate changes from q_0 can be seen from Table 9·I and Figure 9·6.

Table 9·I

Proportionate change from q_0, d	*Proportionate change from K_0*
−0·75	1·13
−0·50	0·25
−0·25	0·04
0	0
+0·25	0·03
+0·50	0·08
+1·00	0·25
+2·00	0·67
+3·00	1·13

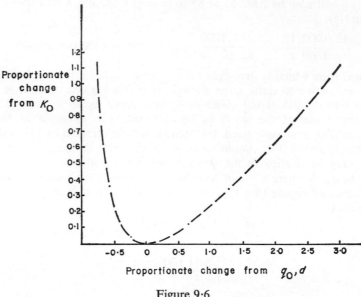

Proportionate change from K_0

Proportionate change from q_0, d

Figure 9·6

It will be noted that total cost is much more sensitive to batch quantities smaller than q_0 in fact by taking twice the EBQ the total cost is increased by only 25 per cent.

(c) *Bulk discounts* The study of the sensitivity of the total cost curve may in some cases give an insight into the discount which should be offered to a customer in an attempt to get him to take larger and less frequent deliveries.

A valued customer purchases 5000 of a particular item costing £20 each during a year. In order to minimize his stock holding costs, he requires delivery of 100 items each week to his works. This creates problems of scheduling transport in addition to the actual high delivery costs involved which total £25 for each trip. Discussions with the customer reveal that he costs his orders at £5 each and uses a stock carrying cost of 25 per cent of the value of stock per annum.

One delivery to the customer fortnightly instead of weekly would be acceptable from a scheduling point of view, but this would involve doubling the batch size and hence would increase the customer's total stock holding cost by 25 per cent.

For the customer $\quad\quad\quad\quad\quad K_0 = \sqrt{2C_1C_2Rp}$
Assuming 50 weeks in the year $\quad K_0 = \sqrt{2.5.0\cdot25.5000.20}$
$$= \text{£500 per annum.}$$

188

For $q = 200$, K would be $1\cdot25K_0$, which is £625 per annum. It could thus be pointed out to the customer that if he would take batches of 200 instead of 100 he would be offered a bulk discount of say, £5 per batch. The customer might well, of course, sense that the saving on deliveries would be much greater than £5. The range £5 to £25 per batch would then be the limits of the negotiating differential.

Figure 9·6 may be used to study the effect on total cost of deviations from the EBQ, and may hence serve as a useful guide in making a decision as to whether or not the offer of a bulk discount should be accepted.

An Example of an Optimizing Approach to a Production and Distribution Problem

A company produces an item valued at £8, the demand for which at the factory averages 1200 per year. A batch of the items can be produced in two days. For marketing purposes three depots, A, B, and C, in the field are utilized, and each of these may be supplied by lorry within twenty-four hours from the factory stores. Depot B is farthest from the factory. There is a labour and materials cost of £300 associated with setting up the production machines at the factory on each occasion, and distribution costs from the factory to A, B, and C for each delivery are respectively £10, £20 and £13. The cost of holding stock differs in respect of that held at the factory stores and that held at the depots, being 25 per cent of the average annual investment in the former case, and 30 per cent in each of the latter.

Mean demand is for 200 items per annum at depot A, 400 at depot B, and 600 at depot C. Appropriate buffer stocks (which are discussed later in this chapter) are held in each case.

The problem is to determine the frequency of given production quantities at the factory, and the timing of deliveries to the depots such that minimum stock holding/distribution costs are achieved.

In the first instance a generalized approach is adopted:

let q = production quantity at the factory
  q_1 = size of batch delivered to depot A
  q_2 = size of batch delivered to depot B
  q_3 = size of batch delivered to depot C
  R = mean annual demand at the factory
  R_1 = mean annual demand at depot A
  R_2 = mean annual demand at depot B
  R_3 = mean annual demand at depot C
  C_1 = production machine set up cost at the factory
  C_{11} = cost of each delivery to depot A
  C_{12} = cost of each delivery to depot B
  C_{13} = cost of each delivery to depot C
  C_{21} = cost of holding stock at the factory
  C_{22} = cost of holding stock at the depots
  p = value of the item.

189

In relation to the period of one year, production and delivery times are very small and the simple 'sawtooth' model used earlier is appropriate. Total cost K for one year is thus

$$K = \text{(sum of set-up and delivery costs)} + \text{(sum of stock holding costs)}.$$

The average stock held at each depot (buffer stocks may be ignored in this analysis of turnover stock) is $q_i/2$, where $i = 1, 2, 3$. The average stock held at the factory is thus

$$\frac{q}{2} - \left(\frac{q_1}{2} + \frac{q_2}{2} + \frac{q_3}{2}\right) = \tfrac{1}{2}(q - q_1 - q_2 - q_3)$$

(this is a reasonable approximation, provided q is greater than the sum of q_i). Therefore

$$K = \frac{C_1 R}{q} + \frac{C_{11} R_1}{q_1} + \frac{C_{12} R_2}{q_2} + \frac{C_{13} R_3}{q_3} + \frac{C_{21} p}{2}(q - q_1 - q_2 - q_3)$$
$$+ \frac{C_{22} q_1 p}{2} + \frac{C_{22} q_2 p}{2} + \frac{C_{22} q_3 p}{2}$$

As we now have five variables (K, q, q_1, q_2, and q_3) compared with only two (K and q) in the development used earlier, a two-dimensional graph cannot be employed for the determination of the minimum value of K. In this illustration no constraints are imposed on the variables and straightforward partial differentiation yields the following results for optimal values of q, q_1, q_2, and q_3.

$$q_0 = \sqrt{\frac{2 C_1 R}{C_{21} p}}$$

$$q_{i0} = \sqrt{\frac{2 C_{1i} R_i}{(C_{22} - C_{21}) p}} \quad \text{for } i = 1, 2, 3$$

An interesting point arises in respect of the expression for the q_{i0} as it will be noted that a practical solution exists only for C_{22} greater than C_{21}. In other words, a solution is possible only if the stock holding cost at the depots exceeds that at the factory. It will be apparent that if the reverse situation applies, advantage will be taken of lower storage costs at the depots by shipping the items as soon as they are produced.

Returning to the particular problem

$$q_0 = \sqrt{\frac{2 . 300 . 1200}{0 \cdot 25 . 8}} = 600$$

That is batches of 600 are produced twice a year. Similarly

$q_{10} = 100$ requiring two deliveries a year
$q_{20} = 200$ requiring two deliveries a year
$q_{30} = 200$ (approx.) requiring three deliveries a year

190

(As required above, q_0 at 600 is greater than the sum of q_{i0} at 500.) Also the minimum value of K is

$$K_0 = 300.2 + 10.2 + 20.2 + 13.3 + 0\cdot25.50.8 + 0\cdot3.50.8 + 0\cdot3.100.8$$
$$+ 0\cdot3.100.8 = £949$$

The Costs C_1 and C_2

To this point it has been assumed implicitly that for any particular item of stock, realistic values for C_1, the ordering or set-up cost, and C_2, the holding cost, may be obtained. In the context of distribution, the administrative cost of ordering has not the significance of the cost associated with making up a load and transporting it to its destination. Again, the implications of stock holding cost may be different when viewed from the distribution angle, particularly if company depots are used. One may construct a model incorporating delivery costs as C_1, but the analysis adopted will depend on whether the value assumed for C_2 differs from factory to depot or alternatively the same value of C_2 applies throughout. The really significant cost which must be considered in the situation where depots or customers are supplied is the cost of being out of stock, C_3. An example relevant to this situation will be given below, when decisions must be made in an environment of demand conforming to a probability distribution.

Returning to the study of C_1 and C_2 in general, it should by now be accepted that a reasonable estimate for C_2 may be derived. Similarly C_1, which at first sight presents considerable difficulties in evaluation, must exist for any given order. Purchasing, stores personnel, and buildings charges can only be laid against the stock which they serve to control and the same considerations apply to all other costs which arise solely on account of materials and goods, which for the time being may be classified as stock. Having said this, it must be appreciated that C_1 and C_2 will not be the same for all stock, and in fact for a given item, C_1 and C_2 may not be constant over time. The latter situation will of course have profound implications in the determination of EBQ for an item.

One of the most useful approaches towards the resolution of difficulties concerning the estimation of C_1 and C_2 is to consider items for which the EBQ would seem to be applicable (a fairly high, statistically stable demand and constant C_1 and C_2). In the case of such an item

$$q_0 = \sqrt{\frac{2C_1R}{C_2p}} \quad \text{using the usual notation.}$$

The number of orders per year is thus

$$\frac{R}{q_0} = \frac{R}{\sqrt{\dfrac{2C_1R}{C_2p}}} = \sqrt{\frac{C_2}{2C_1}} \cdot \sqrt{Rp} \tag{2}$$

Similarly the average investment in stock (neglecting for the moment buffer stocks) is $q_0 p/2$ which may be expressed as

$$\frac{p}{2}\sqrt{\frac{2C_1 R}{C^2 p}} = \sqrt{\frac{C_1}{2C_2}}\cdot\sqrt{Rp} \qquad (3)$$

Multiplying (2) and (3) together we have, assuming the existence of an EBQ, that for a given item the number of orders per year multiplied by the average investment in stock is $Rp/2$. It will be noticed that C_1 and C_2 are not involved in this result. This result in itself is not of much interest, as the item is only one of many in stock. However a different picture emerges for all items of stock to which the considerations of an EBQ and constants C_1 and C_2 apply. For all these items the total number of orders per year N is

$$N = \sum \sqrt{\frac{C_2}{2C_1}}\cdot\sqrt{Rp}$$

and the total average investment in stock I is

$$I = \sum \sqrt{\frac{C_1}{2C_2}}\cdot\sqrt{Rp}.$$

As C_1 and C_2 are constant, the product of N and I is

$$N \times I = \frac{1}{2}\left(\sum \sqrt{Rp}\right)^2$$

Now N and I are significant variables. For example 1000 items may appropriately be included in this study. The total number of orders placed per year are, say, 5000 and the average investment in stock may be £40,000. The question to be answered is whether the stock control policy is an optimal one. To demonstrate the principle of this approach, consider a store containing four items, details of which are given in Table 9·II.

Table 9·II

Item	Demand per year	Price	Orders per year	Average investment in stock
	R	£p		£
A	30,000	3	20	2,250
B	40,000	4	20	4,000
C	10,000	1	20	250
D	20,000	2	20	1,000
Total			80	7,500

Current policy therefore, yields a value of £600,000 for $N \times I$. In order to determine the value of $N \times I$, which arises from pursuing an optimal policy, it is necessary to calculate $\sqrt{Rp}$ for each item.

Table 9·III

Item	$\sqrt{Rp}$
A	300
B	400
C	100
D	200
Total	1,000

Thus $\frac{1}{2}(\Sigma\sqrt{Rp})^2 = £\frac{1}{2}.1,000,000 = £500,000$. (It should be stressed at this point that although the 'dimension' of $N \times I$ is £, this is not of course an actual cost incurred but is simply part of a computational procedure used to determine the optimal stock control policy.)

As the product of N and I is to equal £500,000, it is apparent that N and I are variables and may adopt in theory any appropriate conditional values. These are plotted graphically in Figure 9·7.

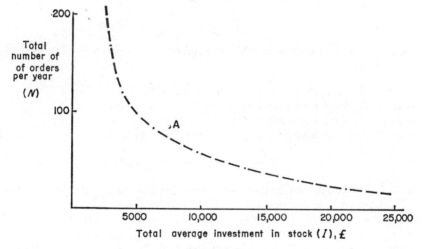

Figure 9·7

The decision maker, again in theory, is free to decide at which point on the curve he will operate. The course to be taken would at first sight appear obvious, namely to select a very low value for I. In practice care must be taken; the current operating point A is shown in Figure 9·7, and it will be seen that for values of I less than £5000 the number of orders to be placed rises sharply. In fact a 25 per cent rise in the number of orders placed (80 to 100) would be required for a value of I equal to £5000. Can an ordering department in practice cope with an increase of this size? If it can, without increasing the working hours of existing staff, this points to the existence of resources which are currently very much under-utilized. If it cannot cope with an increase of 25 per cent presumably additional costs which may amount to several thousands of pounds per annum (salaries, accommodation, equipment, etc.)

must be set against the saving in average investment in stock. This question of the constraints which exist in practice and which must be taken into account in actual stock control schemes will be further discussed below.

Assume that in our case of four items of stock it is felt that an increase of 10 per cent in the number of orders placed would be acceptable. This fixes the value of N at 88 and hence for an optimal policy

$$I = \frac{£500{,}000}{88} = £5682.$$

N and I must now be allocated among the four items, and this is done in proportion to their $\sqrt{Rp}$ values:

Item A Number of orders per year $= 3/10 \times 88 = 26 \cdot 4$
Item B Number of orders per year $= 4/10 \times 88 = 35 \cdot 2$
Item C Number of orders per year $= 1/10 \times 88 = 8 \cdot 8$
Item D Number of orders per year $= 2/10 \times 88 = 17 \cdot 6$

$$\overline{88 \cdot 0}$$

In practice these numbers would be rounded appropriately. Similarly for average investment:

Item A Average investment $= 3/10 \times 5682 = £1704 \cdot 6$
Item B Average investment $= 4/10 \times 5682 = £2272 \cdot 8$
Item C Average investment $= 1/10 \times 5682 = £568 \cdot 2$
Item D Average investment $= 2/10 \times 5682 = £1136 \cdot 4$

$$\overline{£5682 \cdot 0}$$

Several interesting conclusions arise from this analysis. In the first instance it will be noted that the ordering pattern has been completely altered. For those items A and B with a high value of annual usage, the frequency of ordering has been increased and for low value usage items the frequency of ordering is reduced. Again the average investment in each item has changed: a reduction in the case of items A and B and an increase in the case of C and D. It will be seen later that the value of annual usage is of importance in determining which stock control procedure should be adopted.

If now the quotient of N and I is taken instead of the product

$$\frac{N}{I} = \frac{C_2}{C_1}$$

In other words whatever conditional values for N and I are selected, their ratio implies the ratio of holding to ordering cost. Taking $N \times I = £500{,}000$ again consider two theoretical alternatives

(i) $N = 200$ $I = £2500$
(ii) $N = 20$ $I = £25{,}000$

In case (i)

$$\frac{N}{I} = \frac{200}{2500} \text{ or } C_1 = 12.5C_2$$

In case (ii)

$$\frac{N}{I} = \frac{20}{25,000} \text{ or } C_1 = 1250C_2.$$

Thus by selecting an alternative the decision maker is implicitly determining the relative magnitude of the ordering and stock holding costs. It will be noted that in addition to the ratio C_2/C_1 being determined by N/I it is also obtained in the case of each item by taking the ratio of the number of orders for that item per year to the average investment in stock of the item.

Making the number of orders for an item proportional to the square root of the value of annual usage of the item, as developed above, is the basis of a practical procedure known as Coverage Analysis. Although by no means universally applicable, adoption of the technique has produced worthwhile savings in a number of instances.

Safety or Buffer Stocks

The three main aspects of stock control namely the size of deliveries, their frequency, and the size of buffer stocks have been mentioned. The development so far has been concerned with the first two of these, and it has been seen that the approach need not necessarily be one of great precision. The existence of buffer stocks is solely to guard against stock-outs caused by unexpectedly high demand (usually during the lead-time interval when the stock level is low). The cost of stock-out may be so high that an empirical decision may result in the average stock level being excessive. Average stock level is in fact

$q/2+B$ (q is the average order quantity, which will be q_0 if the EBQ approach is used)

where the whole of the buffer stock B contributes to the stock level. In order to determine appropriate values for B it is necessary to study demand and lead time in more detail than has been done up to this point. Also necessary for this analysis is the level of service which it is desired to give for an item.

To establish the size of buffer stock necessary in a given situation two distinct methods of supplying goods into stock must be referred to. Various descriptions are given to these two methods; we shall refer to the first as the re-order level (ROL) method and the second as the periodic review method. They can best be described by reference to Figure 9·8 and 9·9.

The most obvious difference between the two schemes is that, with the ROL method, fixed quantities are ordered at varying intervals (determined by the point in time at which a certain fixed stock level is reached) whereas, with the periodic review method, varying quantities (determined by the difference between the actual level of stock and the maximum stock level) are ordered at fixed intervals of time, T. If the EBQ approach is used then the constant size of the order quantity is determined in the ROL scheme and the interval between

195

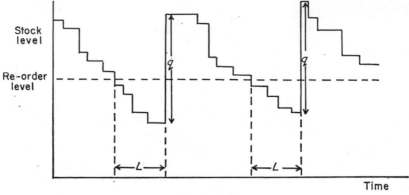

Figure 9·8

orders in the periodic review scheme. Our concern here, however, is how we may compromise between minimum level of stock and an acceptable service level.

A difference may be noted between the two schemes of control. With the ROL scheme varying demand over lead time only must be catered for, whereas with the periodic review scheme (at least where the lead time is less than the review time) varying demand between the placing of an order and the receipt into stock of the next delivery but one (that is a period of $T+L$) must be taken into consideration. A consequence of the latter is a tendency to reduce T below L when the situation corresponds to the ROL requirement. It might be noted that mathematically the periodic review scheme tends to the ROL scheme as the review interval T tends to zero.

It will be apparent that if both demand and lead time are variable the buffer stock must cater for combinations of high lead time and demand. The analysis is simplified if L is taken as constant, and this situation will be considered first.

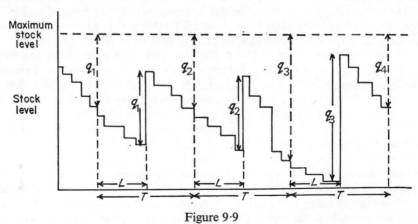

Figure 9·9

Buffer Stocks with L Constant
Take the case of an item for which L or $T+L$, depending upon which scheme is used, is one month. It is necessary to study in some detail the pattern of monthly demand, and to this end historical data for the months in which stable conditions have prevailed is recorded in Table 9·IV.

Table 9·IV

Demand	Number of two-month periods in which stated demand occurred
0–100	3
101–200	3
201–300	12
301–400	9
401–500	3

The probability distribution of demand x is now given in Table 9·V.

Table 9·V

x	$p(x)$	$x.p(x)$
0–100	0·1	5
101–200	0·1	15
201–300	0·4	100
301–400	0·3	105
401–500	0·1	45
	1·0	270

An approximation to average demand during the thirty one-month periods is obtained by summing each average value of x multiplied by the probability of its occurrence $p(x)$, and is seen to be 270. The purpose of the buffer stock can now be seen, for if an order for stock replenishment is made when the stock level falls to 270 the probability of a shortage occurring before the order is received will be over 40 per cent. This level of service would normally be quite unacceptable, and clearly the order must be placed before the level of stock has fallen to 270. The difference between 270 and this higher level of stock is the buffer stock, and its actual size is determined by the decision which is made concerning the level of service to be provided. Assume that a 90 per cent probability of a shortage not occurring is seen as appropriate. Examination of Table 9·V reveals that there is a 90 per cent probability of demand during lead time not exceeding 400. Thus in this example the re-order level would be 400 for the ROL schemes and similarly the maximum stock level in a periodic review scheme would be 400.

The buffer stock is then 400 less 270 which is 130 and in general is:

(Re-order level or Maximum stock level) − (Average demand in L or $T+L$).

Often attempts are made to describe demand by one of the well-known statistical distributions such as the Normal or Poisson probability distributions. The first mentioned requires two parameters, the mean and standard

197

deviation, and the latter only one, the mean, for complete definition. This permits the development of concise and comprehensive models, which include buffer stocks, but the approach to the latter is basically as described in the above numerical example.

Buffer Stocks with L Variable
If, in addition to variable demand, the time taken to replenish a store also varies the problem of determining re-order levels or maximum stock levels becomes much more complex. This situation often arises in practice and in most cases stock control is purely empirical. Assume that demand for one month is as indicated in Table 9·VI but that instead of lead time L being constant at one month it possesses the following probability distribution:

Table 9·VI

L	$p(L)$
months	
0·75	0·1
1·00	0·6
1·25	0·3
	1·0

Thus lead time may be 3, 4, or 5 weeks with an average of 4·2 weeks or 1·05 months. The probability distribution of demand during a period of 1 month is given in Table 9·V. Probability distributions for 3 weeks and 5 weeks cannot be obtained by simply multiplying the demand values by 0·75 or 1·25 and using the same probabilities as would apply in the case of 4 weeks. However certain conclusions may be drawn regarding the re-order level of 400 employed when lead time was constant at 1 month. With variable lead time the probability of a time of one month is 0·6 and the probability of demand exceeding 400 is 0·1. For a lead time of 1·25 months which has a probability of 0·3 it is reasonable to assume that the probability of exceeding 400 will be about 0·4, (0·3+0·1). The combined probability of exceeding 400 is thus:

$$\text{For one month} \quad 0·1 \times 0·6 = 0·06$$
$$\text{For 1·25 months} \quad 0·4 \times 0·3 = 0·12$$
$$\text{Total} = 0·18$$

The probability of not exceeding 400 has thus fallen from 90 per cent in the case of constant lead time to 82 per cent in the case of variable lead time. In order therefore to maintain the same level of service in the latter case the re-order level and hence buffer stock must be raised.

As before, one basis for the practical determination of buffer stocks is the assumption that demand and lead time conform to known statistical distributions such as the Normal when knowledge of the parameters enables appropriate service levels to be determined by combination of the distributions.

198

Another approach, which finds much application in situations of increasing complexity, is simulation. In this case the probability distribution of demand during lead time is established knowing, say, daily demand and lead-time distribution, by simulating day by day the actual stock position. Many months of stock movement may be simulated and the re-order level for a required level of service estimated.

An Example of an Optimizing Approach to the Determination of the Size of Buffer Stock

Consider the earlier example in which depot *C* was one of three supplied from a factory with items valued at £8 each. Demand at the depot was statistically stable with a mean of 600 per year, and the decision was taken to deliver batches of 200 at four monthly intervals.

In order to commence the analysis an indication was required of the way in which demand at the depot varied. Records of monthly demand enabled Table 9·VII to be constructed:

Table 9·VII

Year	1	2	3
Month			
January	48	69	45
February	47	45	43
March	56	35	55
April	51	56	63
May	63	55	56
June	43	42	40
July	51	56	57
August	51	50	43
September	51	62	61
October	49	55	47
November	54	53	26
December	47	45	58
Total	611	623	596

Statistical analysis reveals that monthly demand conforms with the well-known distribution, the Normal. The continuous curve approximating to the demand is shown in Figure 9·10.

The two parameters necessary to describe the Normal distribution, namely the mean and standard deviation, are in this case fifty and ten respectively. Knowing the mean and the standard deviation of demand the probability of exceeding a given demand may be readily determined; that is the implications of various levels of service may be examined.

In this instance deliveries to the depots are scheduled and the buffer stock must be designed to give protection throughout the four-month period. Statistical theory indicates that demand over the four months between deliveries is Normally distributed with a mean of 200 and a standard deviation of twenty.

199

Two alternative approaches are now available. The first of these makes no attempt to evaluate the cost of shortage, but specifies only the level of service required. The second involves an attempt to cost the result of being out of stock when a demand is made. It will become clear that if optimal operating conditions are assumed the cost of a shortage is implicit in the first alternative and one particular level of service is specified in the second.

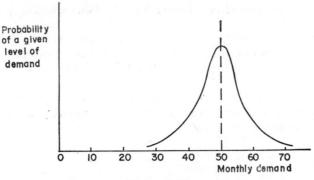

Figure 9·10

The first approach may easily be demonstrated. Consider the two levels of service 80 per cent and 90 per cent. With the former, a stockout would be expected once in five cycles (twenty months) and with the latter once in ten cycles (forty months). A consequence of the Normal distribution in this case is that the 80 per cent level would be achieved if a buffer stock of 0·84 standard deviations is held, and correspondingly 1·28 standard deviations would be necessary for the 90 per cent level. Table 9·VIII may thus be constructed.

Table 9·VIII

Level of service	*Size of buffer stock*
80 per cent	17
90 per cent	26

The second approach requires that an estimate be made of the cost of being out of stock when a demand for an item is made. The normal reaction to this requirement is that no specific estimate can be made as circumstances surrounding the request cannot be predicted. This is correct when one future shortage is considered as it is not known which customer will be involved and hence what his reaction might be. However, statistical theory can be of some help in resolving the difficulty.

In the first place what might the consequence of a shortage be? Alternatives may be listed as follows:

(a) The customer will be quite prepared to wait until the next four-monthly delivery.

200

(b) A special factory to depot delivery will be necessary. This may take two or three days.

(c) The sale will be lost, the customer in this instance satisfying his requirement elsewhere.

(d) In a few instances the customer may place all or part of his business permanently with another buyer.

What is now required is an estimate of the cost and probability of each alternative. Assuming these alternatives for any one shortage to be exhaustive and exclusive the probabilities attached to each when summed must total one. Individual probabilities will, of course, vary from situation to situation and it will be appreciated that for a given situation different distributions will usually arise when independent assessments are made.

Cost and probability estimates may be made on the following assumed lines:

Alternative (a): the cost involved is nil and the probability of this outcome arising is assumed to be 0·25.

Alternative (b): a special delivery from the factory will in general be more costly than a scheduled delivery and in this case is taken as £15. The associated probability assumed here is 0·40. Note that the cost of £15 is incurred for a shortage of any magnitude.

Alternative (c): the profit made on each item averages £2. The cost thus depends on the magnitude of the shortage. An analysis may therefore be appropriate for shortages of various size. However the final total cost of a shortage is not very sensitive to the extent of the shortfall and here an excess demand for 10 items is assumed giving a cost of £20. The probability of this alternative is estimated as 0·25.

Alternative (d): this is the most difficult to assess. The probability of 0·10 is implied and this is by no means high as even if a shortage occurred each cycle, a customer would only on average be lost every forty months. What is required is the cost of losing an average customer, one who will probably purchase items other than the one under consideration. For this purpose a loss of £500 profit is assumed.

All of this information may now be combined to yield the expected cost of being out of stock:

(a) £0 $\times 0·25 = £\ 0$
(b) £15 $\times 0·40 = £\ 6$
(c) £20 $\times 0·25 = £\ 5$
(d) £500 $\times 0·10 = £50$
$$\overline{}$$
Expected Cost $= £61$

As the size of the buffer stock increases the cost of holding stock increases but the expected cost of stockout decreases. Here we have the contra-directional costs necessary for an optimum solution and this is approached in this case by trial and error.

Consider first the cost implicit in accepting a 1 in 4 or 25 per cent chance of a stockout. This situation is indicated in Figure 9·11. For this to occur four-monthly demand must rise to point A. As we are dealing with the Normal Distribution this is 0·68 standard deviations above the average demand of 200.

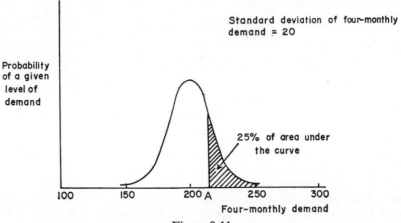

Figure 9·11

A therefore represents a demand of $200 + 20 \times 0 \cdot 68$ which is 214 items; the 14 representing the buffer stock. Throughout the four months therefore the average stock held is thus

$$\frac{200}{2} + 14 = 114.$$

Carrying cost at the depot, as stated earlier, is 30 per cent of the average investment in stock per annum. The charge for one item for four months is therefore

$$£\frac{1}{3} \times \frac{30}{100} \times 8 = £0 \cdot 8.$$

The total cost per four months is the sum of expected holding cost and expected shortage cost:

$$
\begin{aligned}
\text{Holding cost} &= 114 \times 0 \cdot 8 &&= \quad £91 \cdot 20 \\
\text{Shortage cost} &= 61 \times 0 \cdot 25 &&= \quad £15 \cdot 25 \\
\hline
&& \text{Total} &= £106 \cdot 45.
\end{aligned}
$$

Similarly the following results may be derived:

1 in 5 chance of stockout
$$
\begin{aligned}
\text{Holding cost} &= 117 \times 0 \cdot 8 &&= \quad £93 \cdot 60 \\
\text{Shortage cost} &= 61 \times 0 \cdot 2 &&= \quad £12 \cdot 20 \\
\hline
&& \text{Total} &= £105 \cdot 80
\end{aligned}
$$

1 in 8 chance of stockout

Holding cost $= 123 \times 0.8 = $ £98·40

Shortage cost $= 61 \times 0.125 = $ £7·63

Total $= $ £106·03

1 in 10 chance of stockout

Holding cost $- 126 \times 0.8 = $ £100·80

Shortage cost $= 61 \times 0.1 = $ £6·10

Total $= $ £106·90

For the stockout probabilities considered it will be seen that the lowest cost occurs for a buffer stock of 17 when there will be a 1 in 5 chance of a stockout (that is once every twenty months).

In passing it may be noted that if no buffer stock is employed the total cost will be £110·5 which is significantly in excess of the other costs derived.

Tracking and Forecasting Demand

Control methods which have been developed to this point are applicable in situations when demand is constant or has a stable probability distribution. These conditions rarely apply over long periods in practice. Small changes in the pattern of demand can and should be tolerated without resorting to frequent changes of the control system. With respect to both the ROL and periodic review systems, changes in the level of demand will influence the EBQ and the optimum interval between reviews. Similarly the desired level of service will be lowered if demand increases undetected. Even if no long-term increase in demand is taking place a short-term abnormal increase may create stockout in the periodic review system between reviews and to a lesser extent the ROL system is vulnerable during lead time. Thus methods are required for tracking demand in the short term and detecting significant changes in the level of demand in the longer term.

A very common approach, and one which by no means should be under-rated, is to plot the time series of demand on a graph. It is then often possible to detect trends visually and as a result make the necessary decisions whether or not to modify the control. A method which is more sophisticated but at the same time requires considerable computation is the mathematical fitting of a 'best' trend line through the individual values of demand. An extension is to determine 'confidence' limits which may be drawn in one each side of the plotted trend line. So long as values of demand which arise in the future fall within these confidence limits extrapolated it may then be assumed that the trend of demand remains constant. If, of course, the trend in demand is markedly up or down the EBQ approach in the simple form developed in this chapter is inapplicable; methods of dealing with this type of situation will be described below.

If it is desired to check, for example, the constancy of demand for certain items a very sensitive part-graphical method known as the Cumulative Sum (shortened to 'cusum') technique may be employed. The principle of this approach may be demonstrated quite readily.

Assume that demand for an item has been constant for some time at an average of ten per week. Eight weeks' figures are given in Table 9·IX.

Table 9·IX

Week number	1	2	3	4	5	6	7	8
Demand	11	4	13	10	9	13	12	8
Deviation from the average of 10	+1	−6	+3	0	−1	+3	+2	2
Accumulated deviations	+1	−5	−2	−2	−3	0	+2	0

It will be noted that the values vary about an average of ten and the deviation from ten will sometimes be negative and sometimes positive. On average however (and this is the basis for the cumulative sum technique) the deviation will be zero and hence the sum of the deviations will also be zero. If the deviations are accumulated and the accumulated sum plotted week by week the resulting graph will vary about zero.

Assume that from week 9 an increase in demand occurs. For simplicity an average of eleven is achieved by adding one to the demand during each of the first eight weeks. Repeating the procedure used in Table 9·IX, still assuming an average of ten the results obtained are given in Table 9·X.

Table 9·X

Week number	9	10	11	12	13	14	15	16
Demand	12	5	14	11	10	14	13	10
Deviation from an 'average' of 10	+2	−5	+4	+1	0	+4	+3	0
Accumulated deviations	+2	−3	+1	+2	+2	+6	+9	+9

Weekly demand over the sixteen weeks is shown in Figure 9·12 and although the second period of eight weeks is a simple transform of the first period, it is not easy to detect from the graph that demand has risen.

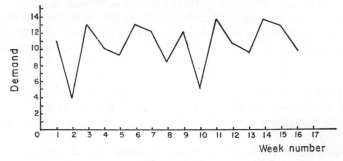

Figure 9·12

Figure 9·13 shows the cusums plotted against the appropriate week number and although a change in average demand is not suggested until week 13 or 14 it is apparent that if the new average is eleven the cusum chart will rise with a slope of one unit per week. It would of course be impracticable to adopt this approach with many different items and in fact severe limitations exist when there is a trend in demand.

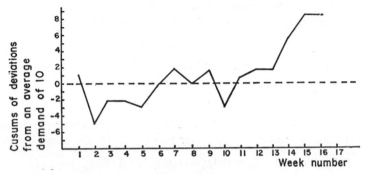

Figure 9·13

Exponential Smoothing

It was stressed earlier in the chapter that examination of the level of stock of an item reveals in general marked fluctuations. So irregular does demand appear that the most usual response to a suggestion that demand should be tracked and a forecast made is that this is not feasible. Experience has shown that a systematic approach using a method such as exponential smoothing is preferable on many counts to *ad hoc* estimates of demand.

Suppose that demand for a good at a depot in week t is forecast as $\hat{x}_{t-1}$ (the forecast is made in week $t-1$) and the actual demand in month t is x_t. Usually the difference between actual and forecast, $x_t - \hat{x}_{t-1}$ is not equal to zero, x_t being either greater or less than $\hat{x}_{t-1}$. It would seem logical that the next forecast $\hat{x}_t$ should be modified in the light of the latest forecast error. The problem is to decide how much of the forecast error to take into account. For the moment this problem may be shelved by stating that the modification to the new forecast should be some proportion α (with $0 \leqslant \alpha \leqslant 1$) of the forecast error (occasionally use is made of the extended range $0 \leqslant \alpha \leqslant 2$). Thus

$$\hat{x}_t = \hat{x}_{t-1} + \alpha(x_t - \hat{x}_{t-1})$$

and this may be rewritten as

$$\hat{x}_t = \alpha x_t + (1 - \alpha)\hat{x}_{t-1} \tag{4}$$

Before proceeding the broad effect of the magnitude of α may be demonstrated:

$$\text{if } \alpha = 0 \quad \hat{x}_t = \hat{x}_{t-1}$$
$$\text{if } \alpha = 1 \quad \hat{x}_t = x_t$$

$\alpha = 0$ implies that whatever the first forecast all succeeding forecasts remain

205

the same and the forecasting system is completely insensitive. $\alpha = 1$ on the other hand implies that the forecast for the next week always equals this week's demand and the forecasting system is fully sensitive.

Apparently the value of α should lie in the range 0 to 1. $\alpha = 0.5$ is not often used in simple exponential smoothing and in fact in sales forecasting where demand is frequently very irregular a low value of α is employed. For reasons which are given below $\alpha = 0.1$ is often the most appropriate ('best' values of α may be determined by simulation on a given set of data).

Returning to relationship (4) $\hat{x}_{t-1}$ may be written in terms of $\hat{x}_{t-2}$ as

$$\hat{x}_{t-1} = \alpha x_{t-1} + (1-\alpha)\hat{x}_{t-2}$$

By repeating the process $\hat{x}_t$ may be written purely in terms of current and past weekly demands as

$$\hat{x}_t = \alpha x_t + \alpha(1-\alpha)x_{t-1} + \alpha(1-\alpha)^2 x_{t-2} + \dots$$

However, as α is a fraction, past values of demand contribute less to the current forecast as their age increases. Consider two values of α, 0.1 and 0.5 then

$$\text{for } \alpha = 0.1 \quad \hat{x}_t = 0.1x_t + 0.09x_{t-1} + 0.081x_{t-2} + \dots$$

and

$$\text{for } \alpha = 0.5 \quad \hat{x}_t = 0.5x_t + 0.25x_{t-1} + 0.125x_{t-2} + \dots$$

It will be apparent that the effect of highly irregular demand on the current forecast will be much less if low values of α are used.

In addition to variations from week to week, trends may be catered for in exponential smoothing. To do this it is necessary to consider the 'age' of the data. It may be shown that this is $(1-\alpha)/\alpha$ and is thus nine periods for $\alpha = 0.1$ and only one period for $\alpha = 0.5$. The procedure is to obtain a smoothed estimate of trend and to modify the 'current forecast' by taking into account the age of the data and the smoothed trend. For example the current forecast may be 42, the smoothed trend $+1.2$ and if $\alpha = 0.1$ is being used the forecast for next week will be $42 + 10(1.2) = 54$. (Note: the current forecast is nine weeks old.)

One factor which must be stressed in any forecasting system is that data should be examined for seasonal effects. If for example it is known that pre-Christmas demand is likely to be three times demand in September/ October it would be ridiculous to carry forward a forecast which ignores this fact. A systematic approach may still be used by establishing seasonal factors, deseasonalizing data and forecasting with the re-introduction of the seasonal factor for the next period.

Exponential smoothing is ideally suited for building into a computerized stock control/forecasting system, as minimum storage (this period's and last period's figures only) is required.

Practical Considerations
It is true to state that no two distribution managers are called upon to perform the same duties. Geography, nature of the market, transport methods, etc. will ensure that this is so. Even if consideration is given solely to inventory

problems, which arise from the particular products distributed, significant differences arise. On the one hand is the distribution manager who may be responsible for complex, bulky and costly machinery and on the other a manager who controls the distribution of very many ranges of a product one item of which may cost only a few pence. The problems of inventory control which arise in the former case often require the application of sophisticated statistical techniques to very limited data.

In the latter case a thorough systems analysis may be necessary in order to suggest alternative methods of control on the basis of which by taking all significant quantitative and qualitative factors into account the most appropriate approach may be adopted by management. In many instances a fully computerized system of control will emerge and in other cases only a portion of items may be controlled in this way. Space limits a full discussion of computer feasibility studies in the field of distribution. Suffice it to state that if the decision is made to install a stock control/accounting system of a high level of sophistication the distribution manager will be provided with information which will enable him to make many decisions based on fact rather than intuition. The type of information provided would include the status of orders to customers and depots, stock movements, categorized sales by depot and various exception conditions. An approach common to most analyses is to consider the differing contributions made by products towards the total value of sales and value of stocks held and then to apply different control methods to the various categories. This is discussed in the following section.

Classification of Products According to Their Sales/Stock Contribution
When the distribution of many items is to be controlled it is worthwhile establishing the pattern of sales and average inventory by product. To this point in the chapter it has been tacitly assumed that all data required for analysis is readily available. In practice accurate sales information is generally available but unfortunately in many instances the same is not true of product stock levels. As companies come to recognize the savings which can be made by controlling inventory efficiently, more are prepared to invest in the equipment and personnel necessary to ensure that accurate records are kept. In fact inventory control between production and final distribution if fulfilled effectively is now seen as imposing a measure of procedural efficiency on these areas as a result of information flows.

Assuming then that requisite sales and inventory information is available the proportional contribution made by each product or group of products to total sales and inventory may be assessed. The results are almost invariably as shown in Figure 9·14.[2]

This is of course common knowledge with regard to sales but it is useful to be able to define exactly say those 25 per cent of items which contribute 50 per cent of sales. The position with regard to inventory requires some explanation. In the first instance the two curves do not correspond laterally, inasmuch as the fact that an item may make a considerable contribution to sales does not necessarily mean that it will make the same contribution to inventory. That is, its sales 'rank' may differ from its inventory rank. However, in general, there is a correlation between sales and inventory contribution, but the inventory curve lies below the sales curve largely as a result of the buffer stock component of the faster selling items being relatively lower than that of slower selling items.

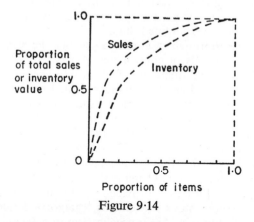

Figure 9·14

The description 'ABC analysis' is often given to the classification of items by sales and is a useful starting point for control purposes, inasmuch as the higher the sales of an item the higher, more usually, is the inventory required. Thus it may be that an 'optimum mix' may result in a reasonably sophisticated forecasting/scheduled delivery system being applied to say 30 per cent of items (Class A), a re-order level/EBQ system to 40 per cent of items (Class B) and a re-order level/empirical batch quantity to the remaining (Class C) items, i.e. the degree of control is directly related to the 'inventory importance' of the item. As stated above, economic considerations will decide whether computer control is applied to all of these classes or, say, only A and B.

The 'uniqueness' of individual distribution systems has been stressed but provided the distribution manager may avail himself of efficient recording/ information procedures application of the scientific techniques outlined in this and other chapters should result in considerable savings as compared with control systems based on empirical reasoning.

References
(1) R. G. Brown, *Statistical Forecasting for Inventory Control*, New York, McGraw-Hill, 1959.
(2) K. Howard and P. B. Schary, 'Inventory Costs and Product Margins—an Aggregate Approach', *International Journal of Physical Distribution*, Vol. II, October 1971.

Chapter C.10

WAREHOUSE/DEPOT LOCATION
by C. Watson-Gandy

The problems involved in distributing goods from factory to customer are receiving increasing attention from both government, industrialists, and management scientists alike. Some measure of this interest can be seen from the setting up by the National Economic Development Office (NEDO) of a committee for the distributive trades, from the publication in the last ten years of some seventy articles and papers on the subject of warehouse location (including many case studies), and from the activities of the Operational Research Society, who have devoted discussion time and attention to warehouse location and the associated problems of vehicle scheduling or journey planning. There are many reasons for this increasing interest, but some of the more important are:

1. The realization of how much distribution is costing. In Great Britain the distribution of goods is costing something of the order of £2010 million a year.[10] [19]. This makes the problem of great importance, both nationally and for the individual firm
2. The changes in consumer patterns; for example, the population swing to the south-east, the development of new towns and the growth of supermarkets and cooperatives
3. The changes in road networks. This includes the vast improvements in trunk and minor roads as well as the ever-increasing length of the motorway system
4. Changes in legislation, including not only the 1968 Road Transport Act, but the ever-increasing burden of taxes, in particular Selective Employment Tax.

These factors and many others, some of which have previously been regarded by management as unvarying, have been causing many companies to rationalize their distribution systems.

In this chapter we will follow such a study through. We begin by examining the distribution function and the role of the warehouse/depot within that function. We then examine some of the methods which have been used to determine the number of warehouses, and where they should be located to serve the purpose of the distribution function most effectively. Also included are some comments on the information required for such a study, and on the implications this study can have for management. Finally, we close with a case history which highlights how some of the problems involved can be tackled in practice.

The Functions of a Distribution System

Any study of an operating system will fall naturally into three main parts. The first step in such a study is to determine the *raison d'être* of the system, its objectives and requirements. The second step is to make the necessary strategic decisions in the light of the broad policy outlined in the first step. The decisions made at this stage would be, for example, the choice of transport alternatives and the determination of the number, size and location of warehouses in the system. The final step in the analysis of the system is to make the tactical decisions without which the system would not operate. Examples of these tactical decisions range from the choice of an operating system for the warehouses, methods to coordinate sales and deliveries, or the selection of a journey planning method right down to the minor, but necessary decisions on such items as the format of inventory control documents and how many copies of the invoices are required.

In this section we are concerned with the first step in the system design process, for it is from this initial study that the role of the warehouse/depot can be isolated as a part of the whole system. In determining the planning policy in outline, a decision must be made on the functions that warehouses are required to perform in the system. However, before examining the many and varied functions that a warehouse/depot can perform, it is necessary to look at the role of the distribution function as whole in the context of the firm, and to consider the relationship between distribution and the other functions of the firm.

The Role of Distribution in the Firm

A close look at the role of distribution in the firm reveals two conflicts of interest. The first of these conflicts is between the production function and the sales function. On the one hand the production department would like very long runs of one particular product; on the other hand the sales department would like many products manufactured in single units in every conceivable variety of colour, shape or model that they can sell. These two objectives cannot be realized simultaneously and, therefore, some kind of compromise is necessary. This is usually done by storing sufficient goods to enable production to be carried out in as long a run as possible, while enabling the sales of individual models to take place.

The second conflict of interest is between sales and distribution itself. The sales department would prefer instant delivery of each item as it is sold; the distribution department would like to deliver the separate items only when they have a lorry going to the appropriate area. Here again a compromise between cost and service is necessary.

Thus it can be seen that distribution is a process lying between the two processes of production and sales, and in this light the objectives of the physical distribution management may be stated as: to deliver goods from
210

the factory to the customer as economically as possible within the service constraints, and to maintain sufficient stock to enable customer demands to be met while allowing production runs to be as long as possible. The functions performed by the warehouse in helping distribution management to meet these objectives now become clearer.

Warehousing Functions
There are probably as many reasons for having a warehouse as there are products passing through them. The reasons put forward by one firm may differ completely from the reasons given by another firm, even in the same industry. However, four functions can be isolated as being of particular significance and are described below. These functions also have a direct bearing on the choice of number and location of the warehouses to be employed in the system.

1. *Storage* This follows directly from the arguments presented earlier. In order to achieve the objectives of physical distribution management it will be necessary to store goods. There are two main reasons for storing goods: (a) Finished goods storage is the stock held to enable production runs to be as long as possible. This stock is usually held in a warehouse in or attached to the factory, but can be held in warehouses in the field. The latter policy can be more expensive because of the extra handling and transportation costs arising from re-shipping to meet demand. (b) Buffer stocks are held in the field as a buffer against variable or erratic demand. It is from this stock that orders are met whenever they occur. Stock can also be held to smooth seasonal demand.

One further reason which is of great importance when the retail outlets are owned by the distributor, is that less inventory need be carried at the outlets and the space so released can be utilized for other purposes, e.g. increased selling space.

2. *Service* The objective here is to move stocks physically closer to the consumer and hence enable the required delivery times to be met. Most firms develop a distribution system to provide a service for the customer, and an improved delivery service can enhance one's competitive position when compared with the service provided by competitors. But apart from considerations of competition, the quality of the service required is frequently dictated by the nature of the product and consumers' buying habits. An example of this is bread in Finland. The Finns will not buy bread unless it is fresh, and as a measure of freshness the bread must be still warm from the oven. This necessitates several deliveries during the day. Other perhaps slightly less perishable goods require delivery within twenty-four hours. This means that a delivery point must be within a maximum of sixty–eighty miles of a depot necessitating a distribution system of a great many small and expensive warehouses.[20] Durable goods on the other hand do not generally require delivery within as short a period as twenty-four hours.

3. *Economics* It is not always for reasons of service that a firm may have a large number of warehouses in its distribution system; it may also be

211

economically sound. Savings can be made by delivering to the warehouses in bulk rather than delivering to each customer direct from the factory. This is particularly true when the drop size at a delivery point is small compared with the size of a bulk load. Another way of using a warehouse to make savings is to take advantage of quantity or special discounts which may be made available during a sales drive by the manufacturers. This will be advantageous to a firm of supermarkets who find it economic to buy in bulk and deliver to their shops themselves.

4. *Processing* In many cases a processing function, which is a continuation of the production function, may be carried out at the warehouse. In this context packaging, labelling and inspection of goods may be performed. Goods may be transferred in bulk to the warehouse where they can be packaged. An example of such a system has been described by Lösch,[14] in which beer was transferred in tankers to the warehouses where it was bottled for despatch to the retail outlets. It was, however, found in the study reported by Lösch that this system was, in fact, uneconomic and that the beer should be bottled at a centralized bottling plant attached to the brewery. In this instance there are economies of scale involved in operating a bottling plant and these outweigh the economies achieved by transporting the beer in bulk tankers. With some other products it may well be economic to package at the warehouses.

It may also be convenient to carry out repairs or the servicing of goods for customers at the warehouse rather than at the retail outlets. This will be particularly worth considering if the work involved requires specialized and expensive equipment or skilled labour of which there may be a shortage. An example of this form of processing is given by the refurbishing of television sets, for which a complete line can be set up at each warehouse.

In general, these are the most important functions that can be performed by a warehouse. They are, of course, not the only reasons for developing a distributive system employing warehouses. Some of these are described in an NEDO publication.[4] In individual cases other functions may be as important to the firm involved as those which have already been described. Some of these are worthwhile mentioning briefly.

5. *Control of local operations* It may be necessary or useful to have local control of sales, invoicing, etc. rather than centralize these operations. This may be for reasons of speed of service to the customer, and these operations can be conveniently performed at the warehouse.

6. *Conditioning* Stocks may be held in storage until they are in a suitable condition to be sold. An example of this is fruit which may be ripened in a warehouse. This may, of course, require special equipment.

7. *Speculation* Firms working in the world commodity market may require warehouses. Commodities, for example sugar, cocoa or copper, may be bought in quantity when the price is low and either converted in a production process or stored and resold when the price is high.

8. *Mixing point* Goods may be received from different points and mixed at the warehouse for shipment elsewhere. This would include the mixing of products from different factories into individual customer orders as well as the break bulk and re-assembly functions of a transit depot. Here the loads are received in bulk from different sources, and recombined into bulk loads according to the destination. This latter type of depot is likely to become more frequent with the increasing use of containers for export.

All the functions described above are by no means exclusive. A warehousing system can be set up to perform any combination of these functions simultaneously, together with the fulfilment of any other needs of individual companies. This list of functions is also not exhaustive, and no doubt other functions will spring to mind. However, if the main purposes of any particular system are isolated, it is felt that, in general, they will be found to be one or a combination of the four major functions described above.

The 'Total Cost' Concept

This concept, or the 'total logistics' concept as it is sometimes called, is probably the most important concept in physical distribution management. The concept itself is quite well known in principle, but is applied surprisingly seldom in practice. An illustration of this is described by Neuschel[15] in which the president of a company called his traffic manager to task for the rapidly increasing size of the distribution bill, only to find that the sharpest increases were caused by a series of top management policy decisions in which the traffic manager had had no part.

This example enables us to put a finger on the areas in which the concepts of physical distribution management are often not employed. These decision areas are those which affect the distribution function in its role as a buffer between the two functions of production and marketing. Here policy decisions are frequently made by management without appreciating or evaluating the effects of such decisions on the distribution function. Examples of this type of decision are—to deliver to all customers within forty-eight hours; to increase the product range; to introduce selling incentives, particularly if the latter causes peaking in sales. These decisions, which at first glance may appear to have little connection with distribution, can prove very costly if taken without considering the possible effects on the distribution costs. However, in recent years there has been a growing appreciation of the total cost concept and this is illustrated by the increasing number of companies who have appointed to their boards a director responsible for distribution, and who can voice the point of view of the distribution function before policy decisions are made.

At a different level a balance must be maintained within the distribution function itself. The distribution function is an extremely complex process involving a large number of problem areas including stock control, number and location of warehouses, control systems, vehicle scheduling and the size and composition of the vehicle fleet. In the present state of knowledge it is convenient to simplify any study of the distribution system by examining these problems singly. However, these problem areas do interact, and great care

213

must be taken not to overlook these interactions, wherein lie all the dangers of sub-optimization.

In general, a global cost function can be built up in the following manner:

F (fixed costs of having warehouses) $+I$ (Stock holding costs) $+T_1$ (cost of trunking) $+T_2$ (cost of local deliveries).

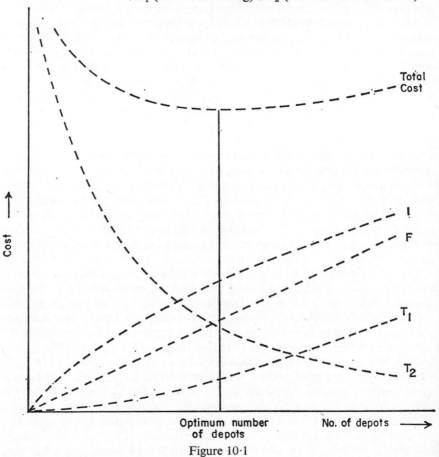

Figure 10·1

These curves and the total cost curve are illustrated in the well-known diagram of Figure 10·1. The curves in this diagram are drawn with broken lines to indicate that they are not strictly continuous or strictly accurate in shape. The curves merely indicate how the costs behave in relation to an increase in the number of warehouses.

From an examination of Figure 10·1, it can be seen that to minimize T_2, the local delivery costs, one requires a depot at the location of every customer. This solution is clearly ridiculous because of the enormous increase in the other costs. Similarly we can minimize I, the stock holding costs, by carrying

214

no inventory at all. This implies that each order causes a run-out and which would have a disastrous effect on the service to customers. Hence it can be seen that the global minimum is that which balances all the costs.

The cost curves such as are illustrated in Figure 10·1 are representative of only one system. The shape of the curves, and of course the optimal solution, will vary from company to company depending on its size, product and distribution policy. One point of major interest about the total cost curve is that as the optimum number of warehouses increases, so the curve becomes increasingly shallower.[18] For example, if the optimum number of warehouses is five, there may be a choice between five or six warehouses; if the optimum number is much larger, say twenty warehouses, the choice of how many warehouses to have may range between eighteen and twenty-three for little or no extra cost. This gives a degree of flexibility, in particular to the larger firm, and the actual number to be employed can be selected for other reasons, e.g. a policy of expansion would indicate the choice of a larger number.

This choice is illustrated in Figure 10·2 which is taken from a case study. In Figure 10·2 the trunking and local delivery costs have been combined to

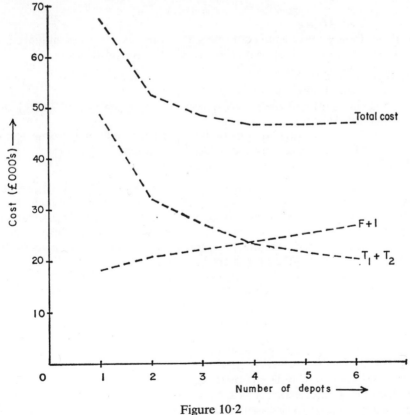

Figure 10·2

215

give one curve (marked $T_1 + T_2$), also the depot and inventory costs have been combined to give one curve (marked $F + I$). Note in this study we were dealing with small quantities of a product which was fairly cheap to store, and hence the $F + I$ curve shows a smaller increase with an increase in the number of depots than would normally be expected. The total cost curve shows that the optimum number of depots is, in this case, four or five and that a system of six depots would be only marginally more expensive.

It is, of course, possible to change the shape of the cost curves within one company either by policy decisions or from the interaction of the other problem areas. This is illustrated by the experience of one company which carried out a rationalization of its vehicle fleet and introduced a better vehicle scheduling system. This had the effect of lowering the T_2 curve, and the company involved found they could reduce the number of warehouses employed.

Thus it can be seen that decisions which effect the distribution function must be taken with care bearing in mind all the different considerations. However, if one can develop a suitable model of the distribution system, the results of possible decisions can be simulated and examined before any change, which might prove very costly, is put into practice.

Depot Location Models

The depot location problem is not one simple problem, but a combination of interrelated problems. It is convenient to identify five of these:

1. How many depots?
2. Where should they be located?
3. What areas should these depots serve or to which depots should customers be allocated?
4. How big should these depots be with particular reference to the economies of scale inherent in warehousing operations?
5. When should the depots be opened?

Consequently, the general approach has been to treat the whole problem as a multi-stage decision process in which decisions are taken for each factor, in turn assuming the other factors to be temporarilly fixed. For example, given a constant number of depots, which are assumed temporarily fixed in location, one can perform an allocation of customers to their currently cheapest depots. Once the customers have been satisfactorily allocated, the depots may now be relocated to serve in a more optimal way this (temporarily fixed) allocation. This procedure is repeated until no further improvement can be made, and then repeated again with a different number of depots.

Because of the complications arising from the interrelations of these factors, it has been necessary to employ simplifying assumptions of various kinds and in fact the last problem mentioned above, i.e. 'When should the depots be opened?' has largely been ignored.

A large number of different methods have been developed to solve the problem. The greater majority of these consider only the static problem. The term 'static' is used to distinguish the single time period problem, i.e. only problems one to four as listed above are considered, whereas 'dynamic' models consider also the problem of when depots should be brought into the system. However, whether the problem examined is static or dynamic, two distinct approaches to the problem can be identified. These two approaches have been called:

1. the 'Infinite Set' approach
2. the 'Feasible Set' approach.

These two approaches differ in the attitude taken on the initial choice of warehouse locations.

The infinite set approach assumes that a warehouse can be located anywhere in the area being examined, i.e. there are an infinite number of possible sites. The main advantage of this approach is that it is very flexible, and although the approach gives a precise location in grid coordinates, because the cost function is very shallow in the region of the optimum, one is not restricted to that exact location. The main disadvantage is that the methods require that the transport costs be directly related to distance, which is not necessarily a valid assumption in all cases.[23] [7]

On the other hand the feasible set approach assumes that only a finite number of known sites are available as warehouse locations. The main advantage here is that if the actual sites are known, then so are the actual costs of buying or leasing. Also it is possible to determine the actual costs of delivering goods from one known site (the depot) to another known site (the customer). The main disadvantage is that not only is a considerable amount of effort and expense involved in building up this list of sites and their costs, but also in a dynamic situation it may not be known what sites are available in, say, five years' time, even if their costs can then be estimated.

Data Requirements

Before discussing the different methods used in solving the warehouse location problem, it may be useful to describe the sort of data that these models require. Note that for a dynamic problem the data listed here should be gathered for each time period in the planning horizon being considered. For example, if the planning horizon is five years, then the data collection should be repeated for each year in turn.

1. *Market data* Assuming that the total region, which is to be served by the system of depots, has been defined, this data is required in two forms. First, because all the methods require to know where the customers are (this is one of the necessary simplifying assumptions made by depot location models), one must have a list of customers and their locations. These can be the actual customer locations, or customers may be grouped into areas and their centre of gravity used either if there are too many customers, e.g. very much more than 1000, or if it is not known precisely where the customers are. In the case of the infinite set approach models these locations are required in the form of grid coordinates. Second, sales forecasts must be obtained for each customer or customer area. Forecasts should be used instead of historical data so that

217

the depot system is developed to cope with future trends, for example, future increases in sales. Data from the immediate past is, however, useful in testing how well the model represents the real world.

2. *Transport costs* The various different modes of transport, both for trunking and local delivery, must be examined to determine their costs, and in relation to the type of service provided. Transport costs are required in the form of point to point costs per ton (or amount carried for each pair of points) in the case of models following the feasible set approach, and in the case of infinite set models the transport costs are required in the form of costs per ton-mile or per mile. All transport costs must be determined for both the current situation and possible future rates.

3. *Warehousing costs* These are usually split into two parts, fixed costs which are the costs of merely having the depot without using it, and variable costs which are proportional to the amount of goods passing through the depot. The variable costs must also include a term which accounts for the cost to the company of any goods stored in the warehouse. This is a cost factor very often neglected, but which can amount to a substantial figure.

4. *Other items* Under this heading is included all the information which may be specific to the operations of an individual company. These items include service requirements, estimated rate of future growth, product mix to be handled, the number of special or emergency deliveries, the cost of overnight stops, the use of haulage contractor warehouses to carry extra stock in periods of peak demand, and if stocks are carried in owned retail shops which might now be stored in the depots, these must also be considered.

This list is by no means exhaustive, but gives some examples of the sort of information that is required.

Static Models
Infinite Set Models

This approach is the older of the two, being based on the work of Weber[24], who published his book on the location of industries in 1909. The models used by all exponents of the infinite set approach are all basically similar, and all make the assumption that transport costs can be related to distance, and usually straight-line distances weighted by the flow along that line. Several methods have been employed and are briefly described.

1. *The centre of gravity method* This method is simply to use the centre of gravity as the depot location. The method has been much used (see Keefer[11] in 1934 and case seven in the NEDO newsletter[4] in 1967) probably because of the simplicity of the calculations involved. The method, however, suffers from three main handicaps.

(i) It does not in general give the optimal location if the costs are measured by the weighted straight-line distances summed over all customers. This has been proved by Vergin and Rogers[25] and is pointed out in the NEDO newsletter mentioned above. The centre of gravity can be quite close to the optimal

218

location and can give the optimal location, but only in certain very special cases or when the costs are proportional to the square of the straight-line distances. It can, on the other hand, be very far out in problems where the customer weights are disproportionate or when one customer or customer area is very important in relation to the others. This is illustrated in the example shown in Figure 10·3.

Figure 10·3 shows seven of the most important market areas in the country, i.e. London, Birmingham, Manchester, Bristol, Cardiff, Newcastle and Glasgow. If these centres are regarded as being equally important, i.e. equally weighted, then the optimum location as given by the sum of the straight-line

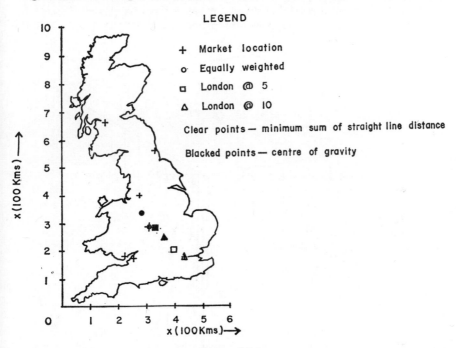

LEGEND

+   Market location

o   Equally weighted

◻   London @ 5

△   London @ 10

Clear points — minimum sum of straight line distance

Blacked points — centre of gravity

Figure 10·3

distances is approximately at Birmingham. The centre of gravity is north of Birmingham with an increase in cost of 2·5 per cent. If London is regarded as much more important in relation to the other centres and is given a weight of five, while the weights of the other towns remain at unity, then the weighted straight-line distances gives a location about twenty-five miles north-west of London. The centre of gravity in this case is about fifteen miles south-east of Birmingham and the difference in cost increases to 5·5 per cent. If London is now given a weight of ten, the other centres remaining at unity, the weighted straight-line distances give a location in London. The centre of gravity is now half-way between London and Birmingham, and the difference in cost is 29·7 per cent, a very substantial figure.

(ii) The centre of gravity method will locate only one depot. Therefore, in multi-depot problems, it is necessary to divide up the total region into areas to be served by single depots. It is not always obvious how this should be done and this can lead to sub-optimal answers.

(iii) The centre of gravity does not give any indication of the costs involved at that location and the costing must be carried out by some other method.

2. *The mechanical analogue*   This is the well-known 'strings and weights' method and is illustrated in Figure 10·4. This is a simple and cheap method with immense visual appeal. It involves drilling holes in a flat board at the locations of the customers (taken from a map). Strings are passed through the holes with one end carrying a weight proportional to the demand of the

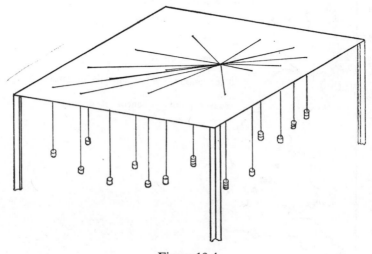

Figure 10·4

customer, while the other end is tied to a ring or washer. Friction can be reduced by using nylon string and nylon washers in the holes. When all is complete, the ring is pulled to one side and, when released, will move to the position of minimum potential energy, which is the optimal depot location. This method has been used and described by Burstall, Leaver and Sussams,[2] and Shea.[17] It suffers, as does the centre of gravity method, from the defects (ii) and (iii) above. It is also not very useful in problems in which the costs can vary depending on where the depot is, for example, district dependent warehousing costs or increased costs due to journeys passing through heavily congested areas (see Burstall, Leaver and Sussams above).

3. *The numeric-analytic method*   This is, in fact, a mathematical representation of the mechanical analogue for solution generally on a computer. It minimizes the cost function by an iterative procedure. In its simplest form the cost function can be represented mathematically by

$$C = \sum_{i=1}^{m} \sum_{j=1}^{n} \alpha_j w_j d_{ij} \delta_{ij} \qquad (10\text{--}1)$$

where m = number of depots

n = number of customers

α_j = cost of serving customer j $(j = 1, 2, \ldots n)$ per ton-mile

w_j = demand of customer j in tons

d_{ij} = distance from customer j to depot i $(i = 1, 2, \ldots m)$

$\quad = \sqrt{(x_j - x_i) + (y_j - y_i)^2}$

where x_j, y_j are the grid coordinates of customer j and x_i, y_i are the grid coordinates of depot i

δ_{ji} = 1 if depot i serves customer j

$\quad = 0$ otherwise.

This cost function is minimized by taking partial differentials of equation (10–1) with respect to the coordinates of each depot in turn. The equations are set equal to zero for a minimum and solved with respect to x_i and y_i $(i = 1, 2, \ldots m)$. Thus

$$x_i^* = \frac{\displaystyle\sum_{j=1}^{n} \alpha_j w_j x_j \delta_{ij}/d_{ij}}{\displaystyle\sum_{j=1}^{n} \alpha_j w_j \delta_{ij}/d_{ij}} \qquad (10\text{--}2)$$

and

$$y_i^* = \frac{\displaystyle\sum_{j=1}^{n} \alpha_j w_j y_j \delta_{ij}/d_{ij}}{\displaystyle\sum_{=1}^{n} \alpha_j w_j \delta_{ij}/d_{ij}} \qquad (10\text{--}3)$$

The locations obtained by solving equations (10–2) and (10–3) are improved locations compared with the original initial locations. Customers are now re-allocated to the depots which can deliver to them in the cheapest way, and the procedure is repeated until no further improvement can be made.

This method can handle multi-depot situations and can be adapted to cater for a variety of different cost functions including those which have discontinuities. A model is also available to minimize the total cost function (as shown in Figure 10·1), and which will give the optimum number of warehouses and their locations in one solution (see Eilon and Watson-Gandy[6]).

This method has multi-optima and there is currently no way of telling how far any solution is from the global optimum. One method used to solve this problem is to make several trials using different initial locations for the depots.

The best solution found is generally, if not the global optimum, at least quite close and this procedure has the advantage of providing alternative solutions to any problem. Numeric-analytic methods have been used successfully in a number of case studies, including one given later.

Feasible Set Methods
The feasible set approach assumes that there are only a finite number of known sites available as warehouse locations. The problem is, therefore, to select from this set of sites that sub-set which minimizes the distribution costs. The approach arose from consideration of two factors that the infinite set approach did not cater for, namely: that transport costs are not necessarily related to distance, and that the costs of buying or renting depots can vary from one part of the country to another. Several methods have been employed and the most important are described below.

1. *Mathematical programming* This method of solving the warehouse location problem has been hampered by the presence of non-linearities in the cost functions, and by the existence of fixed costs, particularly in the warehousing cost function. In general, the problem is formulated as a mixed mode problem consisting of 'strategic' variables indicating whether a depot is open or closed, and 'tactical' variables representing the flow of goods from depot to customer. Mathematically the problem may be stated as:

$$\text{Minimize} \quad \sum_{i=1}^{m} \sum_{j=1}^{n} c_{ij}x_{ij} + \sum_{i=1}^{m} f_i y_i \qquad (10\text{–}4)$$

$$\text{subject to} \quad \sum_{i=1}^{m} x_{ij} = 1$$

$$0 \leq x_{ij} \leq 1$$

$$y_i = 0 \text{ or } 1$$

where c_{ij} = cost of delivering from depot i to customer j the goods he desires. This term can also include the variable costs of operating depot i
x_{ij} = the 'tactical' variable indicating the proportion of the demand of customer j supplied from depot i
f_i = the fixed cost of depot i
y_i = the 'strategic' variable. $y_i = 1$, if depot i is open; otherwise $y_i = 0$.

The method of solution to the problem as expressed in equation (10–4) is generally by branch, and bound on the y_i variables, each node in the tree being represented by certain y_i's fixed at 1, i.e. open, certain other y_i's fixed at 0, i.e. closed and the remainder for which no decision has yet been made, i.e. have values between 0 and 1. The starting point for the branch and bound is obtained by solving equation (10–4) as a linear programme without the integer constraints.

222

This method of solution has been used notably by Efroymson and Ray[5] who point out that because of the absence of capacity constraints $x_{ij} = 1$ or 0 is the optimal solution, i.e. a depot will serve all or none of the demand of any customer. They have also developed three tests which enable them to evaluate nodes very quickly, rather than solve a linear programme at each stage.

The problem of capacity constraints has been examined by Gray.[9] The problem that he has solved, however, is analogous to the problem of determining sites in which to store goods, and is not strictly applicable to problems in which a depot can serve more than one customer.

Although mixed mode programming methods give an optimal solution to the problem that they are set, it is felt that the problem has to be simplified so much in order to present it in a form suitable for solution, that it no longer represents the real problem. This is particularly true if there are any non-linearities in the cost function, which are quite likely to be present, e.g. economies of scale. At present, therefore, other methods are probably better.

2. *Simulation* This technique may be much more widely used in depot location problems than is indicated in the literature. The reason for this may be due to an understandable reluctance to publish figures that may be of value to competitors. However, a simulation study has been published by Shycon and Maffei,[18] and simulation was also used by Shea[17] to cost solutions obtained using the mechanical analogue.

The technique of simulation is too well known to require any introduction. Simulation can be used to examine very complex systems, and such factors as differential transport rates structures, the vagaries of customers' ordering patterns, and even vehicle scheduling routines can be included.

It must be emphasized that simulation will not necessarily give the optimal solution, but only a comparison of costs between those sites being examined. Of course, once the model is built, it can be used to evaluate alternative systems and to compare the effects on the distribution costs of different marketing policies. The accuracy of the model will, however, depend on the availability of suitable data and on the capacity of the computer used. For example, a vehicle scheduling routine can take up to one minute for a fifty customer problem on an IBM 7094. To simulate one year of such a system (i.e. one depot and fifty customers per day, 250 working days) could take over four hours' computer time, which makes a simulation of this detail impractical. It is probably best used either for smaller problems or only in broad outline for larger problems.

3. *Heuristic methods* Heuristics are a set of simple rules which are designed to give a good but not necessarily optimal solution. Heuristics are, at present, the best methods for solving the depot location problem following the feasible set approach, and some quite effective rules have been suggested by Kuehn and Hamburger,[13] Feldman, Lehrer and Ray,[8] and Drysdale and Sandiford.[3]

All three approaches are based on the assumption that a good solution to the depot location problem can be developed by determining the location of

223

depots one by one. Kuehn and Hamburger suggest an approach in which depots are added into the system one by one, that depot which produces the greatest cost saving being selected. They also suggest what they have termed the 'bump and shift' routine, which is used when no further depots can be added. This routine tests if depots selected earlier are still economically viable in view of later additions (bump). It tests also if depots should be moved to other sites in the area it serves (shift). Feldman, Lehrer and Ray suggest starting with all depots in solution and dropping depots one by one as an alternative to the add routine of Kuehn and Hamburger. Drysdale and Sandiford suggest an approach which incorporates ideas from both the two previous methods. They also include an additional heuristic whereby the fixed costs of the depots are increased in steps from zero to their final value. This heuristic is stated to be less likely to remove depots incorrectly, particularly in the early stages of the programme.

Dynamic Planning Policies

Any solution to the depot location problem has a certain degree of permanence. The degree to which a depot system is permanent will, of course, depend on company policy; for example, if it is company policy to build or lease depots, then the results of a depot location exercise may constrain the distribution system for many years, especially as it is not inconceivable that the choice of depots, which is optimal today, will not be optimal in ten or even five years time. On the other hand, if it is company policy to rent space in a public warehouse, it may be much cheaper to 'relocate' the depots in the system and the decision as to where to store and distribute the company's products can be taken much more frequently.

In both cases, however, it may prove very much cheaper to determine an optimal depot location strategy over a planning horizon of a number of years, and solve not only the problem of *where* to locate depots, but also the additional problem of *when* to locate them. This is precisely what the dynamic depot location models set out to do.

The dynamic location models require three pieces of information additional to data requirements listed earlier.

Firstly, a decision must be made on the length of the planning horizon. This will depend in particular on two factors:

(i) How much capital is involved in the system. If only a small amount of capital is involved, as would be the case if space is rented from a haulage contractor, then relocation decisions can be taken fairly frequently and the planning horizon can be short. If the company builds its own warehouses and the product requires specialized and expensive storage or handling facilities, then a considerable amount of capital may be involved in a decision to relocate, and the planning horizon should be as long as possible.

(ii) How accurate one's forecasts are over time. If the forecasts are reliable, then the planning environment is stable and hence the planning horizon can be long. If the forecasts are subject to uncertainty, then the planning horizon should be short and the more uncertain the future the less capital should be put into the distribution system.

Secondly, we require the costs of opening and of closing depots. These costs are required separately as it would be unusual, though not unlikely, that there is a one-to-one correspondence between the number of depots opened and the number closed; for example, in an expanding market one will open more depots than are closed. The costs of opening depots will involve such items as the cost of looking for a suitable site, estate agents' and lawyers' fees, cost of equipment and hiring of staff, and redecorating and installation costs. The costs of closing a depot will include such items as the cost of moving stocks, redundancy payments or removal costs for the staff, sale of equipment costs, and the writing off of any equipment still on the company's books.

Thirdly, a discount rate is required so that the cost of decisions in different time periods can be discounted back to the present and compared.

In addition to this information, all the information required for the static models, i.e. forecasts of market data, transport and warehousing costs, are required for each year of the planning horizon (assuming that one examines the system year by year and not for longer periods).

Dynamic Models
Very little work has been done on dynamic depot location models. This is probably for a number of reasons. Firstly, to consider depot location over time makes the problem very much larger both from the point of view of building the model and also in the data collection problem. Secondly, it is felt that problems suitable to solution by dynamic methods are not that frequently met with. The characteristics of a problem suitable for solution by these methods are that changes in demand are large both in quantity and location, but they must be predictable. An example of this situation would be a company which grows by expanding into other markets as its existing markets become saturated. Another example would be a new company marketing a product for which rapid increases in demand are expected, i.e. the company will grow very fast. In the latter case, however, the increases in demand may not be all that predictable. In a great number of problems the demand is growing at a slow but steady pace, and in these cases one can obtain all the information about the behaviour of the system from sensitivity analyses (of which more later), and it is not worth the additional expense of collecting extra data and building a dynamic model.

The third and probably most important reason for the paucity of effort spent on dynamic models is that all models at present suggested use a static model as a means of determining the cash flows involved, and work on the static models is by no means complete.

At present there are two methods available for solving the dynamic depot location problem:

1. *Dynamic programming* This method is particularly suited to multi-stage decision processes. Ballou[1] has shown that the depot location problem over

225

time can be treated as such a process. The method is as follows: for each year of the planning period a static location method is used to determine the optimum locations for that year, and the cash flows associated with those locations and with the locations optimal in other years are determined. For a static model either an infinite set or a feasible set method can be used; all that the dynamic programme requires is a list of possible locations. The sites and the costs associated with them are fed in as data to the dynamic programme, which is then used to determine the optimal depot location strategy over the planning horizon. A mathematical formulation of the problem can be stated as

$$F_t(I) = \min_J \; [F_{t-1}(J) + G_t(J, I)] + C_t(I) \qquad (10\text{--}5)$$

where I, J = sets describing particular combinations of depot locations

           $F_t(I)$ = accumulated discounted costs of operating at the combination of sites in the set I up to and including time period t

similarly $F_{t-1}(J)$ = accumulated discounted costs of operating at the set of sites J for period $t-1$

       $G_t(J, I)$ = the costs of closing those depots in J which are not in I, and opening those depots in I which are not in J in period t discounted back to year 1. If I is equal to J, then there is no change and $G_t(J, I) = 0$

         $C_t(I)$ = cost of operating from the sites in I in period t discounted back to year 1.

The costs for the first year, i.e. year 1, are given by

$$F_1(I) = C_1(I)$$

This is a more general formulation than that given by Ballou, and is a formulation for the 'forward' algorithm, i.e. start at year 1 and work forwards in time. The 'backward' algorithm, i.e. the version which starts in the final period and works backwards (as described by Ballou) is very similar. Both algorithms contain the same optimal policy and it is a matter of convenience which is selected; for example, if one has a system in operation it may be convenient to use that system as a starting point and employ the forward algorithm.

2. *Mathematical programming*   This method can also be used to determine optimal planning strategies over time. It is a feasible set approach and suffers from the same disadvantages as the static model, perhaps even more so as the problem is now very much larger. The formulation in its simplest form is similar to equation (10–4), but with an additional subscript t to cater for the time periods. Thus

minimize
$$\sum_{t=1}^{T} \sum_{i=1}^{m} \sum_{j=1}^{n} c_{ijt} x_{ijt} + \sum_{t=1}^{T} \sum_{i=1}^{m} f_{it} y_{it} \qquad (10\text{--}6)$$

226

and subject to similar constraints. It can be seen that even a small problem will be very large; for example, a fifty depot, 200 customer problem over five time periods could have as many as $50,000x_{ijt}$ variables.

Alternatively, if there are any pronounced non-linearities in the cost function, then it is better to use a non-linear optimization technique such as the one described by Klein and Klimpel.[12] The problem that Klein and Klimpel used to illustrate the method was a single plant construction problem. The questions they were required to answer were 'where should the plant be located?' and 'how big should it be?' when faced with economies of scale in building, and a changing demand over time. The method they used was the gradient projection technique of Rosen[16] for non-linear optimization with linear constraints. This method starts from an arbitrary solution, and therefore does not guarantee the global optimum. However, several trails can be made using different starting points, and the best solution chosen. This method is also best used with small problems only, though larger problems can be handled using decomposition techniques.

Sensitivity Analyses

The business environment is continually changing, and any company which wishes to survive must be able to adapt to a greater or lesser extent to the changes in the environment in which it operates. Decisions must be made in the present which could have a serious affect on operations in the future. In any planning exercise we are limited to what we know for certain, and to what we can forecast. For example, if we know exactly when the lease on a particular warehouse will expire, we can forecast increases in demand or increases in, say, lorry drivers' wages. On the other hand, it is very difficult to foresee technological changes, and it is almost impossible to forecast such factors as, for example, new tax laws.

Nevertheless, all plans for the future must be made on the basis of what one can forecast, and in the event of something unforeseen occurring it is necessary to re-analyse the situation to examine the best ways of adjusting to the new circumstances. Of course, the more uncertain the future, the more flexibility is required in one's plans. It is, however, quite a simple matter to test the solution to a depot location exercise for its reactions to changes in the operating environment. This is done by carrying out sensitivity analyses.

Sensitivity analysis is a form of simulation on the depot location model. In other words one alters the input to the model, i.e. changes its operating environment, and studies the effects of the change on the solution. The type of questions that are usefully answered in these analyses are as follows:

We have forecast an increase in local delivery costs of 10 per cent because of a predicted increase in drivers' wages. What is likely to happen if the government increase road tax and the price of fuel as well so that local delivery costs increase by 20 per cent and not the predicted 10 per cent? We have forecast a general increase in sales of 8 per cent over the next two years. How far from optimum will our depot system be if the Wales sales area increases by only 2 per cent, but the north-eastern sales go up by 11 per cent?

227

These and many other questions can be examined in a sensitivity analysis. In fact, any of the input data can be altered and the model re-run, the new solutions being examined for changes in the number and location of depots and/or increases in cost. No depot location exercise should be accepted without such tests, for it is in this way that the management of a company can forearm themselves against possible changes.

It is not necessary, of course, to examine the results of changes in every possible item, because this would be very expensive in time and money. But by performing one or two analyses on items which are easy to alter, one can obtain an estimate as to how robust the solution is and also predict how the solution is likely to react to changes in other factors.

An example of a sensitivity analysis is illustrated in Figure 10·5 which shows the response of a depot location model to changes in the local delivery

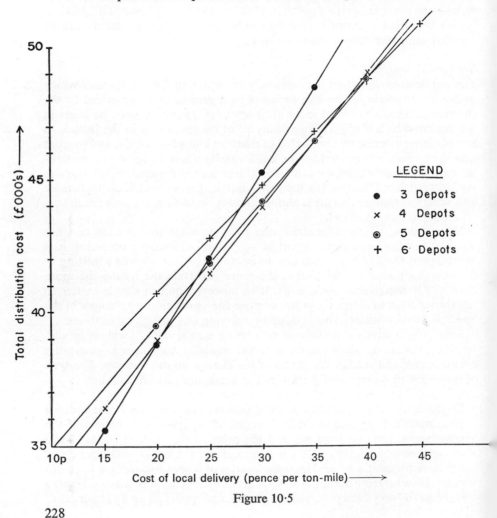

Figure 10·5

rate. In this study the local delivery rate was chosen for an initial sensitivity test as it required the alteration of only one data card. From Figure 10·5 it can be seen that the current rate of 17½p is fairly close to the changeover point at approximately 21p, an increase of just under 20 per cent. From 21p a four-depot system remains optimal until the rate rises as high as 35p. At 40p six depots becomes the optimal solution.

It must be noted that this analysis tested the effects of an increase in the local delivery rate given that all other costs remained constant. Other tests notably with the warehouse costs indicated that a 9 per cent increase in the latter would counteract the effects of a 20 per cent increase in the local delivery costs. The total costs became much larger with these two increases, but the three-depot system remained optimal.

Note also that Figure 10·5 illustrates the remarks made earlier on the shallowness of the total cost curve with a larger number of depots in the optimal solution. The difference in the total costs with four, five and six depots is very small in this case, when the local delivery costs are as high as 35p and 40p.

The Implications for Management

We have examined how the distribution function takes its place among the other functions of a company, and is shown to assist in giving value to the product by placing that product where it is wanted. We have also seen how the warehouse/depot can be employed in the distribution system and how to determine the most effective system in terms of cost within the constraints imposed by the requirements of the system. Before closing this chapter with a case study showing how the methods described earlier can be applied in practice, it will be useful to discuss some of the more important implications that a study of this nature can have for management.

One of the most valuable attributes of a depot location exercise is that it gives to management an opportunity to examine the distribution costs and determine how these should be kept in order to give the best measure of cost effectiveness for the future. Neuschel,[15] in a paper which described a survey of some American companies, reported that the four companies which, according to the measures he used, had the tightest control over distribution costs, were in fact the most profitable companies in the group examined. This, as Neuschel pointed out, indicated that a large number of companies were not operating in the best manner and their management was ignoring a very real area for cost control. There is another question implicit in this survey. If management is not controlling the distribution costs, are they controlling any costs at all?

A depot location exercise also provides a stimulus to examine other aspects of the distribution system. A study of this kind can reveal all sorts of skeletons. Examples of the items that the study might throw up include whether or not the most effective mode of transport, in terms of cost or of service to the customer, is being used; whether or not the lorry fleet, in terms of its size and mix, is the most efficient for the purpose for which it is being used; could a better vehicle scheduling system be introduced? Should lorries be bought or

229

hired? Could the layout of the warehouses be improved? And whether or not alternative handling methods should be considered. All these are items which may not have been examined since the system was first set up. Some related problems which may also come out of the study are whether or not the invoicing system could be improved to give a faster service to customers, or whether the checks on customer credit worthiness are effective.

Another result of the study, which may have important implications for marketing, is that it is possible to examine each area served by individual depots. It may be that the area served by one depot is very sparse in customers. This situation raises two questions:

(i) Is it worthwhile continuing to serve that area at all or could the money spent there be more effectively used elsewhere?

(ii) Should an attempt be made to boost sales in that area and hence make distribution a more profitable exercise?

Similar questions can be asked with reference to individual customers. It may be worthwhile considering relaxing the service constraints in these cases. Some customers are not, and are never likely to be, sufficiently important to warrant deliveries within twenty-four hours. They could, perhaps, be dropped altogether or persuaded to order more, less frequently.

These and many other interesting facts can be thrown up by a study of the distribution system. A close check on all these items can make distribution more effective, and the company more profitable.

A Case Study

In this, the final section of this chapter, we present a case study in warehouse location. This study not only provides an illustration of how the methods described earlier can be used, but also highlights practical problems such as data collection and conversion, and the formulation of the model.

The Company and the Problem

The company concerned in this case study is employed in distributing and marketing consumer durables nationally. The company also manufactures the products sold, but as no distribution could take place from the factories (mainly because of a lack of facilities and space), the manufacturing process can effectively be regarded as being performed by a separate company, and hence the storage of finished goods at the factories is beyond the scope of this study.

The products of the company reached the general public through retail outlets, some of which were wholly owned by the company, but the majority were operated by dealers who were appointed agents.

The problem arose for several reasons, not least of which was the very close check that the company kept on the distribution costs. These costs were increasing, and although some of the extra costs incurred could be explained by increases in such items as fuel or wages, the increases were sufficient to provoke questions as to whether the system could be operated more efficiently.

230

Another reason was that the company was beginning to experience capacity problems at one of its depots. This problem arose not only because of a growing demand for the company's products necessitating a larger inventory, but also because of the lack of storage space at the factories, part of the finished goods store being held in the company's distribution depots.

The study, therefore, had to answer the following questions:

1. Could the present system of depots be improved?
2. Should the present depot which was 'bursting at the seams' be closed and a new, larger depot be opened in the same area?

There was a third question which was in the minds of the management, and which could also be answered by the study. This was: in view of the long trips made to serve the outlets in Scotland and the difficulties of these trips particularly in winter, was it economical to open a depot in Scotland?

Practice prior to the study

Prior to the study, the company distributed their products through a system of four depots. These depots were in London, Bristol, Birmingham and Manchester. The company leased these depots, but as they had been in the company's hands for some time, the rents were in present terms very favourable, and the management was unwilling to relocate unless substantial savings could be achieved.

The products were manufactured in two factories in London and Leeds, each of which made a different range of product. So all depots were served from both factories. Goods were trunked from the factories at least once a week and occasionally more frequently.

For delivery to the retail outlets the company operated a 'bus schedule'. In this type of service a schedule for deliveries is adhered to. This system has the advantage that the manager of the retail outlet knows to the hour when deliveries are going to be made, and can, therefore, have people on hand to help unload. It also means that the lorry driver gets to know his routes very

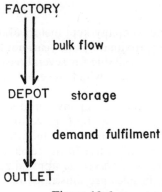

Figure 10·6

well and knows all the short cuts round areas of heavy traffic congestion. On the other hand, by using this system one loses the flexibility of day-to-day vehicle scheduling. In particular, when demand is low extra mileage is incurred in delivering perhaps a single item to a customer which might well have been kept over until the next week.

Thus the whole system operated by the company is concerned with the flow of goods in bulk from the factories to the depots, at which point storage of goods can take place, and another flow of goods in smaller quantities from the depots to the outlets. This is a three-tier system as illustrated in Figure 10·6.

Data collection
We now turn to the problems of the data required, how these were obtained and a description of the work involved in converting the data into a suitable form for the model of the system.

1. *Customer locations* The names and addresses of the retail outlets to which deliveries were made were available from company records. As the model requires the distance from depot to customers (as a measure of the cost of making deliveries to customers), these addresses were transformed into grid references using Ordnance Survey maps. These grid references were not exact as the Ordnance Survey maps do not give the names of streets, but are estimated to be correct to the nearest kilometre, which is sufficiently accurate for the purpose. This was a rather laborious process (as there were several hundred retail outlets), but is considered less lengthy than the alternatives of measuring the exact distances or exact cost for each customer. The computer can be programmed to calculate the distances from the grid references and this is particularly useful if a relocation of the depots is required. The grid references are also available, as a by-product, for use in any future study, and in such a case it will only be necessary to determine the grid references of any additional outlets.

The locations of the customers are illustrated in Figure 10·7. This map does not show all the customers, but gives a very good picture of the concentrations of demand.

2. *Customer demands* The company kept historical data for the demands of individual customers for approximately one year, but total demand figures per month and per annum were available for several past years. Several analyses were performed on these figures, which revealed the following interesting facts.

(a) *Seasonality* The sales of the company's products exhibited the following seasonal pattern. The peak in sales took place in the three months before Christmas. This peak was followed by a three months low in which sales could be down to half the peak period sales. In the remaining six months sales fell in between, and proved to be on average approximately 70 per cent of the peak sales. Typical monthly sales are illustrated in Figure 10·8. Notice that this shows some pre-budget buying.

232

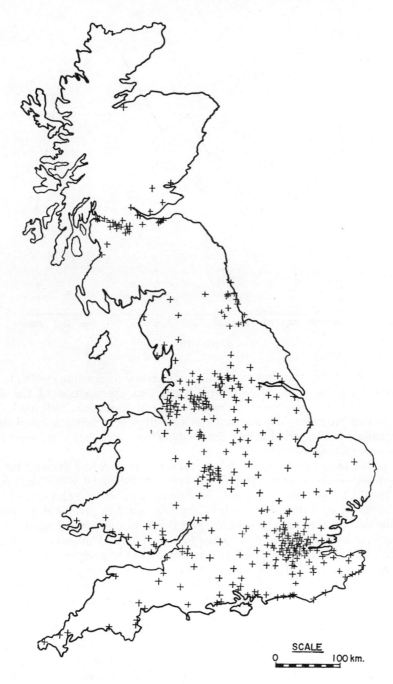

SCALE

0   100 km.

Figure 10·7

233

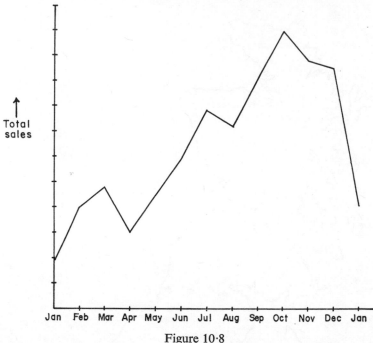

Figure 10·8

(b) *No trend* We tried unsuccessfully to fit several forecasting models to the demand data, but none proved satisfactory. An examination of the data together with the responses of management to questions indicated that trading had become a little uncertain as a result of governmental restrictions on spending in the period before the study. There were, however, signs that sales were picking up again.

In order, therefore, to obtain a suitable estimate of future demand for the company's products, three samples of one week's demand were taken from historical data for each customer. These three samples were chosen as being representative of demands in the peak, average and low periods respectively. All the figures were then grossed to give the annual demand per customer. These were then multiplied by a factor to bring the total annual sales up to a figure which management could reasonably expect to achieve. In this study a single multiplicative factor was used, because it was not possible from the data to tell whether any one part of the country was expanding faster than any other. Management felt, however, that this was not the case.

3. *Local delivery costs* Prior to the study the company delivered to its customers following a 'bus-type' schedule. This means that each customer was visited at least once a week regardless of the size of the order. The management of the company felt that the advantages of this system outweighed the disadvantages, especially in regard to the practical problems of

234

unloading at the customer's premises. As a consequence of this, a cost figure in terms of ton-miles was unrepresentative of the situation.

This system raises two problems; it is necessary firstly to find the cost of a vehicle per mile, and secondly to obtain a measure of the total annual mileage. These two figures can then be multiplied together to give the annual local delivery costs.

The first problem was solved by obtaining average annual costs for a vehicle from the accounts department of the company. These costs included (for the vehicle) depreciation, insurance, road tax, fuel and maintenance, and (for the driver and where necessary a mate) wages, graduated pension, National Insurance and overtime. These figures were summed and divided by the average annual mileage to give a figure in pence per mile.

The second problem involves finding the contribution of each customer to the weekly mileage, based on the distance from depot to customer. This was solved in two steps. First, the crow-flight distance is calculated and multiplied by a factor of 1·2 to give actual road mileage. The use of this factor is now generally accepted and has been confirmed in other studies. A number of analyses were carried out, and some simulations of the vehicle scheduling system were performed to find a suitable function to determine the 'effective' mileage incurred by each customer. The function adopted was to use the road mileage as calculated above, if this was less than eighty miles; otherwise use two-thirds of the road mileage. The fraction chosen was two-thirds because studies of the journeys made by vehicles showed that each vehicle made, on the average, three drops per trip. The 'effective' mileages, when summed for all customers, gave an extremely accurate value for the weekly mileage when compared with the actual mileage travelled in practice.

Inquiries of the depots managers indicated that almost all customers were visited once a week, for fifty-two weeks in the year, but that some customers had sufficient demand to require occasionally more than one visit. To cater for these customers the frequency of visits was estimated by dividing their total annual requirements by the capacity of the vehicles used. If this was greater than fifty-two, then this estimated frequency was used, otherwise the weekly mileage was multiplied by fifty-two to give the weekly mileage. The capacity of the vehicle was measured in 'standard' products by volume, and was calculated using for each product the maximum number of that product which would fit on a vehicle and its percentage of the total sales.

Similar calculations were made for the trunking costs. In this case twice the road mileage (to account for the return journey) was calculated, and as the frequency of visit to depots was not as regular as the local deliveries, this was calculated by dividing the total amount shipped from each factory by the capacity of the trunk vehicles.

4. *Cost of overnight stays* In certain cases the length of the trip made by a vehicle necessitated a night (and in the case of the Scottish trips, more than one night) away from home, and in these cases a subsistence allowance was made to the driver. To find the cost of the overnight stays, the road mileage was divided by eighty miles and integerized (i.e. it is not possible to have 1·25

overnight stays, only the integer value 1 is acceptable). This gave the appropriate number of overnight stays per trip, which was then multiplied by the frequency of visit. The overnight stays were then summed and divided by the average number of drops per trip, which in the case of trips with overnight stays turned out to be slightly over three. The value of eighty miles was calculated from the length of a working day, less the time spent making the required drops, divided by the average speed of the vehicle. These calculations gave a very good approximation of the number of overnight stays.

5. *Warehousing costs* The final data required before the finished model can be described are the cost of running the depots and the costs of the inventory held at the depots. To find the costs of running a depot, it is useful to examine historical data.

Prior to the study the company operated four depots, which is a very small sample. Looking back further into the company's records it was found that the company had operated at one period eleven depots of different sizes. Total annual costs were still available for these depots but these, unfortunately, included the transport costs and drivers' wages. It was found impossible to isolate the purely depot running costs from these figures. However, suitable figures were found for two consecutive years prior to the study. The figures were subjected to regression analysis to determine a suitable function relating the cost of running a depot to the size or, more conveniently, to the annual throughput of the depot. A large number of different curves were postulated, but the curve which proved to be both sensible and gave the best fit to the data, was linear and of the form

$$C = a + bw \tag{10-7}$$

where a = fixed costs of the depot and which were large, i.e. approximately
45 per cent of the total depot costs
b = costs of handling and storing one 'standard' product
w = annual throughput of depot.

An additional term is required to account for the cost to the company of the inventory held at the depots. This is based on the assumption that approximately four weeks' supply is held at the depots. As demand was subject to fluctuations from week to week, a further term was added to account for the variability of demand. As an estimate of the variation likely to occur the standard deviation of the total monthly demand figures (σ_T) was calculated. This is assumed to be related to σ, the standard deviation of the four-weekly variations, according to the expression

$$\sigma = \sigma_T \sqrt{\frac{12w}{13w_T}} \tag{10-8}$$

where w = annual throughput of depot
w_T = total annual throughput
236

The total depot costs are, therefore given by

$$F = a + bw + vr\left(\frac{w}{13} + 2\sigma\right) \tag{10–9}$$

where v = factory cost of the 'standard' product

r = interest assumed of capital employed (10 per cent was assumed in this case).

6. *Warehouse capacity constraints*   It will be recalled that one of the objectives of the study was an examination of the capacity of the depots. For this purpose two items of information are required: the capacity of each depot in 'standard' products and an estimate of the maximum amount of goods in any depot at any time. The first item was available from the company's work study engineers who had, fortunately, just completed a study on this. An estimate for the second figure was obtained in the following manner.

Inquiries indicated that sales followed a seasonal pattern of three months at peak, six months at an average level and three months at a low. An analysis of sales figures gave the ratios of the average and low period sales in the peak period as 70 per cent and 50 per cent respectively. If these figures are multiplied and added, a figure of 8·7 is found. Thus

$$1\cdot00 \times 3 + 0\cdot70 \times 6 + 0\cdot50 \times 3 = 8\cdot7.$$

Hence an estimate of the maximum amount of goods in a depot at any time can be found by dividing the annual throughput of each depot by 8·7. The figures thus obtained can be compared with the depot capacity. Capacity problems are likely to occur just prior to the peak period.

The Model and the Computation Method
The total cost must clearly account for all the different items of cost which have been described earlier. The computation method must be able to determine the optimum number and location of depots to minimize the total cost function, which can be expressed mathematically as

$$C = \sum_{i=1}^{m}\left\{F_i\delta_i + 2\beta\left(\sum_{k=1}^{p} d_{ik}w_{ik}f_{ik}\right) + \sum_{=1}^{n}\alpha\lambda_{ij}d_{ij}v_{ij}\delta_{ij} + \frac{d_{ij}R\mu_j}{80s}\right\} \tag{10–10}$$

where m = total number of depots ($i = 1, 2, \ldots m$)

n = total number of customers ($j = 1, 2, \ldots n$)

p = total number of factories ($k = 1, 2, \ldots p$)

F_i = inventory and running costs of depot i as expressed in equation (10–9)

δ_i = 1 if depot i is open; otherwise $\delta_i = 0$

β = cost of trunking per mile.

d_{ik} = distance from factory to depot i

$\quad = 1\cdot2\sqrt{(x_i - x_k)^2 + (y_i - y_k)^2}$

237

w_{ik} = total amount trunked from k to i

f_{ik} = frequency of visit of trunk vehicles to depot i from factory k

$$= \frac{w_{ik}}{c_t}$$

where c_t = capacity of trunking vehicle in 'standard' products

α = cost of local delivery per mile

λ_{ij} = 1 for $d_{ij} \leq 80$ miles

$\quad = \frac{2}{3}$ for $d_{ij} > 80$ miles

d_{ij} = distance from depot i to customer j calculated as for d_{ik}

v_j = frequency of visit to customer

$$= \max\left(52, \frac{w_j}{c_d}\right)$$

where w_j = annual demand of customer j

c_d = capacity of local delivery vehicle in 'standard' products

δ_{ij} = 1 if customer j is served by depot i; otherwise $\delta_{ij} = 0$

R = subsistence allowance for overnight stay

μ_j = v_j if $d_{ij} > 80$: otherwise $\mu_j = 0$

s = average number of drops per trip with overnight stops.

The method used in this case study was the infinite set approach described by Eilon and Watson-Gandy.[6] In particular their Model 3, which caters for trunking costs linear with distance, was adapted to incorporate the particular characteristics of the model as expressed in equation (10–10). Although warehousing costs are now included in this formulation, the drop routine (this removes depots from the solution starting with the smallest, if it is worthwhile) described by Eilon and Watson-Gandy in their Model 5 was not used because it was felt that as the depots were held fixed in location initially, removing the smallest depot might not achieve the best solution. Further, the depots were initially all very much the same size.

Results

Once the model of the system was developed, a programme was written to simulate the system on the computer. A series of runs were carried out to test how well the model represented the real world system. It was found in this case that only a few minor modifications were required and that the model represented the system remarkably accurately.

A large number of runs were carried out using the programme to study the effects of changes on the system. The first of these was a 'base line' run with the system operating as it was, that is with all four depots fixed in location and with the customers allocated as they were prior to the study. Even this initial run gave some interesting information, namely that there were rather surprisingly some capacity problems at the Bristol depot. However, on making inquiries it was found that the company had been operating a further depot at Cardiff. This depot was in the process of being disposed of, but in the meantime some products were being stored there.

The other runs experimented with possible changes in the system. Different combinations were tried with depots both fixed and allowed to move to their optimum locations. Some of the most interesting results are presented in Table 10·I. This shows for each combination of depots the percentage savings that could be achieved.

Table 10·I

SHOWING THE RESULTS OF THE COMPUTER MODEL

Depot combination	% savings over current system	
	Depots fixed in location	Depots at optimum location
London, Bristol, Birmingham, Manchester (the 'base line')	—	2·13
London, Bristol, Manchester	4·16	6·30
London, Manchester	18·94	20·73
London, Bristol, Manchester, Glasgow*	1·06	3·37
London, Manchester, Glasgow*	7·47	15·67

* For the projected depot in Scotland, a point in Glasgow was selected.

These results were quite surprising to the management of the company. They had anticipated the closing of the Birmingham depot and the study and been carried out in part to confirm or disprove this suggestion. However, if one looks again at the customer configurations shown in Figure 10·7, the concentrations of demand are clearly in London, and in the Liverpool-Manchester-Leeds belt. Hence the conclusion that only two depots are needed is quite reasonable.

A further series of runs were carried out to test the sensitivity of the system to external changes, for example increases in the costs of transportation and increases in demand. The system was found to be very robust and even increases of up to 20 per cent in demand, both as a trend over all existing customers, and also by increasing the number of customers in areas where the company thought it might expand, did not change the location or the number of depots giving the minimum cost. However, in the last case, i.e. with 20 per cent increase in demand, the solutions were very close to each other in cost.

Conclusions

The recommendations to the company were that only two depots should be used for the delivery of goods, one at London, the other at Manchester. The depot at Manchester was considered to have sufficient capacity to cope with the increased throughput, but a very much larger depot was required in London. The Manchester depot was also reasonably close to its optimum location; the optimum location for the London depot was in south-west London, fairly close to Surbiton. If no suitable site is available, then another location may be sought, but it should be on the west of London.

The company accepted these proposals but decided, for reasons of service to their customers, to adopt a three depot system with depots in London, Manchester and Glasgow. This solution gives a considerable saving over the then existing system and also gives increased flexibility for expansion.

239

References

(1) R. H. Ballou, 'Dynamic Warehouse Location Analysis', *Journal of Marketing Research*, Vol. 5, August 1968, pp. 271–6.

(2) R. M. Burstall, R. A. Leaver, and J. E. Sussams, 'Evaluation of Transport Costs for Alternative Factory Sites', *Operational Research Quarterly*, Vol. 13, No. 4, December 1962, pp. 345–54.

(3) J. K. Drysdale and P. J. Sandiford, 'Heuristic Warehouse Location—A Case History Using a New Method', *Journal of the Canadian Operations Research Society*, Vol. 7, No. 1, March 1969, pp. 45–61.

(4) Economic Development Committee for the Distributive Trades, 'Planning Warehouse Locations', National Economic Development Office, Millbank, London, September 1967.

(5) M. A. Efroymson and T. L. Ray, 'A Branch-Bound Algorithm for Plant Location', *Operations Research*, Vol. 14, No. 3, May–June 1966, pp. 361–8.

(6) S. Eilon and C. D. T. Watson-Gandy, 'Models for Determining Depot Location', Report No. 69/4, Management Engineering Section, Imperial College, London, January 1969.

(7) S. Eilon and N. Christofides, 'Expected Distances in Distribution Problems', *Operational Research Quarterly*, Vol. 20, No. 4, December 1969.

(8) E. Feldman, F. A. Lehrer and T. L. Ray, 'Warehouse Location under Continuous Economies of Scale', *Management Science*, Vol. 12, No. 9, May 1966, pp. 670–84.

(9) P. Gray, 'Mixed Integer Programming Algorithms for Site Selection and Other Fixed Charge Problems Having Capacity Constraints', *Technical Report No. 6*, Department of Operations Research, Stanford University, Stanford, California, November 1967.

(10) Highway Statistics 1965, London, HMSO, 1966.

(11) K. B. Keefer, 'Easy Way to Determine the Centre of Distribution', *Food Industries*, Vol. 6, October 1934, pp. 450–1.

(12) M. Klein and R. R. Klimpel, 'Application of Linearly Constrained Non-Linear Optimisation to Plant Location and Sizing', *Journal of Industrial Engineering* (U.S.), Vol. 18, No. 1, January 1967.

(13) A. A. Kuehn and M. J. Hamburger, 'A Heuristic Program for Locating Warehouses', *Management Science*, Vol. 9, No. 4, July 1963, pp. 643–66.

(14) E. G. Lösch, 'Long Range Planning of the Distribution System of a Brewery', Paper 3, Session 12, IFORS Conference, Venice, June 1969.

(15) R. P. Neuschel, 'Physical Distribution—Forgotten Frontier', *Harvard Business Review*, Vol. 45, No. 2, March–April 1967, pp. 125–34.

(16) J. B. Rosen, 'The Gradient Projection Method for Non-Linear Programming—Part 1, Linear Constraints', *Journal of the Society of Industrial and Applied Mathematics*, Vol. 8, No. 1, 1960.

(17) A. Shea, 'Determination of the Optimal Location of Depots', Distributive Systems Sessions, Proceedings 4th International Conference on Operations Research, Boston, 1966.

(18) H. N. Shycon and R. B. Maffei, 'Simulation—Tool for Better Distribution', *Harvard Business Review*, Vol. 36, No. 8, November–December 1960, pp. 65–75.

(19) J. E. Sussams, 'Raising Productivity in Distribution', *Management Decision*, Vol. 1, No. 3, Autumn 1967, pp. 36–9.

(20) J. E. Sussams, 'Some Problems Associated with the Distribution of Consumer Products', *Operational Reaserch Quarterly*, Vol. 19, No. 2, June 1968, pp. 161–74.

(21) C. D. T. Watson-Gandy, 'The Planning and Development of Warehousing Policies', *Freight Management*, Vol. 3, No. 6, June 1969, pp. 37–41.

(22) C. D. T. Watson-Gandy and N. Christofides, 'The Distribution of Consumer Durables —A Case Study in Warehouse Location', Report No. 69/14, Management Engineering Section, Imperial College, London, December 1969.

(23) M. H. J. Webb, 'Cost Functions in the Location of Depots for Multiple-delivery Journeys', *Operational Research Quarterly*, Vol. 19, No. 3, September 1968, pp. 311–20.

(24) A. Weber, 'Über den Standort der Industrien', Tubingen, 1909, translated as 'Alfred Weber's Theory of the Location of Industries', by C. J. Friedrich, Chicago, 1929.

(25) R. C. Vergin and J. B. Rogers, 'An Algorithm and Computational Procedure for Locating Economic Facilities', *Management Science*, Vol. 13, No. 6, February 1967, pp. B-240–B-254.

Chapter C.11

WAREHOUSE MANAGEMENT

by B. McKibbin

THE ROLE OF WAREHOUSING

In the field of warehousing, operational performance and cost control should be based on careful management and a company's attitude towards its own physical distribution policy. Unfortunately, this is sometimes regarded as a discrete activity within the general framework of the organizational structure of the company, and various functional areas interpret policy not on the practicalities of the situation, but rather on the basis of their responsibilities and authority. Good performance requires the integration of operational and inventory management, storage techniques and other processing.

During the last ten years, the image of the warehouse function has altered considerably and many organizations are now operating from well designed, single-storey warehouses. Such developments provide opportunity for operational efficiency at levels of economy hitherto unobtainable. Unfortunately, further opportunities for reduction in costs and capital expenditure are being overlooked due to a management problem of being unable to focus proper attention on those aspects which are closely related to physical movement and storage.

The significance of operational cost cannot be overlooked, whatever the system or product being handled. The relationship of warehousing costs to the sales of the value of the product will indicate the degree of importance sometimes overlooked because of the difficulty of identifying and isolating costs which are attributed to the materials handling operation. An analysis of total distribution costs was published in the *Journal of Industrial Engineering* (of the United States). The percentages recorded are compared with data applying to the United Kingdom and published by the *Financial Times*.

In manufacturing, where the direct cost of materials can vary from 30 to 75 per cent of the sales price, warehousing cost elements may have a different significance to those which apply to food distribution. As an example, the costs at which goods are purchased in this section can vary from 75 to 95 per cent of the eventual selling price. Margins will, therefore, play a significant part in assessing the importance attached to individual warehousing operations.

Table 11·II illustrates the constituent cost elements for a food warehousing operation. With gross profit margins running at 7 per cent, more than half

Table 11·I

Functional activity	United States % of sales	United Kingdom % of sales
Administration	2·4	2·0
Transport		
Inwards	2·1	1·5
Despatch	4·3	4·0
	— 6·4	— 5·5
Receiving and shipping	1·7	0·5
Product packaging	2·6	2·0
Warehousing		
At production source	2·1	1·0
Sub-depots	1·6	1·5
	— 3·7	— 2·5
Inventory costs		
Interest	2·2	2·0
Taxes, insurance, obsolescence	1·6	1·0
	— 3·8	— 3·0
Order processing	1·2	0·5
	21·8	16·0

Source : International Commercial Techniques, usa and *Financial Times* Limited.

the total operational expense is concerned with the warehousing operation and related administration and company overheads.

The concept of total distribution cost, of which warehousing is one of the constituent elements, is normally concerned with the overall cost of moving goods from raw materials source, through production, to the ultimate consumer. In those companies able to control or direct appropriate phases of the material movement, various alternative strategies may be applied. In addition to the permutations and combinations of the movement plan are added the complications of whether a product can be manufactured at more than one source with varying production, transport and storage costs. The ultimate in planning must produce a minimum cost plan.

A comparison of costs for two different distribution plans is shown in *Table* 11·III.

In Table 11·III only three elements—manufacturing, transport and ware-housing—have been taken into consideration. Obviously other factors will influence total distribution costs, for example, plant capacity, quality and levels of service. From the analysis, system 'A' is £5 a ton cheaper than 'B'. The levels of service provided by a field warehouse will obviously be better

Table 11·II

Cost centre	% Sales value
Building occupancy	0·92
Warehouse handling	1·26
Administration	0·17
Company overheads	1·40
Σ	3·75%

Table 11·III

COST COMPARISON FOR DIFFERENT DISTRIBUTION SYSTEMS   £ per ton

Manufacturing or distribution activity	System 'A'	System 'B'	*Difference*
1. Raw material supply	20	18	2
2. Transport costs from raw material to first process	5	6	(1)
3. First process	15	15	—
4. Transport costs from first to second process	3	7	(4)
5. Second process	7	6	1
6. Transport costs from second process to final process	8	4	4
7. Final process	20	20	—
8. Transport costs from final process to consumer	12	—	12
9. Transport costs from final process to field warehouse	—	6	(6)
10. Field warehouse operating costs	—	5	(5)
11. Retail distribution costs from field warehouse to consumer	—	8	(8)
Totals :	£90	£95	£(5)

than the bulk system. The development of a warehousing system can reduce the total distribution costs, normally associated with the movement of small customer orders from factories direct to the consumer. This is not an unusual situation, for in certain cases the most economical way would be to ship in full vehicle loads from the supply point to a regional warehouse.

Whatever the ultimate plan, management must have a proper appreciation of total distribution. The warehouse or distribution manager should be able to recognize the nature of the individual elements normally associated with distribution, and the manner in which these costs are likely to vary when changes occur. This knowledge of cost variation provides a satisfactory framework encompassing the various alternative distribution policies.

Naturally, different warehousing opportunities exist and the warehouse manager must, therefore, identify whether the ultimate form of warehousing will be one provided by a public company or operated by his own organization. Each has merit depending on the objectives of the warehouse plan and the finance and investment policy of the company.

A public warehouse provides services for a number of companies, all of which have different warehousing requirements. It receives stores, despatches, and performs other related services which are provided at rates intended to result in a profit to the warehousing company. Public warehouses fall into a number of different categories, as:

1. Commodity Warehouses—specializing in the storage and handling of specific commodities; wool, cotton or tobacco
2. Bulk Storage Warehouses—providing storage for chemicals and oils
3. Cold Storage Warehouses—providing controlled low temperature storage locations
4. General Merchandise Warehouses—storing a large variety of materials and finished goods

245

To assess the true viability of using a public warehouse, management needs to consider those functions it may be called upon to perform. The complexities of modern distribution will involve not only normal receiving, storage and despatch activity but additional facilities for transit storage and repackaging. At least one distribution network in the UK now provides a sophisticated information system to users, through the use of a computer information system.

It is important to evaluate the advantages and disadvantages of using a public warehousing system over the alternative of operating central (or a series of) regional depots.

Public Warehouse Advantages

1. Minimum investment risk
2. Lower costs for low volume
3. Provision of a warehouse service on an experimental basis
4. Provision of additional or buffer storage to augment existing company systems.

Company Controlled Warehouse

1. Better control
2. Lower costs (though this would have to be proved)
3. Product and market information feed back
4. Warehouse used as regional distribution centre
5. Warehouse as a base for retail delivery and trunk vehicle operations.

Warehousing, by its very nature, adds to the overall cost of materials movement, though it must obviously be employed to meet levels of service, or, by geographical location, reduce total production and transportation costs. The effect of increased customer service provided by the warehouse may improve the turnover to such an extent as to counteract the direct and indirect costs of the additional requirements. A problem in organizations which are sales orientated is the provision of more than the economic number of warehouses in order to provide an equitable level of service within the operational budgets stipulated by distribution management. Warehouse services of this nature will only be warranted when the increased volume in sales offsets the increased distribution costs.

A secondary consideration and a problem not unknown to warehouse management is the one of providing more warehouse space than is essential to hold the planned inventory. The cost of space is normally a fixed and recurring cost, whether it is used or not. Finally, sales motivated warehouses are likely to hold a higher level of stock in order to reduce the problem of non-availability of stock and to improve levels of service.

In the role of warehousing, provided management is aware of these problems and can cope with the demands of the marketing system, there are a number of ways in which a properly designed and operated warehousing system can generate additional sales volume:

1. Minimize out-of-stock occurrences
2. Reduced retail customer inventory requirement
3. Strengthen customer/supplier relationships
4. Increase delivery discount
5. Provide extended market coverage.

WAREHOUSE ORGANIZATION

The principal elements of modern warehouses take account of:

1. Emphasis on the 'Turnover Phases of Operation'
2. The use of the one storey warehouse buildings
3. The use of assembly line picking techniques, supplemented by integrated order selection administration
4. The use of pallets, storage racks and effective mechanical handling operations.

Warehousing philosophy stresses the systematic and orderly movement of goods through the system. Economic levels of expense must be based on the use of the most suitable methods of handling merchandise by:

(a) fewest handlings
(b) proper machine methods
(c) speed of order selection.

The nature of the company's business is the most important factor influencing the organization of the warehouse. A public warehousing company will differ from one engaged in the distribution of consumer durables. The internal organization of a warehouse depends on the specific function which it has been designed to perform. From a geographical standpoint, it may have to encompass a broad scope of activity generally associated with the concept of normal warehousing. What these activities are will be directly related to the type of company business, departmental organization and the management capability of the group as a whole. It is important that within the framework of the organization charts for the company, one individual is made responsible for the total distribution role.

Problems common to most warehousing situations can be regarded as:

1. The nature of the distribution system
2. Building, design and layout
3. Utilization of labour and methods of handling
4. Administration procedures, planning and stock control.

One difficulty encountered is the physical limitations set by existing buildings. A system may be defined from an organizational study of the warehouse requirement and a number of factors will have been taken into account to obtain an optimum solution. But compromise may be needed, for there are always a number of conflicting interests to be balanced. If the storage activity

247

is unproductive and, like handling, only adds cost to the commodity, then a warehouse should be considered as a planned space for the accommodation and handling of materials and goods.

The reasons for warehousing are:

1. To allow for the unbalanced flow of materials from production or external sources
2. To provide adequate buffer facilities against production failures
3. To absorb standard cost production runs
4. To hold buffer stock against seasonal, peak or unknown sales demand
5. To provide physical resources to support economic order quantity buying.

In the economics of warehousing, the lowest operating results will be achieved by the best combination of the following resources:

—finance—operating costs and capital invested
—mechanical handling equipment
—labour utilization
—space utilization.

The provision of storage and handling equipment can usually be justified when, as a result, the combined facility caters for a greater volume of throughput at a total cost lower than would have been the case if the expenditure had not been incurred.

Table 11·IV

UNIT COSTS FOR HANDLING—DIRECT LABOUR

Warehouse division	Direct labour number	Number of units handled per week	Number of hours worked per week	Units handled per hour	Estimated £ cost per hour	£ cost per unit handled
A						
1969	5	2,180	250	8·73	0·50	0·058
1970	4	2,600	160	16·20	0·53	0·033
1973	5	4,000	200	20·00	0·55	0·028
B						
1969	12	4,350	510	8·57	0·45	0·052
1970	11	4,700	440	10·70	0·47	0·043
1973	16	5,900	650	9·10	0·49	0·048
Combined A and B						
1969	17	6,530	760	8·60	0·47	0·055
1970	15	7,300	600	12·20	0·50	0·041
1973	21	9,900	850	11·70	0·52	0·044

Tables 11·IV and 11·V and Figure 11·1 set out the stages for a cost appreciation of a new warehouse outlay and improved methods of handling. The study undertaken in 1969 reviewed the expected warehouse activity from

248

1970 to 1973 and onwards. Expenditure was allocated to the three groups below for the periods in question:

—fixed or overhead
—indirect or semi-variable
—direct or variable.

Table 11·IV records the anticipated direct labour requirements, unit volume and cost per unit handled. Table 11·V summarizes total budget expenditure from which it will be noted that the principal variance in fixed costs arises from a larger investment in handling equipment and certain alterations to the warehouse building.

Table 11·V

WAREHOUSE COSTS

Warehouse costs	1970 £	1973 £
Building insurance	500	500
Rent	2,200	2,200
Heating	2,100	2,100
Electricity	300	350
Water	35	35
Cleaning	550	1,100
Building maintenance	950	950
Depreciation—equipment	4,100	5,900
Depreciation—building	3,800	4,000
Other costs	3,000	3,000
	17,535	20,135
Fixed costs per week	340	410
Indirect costs per week:		
(i) Manager	50	56
(ii) Supervisor	40	44
(iii) Chargehand	40	66
(iv) Administration	40	44
Total fixed and indirect costs, per week	510	620
Variable costs Unit volume × average unit cost	7,300 @ 0·041	9,900 @ 0·044

An important aspect of a warehouse development is concerned with the phasing of the move to new premises. Break-even charts (Figures 11·1 and 11·2) can be used to predict improvement in operating costs for varying levels of investment and unit movement. Increased activity normally corresponds to a time scale. In the example, fixed costs for the present system, if handling in a number of old warehouse premises, are not significantly different to the minimum investment in the first phase of the new warehouse. However, handling costs are considerably better, resulting in an overall improvement of £5200 per annum.

249

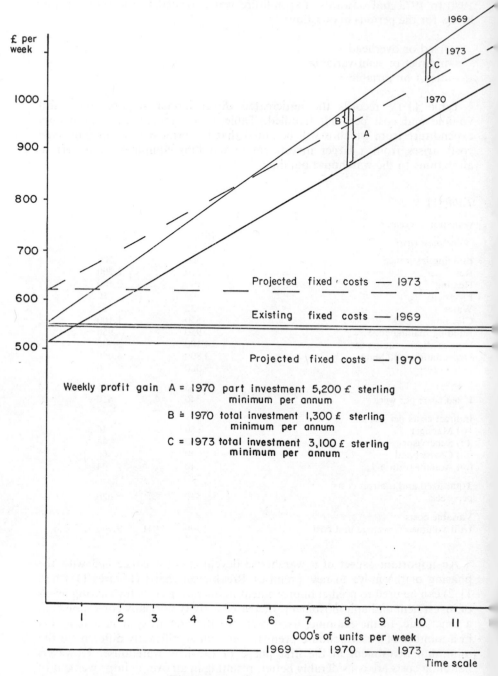

Figure 11·1   Break-even Charts

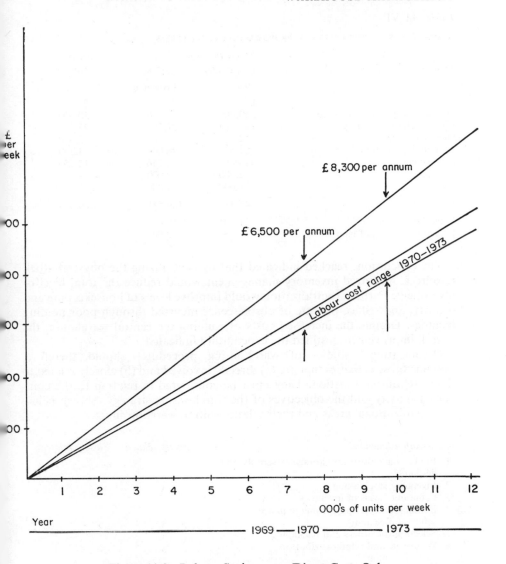

Figure 11·2   Labour Savings—on Direct Costs Only

Another way to quantify optimum utilization of the resources mentioned can be demonstrated by a study recently undertaken to determine whether a £200,000 investment in a new warehouse could be justified. It was decided to analyse the problem in the first instance by defining the constituent cost elements in the holding of the inventory. Annual costs were extracted for the current position and estimated for the future. The total costs, expressed as a percentage of the total inventory value, are known as Annual Inventory Holding Costs, or the K Factor.

Table 11·VI

SUMMARY OF K FACTOR COSTS AND PROPOSED INVENTORY LEVELS

Element of K factor		Stock Investment		Savings
		£1,147,859	£917,859	20%
		1970	Projected	—
		£	£	£
Obsolescence and depreciation		30,000	10,000	20,000
Finance charges @ 10%		114,785	91,785	23,000
Ordering costs		12,000	9,000	3,000
Warehouse handling		81,590	48,000	33,590
Storage costs		(2,000)	12,756	−12,756
Insurance		2,000	2,000	—
Pilferage		7,000	7,000	—
K factor	Σ	247,375	180,541	66,834
K factor	%	21·60%	19·60%	
K factor % of gain			2·00%	

The conclusions reached indicated that by centralizing the physical stock resources, improved inventory management would reduce the total level of investment. Further, centralization would improve levels of housekeeping and security, and reduce the rate of obsolescence incurred through poor holding facilities. Despite the increased costs of running the central warehouse, the overall improvement justified the expenditure indicated.

Organizational studies of warehousing procedures should, therefore, examine those activities that are (a) directly involved and (b) closely related to the warehousing function. They must be considered in relation to the company's activity and the objectives of the warehousing strategy. Shown below are organizational areas and their relationship to warehousing:

Organization functions	*Directly related*	*Closely related*
1. Intake, replenishment, storage, assembly and despatch	√	
2. Inventory stocktaking	√	
3. Economic levels of inventory	√	
4. Building and equipment maintenance, safety and cleaning	√	
5. Selecting for orders and packaging	√	
6. Wholesale and retail distribution	√	
7. Load planning		√
8. Statistical records and management accounting		√
9. Production control and sales activity		√
10. Quality control		√

An effective warehouse stems from good internal organization. Elements essential to warehouse administration and clerical functions are:

(a) Proper inter-relationship of authority with responsibility

(b) Administrative and clerical activities should be coordinated according to function, such as planning, filing, order taking

(c) Through properly constructed training programmes, warehouse management should ensure the correct underpinning of all activities

(d) Correct procedures to maintain effective, physical inventory accountability.

Utilization of Labour

Direct labour costs are usually the largest single item of expenditure associated with handling and storage. The development of an organizational structure for labour control, divided into clearly defined areas of activity, provides the data base for the development of handling cost standards. The Table 11·VII lists activities by defining each job area and allocating a reference number. This can form the basis for departmental labour control within the warehouse and the further development of time and expenditure analysis within each of the related sections.

Table 11·VII

Warehouse activity reference no.	Warehouse activity	Description
H.1	Receiving	Checking, inspecting and signing for all merchandise received
H.2	Road intake/ unloading	To include all activity connected with the discharge of vehicle loads and stacking in warehouse pallets
H.3	Rail intake/ unloading	All work connected with the discharge of rail vehicles and stacking merchandise on warehouse pallets
H.4	Transportation to storage	Includes removing unit loads from unloading area, and transporting to storage and/or stacking areas
H.5	Re-warehousing and stock rotation	Undertaking work in connection with re-location of pallet units and consolidating broken pallet quantities. Includes normal activity associated with stock rotation. Replenishment of stock to the assembly area
H.6	Order assembly	All activities associated with order assembly from racks or shelves or the movement of full pallet quantities from storage to despatch areas
H.7	Transport to despatch area	Covers the activity of movement of full or part assembled pallets containing orders through to despatch area.
H.8	Checking/despatch	Covers checking and where necessary marking of all containers, pallets or boxes prior to vehicle loading
H.9	Loading/vehicle	Includes all work connected with loading trucks and hand stacking merchandise in delivery container
H.10	Loading/rail	
H.11	Recouping	All work connected with the recouping of damage sustained to merchandise either in transit or in warehouse during course of delivery
H.12	Stock control	Includes all time spent on dealing with stock accountability, and other matters relating to physical stock control
H.13	Miscellaneous warehouse activity	A section to cover details of miscellaneous work undertaken in the warehouse

253

The next table records the distribution of labour in a typical warehousing situation. This distribution will, of course, vary for each warehousing operation, as much is dependent on the type, size and method.

Table 11·VIII

Activity ref. no.	Description of activity	Per cent (%)	
H.1	Intake—check	0·50	
H.2	Unloading road vehicles	8·00	23·50
H.3	Unloading rail wagons	9·00	
H.4	Transporting to storage	6·00	
H.5	Replenishment and stock rotation	2·50	
H.6	Order assembly	25·00	
H.7	Transportation to despatch	5·00	41·00
H.8	Checking despatch	3·50	Despatch
H.9	Loading road vehicles	3·00	
H.10	Loading rail wagons	2·00	
H.11	Recouping, damages, returns and empties	4·50	5·50
H.12	Stock control	1·00	Miscellaneous
H.13	Miscellaneous activity	11·00	11·00
	Contingency allowance for inbalance in work activity and rest allowances	18·50	18·50
		Σ 100%	

WAREHOUSE PLANNING

Planning and layout are essential if good operational results are to be achieved. In essence, layout is the planning and integration of the overall materials movement, designed to achieve the most effective and economical relationship between men, equipment and the use of storage space. The main problem in planning is concerned with the flow of material which must not be allowed to develop into a complex or diverse pattern of activity. There are two basic planning requirements:

1. An efficient plan for the flow of materials will produce the most economical operation
2. The material flow pattern becomes the basis for the correct arrangement of facilities and work area within the warehouse.

Before planning commences, management must decide whether to provide a minimum cost warehousing operation, to the detriment of service, or to establish a minimum cost warehouse whilst maintaining desirable levels of service. In defining the objectives, thought must also be given to providing a better level of service than the competition, without regard to cost. When examining the layout objectives, consideration must also be given to the best utilization of space and to the design and selection of the appropriate materials handling system. The correct identification of these factors will help the planners to decide if the ultimate warehouse should be manual, semi-automated or a fully-automated type. In defining the functional requirements of the project, to include short- and long-term considerations, a decision on the type and form of store or warehouse must be the first priority. Secondly, a decision must be taken on whether the warehouse will handle bulk stocks on an 'in and out' basis, or whether the activity will include an element of pallet break up, assembly and repacking. In the case of an assembly operation, it is important to know whether the items are to remain in original outers or to be broken down into individual packs. This form of operation demands a higher degree of control and security.

Figure 11·3 depicts the basic network for layout planning.

In stores relationship, it would also be necessary to consider the location of fast-movers and special requirements for heavy or bulky items. The space requirement is the allocation of stock to one or a number of different storage modes, determined by synthetic projection of the existing inventory. Ancillary considerations would consider optimum aisle widths, positions of columns and the overall shape of the warehouse, governed by the availability of land and road accesses.

When the space requirement is being analysed, various types of storage modes which might be applicable should be viewed:

1. *Random Store*

   This system allows for any line item to be placed in any vacant location. Obviously it provides for greater flexibility in the storage of goods and it is usually possible to obtain a high degree of cubic capacity utilization. However, a rigid control must be maintained on line item location in the system. Computers, a visi-post or bin card control will facilitate the inward and outward movement of stock and its location. This form of storage favours the bulk retention of a large number of line items with relatively low number of pallets per line item.

2. *Fixed Location System*

   This system provides a permanent place in the warehouse of a pre-determined capacity for each line item. A fixed location system must be predetermined from the cubic capacity required to hold the given amount of stock. Locations can be placed at random or, preferably, in sequence of the stock reference number, alphabetical order or a predetermined generic grouping. The main disadvantage in this system is that if the turnover of stock falls below the anticipated demand, the predetermined location may not be capable of accepting the total amount of stock coming forward. This would inevitably involve a second warehousing operation by placing inbalances in a buffer or reserve location system.

3. *Zonal Storage*

   Zonal storage is the predetermined allocation of merchandise or classes of material to a specific zone of the warehouse. Within each zone, goods could then be stored either in fixed location or at random.

255

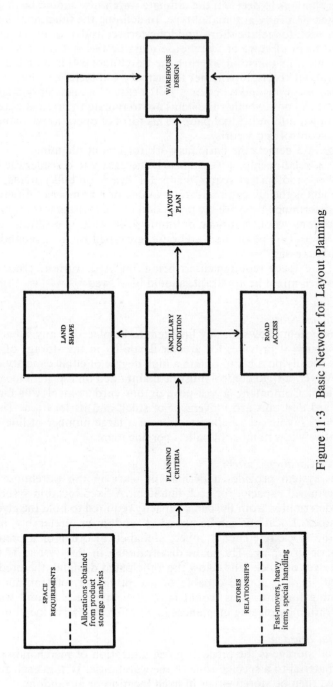

Figure 11·3 Basic Network for Layout Planning

A combination of random and fixed location systems for bulk reserve and assembly picking respectively produces the best compromise solution.

In progressing layout planning, other factors relating to the dimensions of the warehouse, the inventory plan and a summary of sales volume by product, class or line item must be considered. Warehouse throughput should be evaluated in terms of tons, packages, or by sales value. The inventory analysis, or product storage analysis, forms an important part of the study. An accurate determination of the total requirement will produce a statement of overall warehouse size. Analysis would include examination of stock cards or other types of purchase records giving the total movement of individual line items over a sample period of trading and the supporting levels of inventory. This information can be captured in a number of ways. The most suitable one is a predesigned form containing entries relevant to the overall analysis:

(a) Line description
(b) Manufacturing source/supplier
(c) Total unit of sales per annum
(d) Average units of sales per week
(e) Inventory level—average, maximum and minimum (with an indication of seasonal period for fluctuations)
(f) Case dimensions
(g) Cubic feet per case
(h) Weight per outer.

Once data of this nature has been collected, analyses essential to the planning of layout and flow charts can be prepared. A product-quantity histogram (Fig. 11·4) shows the relationship of items or varieties on the horizontal scale, and the quantity on the vertical scale. The quantity can be expressed as units, tons, pallets or the cubic movement per annum. It is

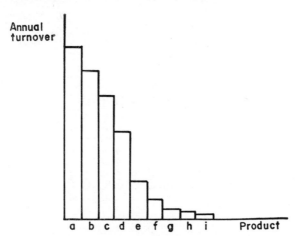

Figure 11·4   Product-Quantity Chart

257

Table 11·IX

MANUFACTURER GROUP ANALYSIS

Section number	Line description manufacturer Group Σ 1–295	Number lines in section	Average units sales per wk	Estimated pallet positions required	% of total rack	Inventory Level			Total cubic space cu. ft.	% Total sales activity	% Total lines nos.	% Cubic storage demand
						Av.	Min.	Max.				
1	Group 1	20	158	3·00	0·61	407	66	739	398	0·43	0·79	0·50
2	Group 2	27	122	2·50	0·51	281	61	491	115	0·33	1·07	0·14
3	Group 3	47	326	4·50	0·89	1,844	399	3,365	1,543	0·89	1·86	1·93
4	Group 4	15	77	4·50	0·43	343	101	576	385	0·21	0·59	0·48
5	Group 5	8	128	2·00	0·45	659	423	952	585	0·35	0·31	0·73
6	Group 6	11	200	2·75	0·56	639	72	1,201	570	0·55	0·44	0·71
7	Group 7	142	3,136	32·00	6·27	4,703	1,183	8,172	4,095	8·61	5·62	5·11
8	Group 8	6	15	0·50	0·10	49	13	82	36	0·04	0·24	0·04
9	Group 9	4	70	1·50	0·22	158	65	248	246	0·19	0·16	0·31
10	Group 10	43	456	7·50	1·47	1,315	247	2,461	1,090	1·25	1·70	1·36

better to express the activity in these units rather than in terms of sales value. This has little meaning in determining the allocation of space. The product quantity chart can be prepared for different manufacturing situations, or for generic groups of product. When one or more line items represent a significant proportion of the total movement, these will obviously warrant special attention in the planning of the stock location positions. In the same way, it would also be important to isolate those items that are large, heavy or difficult to handle—indicating a particular form of mechanical handling equipment. It is obvious that the greater the detail obtained in the inventory analysis, the easier it will be to make a final determination of the layout and location plan. The sum of the individual activities occurring in each line will produce an assessment of the total demand on space and movement within a defined group. It is also wise to examine the location in the warehouse of those groups so defined in relation to their popularity or movement pattern. Conversely, the layout can be based on commodity groups as they occur in the sales order book. Table 11·IX shows the form that a typical summary analysis of individual manufacturer groups would take.

In this analysis, 295 individual manufacturer groups were considered. It was found Group 7 represented 8·61 per cent of the total throughput, but due to the heavy nature of the product and the limited number of lines, only 5 to 5½ per cent of the available space was required for storage. Special consideration would have to be given to such a manufacturer group and to the final location in the warehouse.

This form of product analysis can be extended to provide information on the type of handling unit and ultimately on the method of storage.

Table 11·X shows how the product and unit handling analysis can be combined to obtain a total description of individual line items. In this particular example, all items of the inventory were satisfactorily stored either on wooden pallets or in a specially constructed cage-type pallet. Table 11·XI records the total number of pallet and cage movements, the average weight and the average number of boxes per line item, an essential part of the movement pattern.

When determining the form of storage equipment, a number of alternative strategies might include:

(a) Static racking—fixed or adjustable
                 —drive in
(b) Storage bins —static or mobile
(c) Live storage
(d) Bulk pallet stacking.

Block stacking of pallets, in tiers of four or five in depth, will provide the greatest density per square foot and offer maximum flexibility in warehouse layout. Although this form of storage appears to be beneficial, due to the nature of the goods and the volume of throughput, numerous handlings may be required to maintain adequate stock turn. For example, in an analysis of a warehousing situation, it might be discovered that 10 per cent of line items

259

Table 11·X

PRODUCT AND UNIT HANDLING ANALYSIS

PRODUCT CHARACTERISTICS

Code ref.	Box content	Product description	Boxes per outer	Outer Dimensions L mm	B mm	W mm	Volume per outer litres	Sales per year (est) tons
A 1	2 lb	B 1	1	282	188	75	3·976	90
A 2	1 lb	B 2	3	384	229	72	6·331	115
A 3	1 lb	C 3	3	208	144	118	3·534	17
A 4	4 lb	D 1	1	429	252	74	7·999	—
A 5	2 lb	D 2	1	407	273	69	7·666	23
A 6	1 lb	B 3	3	319	229	103	7·524	12
A 7	1½ lb	D 2	2	302	168	113	5·733	131
A 8	1 lb	C 3	3	194	160	144	4·469	716
					153	181	8·446	973
								183

UNIT HANDLING ANALYSIS

Unit of Movement

Pack wt. lb	Gross wt. outers lb	Strategy P=Pallet C=Cage	Pallet Number outers per pallet	Gross wt. per pallet ton	Volume per pallet m³	Cage Number outers per cage	Gross wt. per cage ton	Volume per cage m³
2	3·08	C				140	0·192	0·556
1	5·00	C				86	0·192	0·544
1	4·74	C				140	0·296	0·494
2	3·08	C				76	0·104	0·582
1	4·74	C				64	0·135	0·481
1½	4·08	C				110	0·200	0·630
1	3·68	P	350	0·575	1·564			
½	7·18	P	168	0·539	1·419			
1	3·64	P	480	0·780	1·622			
½	3·52	P	400	0·629	1·492			
2	3·80	C				60	0·102	0·504
		C				84	0·185	0·585
			270	0·444	1·289			

accounts for 60 per cent of the sales volume. A further 10 per cent of line items accounts for an additional 20 per cent of sales and the remaining 80 per cent of line items the balance. An analysis of this nature, which is really an extension of the product quantity chart, shows how products place widely differing demands on the handling and storage capabilities. The slow moving items, essentially of a static nature, incur substantial costs in storage but only nominal costs in handling. The exact reverse holds for the fast moving line items. As most warehousing situations encompass these extremes storage efficiency must be of a high priority in the case of slow-moving items, and handling efficiency in the case of fast-moving items. To arrive at the right storage mode, these degrees of efficiency must not be overlooked. They can be estimated by considering various strategies. For example, it can be

Table 11·XI

PALLETS

Group Ref.	No. of Lines	No. of pallets/ cages moved per annum	WEIGHTED Outers per pallet/ cages	Gross wt. per pallet cages	Volume per pallet cages	AVERAGES Gross wt. per outer	Outers per gross
				ton	m³	lbs	ton
A	10	6,475	267·86	0·558	1·475	4·67	479·60
B	23	3,053	221·68	0·418	1·555	4·23	529·52
C	—	—	—	—	—	—	—
D	—	—	—	—	—	—	—
E	—	—	—	—	—	—	—
	33	9,528	253·08	0·513	1·500	4·546	492·64
F	19	5,804	142·21	0·180	1·68	2·838	789·20
Σ	52	15,332	211·11	0·387	1·568	4·111	544·854

CAGES

Group Ref.	No. of Lines	No. of pallets/ cages moved per annum	Outers per pallet/ cages	Gross wt. per pallet cages	Volume per pallet cages	Gross wt. per outer	Outers per gross
A	15	6,026	112·52	0·196	0·534	3·913	572·44
B	—	—	—	—	—	—	—
C	4	1,244	138·71	0·142	0·564	2·295	975·75
D	7	11,399	135·06	0·236	0·501	3·91	572·00
E	20	9,951	116·59	0·259	0·530	4·977	450·03
	46	28,620	124·05	0·231	0·521	4·183	535·42
F	—	—	—	—	—	—	—
Σ	46	28,620	124·05	0·231	0·521	4·183	535·42

determined that a line item with four pallets of inventory or less should be placed in static racking. The remaining pallets can be bulk stacked in random pallet quantities, ranging from five to as many as twenty pallet loads per line item. Assuming pallets are capable of being stacked four high, then it is possible to use configurations of three, four or five deep runs for the balance. In the following exercise, designed to determine which configuration is the most suitable, the number of pallets per line item are listed in ascending order, with the calculated square feet for each strategy.

In a purely random condition, it would appear that the five-deep configuration would produce the lowest storage cost. This is based on the assumption that there is only one line item in each of the pallet groups. However, if the inventory analysis shows a preponderance of ten pallet loads per line item, a different strategy must be considered as ten pallet loads per line item or less can be more effectively stored in three deep runs.

In warehouses where a high percentage of storage is in full pallet quantities, recommendation of an incorrect mode for storage can have an adverse effect on storage efficiency, due to the random withdrawal of pallet loads from the bulk storage area. This loss of utilization is sometimes described as 'honeycombing'. Table 11·XIII describes six storage alternatives, showing the space required per pallet for varying pallet quantities for individual lines. In each case, other than for the first condition of static racking, it will be seen that,

261

Table 11·XII

PALLET SIZE 40″ × 48″. GANGWAY WIDTHS 10′ 0″

Number of pallets per line item	*Number of 4-high stacks required*		
	3-deep	*4-deep*	*5-deep*
5	1	1	1
6	1	1	1
7	1	1	1
8	1	1	1
9	1	1	1
10	1	1	1
11	2	1	1
12	2	1	1
13	2	1	1
14	2	1	1
15	2	2	1
16	2	2	1
17	2	2	1
18	2	2	1
19	2	2	2
20	2	2	2
Total number of stacks:	26	22	18
Square feet per pallet run:	70	76	92
Total area square feet:	1,820	1,710	1,650
Average occupancy per pallet square feet:	9·10	8·56	8·25

as the number of pallets is reduced, more square feet of warehouse space are required for each pallet. This increase reflects the relative degrees of inefficiency of the various strategies when the dynamic nature of warehousing is taken into account. A conclusion can only be reached on the form of the storage mode when the dynamic nature of the inventory has been correctly interpreted.

In Table 11·XIV intake of eight pallets is examined under three different types of storage, with an average movement rate of one pallet despatched per day. Each entry under the three strategies represents the total number of square feet required to support the balance of pallets left. In the static rack condition, the requirement decreases at the rate of one pallet or ten square feet per day on the assumption that the space vacated can be made immediately available to another storage requirement. In this analysis, the best solution is probably to use a static rack configuration, four-high, thus showing that lots of eight pallets or less with a regular movement of one pallet per day will cost less than in either of the other two considerations.

Warehouse layout concerns the physical storage of the inventory by one of a number of different methods. It should also meet the requirements of order selection, aisle configuration, intake and despatch areas and their relationships. The planning objective must be to make the warehouse as efficient as possible, to reduce handling costs and to provide for an effective utilization of space. Planning objectives are:

1. Free movement through the order selection area with minimum congestion
2. Shortest overall distance required to pass all items in stock
3. Logical location of items
4. Good lighting and physical facilities to increase accuracy of selection and reduce fatigue
5. Correct and proper use of space
6. Correct selection of materials handling equipment.

Table 11·XIII

	1	2	3	4	5	6
STORAGE: *Mode:*	*Pallet rack*	*Drive-in rack*	*Block*	*Block*	*Block*	*Block*
Height:	4 pallets	4 pallets	4 pallets	4 pallets	4 pallets	4 pallets
Depth:	1 pallet	3 pallets	1 pallet	2 pallets	3 pallets	4 pallets
Storage space plus gangway allowance:	40 sq. ft.	70 sq. ft.	35 sq. ft.	50 sq. ft.	65 sq. ft.	80 sq. ft.
Pallets per load:						
1	10	70·0	35·0	50·0	65·0	80·0
2	10	35·0	17·5	25·0	32·5	40·0
3	10	23·4	11·70	16·6	21·7	26·8
4	10	17·5	8·70	12·5	16·3	20·0
5	10	14·0	14·0	10·0	13·0	16·0
6	10	11·7	11·7	8·3	10·8	13·4
7	10	10·0	10·0	7·10	9·30	11·4
8	10	8·8	8·8	6·20	8·10	10·0
9	10	7·8	11·70	11·10	7·20	8·9
10	10	7·0	10·5	10·0	6·50	8·0
11	10	6·4	9·50	9·10	5·90	7·20
12	10	5·85	8·70	8·30	5·40	6·7
13	10	10·80	10·70	7·70	10·0	6·2
14	10	10·0	10·0	7·10	9·30	5·7
15	10	9·3	9·3	6·70	8·70	5·30
16	10	8·8	8·8	6·20	8·10	5·30

Assembly Area

An assembly line is the physical arrangement of stock planned to facilitate the selection of orders. Under ideal circumstances, it should hold a proportion of the full range of line items in predetermined quantities, considered to be the most suitable for order selection. The assembly line is normally replenished from reserve stocks located in random position above or adjacent to the active picking areas, with bulk stock brought forward from the buffer area. The layout should permit the assembler to collect an order in one complete circuit of the warehouse, and in consequence the sequence of goods on the assembly line must be the same as those in which the goods are called for by the order. This presupposes:

(a) a preprinted order form
(b) a punch card system
(c) computer prepared orders.

263

Table II·XIV

EIGHT PALLETS TO BE STORED

Day	Pallet rack 4 × 1	Block stack 3 deep	Block stack 2 deep
1	80	65	50
2	70	65	50
3	60	65	50
4	50	65	50
5	40	32·5	50
6	30	32·5	50
7	20	32·5	50
8	10	32·5	50
Total	360 sq. ft	390 sq. ft	400 sq. ft

As various assembly line designs require varying space requirements, it is important to have a clear recognition of the policy under which the warehouse is to operate. Loss of storage space may have to be offset against an increase in productivity by the assembly team. However, recent developments in warehouse construction, where height is now a common asset, minimize this particular problem. In theory, there must be a walk of a given minimum distance involved every time an order is selected. Under the ideal circumstances, each order would call for at least one unit from the entire item range. In this case the distance covered by the assembler would be completely effective and kept to a minimum for each line item or picking face visited. The length of this assembly line is governed by the number of items on the inventory list and the pattern of the layout. Table 11·XV shows how the number of lines can be converted to assess different lengths.

In the first condition, it has been assumed that each line item would warrant allocation of 3 feet or a small picking pallet space for each line. Where the warehouse is predominantly a palletized operation, the type of assembly line configuration must be viewed against the costs of replenishment. If all items are palletized on the 36 inch module, the actual replenishment costs will be held to a minimum level. However, many of the 700 or 1400 items in the

Table 11·XV

NO. OF ITEMS ON INVENTORY LIST		*Warehouse with*	
Ref.		1,000 items	2,000 items
1.	Total no. of assembly line items (30% balance to special area)	700	1,400
2.	Linear footage at 36″ per item	2,100′	4,200′
3.	If line is double faced but base	1,050′	2,100′
4.	pallets only *add* 10% clearance factor	1,155′	2,300′
5.	If line is double faced and two tiered on one face only Ret. 3 × 0·66	700′	1,400′
6.	*Add* 10% clearance factor	770′	1,540′
7.	If line is double faced and two tiered on both faces Ret. 3 × 0·5	525′	1,050′
8.	*Add* 10% clearance factor	578′	1,155′

264

assembly line could never warrant a full pallet per line item. By calculating the cubic volume of movement per line item per week, and considering varying replenishment policies, it is possible to reach an optimum point which provides for the minimum length of walk with the minimum cost of replenishment.

While the number of line items in the assembly line must be a basic factor in determining its length, Table 11·XV also shows that the length of the line

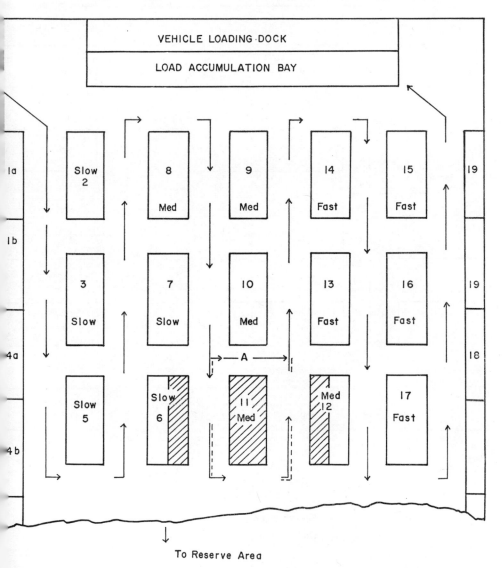

Figure 11·5   Straight line Assembly Pattern. 19 Bays—660′ Assembly Walk

265

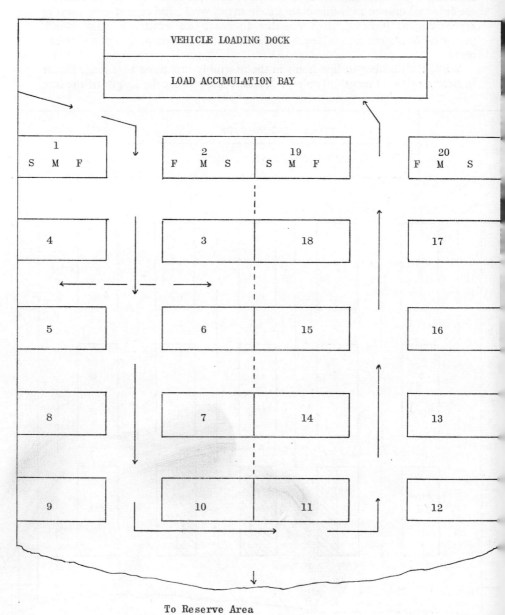

To Reserve Area

Figure 11·6   20 Bays—290′ Assembly Walk

for assembly work can also be affected by the pattern of the line layout, or design. The pattern of line layout falls into one of two principal patterns:

1. Straight line assembly
2. Short line assembly.

In the straight line pattern, the order picker passes all the rack faces on the occasion of each order. Depending on the density of line items called for on each order and their location, it might be possible to use a cross-over aisle to shorten the walk when the assembler knows that there is no item of stock called for in a particular section. Under normal circumstances, where the ratio of lines held to lines called by the order is relatively high, assembly lines designed in this form are longer than they need be. In Figure 11·5 the shaded area accounts for 15 per cent of the assembly storage area but by using the cross-over aisle only 10 per cent of the 600 feet of travel is saved. In Figure 11·6 the short line assembly design produces certain advantages over the previous one, and at the same time can reduce the length of walk per order. The overall length of walk is usually not greater than twice the length plus the width of the area. During the process of order selection, movement may have to be made into the spurs or alleys to select the slower moving items. Each aisle will only contain a limited number of items and so the number of entries will obviously be less than in the previous example. In theory, it is possible to consider locating fast moving goods on the racks adjacent to the gangway, placing the slower moving items deeper in the racking aisles. However, unless the order picking system is controlled by a computer which can convert the sales list to warehouse location, a system of this nature will break down in practice.

In the first of the two designs, the warehouse operator has to accept the fact that he must pass all the stacks on every order picking truck. In the second design, however, the order picker has no alternative than to take the shortest walk. It is obvious that the total distances walked by assemblers will influence the warehouse cost of assembly and the total number of units selected per man hour.

There are certain limitations influencing the order picking processes:

(a) The order picker can only push a certain weight
(b) The selection truck or pallet can only accommodate a certain volume
(c) If the warehouse assembler is provided with an electric truck to ease the problem of one of the above, the limitations of (b) are quite significant, particularly as the size of order increases.

In layout planning, line items should be located to provide reasonable selection loads for the order picker and to minimize the time of unnecessary movement. This is shown in Figure 11·7. The results are based on a study of a warehouse where the distance for a complete circuit of the picking area was 540 ft. When the size of order increases from £60 to £120, two base units were required. In consequence, although the assembly movement remains unaltered for the circuit of the warehouse, a further 480 feet of transportation movement has to be added.

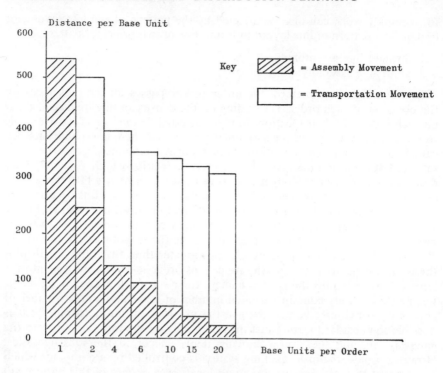

No. o, base units per order	Foot movement per base unit on assembly	Foot movement per order		Total Movement per order	£ Estimated order value
		Assembly	Transportation		
1	540	540	—	540	60
2	270	540	480	1,020	120
4	135	540	1,060	1,600	240
6	90	540	1,620	2,160	360
10	54	540	2,860	3,400	600
15	36	540	4,340	4,880	900
20	27	540	5,870	6,410	1,200

Figure 11·7   Assembly/Transportation Comparison Chart

Any step in planning which reduces or eliminates ineffective activity during assembly is well warranted. Certain guiding principles can be applied to obtain maximum economy and speed in order selection:

1. The assembly line should contain all items of the regular sales list of steady demand, but need not carry everything that the customer orders.
2. Relatively heavy goods should be placed at the end of the assembly line to eliminate long hauls of large accumulative tonnage

268

3. Heavy goods of low velocity should not be placed on the line but held in locations immediately accessible for selection.
4. Heavy goods of high velocity should be kept in the assembly area at the end of an assembly line and adjacent to the load accumulation bay
5. Unit quantities (a split of a full case of regular items sold in less than full case quantities) should be kept on the regular assembly line or in a special shelf area.

Order Analysis

Maximum efficiency in order assembly is obtained by selecting the correct type of handling equipment. This may be a simple pallet with a standard pallet truck, or a highly sophisticated system of selection involving data processing controls and automatic discharge.

The development of the correct method of selection will depend on analysis of the order characteristics to define the size and fluctuations in despatch. The table below details the form of analysis to be considered. In studies of this nature, a sample should be taken for a period of up to one year, on the following:

1. Average number of line items per order
2. Average number of units per item
3. Average number of orders per day
4. Average number of units per order
5. Average number of orders per journey
6. Cubic analysis of items, orders and journeys
7. Weight analysis of items, orders and journeys
8. Frequency distribution analysis of items
9. Methods of delivery.

A typical order might be defined as:

1. 3.5 line items per order
2. 8.6 units per order
3. 2·50 units per line item.

The ratio or relationship between the number of picking faces involved and the number of units selected should be identified. A large proportion of selection cost is related to the movement from one picking face to another. As the number of units selected for each line increases, higher picking rates will be achieved. A further extension of the analysis would take the volumetric and weight factors into account, and this can help define the nature of the order related to the form of order picking unit.

In the following example, a standard pallet box type unit was chosen. This data forms a basis for calculating the man hour requirements in the assembly and loading operation:

1. 1000 units selected per day
2. 400 line items per day

3. 40 pallets handled per day
4. 10 lines items per pallet
5. 25 cases per pallet
6. 25 cu. feet per pallet (@ 1 cubic foot per unit)
7. 450 lb. per pallet (@ 18 lb. per unit).

Work Study Application

Mechanization alone will never solve all handling problems, though certain types of equipment are essential to modern warehousing. It is too easy to formulate a handling policy on the maxim that efficiency increases in relation to the degree of mechanization. It must be accepted that, whilst a fork lift truck is more effective than man power in certain types of operations, it would not necessarily follow that unilateral use of such equipment would be correct when substituted for labour whenever there was a reasonable opportunity. The development of work study standards will facilitate the preparation of synthetic time study analyses for warehouse operations. Through correct identification of elements and associated time standards, management is given an opportunity to consider warehouse efficiency and the development of standards for future equipment purchases. In assembly operations, normal work study procedures will define the methods, allocated between standard and occasional elements. The following example, Table 11·XVI, shows the operation elements associated with conventional order picking operations for a food warehouse. Article selection and transportation are the two most important elements. These should always be identified separately.

Table 11·XVI

EXAMPLE OF WORK SPECIFICATION SHEET AND WORK STANDARDS

Ref.	*Element description*	*Basic minutes per average order 30 units*
	Standard elements	
1.	Select order from control point	0·018
2.	Move to and select empty pallet	0·006
3.	Examine order sheet and move to 1st assembly position	0·019
4.	Read order sheet—move to fixture, select item code box and mark order sheet	0·237
5.	Move pallet truck to next assembly position	0·202
6.	Return full pallet to loading bay	0·106
	Sub total:	0·588
	Occasional elements	
1.	Procure special box of high value items	0·006
2.	Pack high value items into special box	0·008
3.	Query 'out of stock' position	0·009
4.	Request stock replenishment	0·005
5.	Correct assembly error	—
6.	Collect send pallet for completion of order	0·015
	Sub total:	0·043
	Total basic minutes:	0·631

These standards consider the effect of time and cost relationships, but they do not take into account the additional oncost for the type of equipment involved. In this particular study, ordinary hand pallet trucks were used. However, it would also be possible to evaluate an alternative method by applying the same element description and studying the operation with an operator using an electric truck. The order characteristic study would define the number of full pallet loads handled on an 'in' and 'out' basis. Here hand or electric pallet equipment would be no substitute for fork lift trucks.

Effect of Variable Order Size on Order Picking Rates

The basic elements of order assembly have been defined. As each individual order picking operation has a distinctive character closely related to the nature of the product and the size of the warehouse, each operation must be viewed separately. It has already been explained that one of the factors influencing productivity is the order size and the number of line items held on the warehouse floor. The ratio of units to line item visited per order, considered in relation to the total number of picking faces, establishes the ratio of effective to ineffective movement. The element of time to move the picking truck from one location to another becomes more significant than the variable cost of selecting one additional unit at each of the locations visited. Similarly, small orders spread over a large line item inventory will involve the order picker in disproportionate walk to selection time. By isolating the fixed and variable time elements obtained from the work standards, it is possible to predict average units selected per man hour for varying order sizes. Using the standards previously described, Table 11·XVII shows the relationship between fixed and variable time and total time at 100 performance.

Table 11·XVII

Units per order	Fixed basic mins/order	Variable mins/ order (0·484)	Total mins/order	At 100 performance units assembled per man hour
5	2·88	2·42	5·30	56·00
10	2·88	4·84	7·72	77·50
20	2·88	9·68	12·56	95·50
30	2·88	14·50	17·38	103·50
40	2·88	19·30	22·18	108·00
50	2·88	24·20	27·08	111·00
60	2·88	29·00	31·88	113·00
70	2·88	33·90	36·78	114·00
80	2·88	38·70	41·58	115·00
90	2·88	43·50	46·38	116·50

This may be represented more dramatically by the graph, Figure 11·8.

In the smaller order sizes, it may be necessary to consider different methods of selection to reduce the disproportionate amount of ineffective movement.

In line sequence assembly, a summary of units required for a given number of orders in a batch can be extracted line by line.

271

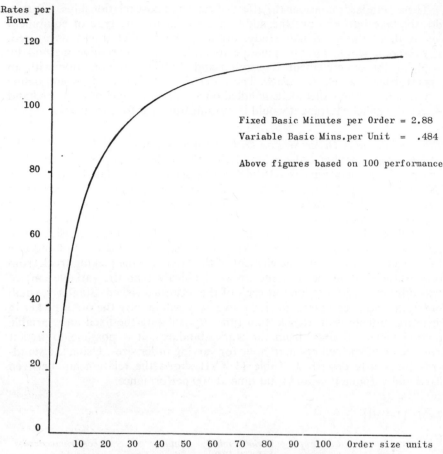

Figure 11·8   Units assembled per man hour. Varying Order Size

The assembler selects the total quantities required for each line item. This eliminates the ineffective and repetitive element of movement. The selection is taken to the loading bay where the items are broken down against the individual orders contained in the original batch summary. A method of this sort has certain disadvantages, for whilst it obviously reduces picking costs, there is an additional sortation activity at the loading bank, and more administration. Finally, no one journey can be completed until the last unit of the last line item has been marshalled to the last order.

The second system, sometimes called order sequence or load summary, is basically the same. A number of orders are batched together and a load summary prepared, which details all the items required in that summary. Quantities per line item are selected normally and brought forward to a bulk assembly area. From this point, normal order picking is undertaken. Where the journey or batches are of a considerable size, much of the inventory can

272

be moved forward from the stock to bulk assembly area by a fork lift truck. This last system can be extended to a bulk assembly operation. In this case, however, there is no need to prepare individual load summaries. Warehouse management, through a knowledge of day-to-day movement, can identify those line items which are the most popular. The bulk assembly is replenished at frequent intervals during the day and records are kept of all movements. Reconciliation of total stock handled is therefore relatively easy. Not all items in the order assembly routine would be handled on this basis and it would be necessary to identify those line items whose volume of movement would justify such operations.

Order Checking

The cost of checking should not exceed the value obtained from the results of checks. Although organizations are dispensing with checking, particularly where their warehouses are serving own outlets, some form of random checking is mandatory to the profitability of the operation. The main points to be considered in determining the need and degree of order checking are:

1. Customers' service factors through lost sales and goodwill
2. The cost of checking
3. The resultant savings through wrong selection or counting
4. The cost of rectification (i.e. additional warehouse time and despatch costs, where they apply)
5. Elimination of damaged goods prior to despatch.

Only a realistic evaluation of costs of checking and a statement of savings can determine correct policy. Four different methods, giving some form of control on all outgoing merchandise, are:

1. A unit count of all cases selected on every order
2. A unit count and 100 per cent item description check
3. A random spot check of item by description
4. A sample item check based on a predetermined arrangement.

Line and order summary assembly patterns also provide for built-in checks. For in both these cases, it is relatively simple to check the total amount of stock assembled in a batch, prior to the commencement of the picking operation.

Warehouse Control Standards and Operational Costs

In common with all other business activities, warehousing is faced with the problem of how to measure and control costs. The preparation of realistic standards is essential to a profitable business. In any event, no one warehouse can be measured in the same terms as could be applied to a similar operation of another company or to other varying conditions. New techniques or concepts obviously require an improved management approach to the methods of control and operation.

273

There are three main areas for cost attention:

1. Reduction of direct costs
2. Reduction of indirect costs
3. Increase of output.

Measurement is essential to identify those areas for cost reduction and to achieve this aim it should be applied to as much of the warehouse system as is considered practicable. Good measurement will highlight those aspects of the system which might otherwise be unobserved. Further, it assists in promoting a better understanding of warehousing problems and consequently creates a positive aid to a more objective approach.

The three principal elements of cost related to all warehousing are:

1. the cost of occupying space
2. the cost of employing labour
3. the cost of operating equipment.

Using these elements as a guide to management accounting, a further division of cost centres, appropriate to the warehousing operation (Table 11·XVIII), describes the way in which this information can be analysed. In this example, expenses are recorded for two warehouses, handling different volumes of carton material.

Following on from standards for the warehouse system, it would be desirable to have a number of simple control reports, analysing the allocation of labour, the total hours of work and a statement of activity associated with the period of analysis.

Basic requirements for the preparation of a warehouse control record would include:

(a) Weekly wage and salary analysis
(b) Labour establishment and returns, with agreed allocation of labour to discrete areas of activity
(c) Return on total hours of work—basic and overtime
(d) Warehouse activity, expressed in units or tons (whatever the basic measurement)
(e) Total deliveries
(f) Total units delivered.

This information would be summarized daily for local management and passed forward to head office on a weekly return. By consultation with accountants, the main areas of cost, either shown in Table 11·XVIII or against the agreed staff allocations, recommended above, would be the development of further financial controls. Management must have a ready means of cost control to identify excess expenditure immediately it occurs. The development of handling costs, expressed in the number of units per man hour or the number of tons per week, forms a simple but effective method of management control.

In Table 11·XVIII the unit of handling was taken as an outer carton. The volume of activity divided into the total cost produces a cost for handling and for individual items.

Table 11·XVIII

	Warehouse A		Warehouse B	
Turnover:	£6·225 m		£2·383 m	
Area:	100,000 sq. ft		51,000 sq. ft	
Cost centres	£	%	£	%
1. *Occupancy*				
Rent	45,300		23,000	
Rates	17,340		6,630	
Building insurance	630		320	
Wages: cleaners and watchmen	4,780		3,140	
Canteen	2,650		1,300	
Building repairs	4,530		2,300	
Light, heat and power	2,830		1,140	
Depreciation—building alterations	8,000		4,000	
Water and drainage	200		100	
	86,260	0·924	41,930	1·173
2. *Handling*				
Staff costs—Management	—		—	
—Supervision	2,630		2,630	
—Chargehands	4,640		4,640	
—Intake labour and checking	6,180		2,060	
—Storage movement	6,180		2,060	
—Stock replenishment	6,180		4,120	
—Assembly	53,560		20,600	
—Load checking	2,060		4,120	
—Loading bay	4,120		—	
—Returns and empties	2,060		—	
—Maintenance	—		—	
Equipment—Mechanical	18,240		9,710	
—Racking	2,170		1,130	
—Pallets	3,050		1,020	
—Containers	6,260		2,600	
—Contingencies	610		300	
	117,940	1·263	54,990	1·538
3. *Office*				
Wages and salaries including handling management	13,670		11,290	
Office equipment	940		500	
Stationery	1,800		900	
	16,410	0·176	12,690	0·355
4. *Overheads*				
(Including Management Recovery Charges)	130,000	1·40	64,000	1·80
Direct handling cost per unit: £–p		£0–1·220		£0–1·21

Cost of Operation

The two graphs, Figures 11·9 and 11·10, record the relative costs of handling and stacking when using different methods and different types of equipment. Fork lift trucks are not economic for long hauls. When loads have to be moved over considerable distances in warehousing, some form of infloor conveyor or tow-tug system might produce a more favourable cost situation.

The fork lift truck should be used to load and unload and locate stock in the storage fixtures and alternative means of moving loads from A to B. In the smaller warehouses where travel distances are relatively short, it is probably better to use a fork lift truck as the means of movement and stacking.

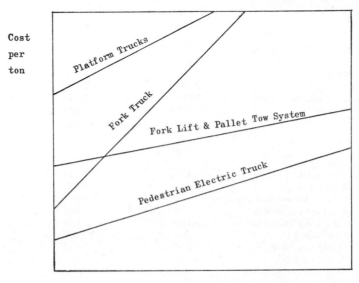

Figure 11·9   Relative Costs of Movement and Stacking

CASE STUDY—AN ANALYSIS OF A HANDLING PROBLEM

In this case study, a warehousing company employed female labour to select and pack small items from an inventory range of 5000 lines. Management were anxious to isolate those activities where immediate improvement could be made to the overall system, resulting in a saving on direct costs. No detailed records of the overall flow pattern existed. It was therefore decided to examine the system from intake to despatch, recording the pattern of movement, handling and inspection in the principal areas of the warehousing activity. In Table 11·XIX, the summary detailed the operation recording the total activity, allocated to the six principal departmental areas. Due to the nature of the warehouse and the positioning of buildings, management were prepared to accept a number of additional handlings to make the best use of the physical facilities. The analysis showed that thirty-two individual handlings occurred when one unit moved through the warehouse. Thought was given to the overall handling problem and the operation was viewed in depth to see what improvements could be made. Each individual area was considered separately, finally being interfaced with the other related sections.

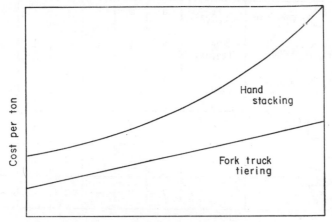

Figure 11·10   As Goods are Stacked Higher

Table 11·XX records the results of a further detailed analysis, based on synthetic work study standards and a reorganization of the system method.

During the course of the studies, it was found that one of the main areas for cost saving surrounded the selection of the small items and their subsequent repacking at packing stations. The current method was described by the following job content:

(a) One girl selected an empty truck from the main truck holding area and, having noted the section number from which goods were to be selected, moved to the first selection point in the relative area

(b) The girl assembler then selected from the stock rack and placed the items picked in a special open container on the hand truck. Each successive section was marked on the order sheet which was a computer print out

(c) The selection operation continued until the hand truck was filled. At this stage it was returned to the main holding area.

The cycle of operation was repeated until the total order for that section had been collected.

(d) The assembled items were then moved to the packing department where the hand trucks were emptied into large open packing benches

(e) After a random check of all items, the cartons were packed with the items selected.

277

Table 11·XIX

OPERATION		TOTAL	I	II	III	IV	V	VI
◯		32	5	4	2	3	7	1
(1) ⬦	Conveyor	11 (2620')	3	2	1	-	1	4
(2) ⬦	Truck	8 (2270')	1	1	1	2	-	3
(3) ⬦	Manual Truck	15 (320')	2	2	1	3	4	3
▢		26	4	4	2	5	4	7
◗		11	3	1	1	2	2	2
▽		5	1	2	-	2	-	-

Summary of current operations

Table 11·XX

OPERATION		TOTAL	I	II	III	IV	V	VI
◯		14	3	1	3	7	**	**
(1) ⬦	Conveyor (Total system)	1 (5800')	2	-	1	4	**	**
(2) ⬦	Truck	3 (150')	-	3	-	-	-	-
(3) ⬦	Manual Truck	7 (170')	-	-	-	-	-	-
▢		9	2	1	2	4	**	**
◗		5	1	1	1	2	**	**
▽		3	-	3	-	-	**	**

** Improved system reduced the actual number of departments required to operate warehouse complex

Proposed operations

278

Where necessary the cartons were stuffed, then sealed, banded and positioned ready for subsequent movement to the despatch bay. A summary of the work study operation showed the following:

Selection

Total studied basic minutes (excluding occasional elements)	—	101·52
Total standard minute value	—	123·00
Total number of units selected	—	372·00
Standard minute value per unit	—	0·33

Packing, sealing and banding

Total studied basic minutes (excluding occasional elements)	—	223·06
Total standard minute value	—	270·00
Total number of units packed	—	372·00
Standard minute value per unit packed	—	0·728

Following the initial time studies for the separate selection and packing operations, a further study was undertaken to determine what additional savings could be made by combining certain elements of the selection and packing. Through work study simulation techniques, a synthetic method of operation was determined and is described as follows:

(a) The female assembly operator selects an empty truck, and having noted the departmental/section number moves to the first selection point

(b) At this stage, the operator selects a number of empty cartons and places these inside the frame of the hand truck. It should be noted that these cartons were identical to the ones used in the packing department, though at this stage they were not made up

(c) The assembler proceeds to the first selection point as indicated on her computer order sheet

(d) Before commencement of assembly, the operator makes up one of the cartons and places this inside the hand selection truck

(e) The operator then selects goods from the racks and places them straight inside the cartons. The assembler moves amongst the racks selecting and packing directly into the carton. When the first carton is filled, she makes up a second one and continues the process of order picking. When the truck is filled, the operator then returns the full truck and cartons to the packing section

(f) She selects another truck and continues to repeat the operation until the whole order is completed.

It was thought that by the elimination of a number of unnecessary rehandling operations occasioned through the packing department, considerable savings in handling standards might result.

279

The results of the time studies showed the following improvements:

Selection and packing

Total studied basic minutes (excluding occasional elements)	— 47·35
Total standard minute value	— 57·20
Total number of units selected	— 158·00
Standard minute value per unit assembled	— 0·362

Sealing and banding

Total studied basic minutes (excluding occasional elements)	— 23·53
Total standard minute value	— 28·40
Total number of units packed	— 158·00
Standard minute value per unit packed	— 0·180

Summary

Total standard minute value for selection and packing
$$= \quad 0·362 + 0·180$$
$$= \quad 0·542$$
standard minutes per unit.

Conclusion

From the above case study, it can be seen that the detailed method study and work standards highlighted the basic weakness of the original system. The company concerned implemented the recommendations and as a result was able to reduce the total labour content of selection and packing by 47 per cent.

RETAIL LOCATION
by Gordon Wills

The selection of appropriate locations for retail activities is fundamental to their success. It is an issue which has attracted the theoretical attention of a long line of economists and geographers, and more recently, sociologists and marketing academics. There is still little evidence of sophisticated approaches amongst the practitioners of retailing in either Europe or North America. Few would deny the hazards of securing accurate estimates of the potential trade for any location at a particular point in time; all would probably concede the greater hazards of any dynamic predictions. Nonetheless, high investment costs are often involved and the procedures which have been developed allow for substantial reductions in the risks to be run. Improved efficiency at the retail sorting level in the total flow of goods and services is essential to retailer, manufacturer and customer alike. This sorting level is just as vitally important in the total PDM process as any other.

At the present time there is no evidence available in Britain to indicate the extent to which any formal analyses of the potential for trade in new or existing locations is conducted, nor its nature. We do have, however, a North American perspective here which we can use as a basic frame of reference. William Applebaum has reported the findings of a study amongst retailing chains in the United States,[1] which included department store, supermarket, clothing, variety store, pharmacy, shoe and car accessory chains. Their average expenditure (in 1963) on new store location research amounted to £2,000 to assess an average investment of £150,000; less than 5 per cent of chains formulated an overall store location strategy within a region—rather they conducted a series of *ad hoc* evaluations of potential sites—and each site selected was normally preceded by four or five rejected locations; finally, 60 per cent of chains sampled did not carry out a follow-up study once their new sites had been constructed.

Table 12·I sets out the agencies which were used in the research which was conducted. It can be readily seen that the heaviest users of consultants were the smaller chains, but that the large chains frequently made use of consultants in conjunction with their own research departments.

This latter finding is perhaps the only theoretically satisfactory element in the management situation. My fundamental purpose here will be to argue that for the effective management of potential trade, a clear policy for retail

281

Table 12·I

AGENCIES FOR LOCATION RESEARCH CONDUCTED BY U.S. RETAILING CHAINS (1963)
(N=60)

Chain sales per annum		*Chain only*	*Chain and consultants*	*Consultants only*	*No systematic research*
Over £175 M	%	72	28	0	0
£35m–£175m	%	62	24	3	11
£6 m–£35 m	%	53	10	24	13
All Chains	%	60	20	10	10

location is essential, and such a policy can only be meaningfully formulated on the basis of adequate retailing research. The chapter will be presented in four sections:

(1) defining a trading area;
(2) assessing its potential;
(3) choosing a specific location;
(4) reviewing performance.

1. DEFINING A TRADING AREA

A trading area may be defined as that area surrounding a trading facility, or group of facilities, in which potential customers have a positive probability that they might trade with the facility or group of facilities.

Trading areas are a phenomenon explained most effectively perhaps by economic geographers. A completely adequate understanding of their patterns of evolution and change is still not available. Nonetheless many of the variables determining their configuration are known, and many of the locational designs which they describe are readily recognizable.

Berry identifies [4] two key analytical concepts which have been developed concerning trading areas in terms of 'centrality' and an 'hierarchy of centres'. Central place theory has been concerned to examine the rationale of the variety of central places which a society develops to meet its trading needs. From this analysis, a clear hierarchy of centres has been discerned, which a range of empirical studies have shown to be meaningful. Simultaneously the interrelationships of the various centres have been discerned. In particular, the differential degree of interrelationship for various products or services provided by a trading facility, and the individual customer's proximity to any particular type of centre have been noted. These points can, perhaps, be illustrated by examples.

In an examination of the customer drawing power of various locations operated by a supermarket chain, Bernard La Londe[17] found three meaningful store clusters from a range of possible combinations. They were:

(a) small urban clusters or strips
(b) small town centres and neighbourhood/community shopping centres
(c) regional shopping centres.

282

The clustering of retail locations giving a meaningful hierarchy within any particular area can be simply accomplished by the technique known as cluster analysis. Applications of this as between towns have been attempted in Britain in a steady stream since Moser and Scott's classic work in 1951.[24] Goddard has applied the technique in describing office locations in London[8] and attempts to delineate true 'development' and 'grey' areas have been made.[35] [33] Christopher [6] has specifically applied such analyses in a marketing context and examined their benefits, for test marketing purposes, as a clustering approach which reflects potential purchasing power.

Significantly, La Londe's study had indicated that the differentials in drawing power were not directly proportional to the level of product offering at the retail site. This is, of course, a fact of considerable importance to our understanding of trading area definition. It has also posed considerable problems to the theoretical approaches which economists have made from time to time. Lewis[19] has perhaps come nearest to taking account of such factors when he rejected the oversimplified models presented by Hotelling[11] and Lerner and Singer.[18] These early models had examined the allocation of patronage between retail outlets on assumptions which were so generalized as to be of no practical value; such assumptions were, e.g. that there were no economies of scale. From a theoretical analysis, Lewis concluded that whilst suburban shops will inevitably be of less than optimum size, central shopping areas should include stores which approach optimality. Although Lewis still made assumptions which the businessman has to question, his model was able to take into account the interrelationship between the various levels in the hierarchy.

The interrelationships between various centres is empirically well highlighted by what has been termed the 'periphery effect'. In analysing the levels of retail sales *per capita* from the Censuses of Distribution, McClelland[21] demonstrated the point that the larger a town grows, the less magnitude proportionately the peripheral trade coming into the town will constitute. In the smaller town, with a population below 10,000, peripheral trade boosts *per capita* sales proportionately much more. A precisely similar analysis, yet separating out shopping and convenience goods, indicates the further crucially important point that the periphery effect is less pronounced in the case of shopping goods. This is hardly surprising bearing in mind the nature of the distribution of many shopping goods trading facilities, and accords with Lewis' views.

Figure 12·1 is a graphical integration of these points drawing on Census of Distribution data for 1961. It indicates not only the lesser significance of main shopping centres in larger towns, but also the relative drawing power of convenience and shopping goods, trading facilities and their decline with town size.

Thus far, we have considered the contribution of economic geographers to a definition of a trading area. (Hood[10] has recently produced an excellent bibliography of value to those who wish to dig deeper.) The theoretical concepts of centrality and an hierarchy of centres have been illustrated in terms of the UK Censuses of Distribution. Whilst the strategic importance of such analysis for retail management must not be overlooked, we must now turn attention to the two major approaches open to management in the operational definition of a trading area. They are, firstly, the gravitational approach and, secondly, the empirical approach.

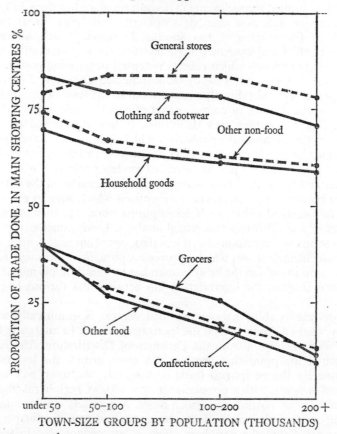

Figure 12·1   Proportion of trade done in main shopping centres by town size and
main trade group (1961)
Source: 1961 Census of Distribution.

Gravitational Approaches

The major advantage of the gravitational approach is that, if a satisfactory formula can be found, it obviates the need for expensive empirical studies. Gravity concepts were developed originally from analogy with Newtonian physics of matter. Although the individual behaviour of molecules is not normally predictable, in large numbers their behaviour can be predicted in terms of mathematical probabilities. The gravitational school of thinking is well summarized by Carrothers[5] who also provides an excellent bibliography. Its earliest formulation in relation to retail location analysis, and one which

284

today is perhaps less satisfactory than ever, took account of just two variables determining a customer's tendency to gravitate towards any particular cluster of trading facilities. These were population and distance, and William Reilly's original formula suggested the following relationships:[27]

$$\frac{Ba}{Bb} = \left(\frac{Pa}{Pb}\right)\left(\frac{Db}{Da}\right)^2$$

where Ba and Bb respectively represent the proportion of trade which two towns, a and b, would draw from an intermediate town. Pa and Pb are the respective populations of towns a and b, and Da and Db are the respective distances of towns a and b from the intermediate town. This formulation was extended by Paul Converse[7] who, by arguing that $Ba = Bb$, i.e. that the split of trade was 50/50, was able to represent the formula to indicate the breaking point for trade gravitation to towns a and b. Converse suggested that:

$$Dbr = \frac{Dab}{1 + \sqrt{\dfrac{Pa}{Pb}}}$$

where Dab = distance between towns a and b, and Dbr = breaking point for trade between towns a and b in miles from b.

Yet a further extension of the formula was made to predict the extent of trade which any town would *retain* in competition with an outside town:

$$\frac{Bo}{Bh} = \left(\frac{Po}{Ph}\right)\left(\frac{i}{Do}\right)^2$$

where Bo is the proportion of trade going outside the town and Bh the proportion retained, Po the population of the outside town, Ph the population of the home town, and Do the distance of the home town from the outside town.

Converse uses i as an inertia factor which will include those factors which militate against travel such as the extent of display, range, transportation methods and so forth.

Reilly's original formula and Converse's modifications have both been extensively tested in North America, and thus far the proof is inconclusive either way. However, the originators have never suggested that they would work in every circumstance. Reilly accompanied his formula with a list of other factors which influence the retail trade of a city. These are listed as Figure 12·2.

The most recent developments in gravitational models have sought to embrace square footages and sales volumes as an element in the drawing power of centres as well, and they have looked particularly at the development of shopping centres.

James Rouse, chairman of a retail chain in the United States, reformulated Reilly's law in the following terms.[30]

Retail shopping centres attract trade from their surroundings in direct proportion to the shopping goods presentation at the centre concerned and in inverse proportion to the square of the driving time between the customer's home and the shopping centre.

1. Lines of transportation
   Public highways
   Railroads and railroad rates—including special rates to commuters
   Electric lines—regular and special rates
   Bus lines—regular and special rates
   Waterways—regular and special rates
   Express and parcel post—regular and special rates
   Air lines
2. Lines of communication
   Circulation of the daily newspaper
     Number of papers distributed
     Geographical territory covered
     Classes of people reached
   Telephone and telegraph lines and rates
3. The class of consumer in the territory surrounding the market
4. Density of population in the territory surrounding the market
5. Proximity of the market to a larger city market
6. The business attractions of the city
   The nature of the leading stores of the city
     The kinds of goods and selections of goods offered by stores in the market
     The delivery, credit, and other services offered by these stores
     The general reputation of these stores as style-goods centres
   The extent to which the city offers storage and a market for the sale and redistribution of goods produced in the surrounding territory
   The banking facilities of the city
7. The social and amusement attractions of the city
   Theatres
   Educational institutions and facilities
   Musical attractions
   Athletic events
   Church, society, or fraternal gatherings
   Fairs and expositions
8. The nature of the competition offered by smaller cities and towns in the surrounding territory
   The kinds of goods and selections of goods offered by stores in smaller locations
   The general attitude of these surrounding cities and towns toward the larger city
9. The population of the city
10. The distance which prospective customers must travel in order to reach the market, and the psychology of distance prevailing in that part of the country
11. The topographical and climatic conditions peculiar to the city and its surrounding territory
12. The kind of leadership offered by the owners or managers of various business interests of the city

Figure 12·2 Outline of Factors Influencing Retail Trading Areas

We have already seen in our earlier discussion of the Census of Distribution data that such generalizations do not hold true throughout the whole range of town sites, and that they vary according to the product or service under consideration. It is one of the major advantages of the most recent gravitational model suggested by David Huff[12] that it can take this into account. However, its significance goes much further. It is a probabilistic approach rather than deterministic. Such an approach is able to take cognizance of the expression of consumer preferences. It no longer looks at trading areas in terms of clean break points (a 0·5 probability contour, however, indicates the same phenomenon). If 0·01 probability represents potential trade for one area, a 0·99 probability must be ascribed to other shopping centres. Huff suggests, therefore, that a contour map should be prepared for customer's probabilities of shopping in any particular group of centres, and that the interlocking nature of the hierarchy of centres will be demonstrated.

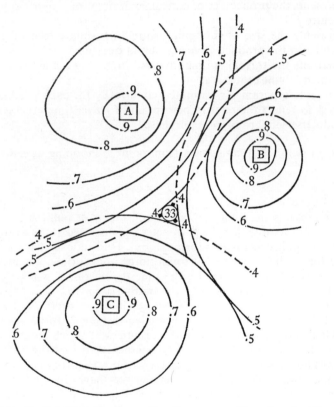

Figure 12·3   Probability Contours for Consumers Shopping in Three Centres

Figure 12·3 shows the probability contours for three shopping centres, A, B and C. The break points suggested by Converse will be seen to be points at which the customer expresses no particular preference for any one centre—where 0·5 or 0·4 contours intersect. This form of analysis, it will be seen, can take account of any number of competing centres simultaneously. The probability that any particular centre will obtain trade in any particular product or service group, is formally expressed by Huff in the following model:

$$Pij = \frac{\dfrac{Sj}{Tij^\lambda}}{\displaystyle\sum_{=1}^{n} \dfrac{Sj}{Tij^\lambda}}$$

where:

  Pij represents the probability of consumer at point of origin i, travelling to a centre j

  Sj represents the size of shopping centre j (in square foot of sales area devoted to the product/service group in question)

  Tij represents the travelling time involved in getting a consumer from his origin at i to the centre at j

  λ represents a parameter estimated empirically for each product/service group to reflect the relative perception of travel time arising from the product/service group to be purchased.

The expected number of consumers from point i, shopping at centre j (Eij), will be

$$Eij = Pij \times Ci$$

where Ci represents the total number of consumers at point i.

It is important to note that the parameter λ is not fixed at the second power as in Reilly's and his successor's formulations. Huff reports that for furniture 2·723 and for clothing 3·191 were found to be appropriate magnitudes. The greater the magnitude, the smaller the time the customer will be willing to spend and hence the smaller will be the trading area.

This latter point is extended by allied findings reported by Donald Thompson[36] on what he terms 'subjective distance'. In an investigation which invited respondents to judge the distances at which shopping centres lay from their home, significant results demonstrated that the perception of distance was affected by whether or not a centre was currently patronized by respondents. When it was, distances were seen as markedly less than by those who did not patronize a centre. Data also indicated a differential perception for store types within and between centres by regular patrons. Discount houses, for instance, were perceived as proportionately farther away subjectively than department stores. The subjective element influencing gravitation has also been raised by sociologists and supermarketeers in Britain. Sofer[34] and McClelland[20] have both identified ways in which societal patterns have been transformed by the changing structure and nature of outlets at various centres at various levels in the hierarchy. The housewife's pattern of gravitation, they hypothesize, and surely correctly, will be subject to social as well as economic pulls.

288

Empirical Approaches

Empirical approaches to the definition of trading areas can be classified as either external or internal to the centre. An external study seeks, by normal consumer survey methods, to interview potential customers throughout a wide area to question them on the pattern of their shopping behaviour. The decision over how wide a net should be cast, however, normally rules this out as an initial empirical approach. It is also considerably more expensive than the two major internal methods of delineation.

Account analysis is usually the least expensive and most frequently used method of defining a hinterland. It can only be of value, however, where a store is already in operation or has access to current data. The method, which can be readily programmed into the conventional integrated data processing system of a store, is described by Plotkin in considerable detail.[26] The major disadvantage of such a method lies in that it only monitors existing trade, rather than the full potential which could be available.

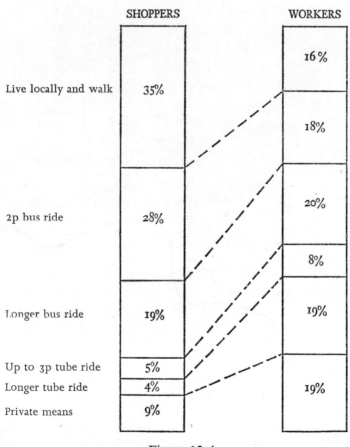

Figure 12·4

This disadvantage is to some, but to a lesser, extent shared by the other major empirical approach. This involves the questioning of customers not just in a particular store, but in the shopping centre generally, to discover where they live and the value of their weekly custom. By interviewing in the centre rather than within a particular store, it is possible to ensure that many potential customers who visit the centre are not overlooked. Sharp[32] reported the origin of custom for Camden Town and demonstrated how a

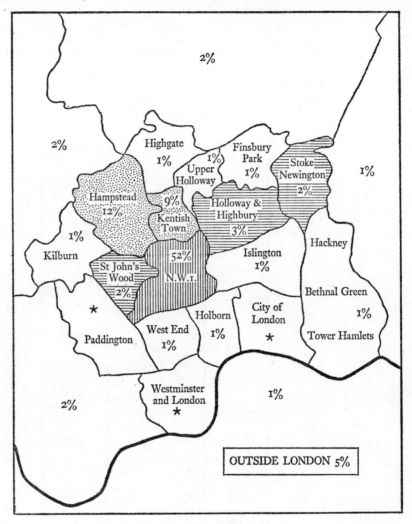

Figure 12·4 (a) Catchment Area

The percentages represent the proportion of shoppers in Camden Town who come from each area. The boundaries represent Postal Districts. Descriptive names have been used in most cases instead of postal numbers, e.g. St Johns Wood for NW8.

large conurbation's custom can come from a very wide hinterland indeed (see Figure 12·4 (a)). Nonetheless, there will still frequently be a substantial group of potential customers who do not visit a centre at all because they feel no attraction towards the extant cluster.

Whether the empirical investigation has located a customer's origin via accounts or via interview procedures, however, the method of charting the trading area will almost invariably be by what is termed 'spotting'. Figure

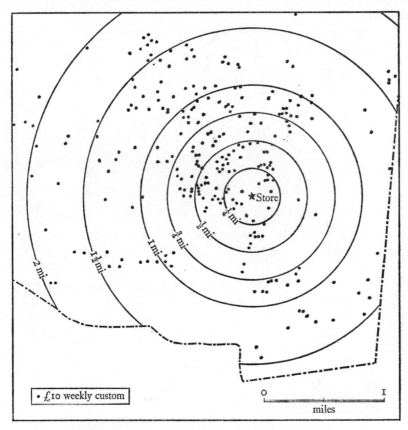

Figure 12·4 (b)   Customer Spotting for Retail Store

12·4 (b) shows such a 'spotting' map. Each spot represents a customer of equal sales value, e.g. £10 of weekly custom. When this spotted map is interpreted in conjunction with the population and land use map shown as Figure 12·4 (c), the rationale of custom can begin to emerge.[2]

Two equally intriguing methods of delineating retail trading areas have been noted. Green[9] has plotted urban hinterlands in England and Wales on the basis of an analysis of bus services, and Richardson,[28] Mooney and Wicks[23] on the basis of provincial newspaper circulation areas. All three are extremely worthwhile studies and provide a useful starting point, particularly since the requisite data is often already available.

We have seen that there are two main approaches to the definition of a retail trading area. In summary, the first suggests that there will be laws of gravitation determining the direction in which trade will flow; the second examines how trade does indeed flow and empirically produces a map of the extant trading area. Both approaches take cognizance of the fact that for different product groups or services the relevant catchment areas for trade will differ.

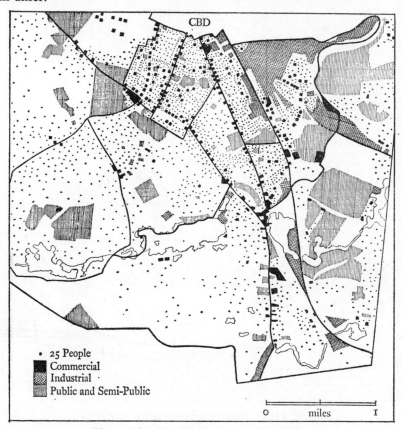

Figure 12·4 (c)   Population and Land Use

2. ASSESSING POTENTIAL WITHIN A DEFINED TRADING AREA

If the crude gravitational formulae for retail trade developed by Reilly and Converse are used, potential trade will be computed in terms of the number of individuals or households living within the determined trading area. This number will be multiplied by the average expenditure in the particular product areas as revealed by Family Expenditure Surveys, the Censuses of Distribution, or trade survey findings.

Although such a procedure may frequently provide an initial method of estimating potential, if either David Huff's probabilistic gravitation model or an empirical approach is employed, a more sensitive analysis will be possible. The method most frequently used here is known as the grid method. Figure 12·5 shows a grid superimposed on a set of contour lines representing either shopping probabilities at the various centres shown (after Huff) or

☐   Location of Shopping Centres

⋀   Contour Lines

Figure 12·5   Grid Method of Analysing Trading Areas

drawing power as measured through an empirical approach. The method has been comprehensively described by Ross Ritland[29] and William Applebaum.[2]

The area included within the squares of a grid for this form of analysis can be varied according to both the nature of the product/service under investigation and the population and expenditure data available for the various localities. Within each grid square, the investigation will:

1. estimate the population
2. determine how great its current relevant expenditure is with the particular store or centre under investigation
3. estimate the total spending of the population on the relevant product/ service group.

From this basic data, the market penetration currently being achieved by the store or centre can be calculated for each grid square, i.e. the extent to which potential trade is being obtained on a comparative basis. Furthermore, the

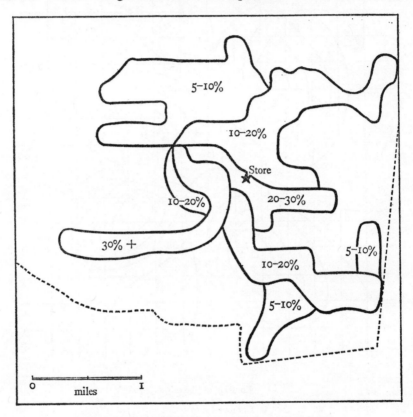

Figure 12·6   Market Penetration for a Retail Store

relative importance of one grid square versus another in terms of total and *per capita* expenditure on a product or service will impart a qualitative understanding to the analysis of potential. Figure 12·6 shows how present market penetration in the area described in Figures 12·4 (b) and (c) might look. It has been prepared by the amalgamation of the various grid squares.

From this analysis one isolates the key target areas for trade development for an existing store, as well as gaining a realistic understanding of the ceiling to trade.

It will have already become apparent that however effective such a method of estimating trade potential and market penetration may be, it will only be of direct relevance to existing stores. As it stands, such a method offers little direct help for assessing the potential for a new store. The translation, nonetheless, is relatively easily achieved.

At the grid stage, rather than considering an actual store, the hypothetical location can be evaluated in terms of probabilities (after Huff) rather than relying on empirically observed behaviour to provide known measures of drawing power. In this way, realistic estimates of potential can be made on the basis of the maximum knowledge about each grid square.

Applebaum has, however, suggested an ingenious method of utilizing existing data from other stores in order to improve on the probabilities one might ascribe. He has called it the 'analog method' because it makes projections on the basis of similar or analogous stores.[2] He suggests that retailing chains should make a point of computing such analogs. Two caveats must at once be entered in using such a method—no two stores are alike and the situation at any analog store is normally subject to continuous change. Nonetheless, an intelligent use of analogous situations has always been, and will remain, a common characteristic of retailing decision taking.

The method involves the selection from all the stores within a chain's control of perhaps two or three, which are apparently most analogous. For each store the actual trading patterns measured are averaged to provide the projection for the proposed location. Through the key measures of population, *per capita* food expenditures and drawing power, the sales forecast is computed.

Implicit Growth/Saturation
It has already been remarked that such an assessment of potential trade is static. It is vitally important that a dynamic perspective be imparted to the data prior to any decision being taken to enter a particular locality. An important review paper has been written on this subject by Applebaum and Cohen,[3] which examines movements towards and away from equilibrium in the provision of retailing facilities.

One can normally expect to be able to establish, from the local planning authority, what population growth is envisaged in the trading area which is to be served. Equally important, however, will be a projection of the growth of disposable incomes of the population, and the likelihood of changes in the pattern of trading competition. In Britain, superficially at least, there would seem to be good reason to expect continuing changes in the pattern of retail trading as urban centres are redeveloped, with concomitant effects on trading areas and potential within them. Equally, the renewed phase of New Town construction will be affecting trading patterns in the areas left behind as well as the new communities the migrants join. Sharp has reported work undertaken by Basildon New Town Corporation to predict future shopping needs.[32]

There will, however, be areas where saturation of retailing facilities will be encountered. Saturation can be defined here as that level of facility which, when related to the potential levels of expenditure available in a trading area, does not give a satisfactory return on investment. This can perhaps be most readily illustrated in the case of supermarkets where sales per square foot of sales area is a widely accepted measure of R.O.I. La Londe[16] suggests the following index of retail saturation (IRS):

$$IRS = \frac{C \times RE}{RF}$$

where:

C = the number of consumers
RE = the average expenditure on the product(s) in question per consumer
RF = the total retail facilities serving the consumers.

In Slough, for example, with some 35,000 households in its estimated trading area, supermarket selling space, i.e. excluding grocery stores of less than 2250 sq. feet sales area, was approximately 180,000 sq. feet. It was estimated that each household spent £6–7 per week on foods.

$$IRS = \frac{35,000 \times £6 \cdot 5}{180,000} = \frac{£227}{180} \text{ per sq. foot}$$

$$= £1 \cdot 23 \text{ per square foot.}$$

Bearing in mind that there were a considerable number of non-supermarkets serving similar needs, such a trading area could well have been deemed saturated. However, Sainsbury was able to make a successful entry into this trading area at the expense of competitors. The newcomer was able to wrest a share of the market at the expense of established chains and even to drive one from the area. Hence saturation is a concept to be treated with caution. It means that, if a new entrant has nothing to offer which can differentiate him from existing facilities, there is no room for him to enter. But if he can differentiate himself sufficiently, and by his entry transform the structure of attitudes which determine the pattern of trade, such an index of saturation is misleading. From the managerial perspective, however, it is important to point out that, *prima facie*, where a high degree of saturation is encountered, in the face of a wide range of alternative opportunities, the most profitable development may well lie elsewhere.

We have seen that by the grid method it is possible to proceed from the delineation of a trading area to an accurate assessment of total potential trade, and our individual penetration of it. In the case of new locations, the review of similar existing locations can provide analogs for the forecast of performance. Finally the need to impart a dynamic to the analysis has been emphasized in terms of growth or saturation patterns in a region. An index of saturation has been suggested to help classify location opportunities in terms of expected R.O.I.

3. CHOOSING A SPECIFIC LOCATION

In the task of selecting a specific location within a defined trading area of known saturation and estimated potential, most of the factors which have hitherto been discussed in general terms come into sharp focus. The first and most significant decision to be taken is that concerning the location type—isolated, small cluster, community centre or major shopping centre. Decisions of this type will have both strategic and tactical dimensions. The two should be clearly separated.

Compatibility

The principle of compatibility postulates that in site selection there should be no interruption of trade and that interchange between one store and another in a complex should be at a maximum, with direct competition at a minimum. Translated into specifics, this principle means, 'Does the business next door help or hinder my sales?' It must also be extended, however, to the totality of any complex to pose the question: 'Does the group of stores in the complex help or hinder my sales?' None better than property developers are aware of this need for the total group to make a satisfactory trading complex. In Britain particularly, the presence of one of the variety stores has frequently been shown to have a make or break effect on a centre's success. Richard Nelson has suggested that a measurable relationship exists between business volumes of any two stores.[25] His model for the relationship is:

$$V = I(V_L + V_S) \times \frac{V_S}{V_L} \times \left(\frac{P_L}{V_L} + \frac{P_S}{V_S} \right)$$

where:

V = the total increase in volume for the two stores
V_L = volume sales in larger store
V_S = volume sales in smaller store
P_S = purposeful purchasing in smaller store
P_L = purposeful purchasing in larger store
I = degree of interchange.

Hence there are two elements to be taken into direct account in the evaluation of compatibility. Firstly, the cumulative attraction of the shopping centre in total; secondly, the immediate compatibility with the store next door.

Interception

Consumers tend to follow traditional patterns of activity in most fields, and trading behaviour is no exception. Hence, besides the obvious use of promotional media to question traditional patterns, the spatial dimension can be deployed. This has been termed the principle of interception.

Essentially it involves the positioning of any particular store at an interception point between the consumer's point of origin and the traditional shopping centre. Harold Imus[14] has suggested that a population living

297

beyond a proposed location will contribute twice as much to sales volume as the population living between the location and the major shopping centre. He argues from the trader's viewpoint for a tight inner-ring of trading locations as the most effective method of interception.

Within the centre, however, attention must also be paid to the principles of interception. The site which is at an extremity and farthest from the car parking or transportation facilities will intercept less trade than one interposed between the car park, say, and a department store, supermarket or variety store.

Interception, however, also has its negative side. All manner of often discussed elements militate against an effective realization of potential trade. Not least amongst these are the traffic configurations. Store accessibility in terms of traffic flows and in pedestrians walking, perhaps with children, is a vital management consideration. Parking, loading, and exits are other sides of the same coin. Traffic circulatory systems are most usefully classified by their effect on location in generating internal, axial, pivotal, external and peripheral sites. Internal sites are normally devoted to comparison goods; axial sites are what is more commonly called urban ribbon development; pivotal sites are to be found at major junctions; external sites are inter-town ribbon development; peripheral sites are clustered at the edge of a community.

Such a classification system is often of considerable value in the use of analogs for new site development. It can also frequently provide a dimension for evaluation in the dynamics of retail trading where new road construction is anticipated. The topic has been well developed by John Mertes.[22]

The Leeds Merrion Centre is an attempt to exploit, *inter alia*, this principle of interception, but first reports from traders in the Centre are an extreme disappointment. It also failed to draw any significant proportion of trade from the city centre due partially to the fact that the area between the Merrion Centre and the city centre is one of dereliction and the journey represents an uphill trek from the city.

In addition, of course, the principle of interception must vary according to whether private or public transport is used. If—as is still the case in Britain —the majority of shoppers use public transport, then interception becomes less relevant since it is as easy to stay on a bus until it reaches the town-centre where traffic congestion and car-parking are problems only for the motorist.

The negative side of location selection, that of closing an uneconomic unit, is not a decision that can be taken without forethought and careful consideration of whether site alone makes the unit unprofitable or whether there are other factors, e.g. the disproportionate labour costs of a small operation, to be considered. There seems to be a reluctance to close an outlet, presumably on the grounds that this would give an opportunity to another retailer and would not be a policy designed to create customer goodwill.

Transfer Effects
In deciding whether or not to adopt a specific location for a new store, retail management are often concerned to measure what has been termed the
298

'transfer effect' which would result from a new store. It will be appreciated that in our earlier analysis of existing patterns of trade, and our suggestions for assessing the potential inherent in any particular location, the methodology for tackling this problem has been demonstrated. Informed estimates can be made on the basis of an understanding of present trade in a parent store, and of potential trade for a new branch.

Murray Sawits has shown[31] from his experience with Federated Department Stores that where the product mix of the parent and branch store are similar, a predictive model can be developed. In any particular trading area delineated for a new branch, the transfer effect will increase with the volume of trade already done by the parent in that area. The model, which has been empirically tested, predicts, however, that the transfer increment becomes proportionately smaller as the parent's share of the branch area increases.

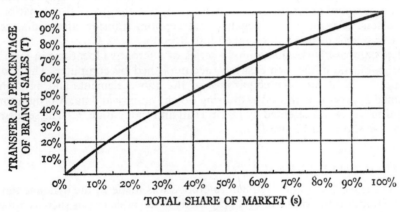

Figure 12·7   Relationship between Transfer Sales to a New Branch from a Parent Store

The predictive model is very sensitive to the accuracy of the market share data. The model is:

$$T = 100p(1 - e^{-s})$$

where T = sales transferred to branch from parent
   p = a proportional factor to scale the transfer from 0–100 per cent
   s = share of market held by the parent.

Better results can be expected by this method of analysis if the trading area is treated by homogeneous segments based on the grid/market penetration methods described earlier.

Figure 12·7 shows graphically the transfer effect relationships which Sawits reports.

Competitive Reaction

The introspective nature of the preceding discussion provides an appropriate stimulus to a consideration of competitive reactions or pre-empting behaviour in the face of the establishment of a new location. Perhaps the most significant factor which must be identified is that the competitive situation will almost invariably be transformed from that which any static trading potential studies indicated. Equally, on one's own part, price and promotional levels may well be set which one would not envisage maintaining.

Alternative strategies must, however, be formulated if the actions of competitors are to be effectively countered. In addition, competitive reaction in spatial terms, i.e. the acquisition of new locations for additional stores, must also be allowed for in the evaluation of estimates of potential. This must normally be in terms of a subjective assessment of the situation once local planning authorities have been consulted about future developments.

We have seen that in the selection of a specific location, not only the nature of the complex in which a store is located, but the internal compatibility, the extent of positive and negative interception, transfer effects, and competitive reactions must all be taken into account.

The comparative evaluation of a series of alternative locations in terms of a probabilistic model can easily be accomplished by computer. The probabilities ascribed can take cognizance of the above elements and any others deemed appropriate, as well as drawing on any empirical data. A programmed solution has been presented by David Huff and Larry Blue.[13] The sequential steps are shown in Figure 12·8.

4. REVIEW PERFORMANCE

In the earlier discussion, frequent reference was made to the dynamic nature of the trading environment. Not only easily discernible trends such as population movements and the entry of new competitors, but changes in the transportation network have been instanced as influencing any analysis conducted. This is what might be termed the 'macro' level of influence. At the 'micro' level, however, retail stores will go through life cycles in customer patronage. We shall look at each of these levels of review in turn.

Macro-Review

A retailing management which has access on a continuing basis to data which enables a continual up-dating of its trading area delineation is in a strong position to measure trends. Perhaps the most practicable method is to use an account analysis approach based on an integrated data processing system.[26] However, such procedures can sometimes resemble post-mortems rather than a diagnostic service enabling management to foresee, then exploit or counter possible developments. A formalized retail intelligence service within each shopping centre is a possible area of cooperative research, which will be designed to give an early warning of any factors which might affect future trading conditions. Frequently, of course, such a function already exists but in an informal way. Many retailers are local people who

300

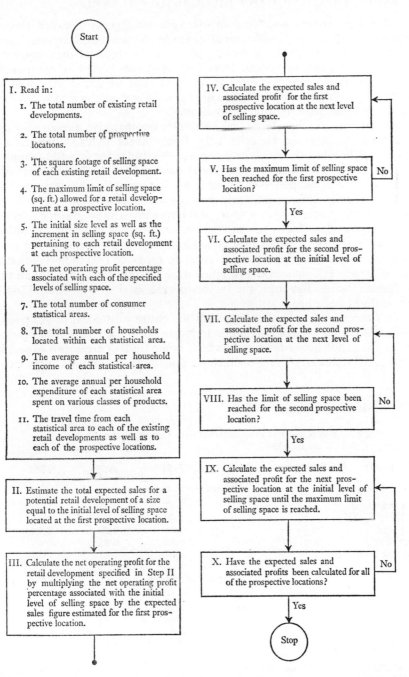

Start

I. Read in:
  1. The total number of existing retail developments.

  2. The total number of prospective locations.

  3. The square footage of selling space of each existing retail development.

  4. The maximum limit of selling space (sq. ft.) allowed for a retail development at a prospective location.

  5. The initial size level as well as the increment in selling space (sq. ft.) pertaining to each retail development at each prospective location.

  6. The net operating profit percentage associated with each of the specified levels of selling space.

  7. The total number of consumer statistical areas.

  8. The total number of households located within each statistical area.

  9. The average annual per household income of each statistical area.

  10. The average annual per household expenditure of each statistical area spent on various classes of products.

  11. The travel time from each statistical area to each of the existing retail developments as well as to each of the prospective locations.

II. Estimate the total expected sales for a potential retail development of a size equal to the initial level of selling space located at the first prospective location.

III. Calculate the net operating profit for the retail development specified in Step II by multiplying the net operating profit percentage associated with the initial level of selling space by the expected sales figure estimated for the first prospective location.

IV. Calculate the expected sales and associated profit for the first prospective location at the next level of selling space.

V. Has the maximum limit of selling space been reached for the first prospective location? — No

Yes

VI. Calculate the expected sales and associated profit for the second prospective location at the initial level of selling space.

VII. Calculate the expected sales and associated profit for the second prospective location at the next level of selling space.

VIII. Has the limit of selling space been reached for the second prospective location? — No

Yes

IX. Calculate the expected sales and associated profit for the next prospective location at the initial level of selling space until the maximum limit of selling space is reached.

X. Have the expected sales and associated profits been calculated for all of the prospective locations? — No

Yes

Stop

Figure 12·8　Sequential Steps in Analysing the Optimum Location Problem

301

read the local papers and have an extensive intelligence network through chambers of trade and professional contacts. Sometimes, however, trends will be less dramatic. Over a decade, perhaps, the status of one centre may be gradually eroded by others. Here only continual review of comparative trading situations can pinpoint the problem. The weakness may well, for instance, be a failure despite a growing sales volume at a centre to maintain a share of these growing total expenditures.

David Thompson has developed a valuable comparative measure for such evaluations to be made. He calls it the Convenience Index.[37] In the area with which he was concerned, he computed this Index for fifty-four shopping areas in 1958 and again in 1963, and for eleven for 1939, 1948 and 1954 in addition. Throughout the period he found not only overall trends but pronounced inter-community differences. Areas which were originally not self-sufficient moved rapidly towards such a state, and larger areas showed some decline.

The Convenience Index for any particular shopping centre is the ratio of its 'total retail sales population equivalent' based on regional *per capita* sales and the resident population. Hence, an Index of 1·00 indicates that the area is largely self-sufficient. For cities over 100,000 resident population in the San Francisco Bay area, the indices moved as shown in Table 12·II for the products described.

San Francisco Bay, in common with the entire west coast of America, is the fastest growth area of population in North America. Hence it can perhaps be seen as a hot house for trends which other trading areas can expect but perhaps at a slower pace. Nonetheless, this study emphasizes most clearly

Table 12·II

CONVENIENCE INDICES FOR CITIES OVER 100,000 POPULATION IN THE SAN FRANCISCO BAY AREA, 1939–63

Central city	1939	1948	1954	1958	1963
		General merchandise			
San Francisco	1·27	1·47	1·71	1·73	1·46
Oakland	1·53	1·69	1·59	1·66	1·31
San Jose	2·04	2·34	2·68	1·66	1·02
Berkeley	0·41	0·45	0·68	0·85	0·45
Average	1·35[a]	1·45[b]	1·67	1·63	1·26
		Apparel accessory			
San Francisco	1·63	1·73	1·75	1·81	1·88
Oakland	1·40	1·42	1·36	1·39	1·39
San Jose	1·88	2·03	2·04	1·45	0·97
Berkeley	0·45	0·78	0·87	0·92	0·99
Average	1·56[a]	1·56[b]	1·59	1·59	1·52

[a]1939 average calculated only for cities then exceeding 100,000 population: Oakland and San Francisco.
[b]1948 average calculated only for cities then exceeding 100,000 population: Berkeley, Oakland, and San Francisco.

how the creation of new shopping facilities as a result of a rapid growth in population or incomes can upset established patterns of town centre trading in a few years.

Micro-Review

The life cycle concept, developed normally in terms of brand marketing, has applicability in performance review procedures for individual stores. Familiar aspects of this to most managements will be the need to redecorate/modernize a store. Such expedients can frequently have a substantial effect on tempting back lost custom and giving a store a new lease of life. More important for our consideration here, however, is the growth towards mature sales levels within any particular store. In particular, we shall examine the development of sales in a newly opened outlet.

The growth and decay of retail patronage is a subject which has not been widely treated in marketing literature. Fortunately diffusion theory for information in society has been carried forward in other areas. The fundamental prerequisite for trade is awareness of any store's existence; thereafter a host of other factors may influence patronage. Once penetration has been achieved, i.e. a customer has made one visit, the opportunity arises for that customer either to continue shopping or not to return.

Robert Kelly[15] has translated the findings of new product purchasing to the analysis of retail trade, using the equation for the function:

$$rx(1-r)^{i-1}+k$$

where r is the rate by which penetration approaches the ceiling of penetration
   x is the ceiling of penetration
   k is a small constant representing the rate of new customer additions once the store reaches a maturity level
   i is the number of time periods passed

and

$rx(1-r)^{i-1}$ = the value of any given increment of penetration.

In Figure 12·9 (a) the comparison between penetration achieved over an eleven-week period and the forecast after three weeks' data was available, is shown. Patronage, i.e. continued purchasing, was predicted using the same function and the fit of prediction is shown in Figure 12·9 (b). The operative definition of patronage used by Kelly in this study was four store visits in five consecutive weeks. This meant it was week eight before patronage data for three weeks was available.

The real value of such a device lies not in the historical analysis, but in the power it gives management to act when, in the early days of a new store opening, the desired levels of penetration and patronage are not being achieved. By week three, for instance, management knows what its penetration will be in two or three months' time and can act to amend any variances from plan.

303

It has been demonstrated that measures of change exist as tools for management review at both the macro and micro level in retailing. It has been suggested that a formal procedure for the review of trends affecting a centre can usefully be established and sustained using continuous intelligence. At the individual store level, models for prediction of penetration and patronage facilitate more effective management control by enabling adjustment to meet planned levels.

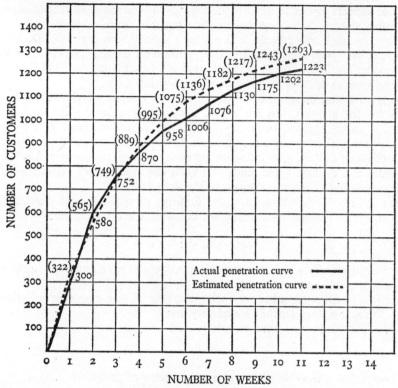

Figure 12·9 (a)   Comparison of Estimated and Actual Penetration Curves (based on the first three weeks' data)

The value of formalized procedures wherever possible has been emphasized, and a reasonable time scale for regular review of all locations should be established by management, taking cognizance of special factors in its own trade and trading area.

Conclusions
In this chapter, four elements of the analysis of potential trade have been considered in relative isolation. Their interrelated nature is, however, always apparent. Effective management of retail trading is impossible without this realization.

Potential trade is by definition tomorrow's business and tomorrow's revenue. No management can afford to neglect the range of techniques which has been developed and which this chapter has surveyed. How many techniques will be employed, how great an expenditure should be contemplated, are vital areas for management decision. They should not be left unconsidered,

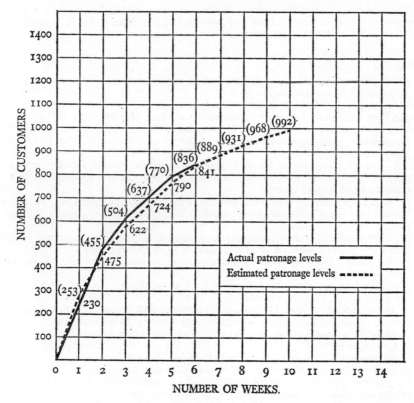

Figure 12·9 (b)   Comparison of Estimated and Actual Patronage Curves (based on three weeks' data)

even if the decision is that insufficient time, and competitive forces, make any such work impracticable. As trading activity becomes more and more subject to change and the average size of investment escalates, the importance of this fact can only be increased.

Management must focus its attention on three specific tasks:

It is the first and the last which are so often overlooked, as management becomes more and more involved in tactics. It requires a conscious effort on the part of management to ensure that strategy and review are given their rightful place. The balance of the knowledge described here, and in retailing literature, clearly bears witness to this fact.

[This chapter is a further development of ideas first presented to the University's Retail Management Forum in October 1967, and published in *New Ideas in Retail Management*, London, Staples, 1970, edited by the author. Extracts used here with permission.]

References
(1) W. Applebaum, 'Stores Location Research—a survey by retailing chains', *Journal of Retailing*, 40, Summer 1964, pp. 53–5.
(2) W. Applebaum, 'Methods for Determining Store Trade Areas, Market Penetration, and Potential Sales', *Journal of Marketing Research*, 3, May 1966, pp. 127–41.
(3) W. Applebaum and S. A. Cohen, 'The Dynamics of Store Trading Areas and Market Equilibrium', *Annals of the Association of American Geographers*, 51, March 1961, pp. 73–101.
(4) B. L. J. Berry, *Geography of Market Centres and Retail Distribution*, London, Prentice-Hall, 1967, reports the work of the pioneers in this field, German geographers Walter Christaller and August Lösch.
(5) G. A. P. Carrothers, 'An Historical Review of the Gravity and Potential Concepts of Human Interaction', *Journal of the American Institute of Planners*, Spring 1956, pp. 94–102.
(6) M. J. Christopher, 'Multi-dimensional Analysis as a Technique for Areal and Ecological Comparison', *British Journal of Marketing*, 3, 3, October 1969.
(7) P. D. Converse, 'New Laws of Retail Gravitation', *Journal of Marketing*, 14, January 1949, pp. 379–84.
(8) J. Goddard, 'Multivariate Analysis of Office Location Patterns in the City Centre; a London Example', *Regional Studies*, 2, 1, 1968.
(9) F. H. W. Green, 'Urban Hinterlands in England and Wales: an analysis of bus services', *Geographical Journal*, July–September 1950, pp. 64–88, plus map.
(10) N. Hood, 'Location Analysis in Economic Geography', *British Journal of Marketing*, 3, 3, October 1969.
(11) H. Hotelling, 'Stability in Competition', *Economic Journal*, June 1929.
(12) D. L. Huff, 'Determination of Intra-Urban Retail Trade Areas', Real Estate Research Programme, University of California, 1962; and 'A Probabilistic Analysis of Consumer Spatial Behaviour', in *Emerging Concepts in Marketing*, American Marketing Association, 1963, pp. 444–50.
(13) D. L. Huff, and L. Blue, (1965), 'A Programmed Solution for Estimating Retail Sales Potential', Centre for Regional Studies, University of Kansas, 1965.
(14) H. R. Imus, 'Projecting Sales Potentials for Department Stores in Regional Shopping Centres', *Economic Geography*, January 1961, pp. 33–51.
(15) R. F. Kelly, 'Estimating Ultimate Performance Levels of New Retail Outlets', *Journal of Marketing Research*, 4, February 1967, pp. 13–19.
(16) B. J. La Londe, 'The Logistics of Retail Location', in *Social Responsibilities of Marketing*, American Marketing Association, 1961, pp. 567–75.
(17) B. J. La Londe, 'Differentials in Supermarket Drawing Power', Marketing and Transportation Paper No. 11, Michigan State University, 1962.
(18) A. P. Lerner and H. W. Singer, 'Some Notes on Duopoly and Spatial Competition', *Journal of Political Economy*, April 1937.
(19) W. Arthur Lewis, 'Competition in Retail Trade', *Economica*, 12, 1945, pp. 202–34.
(20) W. G. McClelland, 'The Supermarket and Society', *Sociological Review*, 10, 1962, pp. 133–44.
(21) W. G. McClelland, *Costs and Competition in Retailing*, London, Macmillan, 1966, pp. 192–201.

(22) J. E. Mertes, 'A Retail Structural Theory for Site Analysis', *Journal of Retailing*, 40, Summer 1964, pp. 19–30.

(23) P. Mooney and A. Wicks, 'Reading Evening Post A and B', in T. Coram, *Cases in Marketing and Marketing Research*, Crosby Lockwood, 1969, pp. 1–14.

(24) C. A. Moser and W. Scott, *British Towns; a statistical study of their social and economic differences*, Edinburgh, Oliver & Boyd, 1961.

(25) E. L. Nelson, *The Selection of Retail Locations*, F. W. Dodge Corporation, 1958, pp. 66–78.

(26) M. D. Plotkin, 'The Use of Credit Accounts and Computers in Determining Store Trading Area' in *New Directions in Marketing*, American Marketing Association, 1965, pp. 261–82.

(27) W. J. Reilly, 'Methods for Study of Retail Relationships', Bureau of Business, Monograph No. 4, University of Texas, 1929.

(28) C. Richardson, 'Bradford's Retail Market Area', *British Journal of Marketing*, 2, 4, January 1969, pp. 260–7.

(29) R. W. Ritland, 'New Methods of Estimating and Forecasting Retail Sales', *Journal of Retailing*, 39, Autumn 1963, pp. 1–9.

(30) J. W. Rouse, 'Estimating Productivity for Planned Regional Shopping Centres', Urban Land Institute, Washington, DC, 1953.

(31) M. Sawits, 'Model for Branch Store Planning', *Harvard Business Review*, 45, July–August 1967, pp. 140–3.

(32) P. Sharp, 'Shopping Centre Surveys in Great Britain', *Commentary, Journal of the Market Research Society*, 9, 4, October 1967, pp. 191–202.

(33) D. M. Smith, 'Identifying the Grey Areas', *Regional Studies*, 2, 2, 1968.

(34) C. Sofer, 'Buying and Selling: a study in the sociology of distribution', *Sociological Review*, Vol. 13, No. 2, 1965.

(35) N. A. Spence, 'A Multi-factor Uniform Regionalization of British Counties on the basis of employment data', *Regional Studies*, 2, 1, 1968.

(36) D. L. Thompson, 'New Concept: Subjective Distance', *Journal of Retailing*, 39, Spring 1963, pp. 1–6.

(37) D. L. Thompson, 'Consumer Convenience and Retail Area Structure', *Journal of Marketing Research*, 4, February 1967, pp. 37–44.

Chapter C.13

RETAIL MANAGEMENT
by Ted Stephenson

Retail distribution stands at the end of the total conversion process, which begins with the raw materials and ends with the finished product in the hands of the retailer. The success of the conversion process, however, is only demonstrated when the customer makes a purchase. This chapter will be concerned with two points which emerge from this preliminary statement: first, the retail operation is itself a conversion process entailing an input and an output[1]; second, it is at the boundary of the total process in that it is in direct contact with the final customer. It is out of these that the general problems of retail management develop and the questions of physical distribution emerge.

The input of the retail organization can be differentiated into:

(a) the generalized factor of finance
(b) manpower, including both staff and management
(c) the raw materials of retailing—the commodities that are to be converted
(d) information relating to the firm and its environment.

The nature of the conversion process rests on the fact that until the commodities are at particular points within the range of the customer, they are of no value to him. Commodities in the factory, the depot and the warehouse do not have customer value until they are in the appropriate situation, that is, when they are accessible to the customer. This implies the effective location of shops, but it also requires that at those sites there are commodities which the customer wants, that the goods are there in appropriate quantities and at appropriate prices, and that they are there at the right time. Retail distribution is thus concerned with place utility, time utility and with arrangements for convenient transactions between customer and seller (possession utility).[2]

In terms of location the right site will depend on a number of factors including the adequacy of the present trading area; the accessibility of the site to the trading area; the growth potential of the area; the possibility of intercepting business by establishing the shop between the people in the trading area and the traditional source of the same goods; the cumulative attraction of a number of shops and the possibility of interchange of customers between them; and the economics of the site.[3]

The ability to develop the right operation depends on the inputs to the system. A first requirement is that the organization has or can obtain the finance which will enable it to build and develop the site or to rent an existing shop. Also the firm must be able to obtain the financial resources to develop the appropriate stock ranges and levels, to secure the necessary raw material input. The relationship between successful conversion and input is highlighted by the fact that some of the finance which the firm depends on is fed back into the firm through its successful selling operations.

The raw material input is not an automatic process, in that the nature of the commodity input is influenced by decisions of management in relation to product mix and pricing policy which are themselves determined by the interaction of the firm's objectives, environmental considerations and the quality of management. In this latter connection the emphasis is on the skill of management to relate its own unit of organization to its relevant environment, and to understand the interaction between the inputs and specifically to consider how far a change in any input affects the operation of the firm and the subsequent output. This pattern operates throughout the management structure in that top management makes strategic and policy decisions which provide a framework for the decisions of lower level managers in such a specific area as buying.

The inputs of finance, manpower and raw materials can be regarded as energy inputs but a further input is that of information, some of which is in the nature of feedback from the firm's existing operations. It is upon the basis of this general information that the management makes its decision with regard to resource allocation and usage, for example, decisions as to the type of outlet to be developed and the derived decisions relating to the type of staff to be employed to provide the appropriate service, either selling goods over the counter, or filling shelves and manning check-out points in self-service shops. These latter decisions clearly affect the manpower input to the firm.

A point that emerges at this stage is that the notion of the right site in physical terms is qualified by the total operation of the retailing unit. That is to say, if the firm's prices are strikingly undercutting those of its competitors with no loss of quality or at least with a price-quality balance that is acceptable, customers may be prepared to suffer some inconvenience to get to that shop. Similarly, given that a firm's goods or services are seen to be significantly superior to those of other shops, customers may be prepared to incur some discomfort to purchase at that particular shop. Thus the appropriate conversion process for a particular shop can be seen to be the product of physical location; of quality-pricing policy; of retailing techniques—for example, self-service, one-stop shopping and so on; of services provided; of the efficiency of the management and staff and of the goods in demand being available as the customer requires. This involves the operational problems of stock-holding, sorting stock to meet customer requirements and of physical transfer to the customer. The output of the conversion process are the goods and services as they have been affected by the various elements in the conversion process.

310

A further output from the conversion system is information about the goods and services converted, and the efficiency of this output will be an important factor in determining whether the main output is sold and so produces a financial feedback sufficient to develop the organization still further. For a general model of the input-conversion-output process, see Figure 13·1.

The Retailing Environment

The conversion process takes place in an environment which may be dynamic or stable; heterogeneous or homogeneous; fragmented or unified; benign or hostile.[4] All of these apply to both the input and output sides of the conversion process. All these factors represent constraints and contingencies on the retail organization as well as representing opportunities to be exploited. In operational terms these different aspects of the environment may be seen in the following examples. A retail organization may operate in a situation in which the input of commodities is stable, the same firms have supplied the organization for a lengthy period and there have been little or no problems of supply. The commodities have been delivered to the retailer at the specified times, in the specified qualities and quantities with few damaged goods, with the result that the retailer has been able to operate with a high degree of certainty and a consequent reduction in stock levels, not having to carry a margin of stocks to meet the uncertainty of supplies. This situation can be contrasted with the position where the retail organization is faced with changing sources of supply and of variations in the supplies input due to the instability of the suppliers' operations and of the distribution system, with the consequent requirement of a higher stock level to avoid customer dissatisfaction.

In addition to the problem of the dynamic/stable input, there is the further problem of the market into which the output goes. Here two questions arise: Is the customer demand stable or dynamic? Is the market stable because of the lack of competition or dynamic because of a highly competitive situation? Here again there arise problems of stockholding: given stability of supplies and of customer demand, the problem of stock level may create little difficulty, but given uncertainty of supply or demand, jointly or individually, the stock level problem increases in severity.

In relation to the question of heterogeneous and homogeneous environments, the problem on the input side of the retail organization arises out of its nature, that is to say, whether it is a specialist organization dealing in limited lines and ranges or whether it is a multi-product organization selling over a wide range of commodities. Even where the organization is operating as a specialist operation, heterogeneity may arise because the organization deals in different price ranges of the commodities in which it specializes. Basically the question of heterogeneity or homogeneity on the input side rests on the number of different kinds of commodities with which the retailer has to deal and the extent to which they have to be obtained from different sources of supply. The more complex this aspect of his operations the greater the possibility of problems arising in achieving spatial and time utility for the customer.

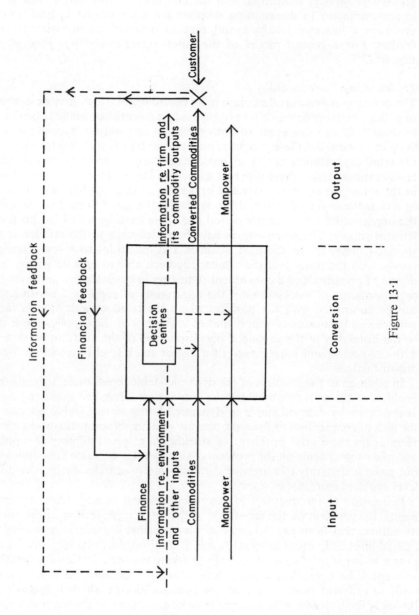

Customer

Information re. firm and
its commodity outputs

Converted Commodities

Manpower

Output

Information feedback

Financial feedback

Decision
centres

Conversion

Figure 13·1

Finance

Information re. environment
and other inputs

Commodities

Manpower

Input

On the output side, the question of heterogeneity and homogeneity is conditioned by the nature of the particular retail organization: if it is a specialist retailer then it is catering substantially to meet a homogeneous customer need; where it offers a wide range of commodities it is seeking to meet heterogeneous customer needs, the situation being further complicated by the degree of heterogeneity/homogeneity that is introduced by its price range policy.

The notion of the fragmented or unified environment relates to the question of whether the firm is dependent on a single or limited number of sources of supply, or on a large number of such sources. If a retail organization is receiving a heterogeneous input this may or may not come from a single or limited number of suppliers, depending on the nature of the supplier. If it is receiving a homogeneous input it may, or may not, come from many suppliers. The range of possibilities is outlined in Table 13·I:

Table 13·I

Environment	Homogeneous	Heterogeneous
Unified	Limited range of commodities from a single or few suppliers	Variety of commodities from a single or few suppliers
Fragmented	Limited range of commodities from many suppliers	Variety of commodities from many suppliers

On the output side it refers to the question of whether the firm sells to a single or few customers, or to a large number of customers. While the retailer is generally faced with a highly fragmented customer environment, there are situations in which a retailer may sell predominantly to a limited number of special customers—this may occur where a retailer deals with some institutional customers in addition to more normal customers.

The benign or hostile nature of the environment refers to the attitudes and actions of both competitors and customers of the firm. It refers to the degree of feeling in the environment towards the firm; that is, how far competitors are prepared to cooperate with the firm and how far there is customer loyalty. The significance of the latter lies not only in the readiness of customers to buy from that particular retail organization, but also the tolerance with which they are prepared to accept spatial and time utility breakdowns which may arise out of stock situations developing, among other things, from failure of the physical distribution system between suppliers and the retailer. On the input side the benign or hostile nature of the environment manifests itself in the readiness or otherwise of suppliers to meet special requirements of given retailers.

All these facets of the environment have significance for the structure of the retail organization and for the behaviour of its management. Where the environment is stable, both in terms of input and output, the structure of the firm can be formalized and can rely on rules to achieve its adaptation to that environment. Routine stock ordering and routine sales procedures can well be the acceptable mode of operation. This can be the least costly form of operation and will tend to make limited demands on its management. Where the environment is dynamic both in terms of input and output, then flexibility of structure and management will be necessary and operation by rule will be inefficient. Greater discretion within a planned framework will become a necessary aspect of the firm, and management capability of using its discretionary ability will be required. To meet this type of dynamic situation, the firm will need to monitor the environment and plan responses to it.

Where the input environment is dynamic and the output environment is stable, and where the converse applies, different organization responses are required. For examples of these see Table 13·II:

Table 13·II

INPUT

Output		Dynamic	Stable
Output	Dynamic	Discretion within plans for both	Rules to cover input Discretion on output
	Stable	Discretion on input Rules on output	Rules to cover both environments

One problem that arises in these cases is that of integrating responses to different environmental conditions facing the same organization, more specifically it highlights the buying/selling stances to be adopted by retail organizations in facing stable and dynamic environments.

Where the environment on the input side of a retail organization is heterogeneous because of the firm's policies, the organization needs to create specialized buying units. Not being able to establish separate buying units for every commodity it purchases, the organization has to identify those product segments which have a high degree of similarity or complementarity, and establish buying units to deal with them. On the input side, where a retail organization is dealing with a homogeneous situation, the need for structural buying divisions is related to the size of its operations and the volume of interaction between itself and the suppliers, and whether the input is fragmented or unified. The problem here is one of surveillance capacity, that is, the ability of the firm to handle the input transactions. Surveillance capacity will vary with differences in data-collection and transmission and processing devices, for example, the degree to which computerization has taken place, but at any given time the available devices set constraints upon the organization's surveillance capacity.

In structural terms, the heterogeneous input will call for specialist buying units and skills, while in the homogeneous input situation where subdivision is required, less specialization is called for, but more repetition of the same buying skills will be demanded. The problem is further complicated by the stability/dynamic dimension of the environment. With a dynamic environment the buyers will have to live with a higher degree of uncertainty than is the case where the environment is stable. On the output side, similar problems of heterogeneity and homogeneity will arise, and will influence structure and management behaviour.

314

Similarly, where the retail organization is faced with fragmented sources of supplies and customers it may well be that the firm will have to establish separate structural units, but this will depend on the surveillance capacity of the organization and the skills of its management and the nature of the fragmentation, that is, a retail organization which deals with normal types of retail trade, and also with a number of institutional customers, may find it necessary to establish separate units to handle the two types of trade.

Where the firm is faced with a benign type of environment there may be exchange of information between itself and similar organizations, but when faced with a hostile environment it may need to undertake much more search activity for information. Similarly when faced with benign customers, it may be able to rely on them to come to it rather than it having to go and search for them. In both of these instances where the retailer has to undertake search either for information or customers, or indeed for any other resources essential to its activities, it will have to devote resources, in terms of time and finance, to the search and where necessary build up the appropriate structural units. It might well use these resources for other purposes in a benign environment.

Emergent Structures
Associated with these different aspects of the environment there is the problem of change, that is, of the environment moving from a stable state to a dynamic state, from a homogeneous condition to one of heterogeneity, from a unified to a fragmented state and from a benign environment to a hostile one, and of course the converse of all these movements. The problem for the retail organization is to be sensitive to these changes and to be aware of the consequences in terms of stock levels, of structural requirements, of changing complexity of the problem of physical distribution in terms of both inputs and outputs, and of managerial skills. Some of these changes in the relation of the retail firm to the environment are induced by changes in the policies of the firm but even here the need is to consider the consequences of these changes along the dimensions outlined above. Failure to recognize the significance of change, whether environment-induced or self-induced, can lead to structures, policies and behaviours that are out of line with the requirements of the new situation with the result that organizational stress and ineffectiveness develop.

From the preceding analysis it will be seen that the nature of the environment will influence the type of structure that the organization requires, and this in turn will influence the type of coordination that is required to bring the different units together into an operating totality. As the retail organization becomes substructured to deal with its environment, so the problem of interdependence arises and specifically raises the question of the nature of the links between the individual sub-units. While these units of the organization are interdependent, it does not necessarily mean that each part is dependent on and supports each other in a direct way. The branches of a retail chain organization may have little contact with each other, yet they are interdependent in that unless each performs adequately the total firm is

315

endangered, so that failure on the part of any one branch can weaken the whole and the other branches. This is an organizational situation in which each part is supported by the whole, and each part renders a separate contribution to the whole: it can be regarded as pooled interdependence.

However, other units of the retail organization may depend upon a different type of interdependence, a sales department dependent upon a buying department; an accounts department dependent upon a sales department. These departments have a pooled type of interdependence, but there is also a direct interdependence which can be regarded as sequential, in that the buying department must perform effectively before the sales department can act, and unless the sales department operates efficiently the accounts department cannot fulfil its task. Viewed in another way, there can be seen to be an element of reciprocal interdependence in that the buying department cannot perform effectively unless it receives an input of information from the sales department.

These three types of interdependence call for different types of coordination. Coordination may be achieved by the establishment of routines and rules which direct the actions of each unit into lines consistent with those taken by others in the interdependent relationship. The rules need to be internally consistent, and this means that the situations to which they are applied are relatively stable, repetitive and not too numerous in order that there may be a matching of situations with appropriate rules. As an alternative to coordination by rule, there can be coordination by plan which involves the development of schedules for the interdependent units against which their activities can be governed. This approach is less rigid and is more appropriate for dynamic situations, especially those involving a changing environment. A final form of coordination is that achieved by mutual adjustment which involves the transmission of new information during the action process—a regulatory feedback operates.

When these types of coordination are related to the different forms of interdependence it would appear that where there is pooled interdependence— rules are appropriate; in the case of sequential interdependence, coordination by plan appears to be suitable, and in the instance of reciprocal interdependence mutual adjustment would appear to be advantageous. A further point of managerial importance which emerges is that the three types of coordination place different burdens on communication and decision-making. It would seem that rule application requires less communication and fewer decisions than does planning, which in turn calls for less decision and communication activity than is required by mutual adjustment. This is important in that each calls for differing degrees of managerial skill. The retail organization faced with a complex of environmental variables needs to be structured not only to deal with these variables, but also to devise the appropriate type of coordination and with it the appropriate skills; for example, in the dynamic environment managers will be required who can exercise discretion and live with a higher degree of uncertainty than in the stable environment. Similarly in a highly heterogeneous and fragmented input environment, the management in charge of the resultant complex of substructures will need to

316

be capable of dealing with a wide range of problems arising out of the nature of the input.

Up to this point the variables in the environment have been examined independently, but all retail organizations face environments which involve complex, interrelated patterns of these variables. This can be demonstrated if attention is concentrated on the dynamic/stable dimension and the heterogeneous/homogeneous dimension.

Where the retail firm faces an environment that is both stable and homogeneous the structure would tend to be relatively simple. There would be a limited degree of subdivision and where it occurred it would lead to the existence of several similar departments. The organization would rely primarily on standardized rules for dealing with change, the various subdivisions would tend to operate on the basis of applying rules and general management would consist substantially of rule enforcement. The danger in such a situation is that a concentration on rule enforcement can make for rigidity in top management with the result that it is incapable of seeing and understanding changes that are occurring. Concern for detail drives out time and ability for planning.[5] Attention to routine stock procedures and stable delivery systems may distract attention from the fact that change has occurred which calls for strategic rather than operating decisions.[6]

In the case of the retail organization facing a heterogeneous but stable environment, the emergent structure would tend to be one of a variety of departments each dealing with a relatively homogeneous section of the heterogeneous environment, and again each would tend to rely on rules to deal with the environment. Each of the major subdivisions may be further subdivided into uniform sections which could again be rule-applying agencies.

When the firm faces an environment that is dynamic rather than stable, new problems arise, for standardized responses are no longer adequate, as the firm now faces contingencies as well as constraints. The firm must decide when and how to act, and its cues in part arise out of the environment.

If the firm faces an environment that is dynamic, but homogeneous, it may be subdivided only to the extent to which its capacity to monitor the environment would be over-extended. The resultant subdivisions would be less concerned with the application of rules than with the planning of responses to environmental changes: thus there would be a need for some decentralization. Where the environment is both heterogeneous and dynamic, the structure of the firm needs to be differentiated to correspond to different segments of the environment, and each must operate on a decentralized basis to monitor and plan responses to fluctuations in its sector of the environment.

In reviewing the position of the organization in relation to its environment, it is clear that the more heterogeneous the environment, the greater are the constraints the firm faces, and the more dynamic the environment the greater the contingencies. Central to this is the fact that the type of environment a firm faces will have a profound influence on its physical distribution system. These situations have implications for the firm in terms of information flows into the firm, and in terms of decisions relating to the physical flow of goods into and out of the firm, and in connection with its stock-holding policies.

317

Problems such as the speed of delivery of supplies and the consistency of delivery have to be seen within the context of the environment of the retail firm, and related to such factors as company policy, itself a product of inter-action between the firm and its environment. To deal with these problems, appropriate information flows have to be built into the organization's relationship with its environment and specifically into the physical distribution system.

Retail organizations need to build up information on the efficiency of their suppliers' physical distribution to them, to work out the cost to themselves of lost sales and lost customers arising from the inefficiency of suppliers' operations and also to estimate those costs which arise when suppliers send the wrong commodities and these have to be returned (this includes not only errors in size, colour or physical attributes, but also the right commodities arriving in damaged condition). To deal with these problems is the task of management; less obviously, but just as necessarily, it is the task of manage-ment to control the amount and scope of organizational adaptation in dealing with a complex environment. Management deals with this problem by establishing structural units which are specialized to face a limited range of contingencies within a limited range of constraints. The more constraints and contingencies the firm faces, the more its structure will be departmentalized. Once it is accepted that a retail organization will face an environment involv-ing a complex pattern of variables, the possibility of varied and complex structures needs to be considered, and the need for retail management to devise such structures becomes a prerequisite of successful operation. These varying structures not only raise design problems, but also raise questions relating to the type of management skills required to operate the departments and sections which are facing different types of environment. It also raises questions of promotion and transferability when management personnel are moving to different types of subdivision designed to meet differing environ-mental conditions. Too little attention is paid to systematic consideration of organizational design by retail organizations, with the consequence that they are often ill-adapted to meet the type of environment facing them.

Environmental Control
Faced with this type of multi-variable environment, the management of a retail organization has to try to establish such control over the environment as is possible, while at the same time recognizing that elements in the environ-ment are seeking to control its operations. Management has to attempt to protect the firm from environmental contingencies by taking certain actions. First, the firm may seek to protect itself by buffering activities, that is, on the input side it stocks goods; the extent to which it needs to do this is influenced by the degree of regularity of supplies and by the extent to which it is depen-dent upon any one supplier. Faced by heterogeneity and fragmentation on its input side, the firm is—given that no one source is pre-eminently dominant—not dependent on any one source, so that a breakdown in a source need not be detrimental to its operations. On the output side the need to carry stocks is influenced by the regularity of the demand. Buffering goes beyond carrying

318

stock levels adequate to meet normal supply-demand situations: its aim is to protect the retailer from being caught short due to contingencies on the input and output sides of the firm. Clearly this raises questions of probability, of the likelihood that a given type of contingency will arise in any meaningful time span for the firm. Buffering, while it protects the firm, does carry costs, and a classic problem arising from it is how to maintain stocks to meet contingency situations without incurring obsolescence, as need changes.

Second, while buffering aims to absorb environmental fluctuations, smoothing involves attempts to reduce fluctuations in the environment. Smoothing is one of the strategies available to management to assist it to control the environment. Retailers faced with seasonal or other fluctuations in demand may offer inducements to their customers in the form of special promotions or sales during periods when demand is depressed.

Third, there are situations where environmental changes cannot be buffered or smoothed. In these instances, where changes can be anticipated, the firm can forecast demand for a given period and so plan and schedule operations to meet the anticipated changes. Retailers learn that some environmental fluctuations are patterned, and in these cases forecasting and adjustment appear almost automatic. For example a retail firm, knowing that it has peak periods for custom, may seek to redistribute that custom by offering special concessions to those who shop at off-peak periods—a smoothing type of operation, but given that this may have a limited effect it can schedule its activities to meet these peak periods through the use of part-time staff. In some situations firms have gained sufficient experience to know that these variations are patterned with a high degree of regularity, but where the environment is more complex there may be need for more than a simple projection of past experience. It is in these situations that forecasting emerges as a specialized and sophisticated activity, requiring the use of elaborate statistical techniques.

It is evident that not all fluctuations in the environment can be anticipated and when this is the case it is clear that the orderly operation of the firm is likely to be upset. The test of management in such situations is its ability to adapt to the circumstances effectively within as short a time span as possible. Where firms have been operating in a stable environment, sudden unanticipated developments are likely to have far-reaching consequences, in that the firms are not geared to meeting such situations: this applies particularly to management attitudes. The 'precipitating event' of unexpected change can have disastrous results for such firms. For example, in areas where the established grocery firms have not faced the competition of powerful supermarket operators, the advent of such competition can create situations which are beyond the understanding and abilities of the existing firm. The result is not inevitable, as the management may respond effectively and the 'precipitating event' may be just what is required to bring the firm into a new phase of acitvity. This can be a 'make or break' situation in that it can upset all preconceived notions of stock holding, commodity mix, price levels and the type of physical distribution appropriate to the situation. What may well happen is that there will be a time-lag before the firm adjusts to the new situation, and in this way the firm will suffer in comparison with those who are more tuned to meet the demands of the situation.

The retail firm will seek to control, or at least influence, the various elements in its environment, particularly sources of finance and labour, suppliers and customers. This it will try to achieve through a variety of methods, and it is here that management must assess the types of dependence which surround it. The Ansoffian[6] assessment of strengths and weaknesses undertaken by a firm must include a survey of the various relationships between the firm and its environmental elements. It also needs to assess the criteria by which those elements judge its performance.

These elements and their criteria are listed in Table 13·III:

Table 13·III

Superordinate systems	Criteria
Shareholders	Price appreciation of securities Dividend payment
Labour force	Wage levels Stability of employment Opportunity
The market: consumers	Value given
The market: competitors	Rate of growth Innovation
Suppliers	Rapidity of payment
Creditors	Adherence to contract terms
Community	Contribution to community development
Nation	Public responsibility

S. Tilles, 'The Manager's Job—A Systems Approach', *Harvard Business Review*, January–February 1963, p. 78.

Central to the concern of the retailer is the 'value-given' criteria of the customers. This relates closely to the question of physical distribution and its efficient management by the retailer, that is, the management of the input of commodities into the firm, the appropriate stock policies, the flow of information to the customers, the location of the shops and of the commodities in the shops, and the distribution arrangements to the customer. Without the efficient management of this system the successful fulfilment of the criteria of the other environmental elements is unlikely. On the basis of the analysis of dependencies and criteria the retail organization needs to determine the strategies which are appropriate to each element, if it is to maintain and increase its influence over them.

In the area of supplies the alternatives available to the firm will be influenced by the variables already outlined, that is, heterogeneity, fragmentation, stability and so on. Within this framework of variables the firm has to determine the extent to which it will enter into contracts (of short, medium or long duration) with suppliers. In entering into such contracts the firm has some security of future supply, but this is at a cost of reduced freedom to deal with others, for it is committed to an exchange with the other party to the contract, and in consequence has fewer resources available for other dealings. Clearly the supplier also gains in that he is given an assured market. For both parties there is a commitment to reduce uncertainty for the other party, and both must demonstrate their ability to do so. Just as the retailer needs to be sure of his supplies (and that includes their delivery at times appropriate to the retailer's trading requirements), so the supplier needs to be sure that he will be paid at the appropriate time. Here the value of past performances becomes important, for a history of reliable deliveries and reliable payments gives confidence to the contracting parties.

It will be seen that dependence on elements in the environment exists (i) in proportion to the organization's need for resources which that element can provide and (ii) in inverse proportion to the ability of other elements to provide the same resources.[4] For example, a retail firm is dependent on a financial organization to the extent that it needs finance, which is not available from other sources. This raises the question for the retail organization of how far it can be self-financing: retaining a sufficient proportion of its profits, so it does not have to go to the market to obtain funds, would reduce its dependence. Hence the decision on how much to retain of its profits becomes an important issue from the dependence point of view.

As dependence introduces constraints upon the firm's freedom of action, the problem for the firm is how to avoid becoming subservient to an element in the environment. To avoid this situation the firm may try to minimize the power of elements in the environment by keeping alternatives open. Instead of becoming dependent upon one source of supply, the organization may deal with a number of suppliers in order to establish a precedent for support with each supplier, so that if any one supplier is unable or unwilling to continue supplies, the firm has already established links with other suppliers. How far it needs to develop these relations will depend on the state of competition between suppliers. A retailer may be dependent upon a single supplier and still not incur too much inconvenience if there are other suppliers who are ready to step in and provide him with the necessary supplies. Even where firms are willing to step in, the establishment of an effective relationship between retailer and supplier can take time, as both parties are concerned to see how far the other will match up in performance to what is claimed at the commencement of the relationship. Furthermore, the problem is complicated by the fact that the environment contains not only many suppliers, but also many who require the supplies. Alternative buyers weaken the dependence of any one supplier on any one buyer. The supplier can always turn to the alternatives, and faced with this situation a firm may be forced to build up buffer stocks. A further possibility is that the suppliers themselves will coalesce to deal with buyers just as the buyers themselves, in certain circumstances, may enter into agreements with other buyers. These are specific examples of the tendency of firms, when faced with the power of those upon whom they are dependent, to seek power themselves. This they may do through informal cooperative action with others, or through some more definite organizational assimilation, for example, by means of formal

321

agreements on specific areas of activities. The point at issue here is that the more formal the machinery that is established to deal with the opposing concentration of power, the more limited is the individual organization's freedom of action likely to be, until such a stage is reached in mergers that the individual firm no longer exists but becomes part of a larger complex. It will be evident that no one prescription to handle the problems of power and dependence can be laid down, but it is clear that firms need to assess their position if they are to protect themselves from contingencies arising out of dependencies. In many cases firms drift into positions of dependence without fully appreciating the consequences that can arise.

Another means of acquiring power is through the acquisition of prestige; this hinges upon the extent to which an element in the environment considers that trading with a given firm will bring it prestige. In these circumstances the firm which confers prestige upon the element has acquired power in relation to that element and has done so without any commitment to it. The cost to the firm lies in the outlay needed to build up its prestige.

A further example of a retail firm's attempt to control or influence the elements on its input side lies in the strategic decision to move back inside the total system. This it may do by entering into production in order to ensure its source of supply, and also to allow it to develop its own products for sale through its own outlets. In this latter case it is also concerned with securing some influence over the customer by creating a product that is in some sense unique to itself. The extent to which a retail firm involves itself in the productive system can vary: on the one hand the commitment may be in the form of a contractual arrangement, by which the retail organization agrees to accept the output of the manufacturing organization if the latter will produce articles to the specifications set down by the retailer, who may provide technical and design advice and possibly capital for the purchase of appropriate machinery. On the other hand the retail organization may purchase the production unit and so ensure full control. Clearly this is the 'make or buy' type of situation in which questions of synergy[6] inevitably occur. The retail organization needs to analyse carefully the various aspects of its own organization and that of the production unit it is contemplating purchasing, to determine what the gains and losses, in synergistic terms, are likely to be.[6] In one sense synergy may appear to be obvious: the operations of the two organizations appear to be complementary, and by bringing them together it would seem that the parent firm will benefit. However, the possibility of negative synergism exists in the situation, for the management skills appropriate to the operation of a retail firm may not be applicable to a production system. Transportation problems once handled by the manufacturer become the problem of the retailer, and again there may be a lack of the appropriate skills. The fact that the retail firm buys the management skills of the other firm does not necessarily obviate these problems, because there are now problems of understanding and coordination which the retail management may find difficult to handle, not least because of the traditional readiness of retailers to over-emphasize the differences between themselves and those in manufacturing. The problems outlined may also develop if the manufacturing firm decides to enter the field of retailing, either through the opening of new outlets or by the purchase of existing outlets.

Another method by which the retail organization can achieve control on its input side is through the use of 'house brands'. If the retailer places bulk orders for goods with 'house names' the supplier achieves an outlet cheaply, having no marketing expenses. In return the dependence on this particular output is increased and hence the influence of the retail organization is increased also. At the same time the retailer seeks to extend his influence on the output side through developing customer attachment to a 'house name'.

On the output side of the firm, management is also concerned to obtain a measure of control or influence over the environment. This it may seek to achieve by 'house names' and by advertising of various types. It may try to build up customer loyalty through its advertising and its general merchandising policy. But the situation is complicated by the volume of manufacturers advertising, whose aim is to build up loyalty to a brand and not to a particular retailer. This is an aspect of the manufacturer's concern to build up environmental control on his output side, for it means that the product is available through many outlets and is not tied to a limited number. The retailer has to try to exert his influence through his own merchandising and other activities, including those of physical distribution, such as special customer delivery services which could range from special facilities for loading commodities on to the customers' own transport to special or speedy deliveries to the customers' homes. The retail organization needs to build up a distinctive competence for itself, and its management needs to review it periodically in the light of changing competition and changing customer needs, tastes, preferences and expectations. Again the need is for retail management to ask itself basic questions relating to its own mission, such as, what is the firm seeking to achieve given the situation and what should it be seeking to become in the future? This in turn means that it needs to assess not only its own performance but also the environment, and to forecast future developments, including such matters as population shifts, property developments, town planning, including the organization of vehicle and pedestrian traffic which involves questions of private car ownership and usage, the growth of new methods of transportation by suppliers, the opening of new regional and national transport networks, future packing and packaging developments, and warehouse patterns and the development of new attitudes to physical distribution as a total system. Behind these various points there lie such questions as how these changes will affect a given retailer's physical distribution operation—will they call for shifts in the location of the firm's outlets, will they mean that suppliers will be able to deliver more promptly or not and what will this mean for the stockholding policy of the firm? Could it mean that the retailer will have to take a greater or lesser part in the physical distribution system? Given changes in packing and packaging, what implications has this for the retailer in terms of order size, problems of warehousing and stock rooms, display and through store traffic? These questions provide guide lines for thinking through the problems that are liable to arise in the physical distribution area and are of sufficiently far-reaching concern to indicate the centrality of physical distribution in the total distribution operation, and of the need for management to give time to consideration of the physical distribution area in a coherent manner.

This represents not simply a passive reaction to environmental change, but of purposefully considering how far the retail organization can exercise control and influence to ensure that in spite of the changes facing it, it can remain a profitable operation. In addition to the specific methods already discussed, a general way to increase influence is through growth. This firms can try to achieve by means of:

(a) expansion within the existing product lines, that is, increasing sales within the same market, through market penetration
(b) expansion within the existing product line, but by moving to new markets, through market development
(c) expansion through entering into a new product line which has close affinity with existing lines in the existing markets, through product development
(d) development through entering new product lines in new markets, through diversification.[6] In this case the decision represents a major stage in the firm's development as it involves the twofold risk of moving into the sale of new product lines in new markets; the uncertainties of both may be great.

Conversion and Physical Distribution
This takes the problem of retail management back to the conversion process stage, raising questions relating to the number of outlets the firm considers necessary to its expansion/diversification programme, to the size of those outlets, and to their nature. These are problems which must be related to the objectives of the firm and its distinctive competence. Once again problems of physical distribution management emerge, for the development of new outlets raises issues relating to the present organization of the distribution system. For example, given that the organization maintains a warehouse, do more outlets or differently located outlets require a greater or lesser number of company vehicles? Changes in the size of outlets will raise questions relating to the present capacity of vehicles and their ability to handle larger loads, and basically the new capacity of the outlets will raise questions relating to the capacity of the existing warehouse. Further problems relate to the extent to which intershop transfers occur and the transport demands these raise, and arise from changing the nature of the outlets, that is, from counter service with house delivery to self-service, which will require re-organization of the transport system.

At this stage it is clear that the tasks of retail management raise questions of relationship which can be considered in terms of dependence and power, of physical aspects and of information aspects. The retailer is involved in a two-way information process: in one direction he is concerned to transmit information to suppliers about the customers' requirements—in placing

324

orders with his suppliers he is providing information based on his expectations of what his customers will buy in the future. Undoubtedly there will be imperfections in this information, for example, it reflects his own perception of the situation and does not explain why customers' preferences are what they are, and why they may be changing. To overcome these and other imperfections, the manufacturer considers it worth his while to carry out his own market research; where this has been developed by manufacturers the retailer as a source of information for the supplier declines. Manufacturer advertising and market research reduce the dependence of the manufacturer on the retailer, and this reduces the latter's influence in the environment unless the retailer is able and willing to take action to maintain his influence. In physical distribution terms the significance of this lies in the fact that if the supplier does not deliver the commodities at the appropriate time and in the appropriate quantity, in line with his advertising and promotional campaign, the retailer is liable to be faced with a loss not only of sales, but of customers. On the stockholding side of physical distribution, manufacturers' advertising may create problems in that retailers may feel forced to hold higher than normal stocks, to meet demands which they have not stimulated and which may not materialize for any one retailer.

In the other direction, the retailer is a supplier of information to the consumer about the commodities he sells. One way in which he performs this function is by stocking commodities so that they can be examined by the customer; another way is by affixing a price, and yet another way is by personal service and the trading policies he pursues. Even in this field it is evident that changes have taken place, and the retailer is bypassed not only by the manufacturer, but by the development of a variety of information sources such as consumer advisory services, women's journals and informative labelling. The position is further influenced by the development of mass communications so that the individual retailer's communication to his customer is frequently superseded. In spite of this the retailer needs to develop a relationship with his customers which will ensure that he maintains a satisfactory customer flow of purchasing power in his outlets. The informational function of the retailer may have undergone a profound change in recent years, but the need to inform the customer of his presence and of the goods he sells remains, and this he achieves through the development of a distinctive competence which includes the location of his outlets in respect to the customers, the layout of commodities within these outlets, and the speed and consistency with which he delivers the goods into the shop and (where applicable) to the customer's home. The retailer's physical distribution system is part of his advertising and his image projection. The location of the shops is itself part of the information process, as it informs people of the existence of certain shopping facilities. The shop may be only a part of the retailer's message, but it is a part that must be seen by those to whom it is directed. Put in another way:

The whole purpose of distribution is to get goods from their places of production to their places of consumption; within this purpose stands the

325

pivotal device of the shop as a place to which the ultimate consumer can conveniently come for the exercise of choice, the performance of the transactions, and the collection of the goods.

From the customer's point of view it matters greatly how far she has to go to shop; what the time, trouble and expense involved in getting there and back will be; and whether, if she wishes to visit several different sorts of shop or compare prices and quality in several different shops of the same sort, she will find them together or dispersed.

From the shopkeeper's point of view it is vital to be where the customers will come, whether because they are passing his door in their hundreds in any case, or because his is the shop in his trade most conveniently near the homes of enough of them. From the point of view also of town planners and other users of land the location of shops is important, particularly because of their traffic-creating characteristics.[7]

The location of the retail outlet is only one part of the logistics problem. The retailing process is made complicated and costly by the fact that production is generally concentrated, while the consumers are dispersed. The shop represents a point of distribution within a system of other distribution points, including depots owned by the manufacturers and warehouses belonging either to wholesalers or to the retailer himself.

Analysis of this aspect of the physical distribution problem must take into account the number of loadings, deliveries and journeys and also the distances involved and their costs. The cost of 'getting goods from a number of sources to a number of destinations depends on the number and geographical pattern of each, the quantities involved from each source to each destination, the cost of movement, of loading and unloading, in vehicles of different capacities, and the cost of running intermediate depots (including retail shops) and of sorting and reassembling within them'.[7] Looking at this total process in relation to retail management the proportion of the total physical distribution system that comes within the province of the retailer is likely to vary, outlets may be dispersed near the customer and be some distance from the supplier, or may be near the supplier and more distant from the customer. The distances involved may not be substantial, but the nature of the journeys and the availability of alternative forms of transport require analysis by the management involved.

Furthermore, the position is complicated on the input side by the question of whether the shops may be large, taking deliveries in bulk from the suppliers, or whether they are small, requiring suppliers to break up containers for small drops. On the output side the customers may be making less frequent purchases on a bulk basis, this being influenced by the extent of refrigeration and deep freeze that has been developed in the community's standard of living. Even with these latter developments the retailer still acts as a breaker-up of quantities into small deliveries which are relatively costly for him to deliver to his customers. The total operation involving the breaking up and reassembling of commodity stocks, their sorting into appropriate geographical areas, their loading into vehicles and their distribution over short distances

326

are all costly to the retailer who provides a delivery service. Where the customer takes on the task of sorting out her order from the racks and sections in the shops and herself loads them onto a trolley and then transfers them to her shopping basket or to her car, the task of the retailer is changed—the content of part of the physical distribution system is altered. This is not to say that the problem has been simplified, for the retailer now has the task of ensuring that racks and sections are properly stocked to facilitate the customer's selection, and that the appropriate transport is available whether these be wire baskets or trolleys—and this means planned floor space so that customers, with their trolleys, can pass between the racks without discomfort.

Self-service in the grocery trade is an obvious example of the problems outlined, and as this development spreads to sections of dry goods in the form of self-selection, so the output side of the physical distribution aspect of retailing alters, and with it the appropriate management skills. The retailer's problems involve not merely the display, shelf-stocking and transportation problems already outlined, but also the problems of transference of commodities from the baskets or trolleys to the customer's container at the check-out points and of the delivery to the customer's car where she has one.

The fact that the customer buys in small quantities and requires variety of choice means that from the logistics point of view the retailer has to receive a variety of articles from different sources, and on the basis of the customer's requests sort them into suitable collections for her which he may, or may not, be required to deliver.

So far attention has been concentrated on the physical movement of goods from the retailer to the customers, but a further area relating to physical movement of goods is that which occurs within the shop itself. The design of shops thus emerges as an influence on the amount of internal transportation required before goods are displayed. Goods have to be unloaded from vehicles, they may then have to be stored or transported direct to their selling area, from where they may be taken by the customer, or, if this is not possible because of inconvenience, they have to be taken to a despatch area where they may be held until the appropriate delivery day, then they have to be loaded onto the delivery van and taken to the customer. All this reveals the need for management to give consideration to the efficient operation of the internal store transportation system, both to avoid unnecessary journeying and to avoid the storage problems that emerge because of a faulty flow of goods from stock room to selling area. The primary task of a shop is to sell goods and this requires, among other things, the efficient use of selling space. Attention to this aspect of shop layout must not, however, blind the retail manager to the problems and requirements of internal transportation, that is, to the most effective types of transport available and the most efficient routing of that transport. The internal system must be considered as a totality: changes in one part of the system can affect the operation of other parts. For example, a change in the size of hand trucks used for conveying goods from different points in a store and between different floors, requires that the width of alleys and turn-round space must be considered, as must the size of lifts for inter-floor movement.

327

On the input side of the physical movement of goods it has been assumed that the commodities purchased by the retailer are delivered by the suppliers at the shop, and that the breaking up of orders occurs at the shop. When this takes place it relieves the retailer of much of his physical distribution problems on the input side. However, the large retail organization with its own warehousing faces the problem that it may have a large number of outlets and must, in consequence, decide how far it should break bulk for its branches and how frequently it should allow its branches to order from its own warehouse.

This is a costing question in which the costs of holding and bulk breaking at the centre must be compared to the costs of holding stocks at the branches, since the less bulk is broken at the central warehouse and the less frequently branches can order, the higher the stocks they must hold. Involved in the costing must be that of transportation between the warehouse and the branches. In addition to length, which involves routing problems and frequency of journeys to multiple outlets, there are also problems relating to the selection of the appropriate size of vehicles, once the types of loads and routes are known. This raises questions of effective capacity utilization and the use of operations research techniques.

Given that some retail organizations need their own warehouse facilities, and remembering the type of problems outlined above, there is clearly a problem of the location of the warehouse (or in some cases the warehouses): 'Where they should be depends upon the geographical distribution of the population and the shape of the transport network; on the average load required at, and the optimum frequency of distribution to, retail outlets; and on the size of the total demand relative to the units of transport being used.'[8]

In the warehouses themselves there are also transportation problems. A major problem is that large quantities of a given commodity enter the warehouse and have to be stored for varying lengths of time, while varying assortments of different items have to go out. An obvious problem is that of space allocation when it is necessary to house slow-moving items and fast-moving items, so as to minimize the cost of assembling. Clearly information is required about the speed of movement of the differing lines and the quantities which need to be held. Again there is a need to study the types of mechanical handling equipment that are available, and to develop the most effective routing procedures for the appropriate equipment. The successful operation of the warehouse, as indeed of the total physical distribution system, rests upon adequate information and the application, where appropriate, of the latest information handling techniques, including that of computerization.

Summary

Retail management is concerned with the problems of input, conversion and output; and at the centre stands the complex of functions which comprise the conversion process. The environment surrounding this process may be dynamic or stable, heterogeneous or homogeneous, fragmented or unified, benign or hostile, and these factors represent constraints and contingencies facing the firm. These varying environmental factors affect both the structure
328

of the organization and the behaviour of its management, calling for differing degrees of structural departmentalization and for varying measures of flexibility. With the substructuring of the firm to deal with the environment, different forms of departmental interdependence develop, each requiring different types of coordination which place differing burdens on managerial communication and decision-making.

Faced with the multi-variable environment the retail firm takes steps to protect itself either by such tactics as buffering, smoothing, or scheduling, or by attempting to control the environmental elements upon which it is dependent. These elements include shareholders, labour force, customers, competitors, suppliers and creditors. To reduce dependence the retailer can develop a number of strategies which include moving back up the total system and seeking growth through expansion, or diversification. A general way in which the retail organization seeks to extend its influence is by building up a distinctive competence which management must regularly review. Not only is the retailer at the centre of a pattern of relationships with environmental elements, he is also involved in an information network of importance to the functioning of the total system.

Central to the functioning of the varying types of environment and the elements in it is the whole question of physical distributions; the more variable and complex the relationships of the retail organization to its environment, the more difficult the problems of physical distribution (problems of transportation, stock, and information). The involvement of the retailer in the total physical distribution system will vary. How much of the input side of his physical distribution system he performs himself will depend upon the nature of his relationship with the input elements, and the size of his operations. On the output side the amount of physical distribution in which he is involved will depend upon his own trading policies, which have themselves been influenced by environmental factors.

Further aspects of the physical distribution system that require the retailer's attention include problems of internal transportation within a shop, which need to be considered within the framework of the shop as a total system, that is, it is necessary to consider how far changes in selling methods and in shop layout affect the internal transportation system and how far changes in the latter affect the former. Where the retail organization has its own warehousing the problems that arise are twofold, those which relate to the relationship of warehouse to shops and those which relate to transportation within the warehouse; again the systems approach is central to the analysis of these issues.

Among the basic requirements of a physical distribution system is an efficient information system which not only involves appropriate information techniques, but also management that is capable of utilizing the information that it receives.

References
(1) A. K. Rice, *The Enterprise and Its Environment*, London, Tavistock, 1963; E. J. Miller and A. K. Rice, *Systems of Organisation*, London, Tavistock, 1967.

(2) Bowersox, Smykay, La Londe, *Physical Distribution Management*, New York, Macmillan, 1968, p. 20.
(3) R. L. Nelson, 'Principles of Retail Location' in R. R. Gist (ed.), *Management Perspectives in Retailing*, New York, Wiley, 1967.
(4) For extended reference see J. D. Thompson, *Organisations in Action*, London, McGraw-Hill, 1967.
(5) J. G. March and H. A. Simon, *Organisations*, New York, Wiley, p. 185.
(6) H. I. Ansoff, *Corporate Strategy*, London, McGraw-Hill, 1965, Chapter 1.
(7) W. G. McClelland, *Costs and Competition in Retailing*, London, Macmillan, 1966.
(8) W. G. McClelland, *Studies in Retailing*, Oxford, Blackwell, 1963, p. 175.

SECTION D

Operational Implications of PDM

Chapter D.14

PDM—AN AMERICAN PERSPECTIVE

by Philip Schary

The management of physical distribution has been a comparatively recent innovation in American business. The functional areas of production, marketing and finance, by contrast, have a much longer tradition and history of development. In the past, the movement of products and materials to market was not generally of major concern to higher levels of management. With the exception of freight rates, it was accepted as an inevitable cost, a necessary burden to the costs of production and marketing. The fact that only a portion of the costs involved were visible, combined with the inherent limitation of approaching distribution problems on a fragmented basis, only permitted management to exert a limited control over any part of the distribution process, and none over that which remained hidden from view.

Only within the last ten to fifteen years has physical distribution management emerged to the point of becoming a comprehensively defined area, where managerial technique and expertise can be applied to the process as a whole. The identification of PDM as a field in itself has been instrumental in focusing new energy on the area. The result has been to generate a strong interest by management in the application of the concepts of the field, and in extending its conceptual base into wider areas. The continuing ferment reflects awareness of possibilities which the act of emergence has created.

The turning point came as a result of several factors. Changes in marketing, awareness of the high costs of distribution, the complexities of evaluating new technological alternatives in distribution, and the development of new integrative managerial tools combined to create new incentives to develop cohesive management of the distribution process. The purpose of this chapter is to assess the contribution of these factors to the development of American physical distribution.

In the remainder of this section, the environmental factors and their influence on the field in America will be examined briefly. The succeeding sections describe the development of the concept of physical distribution, and survey the current development of the field toward customer service as a goal of increasing importance to the system. This section will encompass the organizational changes which increased awareness of the possibilities for management of physical distribution. Succeeding sections will examine the application of the computer and physical processing technologies to the

333

development of the field. The final section will attempt to discern the future direction of American physical distribution management, outlining the elements which are likely to predominate in the future.

Physical Distribution in America

Physical distribution involves the integration of functional activities involved in the movement of goods to market. There is a basic similarity in distribution systems, in that fundamentally they must accomplish parallel tasks: movement, storage, order processing, sorting and assembly. At similar levels of technological application, it would be logical to anticipate a parallel development of distribution systems, were it not for the influence of two dominating factors: products and markets. Product characteristics strongly influence the application of distribution technology. The product variables of physical density and value create specific requirements for system design, regardless of other environmental factors. In general, there appear to be few major differences among the product assortments of advanced societies. Therefore, the characteristics that distinguish American distribution systems from those found elsewhere lie in the influence of environmental forces, both geographic and marketing, on the system output requirements and the development of the system components.

The American environment has created a special set of conditions for business logistics. American marketing has taken much of its characteristic form as a result of both physical and demographic geography. The national markets, which are increasingly common for many products, are the result of a large continental land mass without physical or political barriers. The relative dispersion of population centres, on the other hand, establishes requirements for distribution for long-haul movements of many products to markets. However, the political unity of the area facilitates both the free flow of goods constrained only by the costs of movement and unified control over national distribution systems, made possible under uniform laws and contractual conditions.

Given these geographic and political factors, the remaining area of difference lies in the nature of American marketing practice. The changes which have taken place in marketing have been the primary reasons for the rise of interest in physical distribution. High levels of affluence, accompanied by a high level of availability at the point of sale, have created demands for wide varieties of products. The full statistical measures of the change are not available, but the trends are obvious to even the casual observer. Rising purchasing power on the part of the consumer has led to increased segmentation of consumer product markets. This, in turn, has resulted in a proliferation of products and product variations to satisfy the discernible needs and desires of more narrowly defined groups of customers. At the same time, competition in retailing has led to the practice of 'scrambled merchandising', in which competing types of stores, e.g. drugstores, supermarkets and discount houses, constantly seek new product lines to sell, as part of their efforts in search of more patronage and profit. As an indication of this trend, one authority reported that the typical supermarket in the United States had broadened its product assortment from approximately 2000 items in 1950 to more than 8000 items in the mid-1960s, with much of this growth appearing in non-food items!

At the same time, strong competitive pressures have been generated to increase the economic efficiency of the distribution process. With the appearance of patterns of overlapping retail merchandise lines, there has been an increase in price competition as well as product competition. The result is manifested in higher demands for efficiency in the distribution process in terms of both lower cost and higher convenience. This has occurred at all levels of the process, from the level serving the ultimate consumer of the product, back through the intermediate members of the marketing channel. The market thrust for convenience by itself would spell higher distribution costs in the marketing process, which have already been estimated according to one source to be as high as $100 billion per year.[2] While the proportion of these expenditures to GNP has declined, Professor Heskett found that the total cost of physical distribution for 1960 was 14·9 per cent of GNP.[3] However, there is no certainty in these estimates. Transportation and inventory costs can be estimated with relative precision, but other costs such as order processing, protective packaging, and materials handling systems are not so clearly identifiable, particularly when they are shared with other functions. Expenses, such as the cost of the lost sale as a result of the product not being available, are unknown. The total cost of physical distribution activities may not be known exactly, but it has created an environment calling for more effective managerial control.

One of the major stumbling blocks to the earlier development of physical distribution as a field is the nature of the process. It has not been a clearly defined functional area in the sense of other business activities, such as production, finance, or marketing. Physical distribution has been characterized as a process incorporating many functions. In the case of physical distribution, however, it was traditional among business firms to maintain these functions as separate entities reporting to different areas within the company, without the necessary organizational ties to breach the gap, except on a haphazard basis.

The result was inevitable. Each area served its own master and its own goals, without heed for the other—'suboptimization' in systems terminology. The traffic department, which was responsible for the purchase of transportation services, was charged with minimizing transport costs. The inventory manager was directed to maintain a minimal level of stocks to reduce company investment. The marketing department was oriented to serving customers without regard for the costs of supplying them. In many cases, no decision alternatives were available. There was only a single choice, such as a single mode package, or channel; and therefore no decision to be made in the distribution area.

To illustrate the nature of distribution problem situations, let us examine a hypothetical distribution system of a durable goods manufacturer. The process begins with production of the finished product at a central manufacturing facility. Goods are placed in inventory to be shipped to several regional warehouses located throughout the country, where stock is held in anticipation of customer orders. These orders will come from the retailers selling the product, who operate with limited stocks of merchandise because they rely on the regional warehouses for fast stock replenishment.

In this system, there will be at least two transportation movements, six product handling operations and two order transmission and processing systems, reflecting the connecting links among the three stages of the system. All of these elements have interrelated effects, which in turn will influence the character of the output of the entire system. The choice of transportation will determine protective packaging requirements, the way in which the product is handled, and the level of inventory required. The order processing system can influence the way in which demands are passed through the system, and therefore the inventory stock levels. The form of packaging at the retail level may determine the shipping module at the distribution warehouse and also the costs of transportation.

Few decisions can be made in distribution which do not affect more than one field at a time. The problem, however, is further compounded when the factors which influence these decisions are also changing. The five elements included in this example have undergone considerable change in recent years. Improved transportation has resulted in faster transit times, more specialized equipment and, more recently, in the expanding use of containers and unitized shipping modules. Storage and warehousing have been improved through computer control of inventories and mechanization of the order-picking process. Packaging requirements have changed as a result of both modern marketing and the flexibility of modern distribution. The external environment of logistics has also changed. Public investment in transportation facilities such as the Interstate Highway System, airports and harbours exert a strong influence on the character of the distribution process. The growth of telecommunications facilities has created the potential for logistics system control on a scale which was not possible a few years ago.

Management of distribution processes requires new conceptual skills in order to utilize the advances in the individual components of logistics. Environmental forces, independent in origin, become strongly interactive in their net effect on the distribution system; and effective management begins only when this interaction is recognized. The forces of the market have placed the burden of providing inventory, not on the retailer but on his supplier, in this case through the manufacturer's distribution warehouse. The cost of serving these customers is then manifested in large stocks of inventory, the high costs of premium transportation, or alternatively in a potentially high cost of lost sales through being out of stock. Changes in the way that the product is sold at retail may change packaging requirements, and create additional costs for production, warehousing and transportation. Changing transportation may force revisions in the optimum pattern of warehouse location. The important point is that none of these factors can be considered in isolation: they must be considered together as a systemic entity.

The management of response to technological change is at the heart of the increase in the importance of physical distribution to American business.

Marketing requires higher levels of service, while it generates pressures to reduce the costs of distribution. The achievement of these opposing goals is only possible by constant re-examination of the technology of physical distribution. Physical distribution management provides the only way to consider an integrated response to multifunctional problems in physical distribution.

The Emergence of a Concept

The concept of physical distribution in the United States has deep roots. The academic origins of the field can be traced back to the writings of marketing teachers such as Shaw, White and Beckman in the 1920s.[4] In general, these early writers were concerned with establishing the relationship of demand creation and supply fulfilment activities, although there was some emphasis in their texts on the techniques of operation and strategy development in the area of physical distribution.

At an operational level, there was also a long-standing awareness of the interaction effects of the components of distribution. One piece of recognition appears in the comparative rate structures of differing modes of transportation. Motor carriers did not always have to meet rail carload rates in order to be competitive for the traffic. There was a service differential, which was often recognized by both carriers and shippers as compensation for inventory savings for smaller volume shipments, direct door-to-door delivery, higher frequency of service, and lower protective packaging requirements of motor carrier operations. Similar differentials developed in water-rail competition. Discussions of air express service in the 1930s introduced consideration of inventory saving and damage reduction in shipping by air. However, while the notion of cost exchange or trade-offs was explicit in the discussion of the period, there was no recognition of the systemic character *per se* of physical distribution.

The major push to develop the concept of the total cost of distribution appears to have come in the 1950s, simultaneously with the rise of air freight and less dramatically with the development of the high-speed Interstate Highway System. The comparatively high rates for air freight service forced the air carriers to develop sales arguments for shippers to consider the total costs of distribution, i.e. inventory costs, warehousing, packaging, etc., where the speed of air freight would act as a substitute for other distribution costs. The type of analysis developed to support this effort is described in Lewis and Culletin, *The Role of Air Freight in Physical Distribution*.[5] The air freight argument may not have gained many converts to air freight, but it undoubtedly had the effect of enhancing the awareness among many shippers that distribution costs involved more than transportation.

Direct analysis of the general problem of physical distribution awaited the development of an academic field. The publication of the first text in 1961, Smykay, Bowersox and Mossman, *Physical Distribution Management*,[6] and those that followed, appearing contemporaneously with articles in business and marketing journals, established the direction of the field. For the first time, physical distribution was presented as a unified body of material

337

concerned with the concept of product or material flow. It involved movement, inventory, information processing, and related areas embodied in the supply function of marketing.

The initial development of the field was concerned with the development of physical distribution as a systemic entity, involving the identification of the component functions and their interrelationship. The original emphasis was on the organization and management of the system in order to minimize costs. It soon became apparent, however, that cost minimization was not sufficient by itself. Wendall M. Stewart[7] pointed out that marketing was generating pressures which made service to the customer an important part of the process. Cost minimization implies a specific level of service, and a major development of the field has been to de-emphasize cost minimization exclusively in favour of goals based on service, and the comparative costs of differing levels of service.

The development of the conceptual base of the field has been accompanied by a diffusion of the physical distribution concept within industry. Awareness has been increased by the creation of a professional association, the National Council of Physical Distribution, numerous special seminars sponsored by major industrial groups such as the American Management Association, and the publication of four trade journals[8] devoted to physical distribution. While a wide divergence in the practice of a field between leaders and laggards is normal, there appears to be a greater willingness today to examine physical distribution management for potential application in distribution problem areas.

Service as an Objective
The pressures from the market place have forced this reassessment of goals. Cost minimization is no longer the only objective of the logistics system because minimization implicitly specifies a service level, and not all customers will respond to the same level of service. The role of physical distribution is becoming recognized as another element in marketing strategy, and distribution service may be used as both substitute or complement for the use of product, price, or promotion variables. Marketing strategy has recognized the price of a product as only one of an assortment of competitive weapons, and likewise, there is a recognition that physical distribution involves not the minimum delivered price, but a degree of service as well.

What is service? In the context of distribution, service may be defined as any element offered to a customer which enables him to reduce his costs of doing business, or his time and effort expenditures as a consumer. The costs are generally those of inventory, ordering, physical processing, or managing. The notion of convenience suggests that when these costs are reduced, the product is enhanced and is, therefore, worth more to the customer. However, service only has value where the advantages of these elements have value to the customer. There may be cases where aspects of distribution service are unrecognized, or have no value at all, and merely imply a wasted expenditure.

The shift from costs to service as a major goal of the system recognizes two important facts: that demand can be created by logistic service, and that the cost benefits of differing levels of service can be compared for individual customers. Stephenson and Willett have emphasized this change in orientation, stating, 'It is necessary to treat customer service as an explicit rather than as an implicit variable.'[9]

Use of customer service as a variable is a recognition that customers have options in maintaining patronage in response to differing degrees of service, and a customer's demand is partially a function of his alternatives and his own costs as a result of differing levels of service. The degree of the supplier's monopoly position would appear to be the most significant variable describing this demand. A willingness of customers to absorb service delays may be a function of the alternatives which these customers perceive. Conversely response to new supply services may vary widely among customers based on their perception of alternatives. The ultimate result is that customer service preferences may be aggregated in a curve describing net increases in sales compared to net additional increments of logistic expenditure, i.e. a 'distribution response' function.

This response function rests on customer costs and his awareness of cost savings. The logistic system has two classes of tools to deal with differing customer service levels. Willett and Stephenson have classified these[9] into 'soft', meaning intangible ancillary services, such as training, missionary sales development and assistance in customer reordering, and 'hard' services which have impacts which can be directly measured. These would include inventory parameters such as the order-cycle length and consistency, the preparation and transmission of orders, and the coordination of physical processing activities, such as shipping in standard modules, prepackaging for ultimate users, performing extra deliveries, and similar services.

Each of these elements can be translated into customer cost savings.[9] Order preparation and physical processing services provided by the shipper can result in a direct transfer of cost from the customer. The success of shippers in absorbing these functions depends on the relative costs and the ease with which they can be performed elsewhere. Order cycle time involves three elements over which the supplier has potential control: data transmission time, carrier service, and the actual order filling and processing operations. Reduction in order cycle time can be translated into customer savings, provided it is accomplished with sufficient reliability to become a factor in his planning. How the shipper can accomplish this is open to a variety of strategies.

Strategic options based on order cycle time alternatives are normally based on some combination of transportation, warehousing, order processing, and manufacturing time. One alternative involves the number and location of warehouses. Warehouses and other field stocks located close to the consumer will reduce the customer's order cycle time below those located at a distance. Cycle time may also be reduced by the use of faster transportation. Further alternatives include faster processing of orders at the warehouse, or the use of faster order transmission from the customer. The choice of strategies depends on the degree of service desired and the related costs. The options available to the system designer can be illustrated by an example from the author's experience.

A major appliance manufacturer began to encounter price competition from competing suppliers in his highly profitable spare parts distribution channel. Spare parts are highly service-sensitive items, in which service not only affects the sales of the parts themselves, but frequently the sale of the next appliance as well. Parts also create severe handling problems (and therefore high costs) because they are small and are ordered in limited quantities for any one item. At the time that the problem of competition was occurring, this firm had already introduced a computer inventory control system with automatic vendor reordering, coupled with a customer order processing system which took the customer's order as soon as it was received, converted it to punch cards, and processed the billing order at the same time that it sent the physical processing instructions to the warehouse. The firm was also planning to build a computer-controlled warehouse for automated order-picking. By these measures, the average order cycle time from the distributors had been reduced from approximately three weeks to one. Management, however, was still concerned that this was not enough.

A logical extension of the system was to improve the information gathering link from the distributor. From a mail-delivered manual type system, the firm converted its most important distribution links to electronic data transmission, which would take stock item cards as inputs, linked by telephone to its central computer. In order to create a noticeable change in service, air freight was tried experimentally as the new mode of transporation. This reduced the distributors' cycle time from one week to one day. After a trial lasting several weeks, this firm decided against continuing air shipment as it was too expensive, and negotiated for expedited motor carrier service, which would change the cycle to three days instead of one. The improvement in service was sufficient to retain customer patronage in the face of lower-priced competition.

There are many ways in which higher levels can be achieved. As this incident indicated, there can be an 'overkill' in service, as well as too little. In this case, the cost of air freight was more than the market required at that time, particularly when coupled with the improved communication system.

Customer service as a logistic strategy involves a process analogous to product market segmentation, identifying customers and their needs, and assembling a 'service package'[10] to satisfy the demands of this segment. The dominant variable in service strategies is time, because inventories are calculated in consumption rates over time. Increased service to the customer may mean reduction in stock because order cycle time is reduced. The precise effect will vary with each customer and will therefore require identification of individual customer requirements.

The Managerial Revolution in Physical Distribution

The introduction of physical distribution management into American business has imposed a new set of requirements for coordination on established organizations. The older form of organization, oriented toward compartmentalization by functions, has been under fire because it does not respond to the need for tighter control. In brief it has been argued that function-oriented management is incapable of integrating the tasks of physical distribution into a unified operating entity so that the process can be managed and developed in response to the environmental demands placed on it. This complaint is not unique to physical distribution alone; it has a parallel in a more universal criticism of American management practice. Stanley Young writes in his article, 'Organization as a System':

What appears to be occurring is that our conception of the organization is changing from one of structure to one of process. Rather than visualize the organization in its traditional structural, bureaucratic, and hierarchical motif, with a fixed set of authority relationships, we are beginning to view organization as a set of flows, information, men, material, and behaviour. Time and change are the critical factors.' [11]

A systems approach to organization is more a difference in orientation than in the details of structure. The focus is on the end result of related processes, with the individual functional goals clearly subordinate to the transcendent goal of the larger system. The purpose is to facilitate the coordination of the activities of dissimilar functions which are necessarily related. In turn this should create a more effective response to a changing environment.

Physical distribution as a process affects many areas in different parts of the firm. Under the traditional hierarchical organizations in which these functions and lines of authority are widely dispersed, it is difficult to respond to change, and even more difficult to initiate change. Under these conditions, organizational inertia tends to resist all efforts to cross lines of authority. This becomes a compelling argument for its alternative, the development of a systemic approach to physical distribution. Brewer and Rosenzweig described the contrast between these two positions in reporting the organizational changes resulting from the introduction of the concept of physical distribution management into two firms: Boeing Airplane Company and the Purex Corporation. [12] The contrast between the conditions before and after the change are between those of a specialized, functionally oriented organization, with narrowly defined, ill-coordinated responsibilities, to an organization oriented to the flow of product, in which this systemic relationship was specifically recognized. To this new concept they proposed a name 'rhocremetics', the science of material flow. This was to be the nucleus of a new discipline which would focus on the systemic approach involved in physical distribution.

The implementation of the system approach to the management of physical distribution has been difficult. Robert Neushel of McKinsey and Company reported on a survey of twenty-six large companies in various industries made in 1967, noting that these firms 'vary enormously in their ability to grasp and cope with the myriad decisions and conditions that influence the total distribution problem'. [13] The organizational development of these firms for management of physical distribution was classified on three levels. The first (about one-third of his sample) operated at the level of the traffic department.

Distribution was confined to a single mode, and activities were centred upon rates and routings. About one-half operated at the conceptual level of the transportation department, in which decisions were made in a broader context, involving distribution alternatives in transportation and warehousing. Only five companies were at a level involving distribution at a more comprehensive corporate level where interaction between distribution and the needs of other areas was strongly recognized. These five were highly successful enterprises earning above-average returns, thus implying a high level of managerial efficiency.

There is no chronological accounting for the degree of adoption and the motivation for adopting integrated forms of physical distribution management. A survey of firms of members of the National Council of Physical Distribution indicates that progress has been steady but slow.[14] The survey, taken in 1968, was compared to one made under roughly similar conditions in 1962 and suggests some measure of progress in achieving more integration of functions as shown below:

FUNCTIONAL RESPONSIBILITY IN PHYSICAL DISTRIBUTION

Function	1962	1968
	%	%
Transportation	90	100
Warehousing	66	98
Inventory Management	72	85
Protective Packaging	40	85
Production Planning	36	61
Order Processing	12	89

Even recognizing that functional responsibilities may be shared with other departments, this is an indication of progress. The study further notes that in 70 per cent of the companies surveyed, the individual in charge of physical distribution has direct access to the vice presidential level, or higher.

Beyond these statistics from the membership rolls of a dedicated professional group, it becomes difficult to measure the degree of penetration. From the author's experience, contact even with functionally divided organizations indicates a strong awareness of the concept, with informal lines of communications substituting for a reconstituted organization chart. The problem of how to organize for physical distribution may not have one unique solution. Robert Stolle describes the rush to organize formal distribution organizations as faddism.[15] He raises the question whether the coordinated results of integrated distribution are achieved most efficiently through new organizations or through new procedures for the old. According to Neuschel's[13] survey, effective distribution depends on adequate cost and performance data, personnel actively seeking new answers to distribution problems, some procedure for examining relative costs and benefits in distribution, and finally the managerial authority to make the necessary exchanges of functions, costs and services. These would appear to be prerequisites for any logistics system.

Logistics and the Computer

If the systems concept in management has been responsible for the change to physical distribution, the computer has been the enabling factor. No technological innovation has had as much direct impact on the development of this field as the computer and quantitative control techniques which it made possible. The computer has not only provided the feasibility to solve hitherto insurmountable problems in both data and analysis, but it has also provided management with the capability to operate physical distribution as an integrated process.

The computer has served the logistics process in three different roles: as a data processor, as an analytical tool for the development of decision rules, and as a vehicle to model the total system, testing alternative designs and long-range planning options.

The initial application of the computer was in data processing. The economics of the computer became increasingly attractive in the face of an increasing volume of documentation and related paper work. However, the evolution of computer data systems has made use of the computer desirable on other grounds. As a data link, the computer and its accessory equipment have the ability to provide almost instantaneous transmission and processing of orders. At the same time, the capacity of this system has encouraged the generation of other reports. As John Magee points out, unit costs of data transmission decline rapidly with increased volume, as most costs of computer operation are independent of output.[16] The decline of the cost of information has encouraged higher volumes of information. When the computer is compared to the cost and performance of any other information system such as mail or teletype and processing on hand-posted inventory cards, it becomes even more attractive.

The near instantaneous processing time of computer systems shortens a major component of order cycle time, the communication link, providing a shorter average cycle time plus a reduced variance on message transmission and processing times. This then increases the ability to control inventory stock levels for both supplier and customer. Further, through shorter cycle times, it strengthens the ability of the system to respond to changes in the experienced level of demand.

Logistics data systems are only a part of a larger class of information systems, denoted as management information systems. The degree to which a logistics order system should be integrated with the larger management information system is conjectural at present, although there appear to be some obvious interfaces where close coordination might be desired. A package logistics data system is available today which not only processes routine orders for customers and suppliers, but will screen these customer orders against credit indicators, release orders to the warehouse, and provide detailed reports on daily operations to the warehouse, inventory control, merchandising control, purchasing, accounting, order-processing, and data processing centres.[17]

The logical extension of the logistics data system is to the cash register, to record data at the point of sale. The advantages are the increased control of merchandising decisions which the immediacy of this information provides, the decrease in order transmission time and the improvements in general inventory stock control.

The user of the computer in developing decision rules and scheduling algorithms for logistics has been particularly fruitful. This has been an area of intense interest for the field of management science, particularly in the specific area of inventory management and control. There has been so much activity in this area because inventory problems have proved more tractable to analysis and the use of quantitative tools than possibly any other area in business, resulting in an extensive body of research in inventory decision rules.

For logistics system operation, one of the most practical developments in computer applications has been the creation of integrated inventory control and planning systems, of which the most prominent example has been IBM's IMPACT. IMPACT is a complete basic package of computer inventory order procedures and decision rules, designed so that after an initial stabilizing period, the inventory system can be operated with as much degree of automatic routine as the inventory manager prefers. At the same time, it is able to generate sufficient information so that management has a comprehensive view of the total system, with more specific detail available on command. The use of these programmes has increased rapidly in the last few years and reflects the problem solutions to the need for increased stock control by distribution management.

There have also been other areas in which computer decision models concerned with limited objectives have been applied. A vehicle scheduling programme, VSP, originally developed in the United Kingdom, has been available as a package programme for use in delivery vehicle scheduling.[18] Several computer models have been developed for solution of warehouse location problems. Among these have been the linear-programming model of Baumol and Wolfe, developed in 1956,[19] and the heuristic search routine for warehouse location, by Kuehn and Hamburger.[20] Many others have appeared in the literature as a measure of the level of activity in quantifying and providing solutions to logistics problems.

Comprehensive decision-making in logistics appears to require modelling with increasingly broad scale capabilities. One answer has been the use of computer simulation, which permits the designer to describe the model in quantitative terms. Simulation in the logistics area was successfully applied by Maffei and Shycon over ten years ago.[21] Since that time the number of applications of simulation to logistics operations appear to be quite numerous, although most have not been reported in the journals.

Standard optimization techniques have also been applied to large-scale logistics problems. One linear programming application reported by Gepfer[22] was sufficiently comprehensive to deal with both inbound and outbound transportation, plus the inventory systems for a firm. The programme was run in three successive stages, and the net saving attributed to this programme was over $300,000 per year.

In a problem solution reported to the author, an industrial products manufacturer with world-wide production and distribution activities developed a linear programme to describe the production and distribution system for its major product line. This programme is still regarded as experimental by the distribution group which sponsored it, but it has already led to a decision to close one overseas plant and supply the market that it served from another location.

Computer modelling imposes an intellectual discipline on logistics planning, and in the end this may prove to be its strongest value. The use of process modelling by simulation, for example, forces management to examine their operation with extreme thoroughness. As a result, it produces an awareness of the structure and the interrelationships of the process for management. The most important contribution of the computer may be the environment that it has created for better decision-making.

The Impact of Technology
Comparing surveys of the component costs of the distribution process can be a frustrating task. In the available published material, there is a consensus that transportation costs comprise the largest single class of distribution expenditures. The relative shares of transportation in these surveys differ, not only by the magnitude of costs, but also by the definition of what is included under the heading of distribution costs. Inventory, materials handling, warehouse operation, packaging and administrative activities usually make up the remainder of these costs in approximately this sequence, depending on the survey. Rank ordering of these functional activities suggests a parallel ordering of managerial concern. However, it does not indicate the relationships which exist between these functions and the degree to which the magnitude of one can be affected by the other.

The problem of warehouse location provides an interesting demonstration of the cost exchanges which are possible. A manufacturer usually has many possible alternatives in moving products to a retail market, depending in part on the physical characteristics of the goods, but also on market forces. One alternative is to locate a central stock at the plant and supply all customers directly from the plant. This maintains low inventory and warehousing costs, but it creates high transportation costs because of the movement of smaller shipments to market. In addition, there may be problems of maintaining service, because of the erratic nature of small shipment transportation in this country. Another alternative is to locate warehouses close to the market, operating with a large number of field stocks, increasing inventory and warehousing costs, but possibly reducing transportation costs by shipping in larger quantities. Between these extremes, there may be many other alternatives.

This is obviously a grossly oversimplified example, but it illustrates the difficulty of handling technical problems in physical distribution in isolation. One of the major accomplishments of the new organizational forms of physical distribution has been the increased ability to integrate these technical problem areas for a single solution. In Neuschel's survey the firms which have

345

integrated the physical distribution function most successfully achieved a clear-cut advantage in evaluating technological change.

What types of changes have occurred within the technological environment of physical distribution? It would probably be a fair statement that there is little introduced into American industry which has not also been found in other advanced societies. Warehousing and materials-handling equipment are marketed on a world-wide basis. Possibly the one area where problem solutions have been unique has been in transportation. The special combinations of geography and regulation have created a transportation environment which differs substantially from that elsewhere in the world.

American transportation developed under private ownership, with government regulation permitting only limited competition between modes of transport. The result was a period of slow evolution rather than dynamic change. Within the last few years, however, there have been strong signs of change, both in technologies and in the forces governing the transportation market. It is the ending of an old pattern which makes physical distribution management particularly relevant today.

Two major technological innovations have appeared in transportation in recent years, with both direct and indirect effects on physical distribution: air freight and containerization. Air freight has developed within the last twenty-five years, and the volume of traffic is small compared to all other modes of transport, even though traffic has grown at rates of up to 20 per cent per year. The major impact of air freight has been indirect rather than direct. Because it can only be competitive on a basis of total distribution costs, it has forced the attention of shippers toward the non-transport costs of distribution in order to create a value for the speed of air freight within the distribution system. In this respect it has served as a change agent, promoting an integrated concept of distribution costs, even though much of the promotional activity to increase air freight traffic through total cost analysis may have been directly unsuccessful.

The other innovation, containerization, is more direct in its impact. Unlike Europe, where a large share of commerce moves by water for part of its journey, the bulk of traffic in the United States moves by land. Hence the maritime container has not as yet been the major factor in American transportation that it has been in the United Kingdom. The introduction of broad-scale container service in the United States stems from the intermodal competition that has developed between rail and motor carrier. In the early '50s, trailer-on-flatcar service or 'piggy back' was introduced, and it has since become the fastest growing service offered by the railroads. Originally conceived as an intermodal service between rail and motor carriers, it never developed strongly in that direction, although some motor carrier trailers have moved by rail. From the standpoint of rail service, it provided a flexibility in routing which was not available from the railroads prior to that time.

Accompanying the change in technology has been a change in the nature of the transportation market. This has been manifested in three developments: a lessening of regulatory constraints on intermodal competition, the rise of
346

unregulated transportation and the increasing segmentation of the transportation market. Competition between modes of transportation has been increasing, as a result of these new technological options and a slow relaxation of regulatory controls. Even more important, however, is the rise of proprietary and other forms of non-regulated transportation, which has displaced a considerable share of the traffic formerly carried by publicly regulated carriers. This, in turn, has created concern whether much of this non-regulated traffic may be carried illegally. The net effect is to create further competition in the transportation industry. This has created the spur to increased segmentation of the market. Both shippers and carriers have sought solutions to the movement of goods which are directly tailored to the needs of specific markets. Carriers catering to these needs have been forced to invest heavily in new specialized transport vehicles and terminal facilities. They have offered special services and schedules, exemplified in the concept of the 'unit-train', developed to serve the needs of individual shippers. The result has been that even the public carriers have become more oriented to the needs of specific markets.

The significance of these changes is that shippers are being offered a wider range of options in distribution than ever before. The transportation market is more openly competitive, not only between regulated and unregulated carriers but between differing modes, such as the rivalry of air and surface carriers in which the balance is decided not on comparative rates alone but on the combined costs of transportation and other areas of distribution.

The other areas of technical application in logistics are also open to change. The pressure of rising labour costs has led to interest in automation and mechanization in materials handling and warehousing. This, in turn, is affecting packaging dimension requirements, protection and marketing specifications. There are no patterns to these developments that can be identified for discussion. The dominant factor is the resulting change that any one of these elements creates in the remainder of the system, and which must be included in comprehensive distribution planning.

A trade journal recently reported the case of a curtain rod and drapery hardware manufacturer in which a changing market completely altered the direction of the company and forced a complete redesign of the distribution system.[23] This firm was able to respond because an aggressive management recognized the role of distribution in maintaining its present markets and creating conditions for further expansion.

The retail market for the firm's product line was in evolution from the small drapery shops and variety stores, serviced through local wholesalers, to large chain store and discount house customers, who placed large orders directly with the manufacturer in large quantities for nationwide delivery to serve those customers who were able to adapt to this changing market competition. The firm established seven regional warehouses. However, customer order patterns placed a severe strain on warehouse capacity and delivery service to the warehouses. This led to a decision to rely more heavily on private rather than public transportation for the bulk of its requirements in order to provide more consistent service.

Further gains in market coverage were possible only by acquiring large retail accounts. However, these firms were interested in suppliers who were capable of handling wider product requirements, with more extensive delivery service and computer reordering capabilities. This led to a series of acquisitions of firms manufacturing related products, but only after a thorough reconsideration of distribution, including evaluation of warehousing and transportation, and the installation of computer inventory control systems in the warehouses. By use of a linear-programming analysis of future market demands and the alternatives to supply the market, this firm for the first time was able to plan distribution rationally in anticipation of market demands. By comprehensive analysis this company was able to change its distribution from a factor which limited market development to an enabling factor which encouraged additional sales.

One characteristic of the new technology of physical distribution is the footloose character of many processing functions. There is no reason why many of the activities such as packaging, warehousing, or transportation should be performed by one specific entity in the channel. Many middlemen, such as wholesalers and retail chains, have long operated transportation systems as part of their distribution activities. One major grocery chain operates the largest private trucking fleet in the world. However, there has also been a movement in reverse, in which the carrier now acts as a distribution company, absorbing some of the physical processing functions of the middlemen. One carrier, operating both as a trucker and as an air freight forwarder from the East to the West Coast, has taken on some of the processing functions of his department store clients, placing garments on hangers, wrapping them, and attaching price tags prior to their transportation to the West Coast stores.[24] For the store, this not only saves the acts of processing, but may relieve both congestion in the receiving warehouse and minimize the delay time that would otherwise be incurred before the garments can be sold. When high-fashion garments are moved by air, the time spent in New York between pick-up from the store and delivery to the airport is now used productively for processing, so that the garments can be sold the next day when they arrive in the store in San Francisco or Los Angeles.

A warehousing company has proposed the development of a small shipment service operating by rail container between its chain of national warehouses, which would serve as distribution centres and storage areas. This combination of services joins the conventional services of a public warehouseman to those of a rail freight forwarder, to offer a more useful package of service to the market.

Management of the physical distribution process requires an understanding of the interactions possible, even between technologically dissimilar components of the logistics system. The character of these interactions suggests that it is often possible to approach technical logistics problems with the objective of the system well in mind, seeking ways to reduce total costs by combining functions within a single sub-system. The evaluation of function and cost trade-offs may be a major contribution of systems management to logistics. In a competitive market, the success of a marketing programme may turn on the ability to adapt to the changing technological environment, and the possibilities which these changes present. The choice may be that of new carrier service, modular material handling systems, or the possibility of shifting the performance of a portion of the physical processing activity on to another agency in the distribution channel. The criteria for evaluation should be the alternatives available within the system, and the opportunity cost of the resources which thereby become under-utilized. This in turn requires a capacity to understand the nature of the system itself.

The Future of PDM

What does the future hold for physical distribution management? In general, there appear to be three areas in which change and further development may be expected: service, process control, and interorganizational cooperation. The first is the extension of the service concept as an objective of the system, and as a result, the proliferation of innovations to serve this goal. The second is the development of controls and standards to measure the operating performance of distribution systems, a problem which becomes more critical as service becomes more prominent as an operating objective. The third is the extension of the management of the system beyond the boundaries of the firm in order to satisfy the objective of service.

These areas are not unrelated. The emphasis on service as an element of marketing strategy requires the development of control systems beyond the cost criteria which are used today. To provide service with adequate control requires a knowledge and active participation in the direction of other member firms in the physical distribution channel. Therefore, the future demands coordination which has not been normally achieved in distribution, and which will require interorganizational information flow as well as product flow.

Service, as we have seen, involves segmentation, but in the future it may involve a more specialized treatment of customers than in the past. Marketing institutions change, and the requirements of serving them also change. The tools of service segmentation may not differ from those we have discussed before: absorption of inventory risks and costs, integration of order processing systems, and the use of standard package modules and shipping units. These elements of segmentation will be found in the variety of policies which the dominant members of marketing channels will impose on their cooperating firms. Assuming for the moment that retail chains will maintain their superior position in marketing channels for many products, they would be in a position to shift the costs of heterogeneity in physical processing, i.e. carton sizes, marking, and delivery procedures, as well as ordering procedures back to their suppliers. Successful distribution policy will then involve the ability on the part of the supplier to absorb this heterogeneity at reasonable cost, to meet the needs of individual customers.

Another development of service, which in the long run may have an even greater effect on physical distribution, is the trend for an increasing variety of products to direct home delivery. The phenomenon of mail order is not new in America, nor is the home delivery of many grocery and dairy items. However, in the opinion of knowledgeable individuals, this will be extended

349

into much wider areas of consumer shopping than we are now experiencing. To the physical distribution system, this becomes an area of significant change. It is less relevant whether the retailer becomes a sales agent or a warehouse-man than the change in the physical character of the distribution system. If local retail shelf stocks are to become less important to consumer purchase decisions, then there must be more development of small shipment services to deliver from central stocking points. However, there are also offsetting advantages in better physical utilization of storage space for goods, elimina-tion of retail stocks, and reduction of time lags in responding to changes in demand. The specific description of a home delivery logistics system must wait on the product choice and the introduction of specific ordering and materials handling processes.

Successful development of service as a weapon will require a different type of data system from those now in use. The only continuous monitors of dis-tribution activity available today are costs and measures of unit flow as recorded in stock records and shipping documents. Normally, service has been measured by the frequency of the out-of-stock condition, which becomes a record of intermittent failure rather than a continuous monitor of per-formance. There is a great deal of uncertainty about the type of information which will be required, but it would appear that the general character of such information would monitor performance so that the symptoms of failure to perform would lead to identification of the cause, and the potential cost to the system.

Extension of control through the operating system, whether inside or out-side the firm, appears to be necessary if the objective of service is to be realized. Logistics control must be recognized as an integral part of the overall problem of planning and control within the firm. The problems of co-ordination are at least as extensive as the firm, and frequently are even wider than the firm's boundaries, reaching to outside firms. However, relationships even between cooperating organizations may lead to conflicting goals. Heskett and Ballou[25] have posed this problem in relation to optimal order quantity calculations among seller, carrier, and buyer. One suggestion for resolution, which they have made, is to operate through the price schedules of either seller or carrier. This in itself engenders possible conflicts which can only be resolved by clear knowledge of common objectives within the inter-organizational system. The unresolved question in extending control within the logistics system is whether this will ultimately require vertical integration in ownership, or whether this can be achieved through inter-firm cooperation for distribution profit maximization.

Conclusion

In summarizing physical distribution in America, it should be noted that there is no common well of experience, that innovation takes place within individual firms in differing degrees and at a differing pace, and further in forms that vary specifically from one firm to another. The common dimension of American experience has been the exposure to the development of a con-cept, engendered by the pressures of a market-oriented society, to move goods to their place of sale more efficiently. The development of the concept of physical distribution as a total system has brought an awareness that cost minimization is not in itself a sufficient goal for physical distribution. Cost alternatives also imply alternative levels of service to the market; the ability to control this level of service has direct significance for marketing strategy. To take advantage of the strategic possibilities of physical distribution as a marketing variable, many firms have found that it is necessary to reorganize their logistic activities into an organizational form which takes account of the nature of physical distribution as a process.

Physical distribution is technologically oriented. The computer has been the enabling factor, making problem solutions feasible which would have been too large or difficult to approach before. Of the operating components of the distribution system, the dominant element appears to be transportation. However, no component stands alone, and the recognition of the inter-dependent nature of the process has been characteristic of the applications of physical distribution management.

Distribution in the future appears to be dominated by three elements: service as a dominating goal of the system, the need for more effective control over the process, and the need by the firm to reach out beyond its own corporate boundaries in order to achieve effective system performance.

The American experience in physical distribution has been fundamentally the evolution of this concept, the notion that all of the functions of distribution are interrelated and that they can, therefore, be managed as an integral unit. The technological options available in this country are probably not substantially different from those in other advanced countries. The unique factor may be the strength of the market forces which have encouraged a direct approach to the problems of distribution. These pressures are forcing physical distribution into a new role as an active element in marketing strategy.

References

(1) Theodore N. Beckman and William Davidson, *Marketing*, Eighth Edition, New York, Ronald Press Company, 1967, p. 300.
(2) *Business Week*, September 24 1966, p. 112.
(3) J. L. Heskett, 'Macro-economic Cost of Distribution', *Transportation Research Forum*, 1962, as reprinted in Norton E. Marks and Robert M. Taylor, *Marketing Logistics: Perspectives and Viewpoints*, New York, John Wiley and Sons, 1967, p. 14.
(4) This section relies heavily on material in Donald J. Bowersox, 'Physical Distribution Development, Current Status and Potential', *Journal of Marketing*, XXXIII, January 1969, p. 63–70.
(5) Howard T. Lewis, James W. Culletin and Jack D. Steele, *The Role of Air Freight in Physical Distribution*, Boston, Harvard University Graduate School of Business Administration Division of Research, 1956.
(6) Macmillan Company, New York, 1961.
(7) Wendell M. Stewart, 'Physical Distribution: Key to Improved Volume and Profit', *Journal of Marketing*, XXIX, January 1965, pp. 65–70.
(8) These journals are: *Transportation and Distribution Management, Handling and Shipping, Distribution Manager*, and *Traffic Management*.

(9) P. Ronald Stephenson and Ronald P. Willett, 'Selling with Physical Distribution Service', *Business Horizons*, XI, December 1968, pp. 76–85.
(10) William M. Hutchinson and John F. Stolle, 'How to Manage Customer Service', *Harvard Business Review*, November–December 1968, p. 89.
(11) Stanley Young, 'Organisation as a System', *California Management Review*, Spring 1968, p. 21.
(12) Stanley H. Brewer and James Rosenzweig, 'Rhocremetics and Organisational Adjustments', *California Management Review*, III, Spring 1961, pp. 52–71.
(13) Robert P. Neuschel, 'Physical Distribution—The Forgotten Frontier', *Harvard Business Review*, XLV, March–April 1967, p. 132.
(14) 'Physical Distribution Management, The State of the Art', paper commissioned by Mason and Lines, Kingsport, Tennessee, 1968, p. 8.
(15) John F. Stolle, 'How to Manage Physical Distribution', *Harvard Business Review*, XLV, July–August 1967, p. 100.
(16) John F. Magee, 'The Computer and the Physical Distribution Network' in Wroe Alderson and Stanley Shapiro (eds.), *Marketing and the Computer*, New York, Prentice-Hall, 1963, p. 63.
(17) Charles S. Carew, 'LINCS . . . A Cosmic Concept for your Space-Age Distribution System, *Handling and Shipping*, May 1969, p. 67.
(18) William J. Baumol and Phillip Wolfe, 'A Warehouse Location Problem', *Operations Research*, II, March–April 1958, pp. 256–65.
(19) Alfred A. Kuehn and Michael J. Hamburger, 'A Heuristic Program for Locating Warehouses', *Management Science*, IX, July 1963, pp. 643–66.
(20) G. E. Nace, 'Computerised Truck Scheduling', *Distribution Manager*, March 1969, pp. 37–42.
(21) Harvey N. Shycon and Richard B. Maffei, 'Simulation-Tool for Better Distribution', *Harvard Business Review*, XXXVIII, November–December 1960, pp. 65–75.
(22) Alan H. Gepfer, 'Business Logistics for Better Profit Performance', *Harvard Business Review*, XLVI, November–December 1968, pp. 75–84, 79.
(23) Tom Wilcox, 'How Dan Ferguson Plotted the Revolution', *Handling and Shipping*, August 1969, pp. 59–63.
(24) 'Trucker Tries for Something Extra', *Business Week*, March 4 1969, pp. 112–18.
(25) J. L. Heskett and Ronald H. Ballou, 'Logistics Planning in Inter-Organisational Systems', *Academy of Management Proceedings*, 1967, pp. 124–36.

Chapter D.15

INTRODUCING PDM: CHARRINGTON-UNITED

by T. Morkill

As soon as one tries to generalize on this subject, one discovers immediately that, historically, British companies have been almost equally divided in their approach, i.e. between the 'marketing' and 'production' concepts.

This chapter is produced in the form of a case history of one of Britain's largest brewing companies, showing how the management organization has been adapted to conform to the company's changing overall policy with respect to the distribution function.

By arranging it in this way one will not produce a stereotyped formula for the reorganization of a company's management structure, to provide for the introduction of the physical distribution concept according to whether it is marketing or production orientated. It is very doubtful whether it would be wise even to try to produce such a proposal. However, by analysing carefully the decisions taken by senior management, and the steps made subsequently, it should be possible to anticipate some of the problems which will be encountered, and the results which can be achieved when introducing the physical distribution philosophy into a new company.

Present Company Policy
At the present time the company policy with respect to the distribution function can be described neatly as the 'Broad Range of Activities Concerned with the Movement of Finished Products from the End of the Production Line to the Consumer', and under this general heading the following activities are included:

(i) transportation and traffic problems—including design and purchase of vehicles
(ii) warehousing
(iii) order processing
(iv) warehouse location and material handling outside the factories
(v) inventory control of finished goods.

In implementing this policy, distribution is considered a 'production service', and total control is through the regional company production

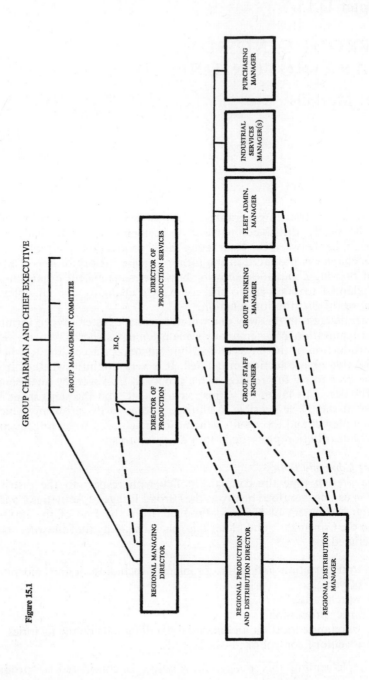

Figure 15.1

directorate. Figure 15·1 shows the group management structure now used, but this has only been reached after many years of education and persuasion: and there will be wide variations in the time required to implement a change of this kind, according to the size of a company, its products, and by no means least, its personalities. It is particularly important to note the relationship between the headquarters section and the regional company. The regional company is responsible for 'profit' and hence the regional distribution manager is responsible to his managing director, and not the functional head of production services. The headquarters section is responsible for coordinating purchasing, administration, technical information and trunking, the last of which is determined largely by group, rather than by regional production activities.

Historical Situation

Stage 1 Having outlined the company's up-to-date policy and explained the present management structure, it is necessary to turn the clock back ten years to the time when this philosophy was first being discussed.

Charrington & Co. operated solely in London and the south-east, and were responsible for the supply of beer only. Figure 15·2 shows the management structure at that time, and one notices how the distribution function is controlled in part by two directors, and four departmental heads. It is worth noting, however, that this developed largely through the accounting procedures being adopted at that time, in so far as the 'brewery' and 'bottling' departments each produced a profit and loss account, with the expenses of the then transport department divided between the two functions according to the number of vehicles being operated. Inevitably this influenced the lack of integration of the distribution function—particularly with respect to transport matters.

Stage 2 Figure 15·3 shows the next stage in the development, which was important in so far as the functions of bottling and transport operating came under the same head, and it represents the last change before the compnay doubled in size. However, this still maintained the separation of vehicle purchasing and maintenance from that of transport operating, whereas the coordination between the two is essential if good vehicle utilization is to be achieved.

Stage 3 The next move came at the time of the merger between Charrington & Co. and United Breweries. This has the effect of almost doubling the size of the company, and in the joint statement to the shareholders justifying the need for such a merger, the chairman made it clear that the chief short-term benefits would be in the rationalization of the production and distribution activities of both companies. The two companies had largely operated in different areas of the country, and two or three other small takeovers took place soon after the merger, to fill in the obvious gaps.

A headquarters section consisting of a director of marketing, director of

355

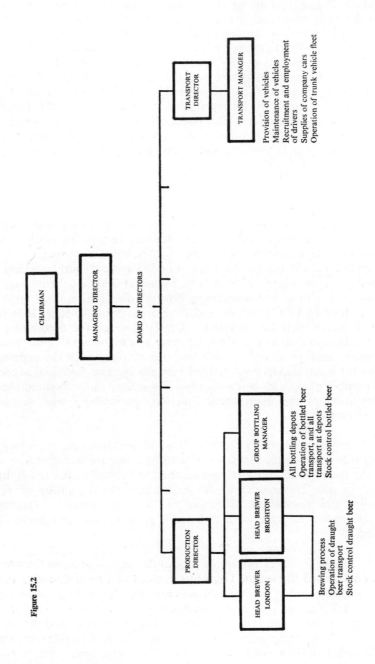

Figure 15.2

CHAIRMAN

MANAGING DIRECTOR

BOARD OF DIRECTORS

PRODUCTION DIRECTOR

HEAD BREWER LONDON

HEAD BREWER BRIGHTON

GROUP BOTTLING MANAGER

Brewing process
Operation of draught
beer transport
Stock control draught beer

All bottling depots
Operation of bottled beer
transport, and all
transport at depots
Stock control bottled beer

TRANSPORT DIRECTOR

TRANSPORT MANAGER

Provision of vehicles
Maintenance of vehicles
Recruitment and employment
of drivers
Supplies of company cars
Operation of trunk vehicle fleet

Figure 15.3

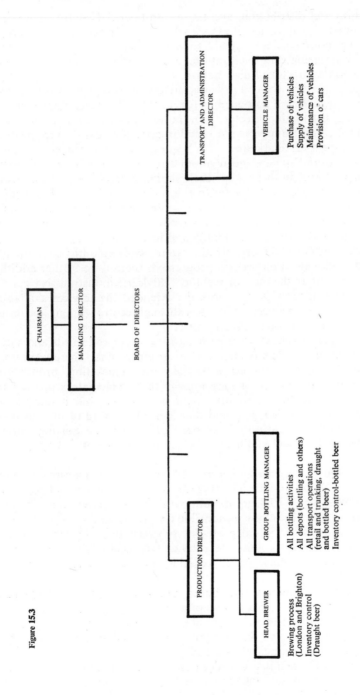

CHAIRMAN

MANAGING DIRECTOR

BOARD OF DIRECTORS

PRODUCTION DIRECTOR

TRANSPORT AND ADMINISTRATION DIRECTOR

HEAD BREWER

Brewing process
(London and Brighton)
Inventory control
(Draught beer)

GROUP BOTTLING MANAGER

All bottling activities
All depots (bottling and others)
All transport operations
(retail and trunking, draught
and bottled beer)
Inventory control-bottled beer

VEHICLE MANAGER

Purchase of vehicles
Supply of vehicles
Maintenance of vehicles
Provision of cars

production and distribution, and the group financial controller was formed to examine the group's activities as a whole, and on the production net three further appointments were made to deal specifically with the three main areas for immediate rationalization, a director of bottling, a director of brewing and a director of distribution.

At the same time the country was divided into regions, with each region having a local board responsible for profit. The local board included a production/distribution director, with the headquarters section acting in a supporting role. This arrangement assisted in getting across the group concepts.

With respect to marketing, the headquarters department concentrated largely on 'brand' policy and regional companies, who were solely responsible for the trade in their area—each submitted their annual sales forecasts. These in turn were made known to the regional and group production and distribution directors, as a safeguard against most eventualities, and made sure breweries, bottling stores and depots were not shut until alternative facilities were known to be available and in working order.

Figure 15·4 shows the organization some twelve months after the merger.

As the rationalization process progressed, there were further additions to the HQ structure in the form of technical advisers, industrial services depots, and project engineers. These additions extended the services available, and at the same time produced economies through centralization, but in no way altered the basic organization structure.

To date there has been no reference to the wines and spirits and soft drink activities, both of which contributed to group profits. These were set up as two quite separate functions with their own marketing, production and distribution departments. It may appear that immediate scope for further rationalization in the distribution field was wasted, but if one adopts the total distribution philosophy, and considers the nature of the business, one will see this step could only have been possible if the existing warehouses had been suitable, and in almost all cases they were not.

Stage 6   With reference to Figure 15·1 the group management committee was formed almost at once. They decided to adopt the regional policy already implemented with CUB group, but with the difference that the regional companies should be totally responsible for profits, and the HQ section should continue to be a services department to assist them in achieving the best results. They would 'continue to provide technical advice, and to negotiate bulk contracts for fuel, parts, vehicles, etc. and to coordinate national advertising'.

Their main function would be to examine afresh the whole range of group activities, and to plan for capital expenditure in the future.

A further change saw the regional companies assuming complete responsibility for the sales and distribution of wines and spirits—with Bass Charrington Vintners acting solely as a production and marketing company. This involved the regional brewery companies in assuming control of wines and spirits warehouses, and depots within their region, and absorbing any transport facilities.

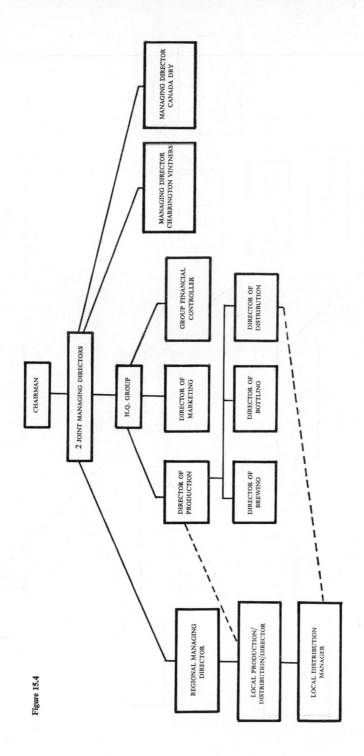

Figure 15.4

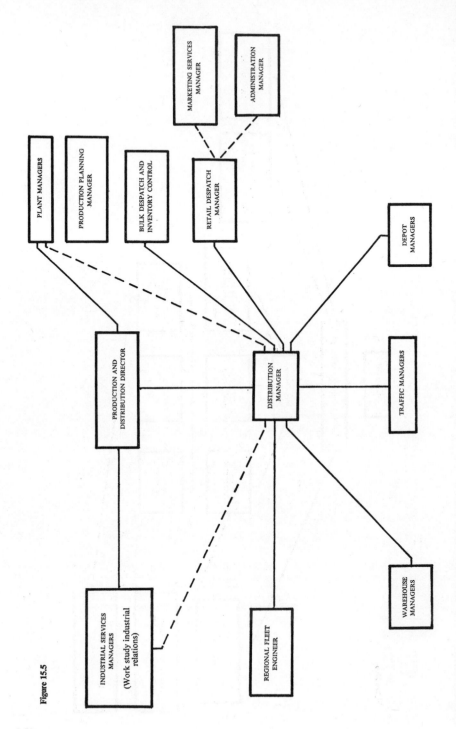

Figure 15.5

360

Day to Day Operations in a Regional Company

To see how the physical distribution system works in practice, it is necessary to examine closely the management structure of the distribution department in a regional company, and to assess its key tasks. Figure 15·5 shows the organization chart.

From this one can see the subdivisions of the distribution function within the distribution department itself, and the relationship between these individual sections and the other major departments. Particularly important are the relationships between the bulk despatch department (trunking) and the production planning section, and the retail despatch manager and the marketing services department. The chief difference between traffic and depot managers is that the traffic manager controls the transport operations at a large production warehousing unit, while the depot manager controls the transport and warehouse functions at a distribution depot.

1. Maintenance of customer service as agreed with marketing department.
2. Economic achievement of programme through:
    (a) Inventory control
    (b) Planning and scheduling of vehicle fleet
3. Worker productivity
4. Administration and communications.

Figure 15·6

Figure 15·6 lists the key tasks of the distribution department of an operating company. It is essential that before determining the transportation requirements the type of customer service required is agreed with the marketing department. It is equally important that the production plan is available—particularly with respect to trunking operations. Once these two units have been defined the numbers of vehicles and depots required can be scientifically evolved.

You may be surprised to find worker productivity as a key task. However, out of the distribution department's annual revenue budget of £2,000,000 for one of the regional companies (representing approximately one-sixth of the group total) wages and salaries represent approximately £1,500,000.

Administration and communications are also important areas. Order despatch departments frequently initiate accounting procedures, and inaccuracies and delays can be very costly, particularly if they affect the 'cash flow'. Similarly poor communications between the despatch and sales departments can frequently lose customers.

Conclusion

So far, we have shown how the distribution policy has evolved, how the management structures have developed with it, and the way the present structure contributes to the company's operations. However, there are one or two further questions to be answered:

(1) Why did top management decide on this policy?
(2) What has been achieved to date and what else is likely to be achieved?
(3) Where do we go from here?

With respect to (1) management believed it was only by defining distribution in their way that one could achieve reliable distribution costings and hence a sound basis for assessing future production and selling policies within the group. At the same time, through the integration of the transport, warehousing, order processing, and inventory control activities, the overall service costs could be kept within economic limits.

Already much has been achieved. Firstly a company 'blueprint' for the future has been built up. Considerable rationalization of production and distribution depots has taken place, and more is in the pipeline. Wage structures have been produced to provide real cohesion between the various sections of the work force—and to ensure that the necessary flexibility is maintained as the company's activities diversify. The roadworthiness of the vehicle fleet has improved beyond all measure.

As to the future—maybe the improved services provided by the distribution department will become a real selling factor. Equally, sales policy may be determined by the economics of distribution. In any event I envisage the economics of distribution making an ever-increasing contribution to the growth of the company and its profit.

Chapter D.16

INTRODUCING PDM: MASSEY-FERGUSON

by J. Houston

To analyse the application of physical distribution within a manufacturing company, it is necessary to consider the organizational structure with particular reference to the decision-making process which determines:

(a) material sourcing for the products
(b) manufacturing location and operation
(c) marketing policy on distribution of the products.

Physical distribution management must reflect and implement the corporate strategy of the business. Sourcing and distribution decisions will have a significant or even critical effect on the ability of the company to sell its products profitably in the markets selected, and physical distribution management must, therefore, be an integral part of all corporate planning and control.

In reviewing physical distribution management in Massey-Ferguson, it is therefore intended to show how the logistics system evolved, and how distribution media have been and are selected as part of the global strategy of the company.

Most of the features of the development and growth of the industrial corporation can be traced in the history of Massey-Ferguson. Through evolutionary changes which have extended over more than a hundred years, Massey-Ferguson has developed from a private, local family enterprise into a global operation—characterized by its integrated nature, the global span of its operations and the organization and control features which it has evolved.

As with most companies, the first step towards becoming international was 'selling abroad'. This in turn led to local assembly and manufacture, with the most important link between the two stages being the sales organization in the territory concerned—whether a company branch or an independent distributor. Through this local organization it was possible to recognize and take care of special environmental factors, and even in many cases to obtain local capital.

The decision to move a local assembly or manufacture was almost always in response to trade restrictions imposed by national governments. Such decisions were therefore defensive in nature, to protect the company's

363

market share, rather than based on purely logistical considerations. However, other factors came into play as a result of a policy of integrating the company's manufacturing activity. To consider these, it is necessary to look briefly at the way in which the present Massey-Ferguson organization was formed.

Massey-Harris, a long-established Canadian Company, had in the period after the Second World War become the world's leading manufacturer of self-propelled combines, as well as continuing to be a major manufacturer of

Figure 16.1

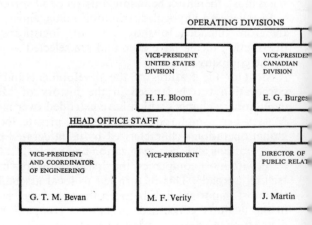

farm tractors and implements. Although it had traditionally pursued a policy of integrated manufacture, this policy had become modified, firstly by the decision in 1938 not to use its own engine in the farm tractors, and later, during the war, when it was decided to assemble tanks in the US factory rather than manufacture tractors. This reduction in manufacturing activity relative to the company's total operations was intensified when the merger took place with Harry Ferguson Ltd in 1953.

The merger was in many ways a natural partnership: the 'Ferguson

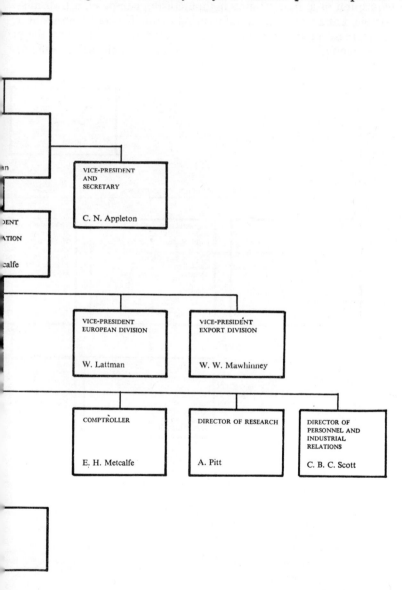

system' had revolutionized the design of farm tractors and implements, making the tractors lighter and more efficient. Just as Massey-Harris was leading the world in self-propelled combine manufacture, Harry Ferguson Ltd was the world leader in farm tractors. Ferguson, however, manufactured only a small proportion of the tractors and implements he sold, with the result that, after the merger, the whole question of manufacture had to be reviewed.

The principal steps taken as a result of the review of manufacturing activity were the acquisition of a diesel engine manufacturing company, a transmission and axle plant and a tractor manufacturing plant. This brought about a considerable increase in the company's manufacturing activity, but there were further developments as a result of an even more significant change in

Figure 16.2

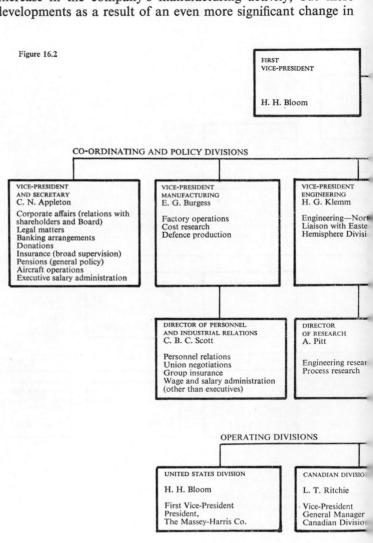

policy. In the past, local assembly and manufacturing programmes had only been undertaken where necessary, to defend the company's share of specific markets. Now such programmes were considered where they seemed likely to provide the opportunity to break into new markets in specific countries. Alongside this new policy, the company also endeavoured to deploy its own manufacturing operations internationally, to minimize costs of supply (including production and distribution costs) rather than merely to protect and develop specific markets. Whereas in 1951 the Board of Massey-Harris had resolved that not more than 10 per cent of its assets should be located outside North America, this new policy of deployment of resources changed the emphasis to the extent that by 1968 more than 50 per cent of the company's assets were employed outside North America.

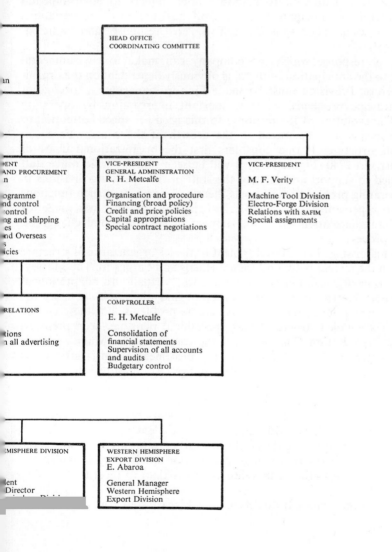

Company Strategy and Corporate Organization

To review in more depth the part which is played by physical distribution management, it is first of all necessary to consider the relationship between the company and its environment. Changes which take place in this relationship are strategic changes, and it is of interest to consider how these alterations in strategy occur, and to what extent adequate resources and management attention are provided to meet the strategic needs of the company.

The interaction between the logistic process and environmental change may be dealt with in several ways. At the simplest level the environmental change may interrupt or disturb the logistic process. The interruption or disturbance is at first considered from an administrative point of view, and only if that fails is a strategic decision taken. As a company becomes more sophisticated, it will attempt to respond more quickly to environmental changes, or even to anticipate them. Ansoff has described the variations in these processes as 'lag response', 'self-triggered response' and 'anticipatory response'.

The rate of response which the company can make to environmental changes, or to the anticipation of them, is obviously dependent on the organization structure. Provision must be made for top management to concentrate on strategic problems, without constant interruption by operating demands. The evolution of the response to this need for special attention to strategic problems may be traced in the growth of the Massey-Ferguson organization structure. If one considers first the organizational chart of Massey-Harris in 1940 (Figure 16·1) it will be seen that the head office staff were intended to support and control the staff of the operating divisions in meeting operating problems; staff posts therefore represented such functions as engineering, personnel and research. No specific allowance was made for providing immediate attention to the impact of environmental change on the logistic process.

The next major stage in the development of the MF organizational structure resulted from the merger between Massey-Harris and Ferguson. The Massey-Harris-Ferguson organization (Figure 16·2) was virtually an adaptation of the old Massey-Harris organization structure and did not fully meet the needs of the new group. Mergers always create problems, but these can be minimized if a detailed structural and operational plan has been prepared for the new organization. This was not the case after the Massey-Harris-Ferguson merger, and policy emerged only piecemeal as crisis after crisis was met—lag response to environmental change. An attempt was made to distinguish between operating functions and coordinating and policy making functions, but there was considerable overlap in these areas with, for example, one of the 'coordinating and policy' vice-presidents being responsible for certain operating activities. Although a vice-president manufacturing was identified at the 'coordinating' level, this position disappeared as soon as the individual concerned was reassigned—a reflection of the way in which the structure was designed around individuals rather than to meet the environmental context.

In terms of organizational structure, the biggest step forward was the

368

change made in 1956 (Figure 16·3) as a result of a change in management. For the first time serious efforts were made to separate explicitly advisory and operational responsibility by clearly identifying staff and line functions. Staff positions, in fact, came to reflect all the major functional divisions— marketing, manufacturing, engineering, planning and procurement, finance, personnel and industrial relations, and public relations. Although the con- tinuing growth of the company caused many changes in the operational divisions, there has been little subsequent need to alter the staff positions.

Establishing a satisfactory management structure makes it easier to take the correct decisions about development of individual markets, based on:

(a) relative costs, taking into account possible alternative supply sources
(b) relative tariff differentials and the existence and strength of local competitive industry
(c) the current and growth pattern of demand
(d) the way in which the development of the market under study will contribute to the global objectives of the company.

After consideration of these factors, the decision can be taken whether to supply from a source outside the market, to establish a new assembly or manufacturing source within the market, or even to arrange for local manu- facture by a licensing agreement. In this way, a global operation can be developed, resulting from the organizational structure, the logistical strategy, and a management control system—an essential part of which must be the planning procedures.

The development of the company's operations on a global scale could only be satisfactorily achieved if certain fundamental policies were observed:

1. To reconcile the requirements of logistics and demand, it was necessary to standardize on products to suit the widest possible range of market segments.
2. A 'common components' policy was desirable, not only to make inventory control simpler and less costly, but also to achieve economies of scale in production runs of components; this could be assisted by interchange of components between manufacturing sources.
3. Economies of scale could also be achieved in the production of whole goods by supplying all 'open' markets from manufacturing plants where production would be grouped on a product type and market segment basis.

Major steps in following these policies were taken in 1959 when Massey- Ferguson acquired F. Perkins Ltd, the diesel engine manufacturers, as well as tractor manufacturing facilities in both England and France from the Standard Motor group. Apart from the general impact on the business, these acquisitions underlined the need for a change in the organizational approach if coordination was to be established and maintained between operations units. Corporate management had to disengage themselves from North

American operations where they had been closely involved, and devote themselves to development and coordination of the group as a whole. The policy governing this development was stated in 1959 in this way:

The organizational structure that best serves total corporate interests will be a blend of decentralized and centralized management. Marketing and manufacturing activities, together with some supporting service functions, should be organized in a way that would bring them as close as possible to

Figure 16.3

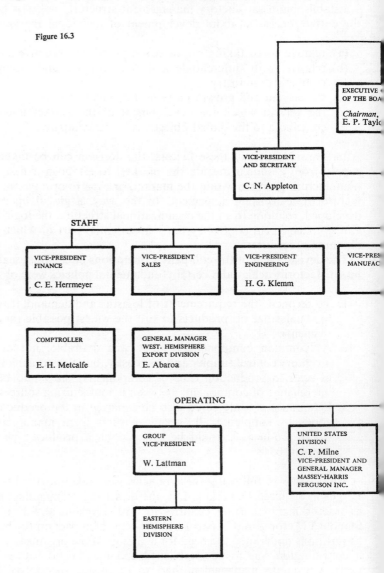

the local market situation. On the other hand, the activities that determine the long range character of the company—such as control of product line, facilities and money and planning the strategy of reacting to changes in the patterns of international trade—should be handled on a centralized basis.

The implementation of this policy resulted in some far-reaching organizational changes. Firstly, those corporate executives who had assumed line responsibilities in North America were disengaged from these activities to

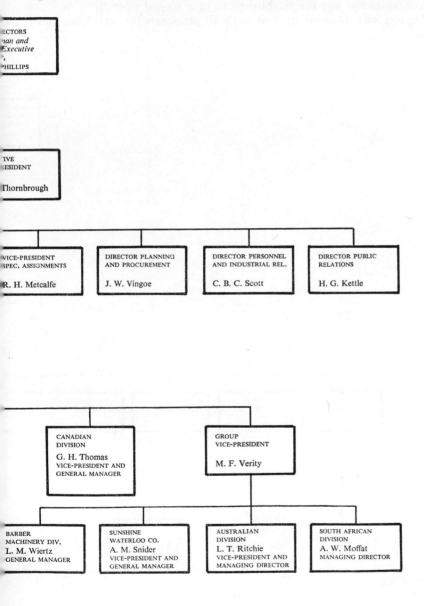

allow them to play the fuller role of coordinating activities in all operations. Secondly, all operations in Canada and the USA were consolidated into one North American operations unit. Thirdly, the Eastern Hemisphere division was replaced by establishing separate French, German and UK operations units. All export activity became the responsibility of an 'International Export Operations' controlled at corporate level by the vice-president of marketing.

From the logistical point of view, another significant development in the 1959 reorganization was the establishment of a special operations division. This division was intended to deal with all proposals for establishing new

Figure 16.4

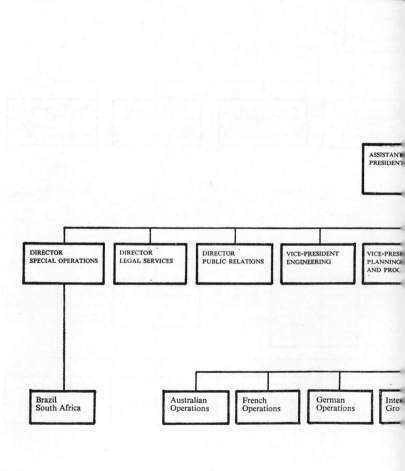

manufacturing centres in countries where the company did not already have an operations unit, or to negotiate manufacturing licensing agreements, and to supervise new manufacturing operations until such activities were ready to take their place as full operations units. Such projects are essentially corporate in nature, and require the input of many different group and staff elements; by the formation of the special operations division the necessary flexibility was provided, as well as building up within the company a specialized body of knowledge on such projects.

In the Corporate Organizational Plan in 1964 (Figure 16·4) the implementation of these changes is reflected; with the exception of export operations's

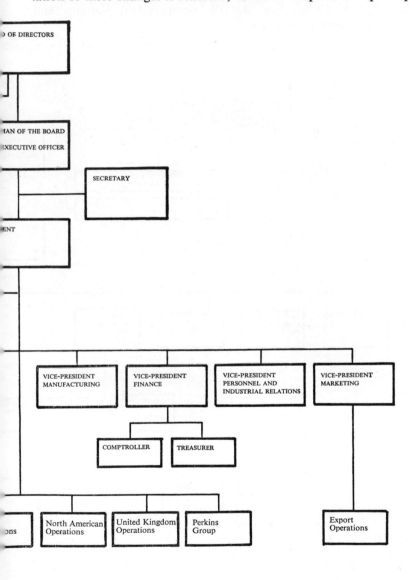

relationship to the vice-president marketing, there is a clear separation of operating responsibilities from the coordinating and policy-making responsibilities. However, in the period from 1959 the geographical dispersion of the company's operations increased and, at the same time, the need was recognized to allow for changes in the balance of the company's product groups with the growth of the engine and industrial and construction machinery activities. This resulted in a further organizational change (Figure 16·5) which divided the company into three operating groups reflecting the three product groups, each with its own group staff. Corporate staff functions were maintained to deal with strategic planning and to coordinate all group activities; one specific change was that the vice-president planning and procurement became director logistics.

Figure 16.5

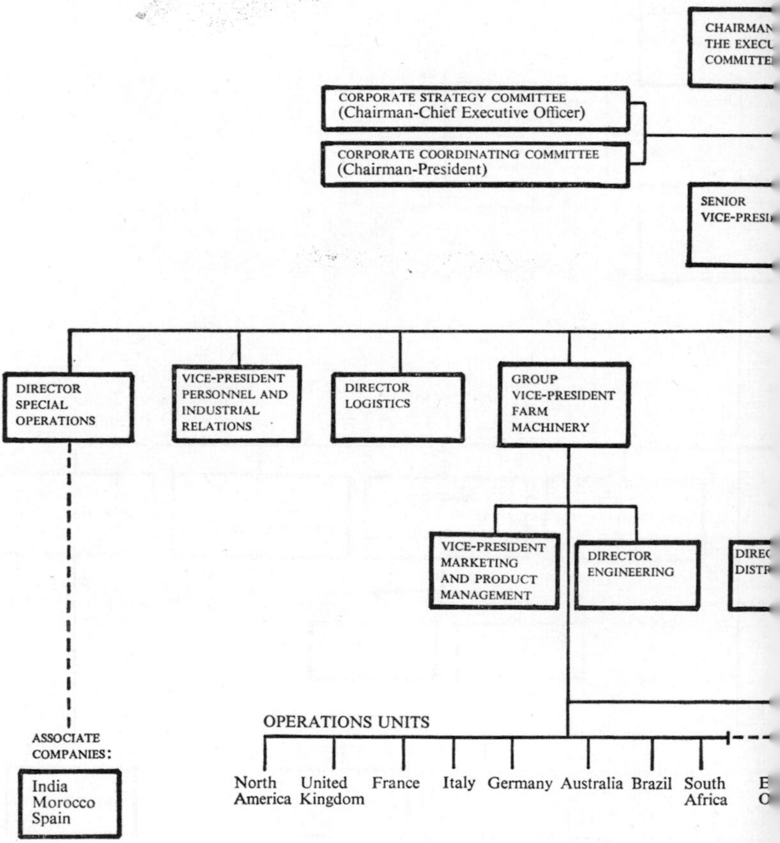

374

Distribution Media

In reviewing the evolution of physical distribution management in Massey-Ferguson attention has been paid, firstly, to the way in which the corporate structure has been developed to provide for making the decisions which are necessary to establish the correct relationship between the company and its environment and, secondly, the organizational changes which have been made to improve the speed of response to environmental changes. It is equally important to consider the effect of marketing policy on physical distribution, as a result of the choice of distribution media.

Virtually all the products manufactured by Massey-Ferguson fall into the category of standard products which require a considerable degree of pre- and post-sales technical and commercial support. Generally speaking, choice

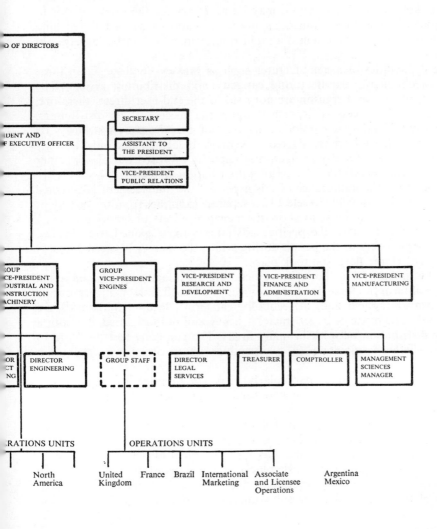

of distribution media depends basically on the interrelationship between: (a) the number of potential end-users, and (b) the requirement for pre- and after-sales service.

Products such as tractors, which are standard items normally bought from stock and requiring considerable service support, cannot be effectively handled by agents whose responsibilities end when the sale is made to the user. The distribution system required for such products must therefore be one which provides for stocking, display, selling and servicing facilities, and preferably for a range of supplementary services. Investment requirement in each market is therefore considerable, in facilities as well as inventory, and unless a manufacturer is content to limit his activities to local markets, it is unlikely that he would be able to undertake the distribution function himself. Where market penetration is poor in a specific area, which represents a key market in overall strategy, it may be necessary for the manufacturer to undertake the distribution functions, but if this happens, the cost of reaching the customer can be high unless a rapid improvement in market penetration is possible.

The capabilities of a manufacturer such as Massey-Ferguson lie in three areas—technology, manufacturing capacity and distribution system. The products of Massey-Ferguson are not sold to the end-user direct; therefore, the company's success is dependent upon the success of its distributors. When diversification is considered as part of the company's strategy, its success will depend on the degree of synergy involved—not only whether existing technology and manufacturing capacity are used but also whether advantage can be taken of the existing distribution system.

To illustrate the importance of this aspect of the management of physical distribution, it is possible to select two separate examples from the history of Massey-Ferguson—firstly, to show the negative effects of ignoring synergy and, secondly, to show the positive advantages to be gained from it. The first example refers to the period during which the merger between Massey-Harris and Harry Ferguson took place.

At that point in time, both companies were manufacturing and marketing a range of farm tractors—the Ferguson range of small tractors incorporating the Ferguson system and, in technological terms, leading the world; the Massey-Harris range of larger tractors, heavy and old-fashioned, but with a strong distribution network in many areas. The company had therefore to choose whether to maintain: (a) two product ranges, or (b) two distribution networks.

The decision was taken, particularly in North America, to maintain two separate franchises, marketing two separate product ranges through two distribution networks thus achieving wider territorial coverage. Only in areas where one or other of the franchises was not represented would the two franchises be placed together, but this process was to be allowed to set its own pace, rather than be regarded as a management objective.

This 'two-line' policy obviously placed tremendous strain, not only on the company's organizational structure, but also on its manufacturing capacity. Much of the work had to be sub-contracted; prices rose and quality fell.

In North America the situation was aggravated by an adverse move in market demand; the deterioration in the merged companies operation is shown in Figures 16·6 and 16·7, illustrating the company's sales volume and profit in North America from 1953–66.

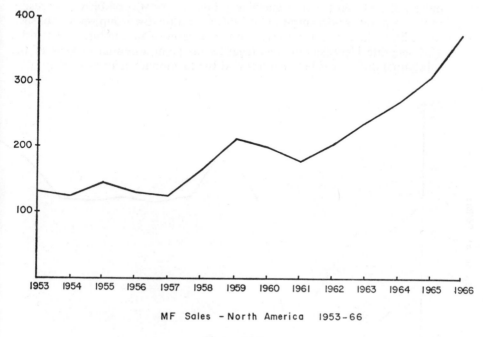

MF Sales – North America   1953–66

Figure 16·6

Unlike the situation in North America and the United Kingdom, the strategy in export territories was a positive move towards one distribution system; in France moves were made immediately after the merger to integrate the two systems. Although market conditions also helped, in that they were more favourable than in North America, it is interesting to note that in the areas where a joint franchise policy was undertaken, both sales volume and profitability improved. The decision to switch from the 'two-line' policy to an integrated distribution network in North America was not taken until immediately after the management reorganization in 1956. The change was not an easy one to make, in view of the anti-trust implications in the US market, and it was recognized that the only solution would be to buy out the independent Ferguson distributors and to operate the business only through the Massey-Harris network of branches and distributors. This was accomplished, with some difficulty, at a cost of $2 million and left the way open not only for an improved organization in North America but also for a dramatic reduction in inventory levels of finished products. As a result of this North American experience, the policy evolved that wherever the company

377

had a manufacturing operation this was used as a marketing branch to supply the distribution network of dealers for all products, including those not manufactured locally.

The second example of selection of distribution media as part of the management of physical distribution concerns the development of the industrial and construction machinery business (ICM) of Massey-Ferguson. In the corporate re-organization of 1966 a separate ICM group was established to facilitate the continued growth and expansion of MF's industrial business. This separate identification was regarded as being essential in view of the substantial differences between ICM and the farm machinery business.

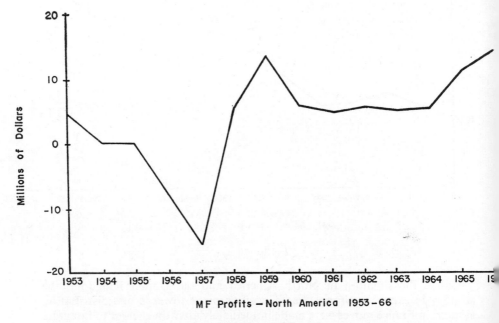

MF Profits — North America 1953—66

Figure 16·7

From the manufacturing point of view, although ICM has certain products such as wheel tractors which are common to the farm machinery businees, the development of the group was largely dependent on products which had little in common with farm machinery. Product specifications have often to be modified to meet customer requirements; production runs are normally short and many model variations may be required. The structure of the market for ICM is different from that for farm machinery; concentrated industrial markets are more important for sales than rural areas, although in terms of product use there must be full availability of parts and service throughout the territory.

To realize the full potential of its ICM business it was necessary for Massey-Ferguson to recognize these special requirements, and to provide sufficient

378

management attention to meet the new circumstances and problems. It was for this reason that a separate ICM group was formed, with parallel organizations to take care of the other two product groups—engines and farm machinery. At the same time, it was important to coordinate the activities of both farm machinery and ICM groups, particularly as some of the responsibility for manufacturing ICM products rested with farm machinery operations units.

In selecting the distribution system for ICM the maximum possible advantage was taken of the existing distribution network—producing synergy by distributing the burden of overhead expenses over a wider range of products. In many markets it was found possible to base distribution of ICM products on the existing farm machinery network. Distributors and dealers had to form separate sales organizations for ICM because of the difference in buying patterns and sales techniques, but advantage could be taken of common facilities such as showrooms, workshops, parts stores and field servicing organizations. ICM offered a diversification and growth opportunity not only for Massey-Ferguson, but also for the company's distributors and dealers.

Of course, the farm machinery distribution network was only used where it was considered that it could cover the market adequately; also, because of the lower sales volume involved, at least initially, only selected parts of the Farm Machinery distribution were used in some areas. In major markets such as the USA, the farm distribution network had to be supplemented. An analysis of construction machinery sales in the USA indicated that 85 per cent of the industry sales occurred in 150 concentrated industrial markets, and of these fifteen key market areas accounted for 55 per cent of all industrial and construction machinery sales. It was in precisely these areas that Massey-Ferguson had the weakest distribution, since MF farm machinery sales were primarily in agricultural areas of the USA.

The process of finding satisfactory distribution in these key areas is a slow one, just as it takes time to adapt the farm machinery distribution to the contrasting economics, equipment needs and buying habits of the ICM business. As an approach to the problem of rapid development of distribution, a vertical franchise concept was adopted by Massey-Ferguson in North America. This involved grouping ICM products by market segment. Dealers were assigned an area of primary responsibility by product group. This permits more than one Massey-Ferguson dealer to offer non-competing product lines in the same geographical area. Dealers are required to provide full sales, service and parts coverage in their area of prime responsibility.

This vertical franchising concept is used by Massey-Ferguson in North America to match the needs of the customer to the capacity of the dealer and, at the same time, to obtain maximum sales coverage even for products with only a limited or specialized application. One example is the use of light industrial tractors as turf tractors: these may be distributed on a limited franchise through specialized turf equipment houses. This degree of specialization is not, however, common in other countries and in most other operations areas Massey-Ferguson has either maintained as its objective the concept of ICM as a single franchise, or has enfranchized a number of dealers to represent

379

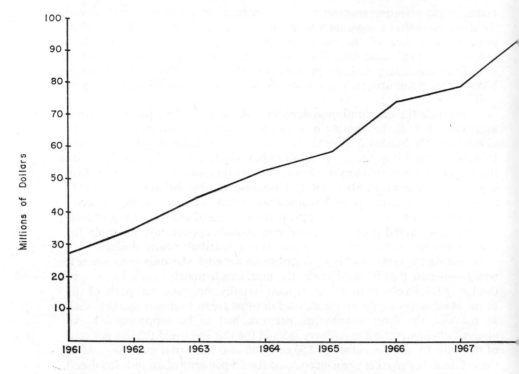

Total MF sales of industrial and construction machinery

Figure 16·8

the industrial (or lighter) end of the range, of whom certain dealers are selected to represent in addition the construction (or heavier) machinery range. The variations in approach to distribution reflect variations in environment rather than inconsistencies of policy; common to all approaches is the desire to make the maximum use of existing resources. The success of the overall policy is reflected in Figure 16·8, showing the growth in MF ICM sales from 1961–8.

Select Bibliography

General Sources

D. J. Bowersox, E. Smykay and B. J. La Londe, *Physical Distribution Management*, New York, Macmillan, 1968.

M. G. Christopher, *Total Distribution*, London, Gower Press, 1971. J. L. Heskett, R. N. Ivie and N. A. Glaskowsky, *Business Logistics*, New York, Ronald Press, 1964.

E. H. Lewis, *Marketing Channels: Structure and Strategy*, New York, McGraw-Hill, 1968.

J. F. Magee, *Physical Distribution Systems*, London, McGraw-Hill, 1967.

B. Mallen (ed.), *The Marketing Channel*, London, Wiley, 1967.

L. W. Stern (ed.), *Distribution Channels: Behavioural Dimensions*, Boston, Houghton Mifflin, 1969.

International Journal of Physical Distribution, IPC Business Press, London, thrice yearly since 1970.

1. *The Total Distribution Concept*

W. Alderson, 'Factors Governing the Development of Marketing Channels', in B. Mallen (ed.), *The Marketing Channel*, London, Wiley, 1967, Chapter 4.

M. G. Christopher, *Total Distribution*, London, 'Gower Press, 1971.

R. Lekashman and J. F. Stolle, 'The Total Cost Approach to Distribution', *Business Horizons*, Winter 1965, pp. 34–46 (reprinted in Bowersox, Smykay and La Londe, *Readings in PDM*).

D. Pettit, 'Physical Distribution Management: The Total Concept', *Management Decision*, Summer 1969, pp. 31–4.

Wendell M. Stewart, 'Physical Distribution: Key to Improved Volume and Profits', *Journal of Marketing*, January 1965, pp. 65–70.

2. *Corporate Planning and Distribution*

T. L. Berg, 'Designing the Distribution System', in B. Mallen (ed.), *The Marketing Channel*, London, Wiley, 1967, Chapter 34.

R. Grant, *Distribution Management*, London, Business Books, 1968, Chapters 1–3.

D. Hussey, 'Appraising the Physical Distribution Environment', in *Developing Policies for Physical Distribution*, Conference Manual, January 1969.

3. *Macro-Distribution*

R. Cox *et al.*, *Distribution in a High-level Economy*, London, Prentice-Hall, 1965.

J. L. Heskett, 'Macro-economic Cost of Physical Distribution', in N. Marks and R. Taylor, *Marketing Logistics*, London, 1967, Chapter 2.

W. Leontief, 'The Structure of Development', in *Technology and Economic Development*, Harmondsworth, Penguin, 1965.

W. G. McClelland, 'The Distributive Sector', in *Three Banks Review*, December 1969.

4. *The Marketing Channel*

R. Breyer, 'Some Observations on Structural Formation and the Growth of Marketing Channels', in B. Mallen (ed.), *The Marketing Channel*.

381

L. P. Bucklin, 'The Economic Structure of Channels of Distribution', in B. Mallen (ed.), *The Marketing Channel*, Chapter 8.

E. H. Lewis, *Marketing Channels: Structure and Strategy*, New York, McGraw-Hill, 1968, Chapters 1 and 7.

B. C. McCammon and R. W. Little, 'Marketing Channels, Analytical Systems and Approaches', in G. Schwartz, *Science in Marketing*, New York, Wiley, 1967, pp. 321–85.

L. Richartz and H. Baligh, *Vertical Market Structures*, Rockleigh, N.J., Allyn & Bacon, 1967, Chapter 1.

5. U.K. Channel Structures

R. Grant, *Distribution Management*, London, Business Books, 1969, Chapters 4 to 7.

N. Stacey and A. Wilson, *The Changing Pattern of Distribution*, Oxford, Pergamon Press, 1965.

6. Channel Intermediaries

(a) Retailing

D. F. Dalrymple and D. L. Thompson, *Retailing: An Economic View*, New York, Free Press, 1969.

J. Goldstucker, 'Trading Areas' in G. Schwartz, *Science in Marketing*, New York, Wiley, 1967, pp. 281–320.

D. L. Huff, 'Defining and Estimating a Trading Area', *Journal of Marketing*, July 1964, pp. 34–8.

W. G. McClelland, *Costs and Competition in Retailing*, London, Macmillan, 1968, Chapters 1, 8 and 10.

G. S. C. Wills, *New Ideas in Retail Management*, London, Staples, 1970.

(b) Wholesaling

J. M. Brion, 'Marketing through the Wholesaler Distribution Channel', in B. Mallen (ed.), *The Marketing Channel*, Chapter 36.

D. A. Revzan, *Wholesaling in Marketing Organisation*, London, Wiley, 1961.

7. The Marketing Channel as an Economic System

W. Alderson, 'Marketing Systems in the Ecological Framework', *International Journal of Production Research*, Vol. 4, 1966, No. 1.

L. Aspinwall, 'The Characteristics of Goods and Parallel Systems Theory', in B. Mallen (ed.), *The Marketing Channel*, Chapter 11.

L. R. Bucklin, 'Postponement, Speculation and the Structure of Distribution Channels', in B. Mallen (ed.), *The Marketing Channel*, Chapter 9.

L. Richartz and H. Baligh, *Vertical Market Structures*, Rockleigh, N.J., Allyn & Bacon, Chapters 2–8.

G. Stigler, 'The Division of Labour is Limited by the Extent of the Market', in B. Mallen (ed.), *The Market Channel*, Chapter 7.

8. The Marketing Channel as a Social System

L. W. Stern and J. W. Brown, 'Distribution Channels: A Social Systems Approach', in Stern (ed.), *Distribution Channels: Behavioural Dimensions*, Boston, Houghton Mifflin, 1969.

L. W. Stern and L. E. Gill, 'Roles and Role Theory in Distribution Channel Systems', in Stern (ed.), *Distribution Channels: Behavioural Dimensions*.

L. W. Stern and F. J. Beier, 'Power in the Channel of Distribution', in Stern (ed.), *Distribution Channels: Behavioural Dimensions*.

9. Conflict and Cooperation in the Marketing Channel

W. Alderson, 'Conflict and Cooperation in Marketing Channels', in Stern (ed.), *Distribution Channels: Behavioural Dimensions*.

B. Mallen, 'Conflict and Cooperation in Marketing Channels', in B. Mallen (ed.), *The Marketing Channel*, Chapter 17.
J. C. Palamountain, 'Vertical Conflict', in Stern (ed.), *Distribution Channels: Behavioural Dimensions.*

10. *Channel Strategy and Management*
W. Alderson and P. E. Green, 'Bayesian Decision Theory in Channel Selection', in B. Mallen (ed.), *The Marketing Channel.*
R. Artle and S. Berghard, 'A note on Manufacturers' Choice of Distribution Channel', in B. Mallen (ed.), *The Marketing Channel.*
H. Baligh, 'A Theoretical Framework for Channel Choice', in B. Mallen (ed.), *The Marketing Channel.*
E. H. Lewis, *Marketing Channels: Structure and Strategy*, New York, McGraw-Hill, 1968, Chapter 6.
M. R. Warshaw, 'Pricing to Gain Wholesaler's Support', in B. Mallen (ed.), *The Marketing Channel.*

11. *Business Logistics: Marketing/Production/Purchasing Interfaces*
B. J. La Londe, 'Integrated Distribution Management: An American Perspective', *Long Range Planning*, December, 1969, pp. 61–71.
J. Magee, 'The Logistics of Distribution', *The Harvard Business Review*, July–August 1960.
J. Magee, *Physical Distribution Systems*, New York, McGraw-Hill, 1967, Chapter 2.

12. *General Systems Theory*
K. Boulding, 'General Systems Theory—The Skeleton of Science' in A. Fiske *et al.*, *Theories for Marketing Systems Analysis*, New York, Harper & Row, 1967, pp. 4–10.
H. L. Gauthier, 'Potential for the Use of Graph Theory in Logistics System Evaluation', in Haas *et al.*, *Science, Technology and Marketing*, Autumn 1966, Proceedings of American Marketing Association.
R. A. Johnson, 'Systems Theory & Management', *Management Science*, Vol. 10, No. 2, January 1964, pp. 367–84.

13. *Physical Distribution System Design*
J. L. Heskett, 'A Missing Link in Physical Distribution System Design', *Journal of Marketing*, October 1966, pp. 37–41.
E. Smykay, D. J. Bowersox and B. J. La Londe, *Physical Distribution Management*, New York, Macmillan, 1968, Chapter 12.
J. E. Sussams, 'Some Problems Associated with the Distribution of Consumer Products', *Operations Research Quarterly*, XIX, June 1968.

14. *Distribution Cost and Revenue Analysis*
T. B. Heckert and R. B. Miner, *Distribution Cost Accounting*, New York, Ronald Press, 1953.
J. Heskett *et al.*, *Business Logistics*, New York, Ronald Press, 1964, Chapter 16.
D. R. Longman and M. Schiff, *Practical Distribution Cost Analysis*, Homewood, Ill., Richard D. Irwin, 1955.
F. H. Mossman and M. Morton, *Logistics of Distribution Systems*, Rockleigh, N.J., Alleyn & Bacon, 1956, pp. 36–69, Chapter 10.
C. H. Sevin, *Marketing Productivity Analysis*, London, McGraw-Hill, 1965.

15. *Role of Service in Marketing*
W. M. Hutchinson and J. F. Stolle, 'How to Manage Customer Service', *Harvard Business Review*, November–December 1968.
P. B. Schary, 'Marketing and Logistics: The Other Side of Physical Distribution', *Freight Management*, July 1970.

P. R. Stephenson and R. Willett, 'Determinants of Buyer Response to Physical Distribution Service', *Journal of Marketing Research*, August 1969, pp. 279–83.
P. R. Stephenson and R. Willett, 'Selling with Distribution Service', *Business Horizons*, December 1968.

16. *Communication in the Channel*

D. J. Bowersox, E. Smykay and B. J. La Londe, *Physical Distribution Management*, Chapter 9.
J. R. Grabner and L. J. Rosenberg, 'Communication in Distribution Channel Systems', in L. W. Stern (ed.), *Distribution Channels: Behavioural Dimensions*.
J. L. Heskett, 'Marketing Time Lags, their Impact on Distribution', in Marks and Taylor, *Marketing Logistics*, Chapter 24.
T. Kaufman, 'Data Systems Which Cross Company Boundaries', *Harvard Business Review*, January 1966, pp. 141–55.
B. J. La Londe and J. F. Grashof, 'The Role of Information Systems in Physical Distribution', in D. J. Bowersox, B. J. La Londe and E. W. Smykay, *Readings in Physical Distribution Management*, Chapter 20.
J. F. Magee, 'The Computer and the Physical Distribution Network', in W. Alderson and S. Schapiro (ed.), *Marketing and the Computer*, London, Prentice-Hall, 1963, Chapter 4.

17. *Inventory Control*

(a) *Order Quantity and Safety Stock*

J. L. Heskett *et al.*, *Business Logistics*, Chapter 11.
E. Koenisberg and J. Buchan, *Scientific Inventory Management*, Chapters 1 and 18 optional, Chapters 2–17).
J. Magee, *Physical Distribution Systems*, London, McGraw-Hill, 1967, Chapter 3.

(b) *Demand Forecasting*

R. G. Brown, 'Less Risk in Inventory Estimates', in Marks and Taylor, *Marketing Logistics*, Chapter 22.
R. G. Brown, *Statistical Forecasting for Inventory Control*, New York, McGraw-Hill, 1959.

(c) *Aggregate Control of Inventory*

R. G. Brown, *Statistical Forecasting for Inventory Control*, New York, McGraw-Hill, 1959, Appendix C.
K. Howard and P. B. Schary, 'Logistics Strategy and Inventory Decisions', *International Journal of Physical Distribution*, Vol. 1, No. 1, 1970.
IBM, *Wholesale Impact: Advanced Principles and Implementation*, Chapter 6.

18. *Warehouse Management*

R. Ballou, 'Improving the Physical Layout of Merchandising in Warehouses', *Journal of Marketing*, July 1967.
G. L. Butcher, 'Distribution: The Ingredients of a Revolution', *The Director*, May 1969.
J. Heskett, *Business Logistics*, Chapter 14.
J. Magee, *Physical Distribution Systems*, pp. 73–81.

19. *Materials Handling and Packaging*

L. M. Guss, *Packaging in Marketing*, American Management Association, 1967.
K. Ruppenthal and C. Whylark, 'Some Problems in Optimising Shipping Facilities', *Logistics Review*, January 1969, pp. 5–22.
R. C. Wilson, 'A Packaging Problem', *Management Science*, Series B, December 1965.

C. J. Zusi, 'An Industrial Packaging Transformation' in Marks and Taylor, *Marketing Logistics*, Chapter 18.

20. *Transport: Technology*
W. J. Baumol and H. D. Vynod, 'An Inventory-Theoretic Model of Freight Transport Demand', *Management Science*, March 1970.
W. J. Baumol and H. D. Vynod, 'Moving Goods in the '70s', *Economist*, September 21, 1968.
R. W. Faulks, *The Elements of Transport*, London, Ian Allen, 1968, Chapters 5, 6, 7, 8, 9, and 10.
C. D. Forster, *The Transport Problem*, London, Blackie.
F. L. Weldon, 'Cargo Containerisation in the West Coast-Hawaiian Trade', *Operations Research*, September–October 1958.
F. Wentworth, *Physical Distribution Management*, London, Gower Press, 1970, Parts III, IV.

21. *Transport: Institutions*
R. W. Faulkes, *The Elements of Transport*, London, Ian Allen, 1968, Chapter 4.
G. W. Quick-Smith, 'Coordination and Integration of Transport', *Commercial Motor*, September 21 1968.
G. L. Reid and K. Allen, *Nationalised Industries*, Harmondsworth, Penguin, 1970, Chapters 5, 6 and 7.
UNCTAD, *Level and Structure of Freight Rates, Conference Practices and Adequacy of Shipping Services*, 1969.
Transport Act 1968, London, H.M.S.O., 1968.

22. *Transport Management*
N. Christofides, 'Modern Methods of Vehicle Scheduling', *Freight Management*, November 1969,
R. Maffei, 'Modern Methods for Local Delivery', *Journal of Marketing*, April 1965, pp. 13–18.
National Computer Centre, *The Impact of Computer Techniques on Transport Planning*. National Computer Centre, 1969.
J. E. Sussams, *Industrial Logistics*, London Gower Press, 1969, Part III.
Transport for Industry, London, H.M.S.O., 1969.

23. *Facilities Location*
W. J. Baumol and P. Wolfe, 'A Warehouse Location Problem', in Marks and Taylor, *Marketing Logistics*, Chapter 13.
E. Feldman, F. A. Lehrer and T. L. Ray, 'Warehouse Location under Continuous Economies of Scale', *Management Science*, May 1966, Series A.
E. Follett, 'New Approach to an Old Problem', *Distribution Manager*, November 1968, pp. 31–6.
J. Heskett *et al*, *Business Logistics*, Chapters 6 and 8.
Kuehn and M. Hamburger, 'A Heuristic Program for Locating Warehouses' in Marks and Taylor, *Marketing Logistics*, Chapter 14.
J. Magee, *Physical Distribution Systems*, New York, McGraw-Hill, 1967, Chapters 5 and 6.
J. E. Sussams, *Industrial Logistics*, London, Gower Press, 1969, Parts I and II.

24. *Setting Service Levels*
J. N. Arbury *et al.*, *A New Approach to Physical Distribution*, New York, American Management Association, 1967.
J. Buchan and E. Koenisberg, *Scientific Inventory Management*, London, Prentice-Hall, 1963, Chapter 19.

25. *Simulation and Systems Analysis of Logistics Systems*

V. C. Hare, *Systems Analysis: a diagnostic approach*, New York, Harcourt Brace Ltd, 1967, Chapters 1 and 3.

R. A. Johnson, F. E. Kast and J. E. Rosenzweig, *The Theory and Management of Systems*, New York, McGraw-Hill, 1963, Chapter 8.

R. Maffei and H. N. Shycon, 'Simulation—A Tool for Better Distribution', *Harvard Business Review*, November–December 1960.

S. Optner, *Systems Analysis for Business and Industrial Problem-Solving*, London, Prentice-Hall, 1965, Chapter 3.

26. *Organization for PDM*

S. Brewer and J. Rosenzweig, 'Rhochrematics and Organisational Adjustment' in Marks and Taylor, *Marketing Logistics*, Chapter 33.

J. L. Heskett and R. Ballou, 'Logistics Planning in Inter-Organisational Systems', *Academy of Management Proceedings*, 26th Annual Meeting 1966, pp. 124–36.

L. W. Stern and J. L. Heskett, 'Conflict Management in Inter-Organisational Relations: A Conceptual Framework', in Stern (ed.), *Distribution Channels: Behavioural Dimensions*, Chapter 19.

J. F. Stolle, 'How to Manage Physical Distribution' in Bowersox, La Londe and Smykay, *Readings in Physical Distribution Management*, Chapter 28.

S. Tilles, 'The Manager's Job—A Systems Approach', *Harvard Business Review*, January–February 1963.

S. Young, 'Organisation as a System', *California Management Review*, Spring 1968.

Subject Index

Name Index